Sex and Sex Education:
A Bibliography

Sex and Sex Education:

A Bibliography

Flora C. Seruya / Susan Losher / Albert Ellis

R. R. BOWKER COMPANY

New York and London, 1972
A Xerox Education Company

For my old friend "Cecilio" with affection and my best wishes

Flor S

1973

Published by R. R. Bowker Co. (a Xerox Education Company)
1180 Avenue of the Americas, New York, N. Y. 10036
Copyright © 1972 by Flora C. Seruya, Susan Losher, Albert Ellis
Printed and bound in the United States of America.

Library of Congress Cataloging in Publication Data

Seruya, Flora C
  Sex and sex education.

  1. Sex—Bibliography.   I. Losher, Susan, joint
author.   II. Ellis, Albert, 1913-   joint
author.   III. Title.
Z7164.S42S38   016.6126′007   72-8333
ISBN 0-8352-0544-4

For my husband, Dominique Seruya,
without whose creative spirit, knowledge,
and guidance this work could not
have been undertaken and accomplished.

F. C. S.

CONTENTS

FOREWORD

Bibliographies are and should be works of great and impressive scholarship, and the one I am about to introduce is no exception to that rule.

With the increasing interest in the discipline of sexology, the need for a comprehensive bibliography was an obvious one. That need is now fulfilled with the excellent work conceived by Mrs. Flora C. Seruya five years ago when she asked my advice about her idea of writing a bibliography of sexology, a project in which I encouraged her wholeheartedly. Her desire for self-expression in this particular field took form in the compilation of this bibliography.

Carried out with the collaboration of her colleague Mrs. Susan Losher and the assistance of Dr. Albert Ellis, the bibliography shows how far we have come since the two great pioneers in sexology, Magnus Hirschfeld and Richard von Krafft-Ebing, started their work in the nineteenth century. If anything, it shows us the impressive growth in sexual research during the last decades. Much of this research has been stimulated and supported by the Institute of Sex Research, but there are many individual scholars who have taken it upon themselves to investigate the manifold and rich aspects of sexology.

Many of us in the field of sexual research will find this bibliography a welcome addition to our libraries.

HENDRIK M. RUITENBEEK

Advisory Council and Faculty,
American Institute for Psychotherapy
and Psychoanalysis

PREFACE

Sexology — as seen by the authors — is the science that no person can afford to ignore today. The fact that we are able to breathe, to move, to think and communicate, in effect the simple act of existing, forces us to focus our attention on the fascinating process of how we came into being and how we behave when motivated by our inherent sexuality.

One could compare the science of sexology to a beautiful, gigantic tree whose branches and leaves represent the myriad of aspects and facets of our own complex sexuality — a source of so much happiness to man, but also one of untold tragedies at times. Hence, it was desired to bring together the most significant material on the subject and decided to utilize the authors' experience and knowledge as librarians and researchers toward this end.

The bibliography, conceived by Mrs. Seruya, came to fruition through her planning and efforts and those of her friend and colleague Mrs. Losher. Yet, they realized that no bibliography is complete without the expertise of a subject specialist and they were fortunate to have Dr. Albert Ellis, a world-renowned sexologist, participate in their plan as their consultant.

Nearly twenty-five years have passed since the publication of the first Kinsey Report, a milestone in the study of sex, and the flood tide of books which have followed in its wake prompted the writing of this bibliography. In gathering the titles, it has been interesting to observe the change in approach to the subject from the humanistic to the scientific.

The plethora of works written on the various aspects of sex and the limitations of time and space have forced us to select those titles which seemed to us to be among the more significant, and to withhold many more titles for possible future inclusion.

Our aim in this work is to reach anyone confronted with the teaching or learning of sex, be he parent, educator, an adult who wishes self-instruction, or a professional who is seeking information or materials for recommended reading. Therefore, the bibliography is to serve as indicator or guide to the variety of books written on sexology in all its aspects and those related to it.

An attempt has been made to include a wide range of viewpoints. Older works have been included for historical perspective in order to reflect the changes in attitude on sex and sex education. Lack of space has forced us to place some titles, which might belong in more than one classification, into one category only. However, the comprehensive indexes should aid the reader in locating them. Many government publications have been omitted.

Under each chapter and subject heading, works are arranged alphabetically by author. In the case of pseudonymous authors, works will be found under the author's real name, with the pseudonym given in brackets following the name.

The chapter on Sex in Literature consists chiefly of works treating this subject from a historical or critical point of view. It is through these works that the original writings of classical authors and others may be located.

The researcher interested in books on sex education is not to limit himself or herself to the chapter of that title, as many useful titles are scattered throughout other chapters as well. The detailed cross-references in the subject index are also to be consulted.

The relatively few bibliographies which have been written on various aspects of sex have all been placed together in the chapter on General Works on Sex. It is recommended that the reader begin his or her search for literature in that chapter.

Descriptive annotations have been given when titles did not seem clear enough. We have used *Book Review Digest*, publications of the Sex Information and Education Council of the United States (SIECUS), and *Bibliography* of the Society for Sex Education and Guidance.

In the compilation of this bibliography we have used the resources of many libraries in the New York City area, in particular American Cancer Society Library, City College of New York Library, Columbia University Libraries, Fort Lee, N.J., Public Library, Mattachine Society Education Research Library, National Health Agencies Library, New York Academy of Medicine Library, New York Psychoanalytic Institute Library, and the Research Libraries of the New York Public Library.

The magnitude of the project brought us into contact with many people, directly and indirectly, whose aid we would like to acknowledge here. Some deserve particular mention, for they have given more of themselves than we can ever adequately acknowledge. Our mates were ever-encouraging, being our chief and best critics. In particular, Dominique Seruya, to whom this book is dedicated, was most instrumental in helping to lay the foundation of this bibliography.

We give special thanks to Mrs. Carola Ehrlich, Mr. Morton Losher, and Miss Laura Carracino for their assistance in preparing the manuscript; and to Mrs. Aldonsa Seruya for her continual encouragement. Great gratitude is felt toward Dr. Sourya Henderson, Medical Librarian of the American Cancer Society, for her valuable advice always given when most needed. Mrs. Losher's colleagues of the Fort Lee Public Library, and in particular Mrs. Helen McManus, Director, deserve the expression of her appreciation for their kind cooperation when she took a leave of absence to help complete the manuscript. We extend our recognition to Dr. Mary S. Calderone, Executive Director of SIECUS, as well as to Mr. Peter Heggie, Executive Secretary of the Authors Guild, Inc., for their advice on our professional problems. A last tribute is fondly acknowledged to the memory of Dr. Isadore Rubin, late editor of *Sexology* magazine, who was so kind to us when we were in the planning stages of our bibliography.

FLORA C. SERUYA, *Medical Librarian*

SUSAN LOSHER, *Head, Technical Services,*
Fort Lee Public Library

ALBERT ELLIS, *Executive Director,*
Institute for Advanced Study
in Rational Psychotherapy

1.
GENERAL WORKS ON SEX

BIBLIOGRAPHIES

Abstracts of Current Literature on Venereal Disease. Atlanta, Ga.: 1952-
present.

Published irregularly.

ALDOUS, JOAN, and R. HILL. International Bibliography of Research in Marriage and the Family, 1900-1964. Minneapolis, Minn.: Minnesota Family
Study Center and the Institute of Life Insurance, 1967. 508 pp.

AMERICAN FEDERATION FOR SEX HYGIENE. Publications of the Constitu-
ent Societies of the American Federation for Sex Hygiene. New York: The
American Federation for Sex Hygiene, 1913. 15 pp.

AMERICAN SOCIAL HYGIENE ASSOCIATION. What Shall We Read: A List of
Books on Social Hygiene and Related Topics. American Social Hygiene
Assn. Publication No. 97. New York: American Social Hygiene Assn.,
1917. 11 pp.

"1914 edition reprinted from 'Social Hygiene,' Vol. 1., No. 1, pp. 108-120."

AMERICAN SOCIAL HYGIENE ASSOCIATION. What to Read on Social Hygiene.
New York: American Social Hygiene Assn., 1920. 8 pp.

ASHBEE, HENRY SPENCER [Pisanus Fraxi]. Catena Librorum Tacendorum:
Bio-biblio-icono-graphical and Critical Notes on Curious, Uncommon, and
Erotic Books. Bibliography of Prohibited Books, Vol. 3. New York:
Brussel, 1962. 593 pp.

"A reissue, without original title page or illustrations, of the 1960 London
facsimile of the work first published in London in 1885."

ASHBEE, HENRY SPENCER [Pisanus Fraxi]. Centuria Librorum Absconditorum: Bio-biblio-icono-graphical and Critical Notes on Curious, Uncommon, and Erotic Books. Bibliography of Prohibited Books, Vol. 2. New
York: Brussel, 1962. 593 pp.

"A reissue, without original title page or illustrations, of the 1960 London
facsimile of the work first published in London in 1879."

ASHBEE, HENRY SPENCER [Pisanus Fraxi]. A Complete Guide to Forbidden Books. North Hollywood, Calif.: Brandon, 1966. 447 pp.

ASHBEE, HENRY SPENCER [Pisanus Fraxi]. Index Librorum Prohibitorum: Bio-biblio-icono-graphical and Critical Notes on Curious, Uncommon, and Erotic Books. Bibliography of Prohibited Books, Vol. 1. New York: Brussel, 1962. 542 pp.

"A reissue ... of the 1960 London facsimile of the work first published in London in 1877."

BAILEY, DERRICK SHERWIN. The Theology of Sex and Marriage: A Short Guide for Readers and Students. London, Eng.: Published for the Church of England Moral Welfare Council by the Church Information Board, 1953. 28 pp.

BELL, ROBERT R. A Bibliography of American Family Problem Areas: A Project of Marriage, Family, and Divorce Section, Society for the Study of Social Problems. Philadelphia, Pa.: Temple University, 1964. 99 pp.

BRADLEY, MARION ZIMMER, and G. DAMON. Checklist: A Complete, Cumulative Checklist of Lesbian, Variant and Homosexual Fiction, in English, or Available in English Translation, with Supplements of Related Material for the Use of Collector, Students, and Librarians. Rochester, Tex.: n.p., 1960. 69 pp.

CARY, HENRY NATHANIEL, comp. Bibliography of the Sources of the Author's "The Slang of Venery and its Analogues," and of his "Synonyms of the Slang of Venery." Chicago, Ill.: n.p., 1919. 45 leaves.

CARY, HENRY NATHANIEL, comp. Bibliotheca Erotica. Chicago, Ill.: n.p., 1918. 22 leaves.

Proofsheets, with manuscript corrections.

CHILD STUDY ASSOCIATION OF AMERICA. Sex Education: Recommended Reading. New York: Child Study Assn. of America, 1969. 16 pp.

CISLER, LUCINDA, comp. Women: A Bibliography. 5th ed., rev. and enl. New York: Lucinda Cisler, 1969. 16 pp.

Updated frequently.

CRAIG, ALEC. The Bibliography of Nudism. London, Eng.: Progressive League, 1954. 2 pp.

"Off-printed from 'Sun and Health,' No. 14 (1954) — Aarhus, Denmark."

DAMON, GENE, and L. STUART. The Lesbian in Literature: A Bibliography. San Francisco, Calif.: Daughters of Bilitis, 1967. 79 pp.

DARROW, WILLIAM W. Selected References on the Behavioral Aspects of Venereal Disease Control; An Annotated Bibliography for Behavioral Scientists, Epidemiologists, and Venereal Disease Casefinding Personnel. Atlanta, Ga.: Center for Disease Control, 1970. 59 pp.

DEAKIN, TERENCE J. Catalogi Librorum Eroticorum: A Critical Bibliography of Erotic Bibliographies and Book-Catalogues. London, Eng.: Woolf, 1964. 28 pp.

DOLLEN, CHARLES, comp. Abortion in Context: A Select Bibliography. Metuchen, N.J.: Scarecrow, 1970. 150 pp.

DOLLEN, CHARLES. Sexuality in America: A Bibliography. Honolulu, Hawaii: Hogarth, 1970. 125 pp.

Family Planning Educational Materials: An Annotated Bibliography of Selected Items. Chapel Hill, N.C.: Carolina Population Center, 1968. 89 pp.

GEIJERSTAM, GUNNAR AF, ed. An Annotated Bibliography of Induced Abortion. Ann Arbor, Mich.: Center for Population Planning, University of Michigan, 1969. 359 pp.

GOODLAND, ROGER. A Bibliography of Sex Rites and Customs: An Annotated Record of Books, Articles, and Illustrations in All Languages. London, Eng.: Routledge, 1931. 752 pp.

Reprinted in 1971 by Milford, Kennebunkport, Maine.

HAIGHT, ANNE LYON. Banned Books: Informal Notes on Some Books Banned for Various Reasons at Various Times. New York: Bowker, 1970. 166 pp.

First published in 1935.

HEARTMAN, CHARLES FREDERICK. The "Blue Book": A Bibliographical Attempt to Describe the Guide Books to the Houses of Ill Fame in New Orleans. By Semper Idem, pseud. Heartman's Historical Series, No. 50. Privately printed, 1936. 77 pp.

HIMES, NORMAN EDWIN. Guide to Birth Control Literature: A Select Bibliography on the Technique of Contraception and on the Social Aspects of Birth Control. London, Eng.: Douglas, 1931. 46 pp.

"Classified and annotated."

ILLINOIS. SEX EDUCATION ADVISORY BOARD. Resource Materials on Family Life and Sex Education. Springfield, Ill.: Office of the Superintendent of Public Instruction, 1968. 51 leaves.

IRELAND (EIRE). CENSORSHIP OF PUBLICATIONS BOARD. Register of Prohibited Publications. Dublin, Ireland: Stationery Office, 1929-present.

"A listing of prohibited books, issued periodically."

JOINT COMMITTEE OF THE AMERICAN MEDICAL ASSOCIATION AND AMERICAN LIBRARY ASSOCIATION. Books about Sex and Marriage. Chicago, Ill.: American Library Assn., 1940. 6 pp.

JOOST, LAURA REED. Bibliography on Marriage, Family Relations: A Select List of Books and Recent Pamphlets and Periodicals Articles. Evanston, Ill.: Northwestern University Library, 1948. 30 pp.

KASDON, DAVID L. International Family Planning; 1966-1968: A Bibliography. Public Health Service Publication, No. 1917. Washington, D.C.: Superintendent of Documents, U.S. Government Printing Office, 1969. 62 pp.

KENYON, CARLETON W., comp. A Selective Bibliography on Population Control — Abortion, Birth Control, Euthanasia, and Sterilization. Sacramento, Calif.: California State Library, Law Library, 1966. 17 pp.

"A six-page supplement to this work was compiled by Lorna Flescher in 1969."

KIRKENDALL, LESTER ALLEN. A Reading and Study Guide for Students in Marriage and Family Relations. 4th ed. Dubuque, Iowa: Brown, 1968. 177 pp.

"Composed of thirty-nine reading-study guides." First edition published in 1960.

LORINCZI, RHONDA GOODKIN. Marriage Counseling and Conciliation: Known Court-Connected Services, with Summaries of Statutes and a Bibliography. Chicago, Ill.: American Bar Foundation, 1970. 41 pp.

LUDLOW, WILLIAM LINNAEUS. A Syllabus and a Bibliography of Marriage and the Family. New Concord, Ohio: Radcliffe, 1951. 309 pp.

McKUSICK, VICTOR A. Mendelian Inheritance in Man: Catalogs of Autosomal Dominant, Autosomal Recessive, and X-Linked Phenotypes. 2nd ed. Baltimore, Md.: Johns Hopkins, 1968. 521 pp.

First edition 1966.

MEEK, OSCAR. A New Selected Bibliography on Homosexuality: Including Listings of Publishers, Periodical Articles, and other Informational Sources. Santa Fe, N.Mex.: New Mexico Research Library of the South-West, 1969. 34 pp.

MEEK, OSCAR. Pornography, Obscenity and Censorship: A Selective Bibliography. Santa Fe, N.Mex.: New Mexico Research Library of the South-West, 1969. 35 pp. Illus.

MICHIGAN. DEPARTMENT OF MENTAL HEALTH. Films Concerning Home and Family Living. Lansing, Mich.: Dept. of Mental Health, Education Section, 1962. 20 leaves.

MILLET, ANTONY PERCIVAL UPTON. Homosexuality: A Bibliography of Literature Published since 1959 and Available in New Zealand. Wellington, New Zealand: Library School, 1967. 55 pp.

MINNESOTA COUNCIL ON FAMILY LIFE. Family Life Literature and Films: An Annotated Bibliography. Minneapolis, Minn.: Minnesota Council on Family Life, 1964. 74 pp.

Revised in 1967.

MINNESOTA. DIVISION OF CHILD WELFARE. Bibliography: Unmarried Parenthood. St. Paul, Minn.: Division of Child Welfare, 1969. 14 leaves.

"Prepared by the Division of Child Welfare and Department of Public Welfare Library."

MOGEY, JOHN M. Sociology of Marriage and Family Behaviour, 1957-1968: A Trend Report and Bibliography, Prepared for the Intl. Sociological Assn., Committee on Family Research. The Hague, The Netherlands: Mouton, 1971. 364 pp.

"Text in English, summary in French under title 'Sociologie du mariage et du comportement familial 1957-1968.' First published in 'Current Sociology,' Vol. 17, Nos. 1-3, 1969."

MOORE, COYLE ELLIS, and E. R. HARTZ. Suggested Readings on Marriage, Family Living, and Character Education. 4th ed. Gainesville, Fla.: Dept. of Auditory Instruction and Women's Activities, General Extension Division of Florida, 1950. 21 leaves.

NEW YORK (CITY) BOARD OF EDUCATION. Some Resources for Family Life Education. Curriculum Research Report. New York: Board of Education, 1963. 84 pp.

NEW YORK. STATE LIBRARY, ALBANY. LEGISLATIVE REFERENCE LIBRARY. Abortion: A Survey of the Literature. Albany, N.Y., 1969. 14 pp.

"Prepared jointly by the Legislative Reference Library and the State Medical Library of the New York State Library."

OETZEL, ROBERTA LEILANI MILES. Selected Bibliography on Sex Differences. Stanford, Calif.: Stanford University, 1962. 80 leaves.

"Sponsored by Social Science Research Council Committee on Socialization and Social Structure."

OKLAHOMA. STATE BOARD OF VOCATIONAL EDUCATION. Resource Materials for Personal and Family Relationships and Child Development. Oklahoma City, Okla.: Oklahoma State Board for Vocational Education, Home Division, 1956. 157 pp. Illus.

PARKER, WILLIAM. Homosexuality: Selected Abstracts and Bibliography. San Francisco, Calif.: Society for Individual Rights, 1966. 107 pp.

PARKER, WILLIAM. Homosexuality: A Selective Bibliography of Over 3,000 Items. Metuchen, N.J.: Scarecrow, 1971. 323 pp.

PETERS, HERMAN JACOB. Marriage: A Topical Outline with Self-Evaluation Instruments for a Course in Marriage and Family Relations. Palo Alto, Calif.: Pacific, 1952. 112 pp.

REISNER, ROBERT GEORGE. Show Me the Good Parts: The Reader's Guide to Sex in Literature. New York: Citadel, 1964. 340 pp.

SAVITZ, ROBERTA JOYCE ASPEL, et al. Childbearing in and before the Years of Adolescence. Washington, D.C.: U.S. Dept. of Health, Education, and Welfare, Welfare Administration, Children's Bureau, 1966. 28 pp.

"A selected, annotated bibliography covering 1960 to May 1965, with several references to earlier pertinent works."

SCHLESINGER, BENJAMIN. The One-Parent Family: Perspectives and Annotated Bibliography. Toronto, Canada: University of Toronto, 1969. 132 pp.

SCHROEDER, THEODORE ALBERT. List of References on Birth Control. New York: Wilson, 1918. 52 pp.

SHARMA, UMESH D., and W. C. RUDY. Homosexuality: A Select Bibliography. Waterloo, Ont., Canada: n.p., 1970. 114 pp.

SINGER, LAURA J., and JUDITH BUSKIN. Sex Education on Film: A Guide to Visual Aids and Programs. New York: Teachers College, 1971. 170 pp.

SOCIETY FOR SEX EDUCATION AND GUIDANCE. Bibliography of Sex Guidance and Human Relationships. London, Eng.: The Society, 1952. 43 pp.

SPIEGEL, JEANNE. Sex Role Concepts: How Women and Men See Themselves and Each Other; A Selected Annotated Bibliography. Washington,
D.C.: Business and Professional Women's Foundation, 1969. 31 pp.

STANTON, HERBERT EDWARD. Censor's Choice: A Checklist of Banned
Books. Delray Beach, Fla., 1953. 2 leaves.

TIETZE, CHRISTOPHER. Bibliography of Fertility Control, 1950-1965. New
York: National Committee on Maternal Health, 1965. 198 pp.

TIETZE, CHRISTOPHER. Selected Bibliography of Contraception, 1940-1960.
New York: National Committee on Maternal Health, 1960. 76 pp.

Also Supplement: 1960-1963.

TIETZE, CHRISTOPHER, ed. Surgical Sterilization of Men and Women: A
Selected Bibliography. National Committee on Maternal Health. Publication, No. 11. New York: National Committee on Maternal Health, 1962.
38 pp.

U. S. PUBLIC HEALTH SERVICE. DIVISION OF SPECIAL HEALTH SER-
VICES. Current Literature on Venereal Disease. Washington, D.C.: U.S.
Public Health Service, 1952-present.

Published irregularly.

WATT, LOIS BELFIELD, and M. H. THOMAS. Family Life and Sex Education:
A Bibliography. Washington, D.C.: Office of Education, U.S. Dept. of
Health, Education, and Welfare, 1967. 7 pp.

Compiled by personnel of the Education Materials Center, Office of Education, from books sent to the Center during 1963-1966.

WATTS, MARY ELIZABETH. Selected References for Social Workers on
Family Planning: An Annotated List. Washington, D.C.: U.S. Dept. of
Health, Education, and Welfare, Children's Bureau, 1968. 23 pp.

WEINBERG, MARTIN, and A. BELL. Homosexuality: An Annotated Bibliography. New York: Harper, 1971. 704 pp.

Lists 1,265 books and articles written in or translated into English between
1940 and 1968 and deals basically with psychological, psychiatric, and sociological aspects of male and female homosexuality.

YOUNG WOMEN'S CHRISTIAN ASSOCIATIONS. MONTREAL. ROLES OF
WOMEN STUDY COMMITTEE. Bibliography. Rev. ed. Montreal, Canada:
Young Women's Christian Assn., 1966. 47 pp.

DICTIONARIES AND ENCYCLOPEDIAS

BEIGEL, HUGO G. Encyclopedia of Sex Education: The Biological, Physiological, Psychological, Social, Legal, and Medical Aspects of Sexual Development. New York: Daye, 1952. 441 pp.

BEIGEL, HUGO G. Sex from A to Z: A Modern Approach to All Aspects of
Human Sex Life. New York: Daye, 1961. 444 pp.

"An extended discussion of terms and concepts relating to sexuality."

BRANT, HERBERT A., and M. BRANT. Dictionary of Pregnancy, Childbirth, and Contraception. London, Eng.: Mayflower, 1971. 256 pp. Illus.

CARY, HENRY NATHANIEL. The Slang of Venery and its Analogues: Compiled from the Works of Ash, Bailey, Barrere, etc. Chicago, Ill.: Privately printed, 1916. 2 vols.

"Multigraphed."

CARY, HENRY NATHANIEL. Synonyms of the Slang of Venery: Collated from the "Slang of Venery and its Analogues." Chicago, Ill.: Privately printed, 1916. 208 leaves.

ELLIOT, ANDREW GEORGE [Rennie MacAndrew]. Encyclopedia of Modern Sex and Love Techniques in Seven Parts. Hollywood, Calif.: Wilshire, 1967. 352 pp.

Earlier edition published in 1944 by Wales, London, England.

ELLIS, ALBERT, and A. ABARBANEL. The Encyclopedia of Sexual Behavior. 2nd ed., new and rev. New York: Hawthorn, 1967. 1,072 pp. Illus.

First edition published in two volumes in 1961. Also published by Ace, New York, in five volumes under different titles.

GILLETTE, PAUL J. The Complete Sex Dictionary. Intro. by Eustace Chesser. London, Eng.: Tandem, 1969. 256 pp.

GOLDSTEIN, MARTIN, et al. The Sex Book: A Modern Pictorial Encyclopedia. New York: Herder, 1971. 203 pp. Illus.

HAIRE, NORMAN, ed. Encyclopedia of Sexual Knowledge, by A. Costler [pseud.], A. Willy [pseud.], and others. New York: Coward-McCann, 1934. 636 pp. Illus.

Translation of "Encyclopédie de La Vie Sexuelle." Several other versions in existence, in French and English, some under the title "Encyclopaedia of Sex Practice."

HEGELER, INGE, and S. HEGELER. An ABZ of Love. New York: Medical Press of New York, 1963. 288 pp. Illus.

Translation of the Danish work "Kaerlighedens ABZ," 1961, Copenhagen. "Handbook of practical advice on sexual relationships. About 600 separate sexual-phases discussed and arranged alphabetically—with over 120 instructive drawings."

LEGMAN, GERSHON. The Language of Homosexuality: An American Glossary. New York, 1941? leaves 1149-1179

Photocopy of Appendix 7 of G. W. Henry's "Sex Variants," 1941.

NIEMOELLER, ADOLPH FREDRICK. American Encyclopedia of Sex. New York: Panurge, 1935. 277 pp.

REISSNER, ALBERT, and C. WADE. Dictionary of Sexual Terms. Bridgeport, Conn.: Associated Booksellers, 1967. 158 pp. Illus.

ROBINSON, VICTOR, ed. Encyclopaedia Sexualis: A Comprehensive Encyclopaedia-Dictionary of the Sexual Sciences. New York: Dingwall-Rock, 1936. 819 pp.

ROBINSON, WILLIAM JOSEPHUS. Medical and Sex Dictionary. New York:
Eugenics, 1937. 187 pp.

Also 1933 edition.

SCHMIDT, JACOB EDWARD. Cyclopedic Lexicon of Sex: Exotic Practices,
Expressions, Variations of the Libido. 2nd ed. New York: Brussel, 1967.
389 pp.

Originally published under the title "Libido," by Thomas, Springfield, Ill.,
1960. "A dictionary of sex slang and underworld terms by a medical
lexicographer."

SCHMIDT, JACOB EDWARD. Sex Dictionary, and Lexicon of Related Emotions. La Crescenta, Calif.: Hannah, 1954. 106 pp.

SCOTT, GEORGE RYLEY. Scott's Encyclopaedia of Sex: A Practical Encyclopaedia arranged in Alphabetical Order, Explanatory of Everything Pertaining to Sexual Physiology, Psychology and Pathology. London, Eng.: Laurie,
1939. 351 pp. Illus.

SCOTT-MORLEY, A. Encyclopaedia of Sex Worship. London, Eng.: Walton
Press, 1967-1968. 4 vols. Illus. Plates.

STILLER, RICHARD. Illustrated Sex Dictionary: A Compilation of the Most
Significant Sexual Terms and Definitions, with More than 100 Illustrations.
Intro. by Le Mon Clark. New York: Health Publications, 1967. 112 pp.
Illus.

TEEHAN, MICHAEL FABIAN. Standard Sex Knowledge and Health Encyclopedia. Topeka, Kans.: Standard Publishing Co., 1922. 157 pp.

TRIMBLE, JOHN. 5,000 Adult Sex Words and Phrases. North Hollywood,
Calif.: Brandon, 1966. 235 pp.

WEDECK, HARRY EZEKIEL. Dictionary of Aphrodisiacs. New York:
Philosophical Library, 1961. 256 pp. Illus.

WILLY, A. [pseud.], et al. The Illustrated Encyclopedia of Sex. Rev. ed. New
York: Cadillac, 1967. 449 pp. Illus.

Earlier edition published in 1950 under the same title, being the illustrated
second volume of the "Encyclopaedia of Sexual Knowledge," with revisions
and additions.

2.
BIOLOGY OF SEX

AIROLA, PRAVO O. Sex and Nutrition: A Modern Study of Nutritional Aspects of Sexuality. New York: Information, Inc., 1970. 220 pp.

ALLISON, ANTHONY, ed. Penguin Science Survey, 1967: The Biology of Sex. Baltimore, Md.: Penguin, 1967. 288 pp. Illus.

AUSTIN, COLIN RUSSELL, ed. Sex Differentiation and Development. Memoirs of the Society for Endocrinology, No. 7. Cambridge, Eng.: Cambridge University Press, 1960. 198 pp. Illus.

Proceedings of a symposium held in London, England in 1958.

BEVAN, JAMES STUART. Sex: The Plain Facts. London, Eng.: Faber, 1966. 96 pp.

BISHOP, PETER MAXWELL FARROW. Chemistry of the Sex Hormones. American Lecture Series, No. 488. American Lectures in Living Chemistry. Springfield, Ill.: Thomas, 1962. 100 pp.

BRECHER, RUTH, and E. BRECHER, eds. An Analysis of Human Sexual Response. New York: New American Library, 1966. 318 pp.

"The goal of this work, written by many specialists is to translate the Masters-Johnson research into layman's English."

BROSTER, LENNOX ROSS. Endocrine Man: A Study in the Surgery of Sex. London, Eng.: Heinemann, 1945. 144 pp.

"Stresses the important part played in the automatic regulation of our functions by the endocrine glands. The problems of the close interrelation between the glands and the three primitive instincts of growth, self-preservation, and reproduction are considered in their wider biological aspects, particularly the evolution of species."

BURROWS, HAROLD. Biological Actions of Sex Hormones. 2nd ed., entirely rev. and reset. Cambridge, Eng.: Cambridge University Press, 1949. 615 pp.

Previous edition 1945.

BUSCHKE, ABRAHAM, and F. JACOBSOHN. Sex Habits, a Vital Factor in Well-Being. Rev. ed. New York: Emerson, 1948. 224 pp. Illus.

Translation of "Geschlechtsleben und Sexuelle Hygiene." London edition published by Routledge has the title "Introduction to Sexual Hygiene."

CHASE, HERMAN BURLEIGH. Sex: The Universal Fact. New York: Dell, 1965. 190 pp.

"Deals with anatomy and physiology, mating behavior, sex determination and differentiation. Also discusses how sex affects an individual and the new role of sex and love in society."

CLARK, Le MON, ed. Illustrated Sex Atlas. Comp. by Richard Stiller. Fwd. by Hugo Gernsback. New York: Health Publications, 1963. 128 pp. Illus.

"Charts, diagrams, and clear anatomical artwork that provides a wealth of visual material on human sexuality."

COLE, FRANCIS JOSEPH. Early Theories of Sexual Generation. Oxford, Eng.: Clarendon, 1930. 230 pp.

CREW, FRANCIS ALBERT ELEY. Introduction to the Study of Sex. London, Eng.: Gollancz, 1932. 160 pp.

De KRUIF, PAUL HENRY. Male Hormone. New York: Harcourt, 1945. 243 pp.

Reprinted by Permabooks, New York, 1948.

De MERRE, LEON J. The Female Sex Hormones. New York: Vantage, 1954. 219 pp.

DICKINSON, ROBERT LATOU. Human Sex Anatomy: A Topographical Hand Atlas. 2nd ed. Medical Aspects of Human Fertility. Baltimore, Md.: Williams & Wilkins, 1949. 145 pp. Illus.

First edition, 1933.

DOISY, EDWARD A., et al. Female Sex Hormones. Philadelphia, Pa.: University of Pennsylvania Press, 1941. 58 pp.

Partial Contents: Gonadotropic Hormones, by P. E. Smith; Diagnostic Procedures in Female Sex Endocrine Problems, by R. T. Frank; Uses and Limitations of Female Sex Endocrine Therapy, by E. L. Sevringhaus.

DOISY, EDWARD ADELBERT. Sex Hormones. School of Medicine; Porter Lectures, Series 5. Girard, Kans.: University of Kansas, 1936. 64 pp.

Contents: Some Aspects of the Study of Internal Secretions; The Ovarian Follicular Hormone and Related Compounds; Sex Hormone Therapy from the Experimental View-point.

FAST, JULIUS. What You Should Know about Human Sexual Response. New York: Putnam, 1966. 167 pp.

"The author has written an explanation of the findings in 'Human Sexual Response' by Masters and Johnson and added his own independent commentaries."

FILLER, JULIET PARKER. The Female Hormones. New York: Booktab, 1947. 184 pp.

FINK, PAUL J., and V. O. HAMMETT. Sexual Function and Dysfunction. Philadelphia, Pa.: Davis, 1969. 205 pp.

"A series of papers given at a symposium. It includes sections on sex education and conception control, as well as sexual functioning."

FROMME, ALLEN. Understanding the Sexual Response in Humans: Containing a Critical Review of the Masters-Johnson Research. New York: Pocket Books, 1966. 79 pp.

GEDDES, PATRICK, and J. A. THOMSON. The Evolution of Sex. Rev. ed. New York: Scribner, 1914. 342 pp. Illus. Diagrams.

"Half-title: The Contemporary Science Series, ed. by Havelock Ellis." Earlier edition published in 1889.

GRIFFITH, EDWARD FYFE. Sex in Everyday Life. London, Eng.: Allen & Unwin, 1938. 379 pp.

"Seeks to present to the thinking public the scientific background on which our present knowledge of sex is based. Starts from a biological basis and proceeds by frank, unemotional, unsensational statements to build up a physiological and ethical concept of sex. Includes appendices dealing with a number of aspects of the subject."

HARRISON, GEOFFREY AINSWORTH, and J. PEEL, eds. Biosocial Aspects of Sex. Journal of Biosocial Science. Supplement, No. 2. Oxford, Eng.: Blackwell, 1970. 164 pp. Illus.

"Proceedings of the sixth annual symposium of the Eugenics Society, London, England, 1969. Published for the Galton Foundation."

HECKEL, NORRIS J. The Effects of Hormones upon the Testis and Accessory Sex Organs. American Lecture Series, No. 110. American Lectures in Endocrinology. Springfield, Ill.: Thomas, 1951. 73 pp. Illus.

IRVINE, WILLIAM JAMES, ed. Reproductive Endocrinology. Baltimore, Md.: Williams & Wilkins, 1971. 182 pp. Illus.

"Proceedings of a symposium of the section of endocrinology of the Royal Society of Medicine, held in Edinburgh, Scotland in May 1969."

JOLLY, HUGH. Sexual Precocity. American Lecture Series, No. 200. A monograph in the Bannerstone Division of American Lectures in Endocrinology. Springfield, Ill.: Thomas, 1955. 276 pp. Illus.

"A study of sixty-nine children under ten years of age. Originally presented as M.D. thesis at the University of Cambridge, England."

KAUFMAN, SHERWIN A. The Ageless Woman: Menopause, Hormones and the Quest for Youth. Englewood Cliffs, N.J.: Prentice-Hall, 1967. 191 pp.

"Presents facts about the aging process which are medically sound and helpful in their mental health aspects. Includes a bibliography of the medical literature on which each chapter is based." Also published by Dell, New York.

KRETCHMER, NORMAN, et al. Environmental Influences on Genetic Expression: Biological and Behavioral Aspects of Sexual Differentiation. Fogarty International Center Proceedings, No. 2. Bethesda, Md.: National Institutes of Health, for sale by the Superintendent of Documents, U.S. Government Printing Office, Washington, D.C., 1970. 278 pp. Illus.

"A symposium held by the National Institutes of Health in 1969."

Le CONTE, JOSEPH. The Genesis of Sex. New York: Appleton, 1879. 15 pp. Diagrams.

"Reprinted from the 'Popular Science Monthly,' December, 1879."

LEHRMAN, NAT, comp. Masters and Johnson Explained. Chicago, Ill.: Playboy, 1970. 223 pp. Illus.

"Includes texts of interviews with Masters and Johnson."

LINDEGÅRD, BENGT, et al. Male Sex Characters in Relation to Body-Build, Endocrine Activity, and Personality. Lunds universitets årsskrift, n. f., avd. 2, bd. 52, nr. 10. Lund, Sweden: Gleerup, 1956. 15 pp. Illus.

"Read before the Royal Physiographic Society, February 8, 1956."

LLEWELLYN-JONES, DEREK. Everywoman and Her Body. New York: Taplinger, 1971. 317 pp. Illus.

London edition, Faber and Faber, has the title "Everywoman: A Gynaecological Guide for Life." "The author, a gynecologist and obstetrician, answers the questions women most frequently ask about themselves and their bodies."

McCURDY, ROBERT NIGEL CHARLES. The Rhesus Danger: Its Medical, Moral, and Legal Aspects. London, Eng.: Heinemann, 1950. 138 pp.

"A valuable summary, for professional and lay readers, of the problem of Rhesus incompatibility, in its medical and social aspects."

McKUSICK, VICTOR A. On the X Chromosome of Man. Washington, D.C.: American Institute of Biological Sciences, 1964. 141 pp. Illus.

"Originally published in abbreviated form in the 'Quarterly Review of Biology,' Vol. 37, no. 2."

MacLAURINE, ALEXANDER H. A. Sexual Waste of Vital Energy. Binghamton, N.Y.: Putnam, 1896. 431 pp.

"Furnishing exhaustive information about the temptations and effects of excessive indulgence of the sexual appetite from childhood to old age. Compiled from twenty-seven eminent medical authorities."

MARTIN, CECIL PERCY. Psychology, Evolution, and Sex. Springfield, Ill.: Thomas, 1956. 166 pp.

MASTERS, WILLIAM H., and V. E. JOHNSON. Human Sexual Response. Boston, Mass.: Little, Brown, 1966. 366 pp. Illus.

"The research director and the research associate of the Reproductive Biology Research Foundation in St. Louis, Missouri, present their findings of research done on 118 female and twenty-seven male prostitutes on whom they studied the various aspects of sexual response, also during pregnancy and old age."

MERRIGAN, JOHN. The Sixth Day: A Guide to Evolution, Sex and Reproduction. London, Eng.: Darton, 1968. 176 pp.

Also published by Morehouse, New York, 1971. Suitable for grades 9-12.

MITTWOCH, URSULA. Sex Chromosomes. New York: Academic Press, 1967. 306 pp. Illus.

MOORE, KEITH L., ed. The Sex Chromatin. Philadelphia, Pa.: Saunders, 1966. 474 pp. Illus.

OHNO, SUSUMU. Sex Chromosomes and Sex-Linked Genes. Monographs on Endocrinology, Vol. 1. New York: Springer, 1967. 192 pp. Illus.

PARSHLEY, H. M. The Science of Human Reproduction: Biological Aspects of Sex. London, Eng.: Allen & Unwin, 1933. 319 pp.

"Treats sex as fundamentally a biological problem to be explored by scientific methods, while recognizing the importance of the psychological and emotional aspects of sex. Describes the functioning of sex-cells (chromosomes), organs of reproduction, development of the embryo, endocrine glands and hormones, eugenics, and the biology of sex behaviour. Arrives at the conclusion that the sex impulse in its primitive form still exists in the human species, that its repression has never really succeeded, and that our race is mentally and physically vigorous enough to accomplish the revolt against mythological lore and follow the light of scientific truth."

REITALU, JUHAN. Chromosome Studies in Connection with Sex Chromosomal Deviations in Man. Lund, Sweden: n.p., 1967. 48 pp. Illus.

SALHANICK, HILTON A., et al. Metabolic Effect of Gonadal Hormones and Contraceptive Steroids. New York: Plenum, 1969. 762 pp. Illus.

"Based on workshop held in Boston, Massachusetts December 1-5, 1968 and sponsored by the National Institute of Child Health and Human Development and the Center for Population Studies of the Harvard University School of Public Health."

SCHERING CORPORATION. Handy Index to Sex Hormones Therapy. Bloomfield, N.J.: Schering Corporation, 1956. 1 vol. unpaged.

SMITH, D. ROBERTSON, et al. Symposium on Nuclear Sex. London, Eng.: Heinemann, 1958. 188 pp. Illus.

This symposium was held at King's College Hospital Medical School in 1957. Also published in New York by Interscience.

STEINACH, EUGEN. Sex and Life: Forty Years of Biological and Medical Experiments. College Park, Md.: McGrath, 1970. 252 pp. Illus.

Reprint of 1940 edition.
"The scientific values adapted to the lay reader by Josef Loebel."

STENCHEVER, MORTON A. Human Sexual Behavior: A Workbook in Reproductive Biology. With testing by William T. Stickley. Chicago, Ill.: Case Western Reserve University, 1970. 110 pp. Illus.

Prepared in cooperation with the Division of Research in Medical Education, the School of Medicine, Case Western Reserve University.

STOPES, MARIE CHARLOTTE CARMICHAEL. Change of Life in Men and Women. New York: Putnam, 1936. 239 pp.

TRALL, RUSSELL THACHER. Sexual Physiology and Hygiene. New York: Holbrook, 1885. 266 pp.

Several editions in existence.

WHARTON, LAWRENCE RICHARDSON. Ovarian Hormones: Safety of the Pill, Babies after Fifty. Springfield, Ill.: Thomas, 1967. 319 pp.

WHITE, MARGARET MOORE. Womanhood. London, Eng.: Deslisle, 1958. 143 pp. Illus.

"Seeks to help women to understand something about themselves. Describes puberty, marriage, births and their spacing, problems of infancy, and, finally, the change of life." Previous edition published by Cassell, London, 1947.

WILSON, ROBERT A. Feminine Forever. New York: Pocket Books, 1968. 176 pp. Illus.

"Discusses the theory that menopause is a hormone deficiency disease totally preventable and entirely curable by the treatment of estrogen therapy." Previous edition published in 1966.

YOUNG, WILLIAM CALDWELL, et al. Sex and Internal Secretions. Fwd. by George W. Corner. 3rd ed. Baltimore, Md.: Williams & Wilkins, 1961. 1,609 pp. Illus.

"This treatise is the co-operative work of a group of twenty-seven investigators. Its purpose is to survey the most important researches in problems of sex, especially those concerned with internal secretions. It is intended for the reader with a moderate biological background. Physicians who are interested in fundamentals will find much valuable material, and it should also attract the interest of serious students of sex."

First published in 1932. Earlier editions edited by Edgar Allen.

3.
FAMILY LIFE

DIVORCE

AMRAM, DAVID WERNER. The Jewish Law of Divorce: According to Bible and Talmud with Some Reference to Its Development in Post-Talmudic Times. 2nd ed. New York: Hermon, 1968. 224 pp.

Previous edition, 1896.

BACAL, JACQUES W., and L. SLOANE. The ABC of Divorce. New York: Dutton, 1947. 128 pp.

BARTLETT, GEORGE ARTHUR. Is Marriage Necessary: Memoirs of a Reno Judge. New York: Penguin Books, 1947. 179 pp.

First edition published in 1931 under the title "Men, Women and Conflict."

BECKER, RUSSELL J. When Marriage Ends. Philadelphia, Pa.: Fortress, 1971. 56 pp.

BERGLER, EDMUND. Divorce Won't Help. New York: Hart, 1970. 240 pp.

Original edition, 1948.

BLAINE, THOMAS ROBERT. Marriage Happiness or Unhappiness: Based on the Author's Experiences as the Trial Judge in More Than Ten Thousand Divorce Cases. Philadelphia, Pa.: Dorrance, 1955. 197 pp.

CANTOR, DONALD J. Escape from Marriage: How to Solve the Problems of Divorce. New York: Morrow, 1971. 191 pp.

CURRAN, GRACE B. The Americarers: A Cure for the Cancer of Divorce. North Quincy, Mass.: Christopher, 1968. 64 pp. Illus.

DAVIS, MILTON L. The Other Side of Divorce. Boston, Mass.: Badger, 1930. 141 pp.

DONELSON, KENNETH, and I. DONELSON. Married Today, Single Tomorrow: Marriage, Breakup and the Law. Garden City, N.Y.: Doubleday, 1969. 320 pp.

FELDER, RAOUL LIONEL. Divorce: The Way Things Are, Not the Way They Should Be. New York: World, 1971. 263 pp.

FREID, JACOB, ed. Jews and Divorce. New York: Ktav, 1968. 208 pp.

Published for the Commission on Synagogue Relations of the Federation of Jewish Philanthropies of New York.

"Proceedings of a conference sponsored by the Commission on Synagogue Relations of the Federation of Jewish Philanthropies of New York."

FROHLICH, NEWTON. Making the Best of It: Or Common-sense Guide to Negotiating a Divorce. New York: Harper & Row, 1971. 132 pp.

GARDNER, RICHARD A. The Boys and Girls Book about Divorce, with an Introduction for Parents. New York: Science House, 1970. 159 pp. Illus.

GOODE, WILLIAM JOSIAH. Women in Divorce. New York: Free Press, 1965. 381 pp.

Earlier edition published as "After Divorce" in 1956.

GROVES, ERNEST RUTHERFORD. Conserving Marriage and the Family: A Realistic Discussion of the Divorce Problem. New York: Macmillan, 1944. 138 pp.

HUNT, MORTON M. The World of the Formerly Married. New York: Mc-Graw-Hill, 1966. 326 pp.

KOHUT, NESTER CLARENCE. Therapeutic Family Law: A Complete Guide to Marital Reconciliations. 2nd ed. Chicago, Ill.: Family Law Publications, 1968. 436 pp.

Earlier edition published in 1964 with the title "A Manual on Marital Reconciliations."

LICHTENBERGER, JAMES PENDLETON. Divorce: A Social Interpretation. New York: McGraw-Hill, 1931. 472 pp.

"Argues that the rapid increase in divorce during recent years has not been due to degeneracy nor to a decline in social morality, but to the changes in our social system which have imposed increasing stresses on the marriage relation."

LICHTENBERGER, JAMES PENDLETON. Divorce: A Study in Social Causation. Columbia Studies in the Social Sciences, No. 94. New York: AMS Press, 1968. 231 pp.

Earlier edition published in 1909 by Columbia University, New York.

LYMAN, HOWARD BURBECK. Single Again. New York: McKay, 1971. 312 pp.

MELGAREJO RANDOLPH, ANTONIO DAMASO. Is Divorce Necessary? New York: Associated Features, 1930. 241 pp.

RESNICOFF, SAMUEL. M. D. A.: Marriage, Divorce, Annulment. New York: Pageant, 1968. 102 pp.

ROSENBLATT, STANLEY. The Divorce Racket. Los Angeles, Calif.: Nash, 1969. 153 pp.

1970 reprint under the title "Instant Divorce."

SHERWIN, ROBERT VEIT. Compatible Divorce. Intro. by Wardell B. Pomeroy. New York: Crown, 1969. 308 pp.

Also 1970 reprint.

WALLER, WILLARD WALTER. The Old Love and the New: Divorce and Readjustment. Carbondale, Ill.: Southern Illinois University Press, 1967. 331 pp.

Earlier edition published in 1930, by Liveright, New York.

WINNETT, ARTHUR ROBERT. The Church and Divorce. London, Eng.: Mowbray, 1968. 110 pp.

Deals with marriage and divorce in relation to the Church of England.

FREE LOVE UNIONS

DICKSON, RUTH. Marriage Is a Bad Habit. Los Angeles, Calif.: Sherbourne, 1968. 191 pp.

"Looks at the possibilities for future arrangements between adults which are more flexible than marriage."

DIXON, WILLIAM HEPWORTH. Spiritual Wives. 2nd ed. New York: AMS Press, 1972. 2 vols.

Reprint of 1868 edition, published in London by Hurst & Blackett.

ELLIS, JOHN B. Free Love and Its Votaries: Or, American Socialism Unmasked. New York: AMS Press, 1971. 502 pp. Illus.

Reprint of 1870 edition published by U.S. Publishing Company, New York.

"Being an Historical and Descriptive Account of the Rise and Progress of the Various Free Love Associations in the United States, and the Effects of Their Vicious Teachings upon American Society."

HOFMANN, WALTER. The Contraceptive Revolution: Bearings on Social Reality. 2nd ed. New York: Sylvania, 1969. 132 pp.

Deals with free group relationship as opposed to the institution of marriage.

KRONHAUSEN, PHYLLIS, and E. KRONHAUSEN. Freedom to Love: A Film. New York: Grove, 1971. 191 pp. Illus.

Background information. (Consists of interviews conducted by the authors with various persons.)

McCORMICK, DONALD. Temple of Love. New York: Citadel Press, 1965. 221 pp.

Published in 1962 by Jarrolds, London, England.

WILE, IRA SOLOMON, ed. The Sex Life of the Unmarried Adult: An Inquiry into and an Interpretation of Current Sex Practices. New York: Vanguard, 1934. 320 pp.

Reprinted, 1971.

MARRIAGE

ADAMS, CLIFFORD ROSE, and V. O. PACKARD. How to Pick a Mate: The Guide to a Happy Marriage. New York: Dutton, 1946. 215 pp.

AGRIPPA VON NETTESHEIM, HEINRICH CORNELIUS. The Commendation of Matrimony. Tr. by David Chapman. London, Eng.: T. Bertheleti, 1545. 48 pp.

Original at the British Museum.

ANDERSON, CARL LEONARD. Physical and Emotional Aspects of Marriage. St. Louis, Mo.: Mosby, 1953. 234 pp.

ARD, BEN NEAL, and C. C. ARD, eds. Handbook of Marriage Counseling. Palo Alto, Calif.: Science and Behavior Books, 1969. 474 pp.

Theories, techniques, and subject matter of marriage counseling are discussed by professionals in many disciplines.

ASTELL, MARY. Some Reflections upon Marriage. London, Eng.: W. Parker, 1730. 180 pp.

Reprinted in 1971 by Source Book Press, New York. "Contrary to the traditional view, she maintained woman was not under obligation to marry and should do so only if she could love and respect her husband."

AUGSBURGER, DAVID W. Cherishable: Love and Marriage. Scottdale, Pa.: Herald, 1971. 174 pp.

AVERY, CURTIS E., and T. B. JOHANNIS. Love and Marriage: A Guide for Young People. New York: Harcourt, 1971. 176 pp. Illus.

BABER, RAY ERWIN. Marriage and the Family. New York: McGraw-Hill, 1939. 656 pp. Diagrams.

"Should be helpful to teachers and youth leaders."

BACH, GEORGE ROBERT, and P. WYDEN. The Intimate Enemy: How to Fight Fair, in Love and Marriage. New York: Morrow, 1969. 405 pp.

BALZAC, HONORÉ DE. The Physiology of Marriage. New York: Liveright, 1932. 358 pp.

Originally published in France, 1829.

BASSETT, MARION PRESTON. A New Sex Ethics and Marriage Structure, Discussed by Adam and Eve. New York: Philosophical Library, 1961. 332 pp.

BECKER, HOWARD, et al. Family, Marriage and Parenthood. 2nd ed. Boston, Mass.: Heath, 1955. 849 pp.

Earlier edition, 1948.

BELL, ROBERT R. Marriage and Family Interaction. 3rd ed. Homewood, Ill.: Dorsey, 1971. 573 pp.

Earlier edition, 1963.

BELL, ROBERT R. Studies in Marriage and the Family. New York: Crowell, 1968. 229 pp.

BERGLER, EDMUND. Conflict in Marriage: The Unhappy Undivorced. New York: Harper, 1949. 216 pp.

British edition, 1951.

BERGLER, EDMUND. Unhappy Marriage and Divorce: A Study of Neurotic Choice of Marriage Partners. New York: International Universities Press, 1946. 167 pp.

BERNARD, JESSIE SHIRLEY, et al. Dating, Mating, and Marriage: A Documentary Case Approach. Cleveland, Ohio: Allen, 1958. 410 pp.

Second edition, 1959.

BERNARD, JESSIE SHIRLEY. Marriage and Family among Negroes. Englewood Cliffs, N.J.: Prentice-Hall, 1966. 160 pp. Illus.

BERNARD, JESSIE SHIRLEY. Remarriage: A Study of Marriage. New York: Russell & Russell, 1971. 372 pp.

Originally published by Dryden, 1956.

BESANCENEY, PAUL H. Interfaith Marriages: Who and Why. New Haven, Conn.: College & University Press, 1970. 233 pp.

BEYFUS, DRUSILLA. The English Marriage: What It Is Like to Be Married Today. London, Eng.: Weidenfeld, 1968. 162 pp.

BHARADWAJ, B. M. Astro Analysis of Matrimonial Concord: A Book on Astrological Exposition of Marital Happiness. New Delhi, India: Sagar Publications, 1970. 80 pp.

BILLINGSLEY, ANDREW. Black Families in White America. Englewood Cliffs, N.J.: Prentice-Hall, 1968. 218 pp.

"A discussion by a sociologist of the historical background of the black family and some of the major dimensions of black family life today."

BIRD, JOSEPH, and L. BIRD. Marriage Is for Grownups. Garden City, N.Y.: Doubleday, 1969. 288 pp.

"Offers suggestions for improving relations between husband and wife."

BJERRE, POUL CARL. The Remaking of Marriage: A Contribution to the Psychology of Sex Relationship. New York: Macmillan, 1931. 257 pp.

BLAINE, THOMAS ROBERT. How to be Happily Married. Minneapolis, Minn.: Denison, 1968. 170 pp.

BLAINE, THOMAS ROBERT. Marriage Happiness or Unhappiness; Based on the Author's Experiences as the Trial Judge in More Than Ten Thousand Divorce Cases. Philadelphia, Pa.: Dorrance, 1955. 197 pp.

BLANCK, RUBIN, and G. BLANCK. Marriage and Personal Development. New York: Columbia University Press, 1968. 191 pp.

BLOOD, ROBERT O. Marriage. 2nd ed. New York: Free Press, 1969. 535 pp. Illus.

"First published in 1955 under the title 'Anticipating Your Marriage.' "

BLUM, LEON. Marriage. Tr. by Warre Bradley Wells. Philadelphia, Pa., London, Eng.: Lippincott, 1937. 330 pp.

First published in France, 1907.

"The French statesman and philosopher suggests that young people are at first polygamous . . . but they eventually come to a time of life when they are ready to settle down in monogamous marriage."

BOSSARD, JAMES HERBERT SIWARD. One Marriage, Two Faiths: Guidance on Interfaith Marriage. New York: Ronald, 1957. 180 pp.

BOSSARD, JAMES HERBERT SIWARD, and E. S. BOLL. Why Marriages Go Wrong: Hazards to Marriage and How to Overcome Them. New York: Ronald, 1958. 224 pp.

BOWMAN, HENRY ADELBERT. Marriage for Moderns. 6th ed. Fwd. by David R. Mace. New York: McGraw-Hill, 1970. 628 pp. Illus.

Earlier edition, 1942.

"Emphasis throughout is upon a functional rather than historical approach."

BRIFFAULT, ROBERT STEPHEN. The Mothers: A Study of the Origins of Sentiments and Institutions. New York: Johnson Reprint, 1969. 3 vols. Illus.

Originally published by Macmillan in 1927.

Abridged edition, Universal Library, 1963.

BRINK, FREDERICK WRIGHT. This Man and This Woman: A Guide for Those Contemplating Marriage. New York: Association Press, 1948. 79 pp.

BRUCE, ANN. Love and Marriage: The Art of Winning and Holding the One You Love. Chicago, Ill.: Franklin, 1931. 256 pp.

BUCK, PEARL SYDENSTRICKER. Of Men and Women. New York: J. Day, 1941. 203 pp.

Contents: The Discord; The Home in China and America; The American Man; The American Woman; Monogamy; Women as Angels; Women and War; The Education of Men and Women for Each Other; Women and Freedom.

Revised edition, 1971.

BURGESS, ERNEST WATSON, and L. S. COTTRELL. Predicting Success or Failure in Marriage. New York: Prentice-Hall, 1939. 472 pp.

CALVERTON, VICTOR FRANCIS. The Bankruptcy of Marriage. New York: Macaulay, 1928. 341 pp.

"Stresses the impermanence of sex attitudes."

CHESSER, EUSTACE. How to Make a Success of Your Marriage. New York: Roy, 1953. 103 pp.

First published in London, 1952.

CHRISTENSEN, HAROLD T., ed. Handbook of Marriage and the Family. Chicago, Ill.: Rand McNally, 1964. 1,028 pp.

"Reviews the major research in marriage and the family, dealing also with sex as it pertains to premarital and marital behavior and adjustment."

CHRISTENSEN, HAROLD T., and K. P. JOHNSON. Marriage and the Family. 3rd ed. New York: Ronald, 1971. 546 pp.

First and second editions published under the title "Marriage Analysis."

CLARK, LeMON. Emotional Adjustment in Marriage. St. Louis, Mo.: Mosby, 1937. 261 pp.

Reprinted, 1946.

CLEMENS, ALPHONSE HENRY. Design for Successful Marriage. 2nd ed. Englewood Cliffs, N.J.: Prentice-Hall, 1964. 363 pp. Tables.

"First published in 1957 under the title 'Marriage and the Family.' "

CLEMENS, ALPHONSE HENRY, ed. Marriage Education and Counselling. Washington, D.C.: Catholic University of America, 1951. 153 pp.

"Selected papers from the workshops on Marriage and the Family and from the Cana Institute conducted at the Catholic University of America, June 1947, 1948, 1949, 1950."

CLINEBELL, HOWARD JOHN, and C. C. CLINEBELL. The Intimate Marriage. New York: Harper & Row, 1970. 231 pp.

COHN, DAVID LEWIS. Love in America: An Informal Study of Manners and Morals in American Marriage. New York: Simon & Schuster, 1943. 236 pp.

COLE, MARGARET. Marriage: Past and Present. London, Eng.: Dent, 1939. 306 pp.

"Discusses what marriage has been in the past and the position of women at different times."

COOPER, JILLY. How to Stay Married. New York: Taplinger, 1970. 127 pp. Illus.

COX, FRANK D., comp. American Marriage: A Changing Scene? Dubuque, Iowa: W. C. Brown, 1971. 272 pp.

CRAWLEY, ALFRED ERNEST. Mystic Rose: A Study of Primitive Marriage. Rev. and enl. by Theodore Besterman. 4th ed. London, Eng.: Watts & Co., 1932. 505 pp.

Earlier edition, 1902.

Reprinted by Peter Smith, Gloucester, Mass.

CRAWLEY, LAWRENCE Q., et al. Reproduction, Sex, and Preparation for Marriage. Englewood Cliffs, N.J.: Prentice-Hall, 1964. 231 pp.

CRESPY, GEORGES, et al. Marriage and Christian Tradition. Tr. by Sister Agnes Cunningham. Techny, Ill.: Divine Word Publications, 1968. 178 pp.

DANIELSSEN, BENGT. Love in the South Seas. Tr. by F. H. Lyon. New York: Reynal, 1956. 240 pp. Illus.

Deals with Polynesian marriage customs and rites.

Translated from the Swedish "Söderhavskarlek."

DAVIES, EDMUND. Tell Us Now: Open Answers to the Actual Questions of the Young, on Sex and Marriage. London, Eng.: Tandem, 1966. 155 pp.

DEFOE, DANIEL. Conjugal Lewdness: Or, Matrimonial Whoredom. Intro. by Maximillian E. Novak. Gainesville, Fla.: Scholars' Facsimiles and Reprints, 1967. 406 pp.

A facsimile reproduction.

Original edition, 1727, entitled "A Treatise Concerning the Use and Abuse of the Marriage Bed."

DEWAR, LINDSAY. Marriage without Morals: A Reply to Mr. Bertrand Russell. London, Eng.: Society for Promoting Christian Knowledge, 1931. 48 pp.

DICKINSON, ROBERT LATOU, and L. BEAM. A Thousand Marriages: A Medical Study of Sex Adjustment. Fwd. by Havelock Ellis. Westport, Conn.: Greenwood, 1970. 482 pp. Illus.

Reprint of 1931 edition, published by Williams & Wilkins.

DICKS, RUSSELL LESLIE. Premarital Guidance. Englewood Cliffs, N.J.: Prentice-Hall, 1963. 141 pp.

Reprinted by Fortress, Philadelphia, Pa., 1967.

DITZION, SIDNEY HERBERT, 1908- . Marriage, Morals, and Sex in America: A History of Ideas. New York: Octagon Books, 1969. 460 pp.

Earlier edition, 1953.

A history of the attitudes toward sex from colonial times to the present.

DOLAN, ALBERT HAROLD. Happiness in Marriage. Chicago, Ill.: Carmelite Press, 1940. 82 pp. Illus.

"A companion volume to 'A Modern Messenger of Purity.' "—Author's Preface.

DOMINIAN, JACOB. Christian Marriage: The Challenge of Change. London, Eng.: Libra, 1968. 256 pp.

DOMINIAN, JACOB. Marital Breakdown. Baltimore, Md.: Penguin, 1968. 172 pp.

Deals with marriage counseling.

DUVALL, EVELYN RUTH MILLIS, and R. HILL. When You Marry. With Chapters in Collaboration with Sylvanus M. Duvall. Rev. ed. for older teens. New York: Association Press, 1962. 337 pp. Illus.

Revised High School edition, Heath, 1967. Earlier edition, 1945.

DUVALL, EVELYN RUTH MILLIS, and S. DUVALL. Saving Your Marriage. New York: Public Affairs Committee, 1954. 28 pp. Illus.

DUVALL, SYLVANUS MILNE. Before You Marry. New rev. ed. New York: Association Press, 1959. 252 pp.

Earlier edition, 1949.

"The author has chosen the 101 questions which people ask—or should ask—before they marry."

EISENSTEIN, VICTOR W., ed. Neurotic Interaction in Marriage. New York: Basic Books, 1956. 352 pp. Illus.

ELLIS, ALBERT, and R. A. HARPER. A Guide to Successful Marriage. Fwd. by Melvin Powers. Hollywood, Calif.: Wilshire, 1968. 288 pp.

Earlier edition has the title "Creative Marriage," Lyle Stuart, 1961.

ELMAN, PETER, ed. Jewish Marriage. London, Eng.: Soncino, 1968. 231 pp.

"Published for the Jewish Marriage Education Council."

EPSTEIN, LOUIS M. Marriage Laws in the Bible and the Talmud. Cambridge, Mass.: Harvard University, 1942. 362 pp.

Reprinted by Johnson Reprint, New York.

EPSTEIN, LOUIS M. The Jewish Marriage Contract: A Study in the Status of the Woman in Jewish Law. New York: Jewish Theological Seminary of America, 1927. 316 pp.

EVELY, LOUIS. Lovers in Marriage. Tr. by John Drury. New York: Herder, 1968. 144 pp.

Translation of "Amour et Mariage."

"The author sees marriage as part of a whole constellation of other relationships, including the new role of women today, premarital sex and trial marriage."

FIRSTMAN, HAZEL R., et al. A Study on Catholic Marriage in the United States. Pacific Palisades, Calif.: 1968. 166 pp.

"A Marriage and Family Research Project."

FISHBEIN, MORRIS, and J. M. FISHBEIN, eds. Successful Marriage: A Modern Guide to Love, Sex, and Family Life. 3rd rev. ed. Garden City, N.Y.: Doubleday, 1971. 478 pp. Illus.

Earlier edition, 1947.

1957 edition has the title "Modern Marriage and Family Living."

FITCH, WILLIAM. Christian Perspectives on Sex and Marriage. Grand Rapids, Mich.: Eerdmans, 1971. 214 pp.

FOLKMAN, JEROME D., and N. M. K. CLATWORTHY. Marriage Has Many Faces. Columbus, Ohio: Merrill, 1970. 436 pp. Illus.

FOLSOM, JOSEPH KIRK, ed. Plan for Marriage: An Intelligent Approach to Marriage and Parenthood. New York, London, Eng.: Harper, 1938. 305 pp.

"Proposed by members of the staff of Vassar College and dealing with preparation for marriage and family life."

FOSTER, ROBERT GEIB. Marriage and Family Relationships. Rev. ed. New York: Macmillan, 1950. 316 pp. Illus.

Earlier edition, 1944.

GALLICHAN, WALTER MATTHEW. The Psychology of Marriage: A Revised and Enlarged Edition with a Chapter on Birth Control. New York: Stokes, 1930. 303 pp.

Earlier edition, 1918.

GANGSEL, LYLE B. Manual for Group Premarital Counseling. New York: Association Press, 1971. 251 pp.

GENNÉ, ELIZABETH, and W. GENNÉ. Christians and the Crisis in Sex Morality: The Church Looks at the Facts about Sex and Marriage Today. New York: Association Press, 1962. 123 pp.

GENNÉ, ELIZABETH, and W. GENNÉ, eds. Foundations for Christian Family Policy. New York: National Council of Churches, 1961. 272 pp.

"A report of the North American Conference on Church and Family held in 1961 covering marriage problems, teenage relationships, masturbation, birth control, adultery, and some issues these raise for churches today."

GITTELSOHN, ROLAND B. Consecrated unto Me: A Jewish View of Love and Marriage. New York: Union of American Hebrew Congregations, 1965. 232 pp.

GOLDSTEIN, SIDNEY E. Meaning of Marriage and Foundations of the Family: A Jewish Interpretation. New York: Bloch, 1942. 214 pp.

"Deals with problems of marriage and family life from the Orthodox Jewish point of view."

GOTTLIEB, SOPHIE B., and B. S. GOTTLIEB. What You Should Know about Marriage. Indianapolis, Ind.: Bobbs, 1962. 192 pp.

GRANBERG, LARS I. Marriage Is for Adults Only. Grand Rapids, Mich.: Zondervan, 1971. 96 pp.

GREENE, BERNARD L. A Clinical Approach to Marital Problems: Evaluation and Management. Springfield, Ill.: Thomas, 1970. 445 pp.

GREY, ALAN L., ed. Man, Woman, and Marriage: Small Group Process in the Family. New York: Atherton, 1970. 225 pp.

GRIFFIN, GLEN C., and W. D. BELNAP. About Marriage and More. Salt Lake City, Utah: Deseret, 1968. 222 pp. Illus.

Deals with marriage and Christian life from a Mormon point of view.

GRIFFITH, EDWARD FYFE. Marriage and the Unconscious. 2nd ed. Springfield, Ill.: Thomas, 1967. 273 pp. Illus.

Earlier edition, London, Secker, 1957.

GRIFFITH, EDWARD FYFE. Ups and Downs in Married Life. London, Eng.: Methuen, 1966. 355 pp. Illus.

GROVES, ERNEST RUTHERFORD. Marriage. Rev. ed. New York: Holt, 1941. 671 pp.

Earlier edition, 1933.

GROVES, ERNEST RUTHERFORD. Preparation for Marriage. 2nd ed. New York: Emerson, 1944. 130 pp.

Earlier edition published by Greenberg, 1936.

GROVES, ERNEST RUTHERFORD, and W. F. OGBURN. American Marriage and Family Relationships. New York: Holt, 1928. 497 pp.

GROVES, GLADYS HOAGLAND. Marriage and Family Life. Boston, Mass.: Houghton Mifflin, 1942. 564 pp.

GROVES, GLADYS HOAGLAND, and R. A. ROSS. The Married Woman: A Practical Guide to Happy Marriage. Cleveland, Ohio: World, 1951. 278 pp.

Reprint of 1936 edition published by Greenberg.

HAIRE, NORMAN. Hymen: Or, The Future of Marriage. New York: Dutton, 1928. 78 pp.

HAMILTON, CICELY MARY. Marriage as a Trade. Detroit, Mich.: Singing Tree, 1971. 257 pp.

"Facsimile reprint of the 1909 edition."

"Advocates woman's economic independence, and constructs a theory of marriage which would make it a real partnership."

HAMILTON, GILBERT Van TASSEL. A Research in Marriage. New York: Lear, 1948. 570 pp.

"Examination of one hundred married couples, residents of New York City . . . on the question whether marriage is in itself a faulty institution, or to what extent the difficulties in marriage are due to environmental influences."

Reprint of 1929 edition, published by Boni.

HAMILTON, GILBERT Van TASSEL, and K. MacGOWAN. What Is Wrong with Marriage? New York: Boni, 1929. 319 pp.

"An interpretation of the results of Dr. Hamilton's 'Research in Marriage' from a less theoretical and more human standpoint; with a summary of the facts, and conclusions as to their significance."

HARPER, ROBERT ALLAN. Marriage. New York: Appleton, 1949. 308 pp.

"A textbook planned for the practical preparation-for-marriage type of course."

HARRELL, IRENE BURK. Good Marriages Grow: A Book for Wives. Waco, Tex.: Word Books, 1968. 102 pp.

HARRINGTON, WILFRED JOHN. The Promise to Love: A Scriptural View of Marriage. New York: Alba, 1968. 141 pp.

HART, S. L. Lifetime of Love. Boston, Mass.: St. Paul, 1969. 525 pp. Illus.

HERBERT, W. L., and F. V. JARVIS. Marriage Counselling in the Community. Oxford, Eng. and New York: Pergamon, 1970. 79 pp.

HIMES, NORMAN EDWIN. Your Marriage. Rev. and ed. by Donald L. Taylor. New York: Rinehart, 1955. 384 pp. Illus.

1940 edition has the subtitle "A Guide to Happiness." 1950 British edition has the title "Happy Marriage."

"Gives valuable advice as to success and happiness in marriage, for young people thinking of marriage or those already married."

JACKSON, WILLIAM J. How to Have a Happy Marriage. Fort Worth, Tex.: Tampa Publications, 1972. 79 pp.

JENNER, HEATHER, and M. SEGAL. Men and Marriage. New York: Putnam, 1970. 223 pp.

Originally published in London.

Deals with marriage brokerage in Great Britain.

KATZ, BARNEY. You Can Have a Better Marriage. New York: American Press, 1956. 177 pp.

KEENAN, ALAN, and J. RYAN. Marriage: A Medical and Sacramental Study. London, Eng.: Sheed, 1956. 337 pp. Illus.

KELLEY, ROBERT K. Courtship, Marriage, and the Family. New York: Harcourt, Brace, 1969. 629 pp. Illus.

KEY, ELLEN KAROLINA SOFIA. Love and Marriage. Critical and biographical Intro. by Havelock Ellis. Tr. from Swedish by Arthur G. Chater. New York: Source Book Press, 1970. 399 pp.

Earlier edition published by Putnam in 1911.

KEYSERLING, HERMANN ALEXANDER. Book of Marriage: A New Interpretation by Twenty-Four Leaders of Contemporary Thought. New York: Harcourt, 1926. 511 pp.

"The essays by Beatrice M. Hinkle, Havelock Ellis, and Rabindranath Tagore were originally written in English. The remainder were translated from the German by Therese Duerr and others."

KIRKENDALL, LESTER ALLEN, and W. J. ADAMS. The Students' Guide to Marriage and Family Life Literature: An Aid to Individualized Study. 5th ed. Dubuque, Iowa: W. C. Brown, 1971. 147 pp.

Earlier edition has the title "A Reading and Study Guide for Students in Marriage and Family Relations."

KITCHENER, HENRY THOMAS. Letters on Marriage, on the Causes of Matrimonial Infidelity, and on the Reciprocal Relations of the Sexes. London, Eng.: Chapple, 1812. 2 vols. in 1.

KLOCK, FRANK. Apes and Husbands. Alhambra, Calif.: Borden Publishing Co., 1970. 364 pp.

Deals with the history of marriage.

KOHUT, NESTER CLARENCE. Therapeutic Family Law: A Complete Guide to Marital Reconciliations. 2nd ed. Chicago, Ill.: Family Law Publications, 1968. 436 pp.

Earlier edition published in 1964 with the title "A Manual on Marital Reconciliations."

KOMAROVSKY, MIRRA. Blue-Collar Marriage. With the collaboration of Jane H. Philips. New York: Random House, 1964. 395 pp.

KUNZ, FREDERICK A. Responsible Family Living: A Study Course for Adults. Independence, Mo.: Herald Publishing, 1971. 64 pp.

LAMBETH CONFERENCE. What the Bishops Have Said about Marriage: A Resolution Together with the Report of Committee 5 of the Lambeth Conference, 1958, "The Family in Contemporary Society" and the Text of Certain Relevant Resolutions Passed by the Conference. London, Eng.: Society for Promoting Christian Knowledge, 1968. 45 pp.

Marriage and family as viewed by the Church of England.

LANDIS, JUDSON TAYLOR, and M. G. LANDIS. Building a Successful Marriage. 5th ed. Englewood Cliffs, N.J.: Prentice-Hall, 1968. 557 pp.

Earlier edition, 1948. Also published under the title "The Marriage Handbook."

LANDIS, PAUL H. Your Dating Days: Looking Forward to Successful Marriage. 2nd ed. New York: McGraw-Hill, 1971. 156 pp.

"Discusses the dating patterns and considerations most likely to lead to a successful marriage. Based on the author's 'Your Marriage and Family Living.'"

LANDIS, PAUL H. Your Marriage and Family Living. 3rd ed. New York: McGraw-Hill, 1969. 488 pp. Illus.

Earlier edition, 1946.

LEDERER, WILLIAM J., and D. D. JACKSON. The Mirages of Marriage. New York: Norton, 1968. 473 pp.

"Describes the nature of the need to realize that the marital relationship is an interlocked system in itself rather than a function of individual partners."

LEE, ROBERT, and M. CASEBIER. The Spouse Gap: Weathering the Marriage Crisis during Middlescence. Nashville, Tenn.: Abingdon, 1971. 222 pp.

LESHAN, EDA J. Mates and Roomates: New Styles in Young Marriages. Public Affairs Pamphlet, No. 468. New York: Public Affairs Press, 1971. 28 pp. Illus.

LINDSEY, BENJAMIN BARR, and W. EVANS. The Companionate Marriage. New York: Boni, 1927. 396 pp.

"Judge Lindsey believes that legal marriage with legalized birth control, which may terminate in divorce, by mutual consent, provided there are no children, is the cure for the maladjustments in present-day marriage."

LIPKE, JEAN CORYLLEL. Marriage. Minneapolis, Minn.: Lerner, 1971. 61 pp. Illus.

Discusses the important considerations of marriage including housing, in-laws, sexual adjustment, and children.

LOBSENZ, NORMAN MITCHELL, and C. W. BLACKBURN. How to Stay Married: A Modern Approach to Sex, Money, and Emotions in Marriage. New York: Cowles, 1969. 215 pp.

LOCKE, HARVEY JAMES. Predicting Adjustment in Marriage: A Comparison of a Divorced and a Happily Married Group. Westport, Conn.: Greenwood, 1968. 407 pp.

Reprint of 1951 edition published by Holt.

Love and Marriage. Man through His Art, Vol. 5. Greenwich, Conn.: New York Graphic Society, 1968. 64 pp. Illus.

"Endorsed by the World Confederation of Organizations of the Teaching Professions."

LUDOVICI, ANTHONY MARIO. The Choice of a Mate. Intro. by Norman Haire. The International Library of Sexology and Psychology, ed. by Norman Haire. London, Eng.: Lane, 1935. 510 pp.

"Makes a number of unconventional and stimulating suggestions as to the choice of a mate, including a recommendation of inbreeding."

LYS, CLAUDIA DE. How the World Weds: The Story of Marriage, Adultery, and Divorce. New York: Martin, 1929. 279 pp. Illus.

MacAVOY, JEAN. Husband and Wife. New York: Hawthorne, 1968. 207 pp. Illus.

MACE, DAVID ROBERT. Success in Marriage. New York: Abingdon, 1958. 158 pp.

Designed for young adults.

MACE, DAVID ROBERT. What Is Marriage Counseling? Public Affairs Pamphlet, No. 250. New York: Public Affairs Committee, 1957. 28 pp. Illus.

MACE, DAVID ROBERT. What Makes a Marriage Happy? Public Affairs Pamphlet, No. 290. New York: Public Affairs Committee, 1959. 20 pp. Illus.

McGINNIS, TOM. Your First Year of Marriage. Fwd. by David R. Mace. Garden City, N.Y.: Doubleday, 1967. 202 pp.

McHOSE, ELIZABETH. Family Life Education in School and Community. Teachers College Studies in Education. New York: Bureau of Publications, Teachers College, Columbia University, 1952. 182 pp.

McLENNAN, JOHN FERGUSON. Primitive Marriage: An Inquiry into the Origin of the Form of Capture in Marriage Ceremonies. Edinburgh, Scot.: Black, 1865. 326 pp.

MAIR, LUCY PHILIP. Marriage. Harmondsworth, Eng.: Penguin, 1971. 221 pp.

MASON, PAMELA OSTRER. Marriage Is the First Step Toward Divorce. New York: Erikson, 1968. 184 pp.

Reprinted by Avon, New York, 1970.

"An appraisal of males in general and husbands in particular, written from the female point of view."

MILLER, LEVI, ed. The Family in Today's Society. Scottdale, Pa.: Herald, 1972. 109 pp.

NASH, ARNOLD SAMUEL, ed. Education for Christian Marriage: Its Theory and Practice. London, Eng.: Student Christian Movement Press, 1939. 304 pp.

"The various authors approach this subject from the Christian viewpoint, and deal with every aspect of marriage, including the educational and legal problems."

NASH, ETHEL MILLER, et al. Marriage Counseling in Medical Practice: A Symposium. Chapel Hill, N.C.: University of North Carolina Press, 1964. 368 pp.

NELSON, JANET FOWLER. Marriages Are Not Made in Heaven. New York: The Woman Press, 1939. 158 pp. Illus.

On the cover: "Education for Marriage Series."

NOVAK, MICHAEL, ed. The Experience of Marriage: The Testimony of Catholic Laymen. New York: Macmillan, 1964. 173 pp.

For young adults, grade 7 and up.

NUTINI, HUGO G. San Bernardino Contla: Marriage and Family Structure in a Tlaxcalan Municipio. Pittsburgh, Pa.: University of Pittsburgh, 1968. 420 pp.

O'NEILL, NENA, and G. O'NEILL. Open Marriage: A New Life Style for Couples. New York: Evans, 1972. 287 pp. Illus.

OTTO, HERBERT A., ed. The Family in Search of a Future: Alternate Models for Moderns. New York: Appleton, 1970. 204 pp.

PETERSON, JAMES ALFRED, ed. Marriage and Family Counseling: Perspective and Prospect. New York: Association Press, 1968. 188 pp. Illus.

"Revision of papers presented by R. Hill and others at a meeting in Washington, D.C., during October, 1967, commemorating the 25th anniversary of the American Association of Marriage Counselors."

PETERSON, JAMES ALFRED. Married Love in the Middle Years. New York: Association Press, 1968. 157 pp.

"Deals with identity crises, sexual problems, and problems of relationships in the mature years."

POMERAI, RALPH DE. Marriage, Past, Present and Future: An Outline of the History and Development of Human Sexual Relationships. London, Eng.: Constable, 1930. 370 pp.

POPENOE, PAUL BOWMAN. Divorce — 17 Ways to Avoid It! Los Angeles, Calif.: Trend Books, 1959. 128 pp. Illus.

"Abridged from the original book 'Marriage Is What You Make It.' "

POPENOE, PAUL BOWMAN. Marriage, Before and After. New York: W. Funk, 1943. 246 pp.

POPENOE, PAUL BOWMAN. Marriage Is What You Make It. New York: Macmillan, 1969. 221 pp.

Reprint of 1950 edition. Also reprinted in 1970 by Abbey, St. Meinrad, Ind.

POPENOE, PAUL BOWMAN. Modern Marriage: A Handbook for Men. 2nd ed. New York: Macmillan, 1940. 299 pp.

"Earlier edition, published in 1925, had slightly different subtitle."

POPENOE, PAUL BOWMAN, and D. C. DISNEY. Can This Marriage Be Saved? New York: Macmillan, 1960. 299 pp.

REIMER, GEORGE R. Dialog: Dating and Marriage. New York: Holt, 1968. 307 pp.

Designed for young adults.

"Although it is addressed to Catholics, it is almost completely nonsectarian in its approach."

REISS, IRA L. The Family System in America. New York: Holt, Rinehart and Winston, 1971. 493 pp. Illus.

RIKER, AUDREY PALM, and H. E. BRISBANE. Married Life. Peoria, Ill.: Bennett, 1970. 543 pp. Illus.

Designed for young adults.

RODMAN, HYMAN, ed. Marriage, Family and Society: A Reader. New York: Random House, 1965. 302 pp.

ROSENBAUM, SALO, and IAN ALGER, eds. The Marriage Relationship: Psychoanalytic Perspectives. New York: Basic Books, 1968. 366 pp.

Deals with all aspects of marriage.

ROTHENBERG, ROBERT EDWARD, ed. The Doctors' Premarital Medical Adviser. New York: Grosset & Dunlap, 1969. 244 pp. Illus.

Also 1971 reprint.

RUSSELL, BERTRAND. Marriage and Morals. New York: Liveright, 1970. 316 pp.

"A survey of the changes in marital morality resulting from changes in social conditions from the dawn of history to the present day."

Reprint of 1929 edition.

RYAN, MICHAEL. The Philosophy of Marriage in its Social, Moral, and Physical Relations . . . with the Physiology of Generation . . . . 3rd ed. London, Eng.: Bailliere, 1839. 338 pp.

SAKOL, JEANNE. What about Teen-Age Marriage? New York: Messner, 1961. 190 pp.

"Addressed primarily to girls, this book discusses the arguments against early marriage and presents some guidelines for considering the ingredients of a mature marriage relationship."

SANCTUARY, GERALD. Marriage under Stress: A Comparative Study of Marriage Conciliation. Lawrence, Kans.: Verry, 1968. 197 pp.

"A comparative study of the services offered for marriage counseling in the U.S., England, Scandinavia and other countries."

SARGENT, WILLIAM EWART. The Psychology of Marriage and the Family Life. 3rd ed. London, Eng.: Independent, 1945. 154 pp.

Earlier edition, 1940.

SAXTON, LLOYD. The Individual, Marriage and the Family: Current Perspectives. Belmont, Calif.: Wadsworth, 1970. 457 pp. Illus.

SCHIMEL, JOHN LOUIS. Your Future as a Husband. Rev. ed. New York: Rosen, 1968. 159 pp.

Earlier edition, 1964.

Intended for grade 7 and up.

SCHIMEL, JOHN LOUIS. Your Future as a Wife. Rev. ed. New York: Rosen, 1968. 157 pp.

Earlier edition, 1963.

For grade 7 and up.

SEYMAR, WILLIAM. Conjugium Conjurgium, or Some Serious Considerations on Marriage, wherein (by Way of Caution and Advice to a Friend) Its Nature, Ends, Events, Concomitant Accidents, Etc., Are Examined. London, Eng.: J. Amery, 1675. 92 pp.

SHEDD, CHARLIE W. Letters to Karen: On Keeping Love in Marriage. New York: Avon, 1968. 159 pp.

Reprint of 1965 edition, published by Abingdon, Nashville, Tenn.

Intended for young adults.

SHOSTROM, EVERETT L., and J. KAVANAUGH. Between Man and Woman: The Dynamics of Intersexual Relationships. Los Angeles, Calif.: Nash, 1971. 285 pp. Illus.

SILVERMAN, HIRSCH LAZAAR, ed. Marital Counseling: Psychology, Ideology, Science. Springfield, Ill.: Thomas, 1967. 530 pp.

"A comprehensive volume by a large group of experts in various counseling fields."

SLATER, ELIOT O. TREVOR, and M. WOODSIDE. Patterns of Marriage: A Study of Marriage Relationships in the Urban Working Classes. London, Eng.: Cassell, 1951. 311 pp.

"A psychiatric investigation into the married life of working-class Londoners during the years 1943-1945."

STERN, BERNHARD JOSEPH. The Family: Past and Present. New York: Appleton, 1938. 461 pp. Illus.

A manual on the American family, its backgrounds in primitive societies, history, and present status, written for the Commission on Human Relations, Progressive Education Association.

STRAIN, FRANCES BRUCE. Marriage Is for Two: A Forward Look at Marriage in Transition. New York: Longmans, 1955. 250 pp.

Listed in ALA Basic Book Collection for High School.

SUSSMAN, MARVIN B., ed. Sourcebook in Marriage and the Family. 3rd ed. Boston, Mass.: Houghton Mifflin, 1968. 594 pp. Illus.

Earlier edition, 1955.

Presents 62 articles organized around the family-life-cycle approach.

TENENBAUM, SAMUEL. A Psychologist Looks at Marriage. South Brunswick, N.J.: Barnes, 1968. 405 pp.

TERMAN, LEWIS MADISON, et al. Psychological Factors in Marital Happiness. New York: McGraw-Hill, 1938. 474 pp.

An investigation of the psychological and psychosexual factors in the marital satisfaction and happiness of 2,484 subjects including 1,133 married couples and 100 divorced couples.

"This study is based on the results of a questionnaire answered by husbands and wives."

TIZARD, LESLIE JAMES. Guide to Marriage. London, Eng.: Allen & Unwin, 1948. 184 pp.

"Completely frank and scientific in its treatment of sex from both the physical and psychological points of view."

UDRY, JOE RICHARD. The Social Context of Marriage. 2nd ed. Philadelphia, Pa.: Lippincott, 1971. 512 pp. Illus.

Earlier edition, 1966.

VAYHINGER, JOHN MONROE. Before Divorce. Philadelphia, Pa.: Fortress, 1972. 56 pp.

WALKER, KENNETH MacFARLANE, ed. Preparation for Marriage. A Handbook Prepared by a Special Committee on behalf of the British Social Hygiene Council. London, Eng.: Cape, 1932. 191 pp.

"The editor made use of material supplied by a committee of scientists, including a clergyman."

WALKER, KENNETH MacFARLANE. Your Marriage: A Book for the Married and the About To Be Married. 2nd ed. London, Eng.: Transworld Publishers, 1957. 189 pp.

Earlier edition published in 1951 under the title "Marriage."

WALLIS, JACK HAROLD. Marriage Guidance: A New Introduction. London, Eng.: Routledge, 1968. 256 pp.

Also published by Humanities, New York.

WALLIS, JACK HAROLD. Sexual Harmony in Marriage. New York: Roy Publishers, 1965. 132 pp.

"A discussion of the emotional relationships between husband and wife and their effect upon sex."

WEIL, MILDRED W. Marriage, the Family, and Society: Toward a Sociology of Marriage and the Family. Danville, Ill.: Interstate, 1971. 268 pp.

WESTERMARCK, EDVARD ALEXANDER. The Future of Marriage in Western Civilization. Freeport, N.Y.: Books for Libraries, 1970. 281 pp.

Reprint of 1936 edition published by Macmillan.

"Predicts the survival of marriage and the family, freer divorce, and the acceptance of the opinion that sexual acts are morally indifferent."

WESTERMARCK, EDVARD ALEXANDER. The History of Human Marriage. 5th ed., rewritten. Landmarks in Anthropology. London, Eng.: Macmillan, 1921. 3 vols.

New York, Johnson Reprint, 1971.

Earlier edition, 1889.

WESTERMARCK, EDVARD ALEXANDER. A Short History of Marriage. New York: Humanities, 1968. 327 pp.

First published in 1926.

"Based on the fifth edition of 'History of Human Marriage,' but is not an abridged edition."

WESTERMARCK, EDVARD ALEXANDER. Three Essays on Sex and Marriage. New York, Macmillan, 1934. 353 pp.

Contents: The Oedipus Complex; Recent Theories of Exogamy; "The Mothers," a Rejoinder to Dr. Briffault.

WHITE, ERNEST. Marriage and the Bible. Nashville, Tenn.: Broadman, 1965. 149 pp.

WHITNEY, JAMES LYMAN. Love and Marriage in a Changing World. San Francisco, Calif.: Parker Printing, 1958. 477 pp.

WILE, IRA SOLOMON. The Man Takes a Wife; A Study of Man's Problems in and through Marriage. New York: Greenberg, 1937. 277 pp.

WINCH, ROBERT FRANCIS. Mate-Selection: A Study of Complementary Needs. New York: Harper, 1958. 349 pp.

WINCH, ROBERT FRANCIS, and L. W. GOODMAN, eds. Selected Studies in Marriage and the Family. 3rd ed. New York: Holt, 1968. 630 pp.

Earlier edition, 1953.

ZIMMERMAN, CARLE CLARK, and L. F. CERVANTES. Marriage and the Family: A Text for Moderns. Chicago, Ill.: Regnery, 1956. 712 pp. Illus.

4.
PSYCHOLOGY OF LOVE AND SEX

ABRAHAM, KARL. On Character and Libido Development: Six Essays. Ed. with Intro. by Bertram D. Lewin. Tr. by Douglas Bryan and Alix Strachey. New York: Norton, 1966. 206 pp.

ADLER, ALFRED. Individual Psychology and Sexual Difficulties. Individual Psychology Pamphlets, Medical Pamphlets, No. 3. London, Eng.: Daniel, 1932. 71 pp.

ANCHELL, MELVIN. Understanding Your Sexual Needs. New York: Fell, 1968. 277 pp. Illus.

ATKINSON, WILLIAM WALKER, and E. E. BEALS. Sexual Power: Or, Vital Rejuvenation. New York: Fenno, 1922. 172 pp.

Also published under the title "Regenerative Power."

AYAU, A. E. The Social Psychology of Hunger and Sex. Cambridge, Mass.: Sci-Art, 1939. 160 pp.

BACH, GEORGE R., and R. DEUTSCH. Pairing. New York: Wyden, 1970. 241 pp.

"A psychologist shows how to achieve genuine intimacy."

1971 edition, Avon.

BAKER, ELSWORTH F. Man in the Trap. New York: Macmillan, 1967. 354 pp. Illus.

Also published in London by Collier-Macmillan.

BALINT, MICHAEL. Primary Love and Psychoanalytic Technique. International Psycho-analytical Library, No. 44. London, Eng.: Hogarth, 1952. 288 pp.

Collected papers written from 1930 to 1952 and issued in various journals.

BAUER, BERNHARD ADAM. Woman and Love. Tr. from the German by Eden and Cedar Paul. New York: Boni & Liveright, 1927. 2 vols.

Vol. 2 has the subtitle: "A Treatise on the Anatomy, Physiology and Sexual Life of Woman, with an Appendix on Prostitution," translated by E. S. Jerdan...and Norman Haire. This volume is a translation of "Wie bist du, weib?"

BEAUVOIR, SIMONE DE. The Second Sex. Tr. and ed. by H. M. Parshley. New York: Bantam, 1961. 705 pp.

Reprint, 1970.

Several versions published.

Original French edition, 1949.

"A comprehensive book that attempts to explain the role and position of women in society."

BENDA, CLEMENS ERNST. The Image of Love: Modern Trends in Psychiatric Thinking. New York: Free Press, 1961. 206 pp.

BENNETT, EDWARD M., and L. R. COHEN. Men and Women: Personality Patterns and Contrasts. Provincetown, Mass.: 1959. pp. 101-155

In "Genetic Psychology Monographs," Provincetown, Mass., Vol. 59, 1959.

BENOIT, HUBERT. The Many Faces of Love: The Psychology of the Emotional and Sexual Life. Tr. by Philip Mairet. New York: Pantheon, 1955. 308 pp.

Translation of "De l'Amour."

BERGLER, EDMUND. Counterfeit Sex: Homosexuality, Impotence, Frigidity. 2nd enl. ed. New York: Grune & Stratton, 1958. 380 pp.

First edition published in 1951 under the title "Neurotic Counterfeit Sex."

BERLOW, NATHAN. Psychosexual Indicators on the Rorschach Test. Ann Arbor, Mich.: University Microfilms, 1953.

Thesis, University of Michigan.

Abstracted in "Dissertation Abstract," Vol. 13 (1953), No. 3, pp. 429-430.

BERNARD, JESSIE SHIRLEY. The Sex Game. Englewood Cliffs, N.J.: Prentice-Hall, 1968. 372 pp.

BEYLE, MARIE HENRI [Stendhal]. On Love. Tr. from the French by H. B. V. under the direction of C. K. Scott-Moncrieff. New York: Liveright, 1947. 420 pp.

Translation of "De l'Amour," 1822.

Several translations published.

BIER, WILLIAM CHRISTIAN, ed. Personality and Sexual Problems. Pastoral Psychology Series, No. 1. New York: Fordham University Press, 1964. 256 pp.

"Revised edition of some of the papers of the 1955 and 1957 Institutes of Pastoral Psychology held at Fordham University, New York, the proceedings of which were published in limited editions."

BILLER, HENRY B. Father, Child, and Sex Role: Paternal Determinants of Personality Development. Lexington, Mass.: Heath Lexington, 1971. 193 pp.

BJERRE, POUL CARL. The Remaking of Marriage: A Contribution to the Psychology of Sex Relationship. New York: Macmillan, 1931. 257 pp.

BLUM, GERALD S. A Study of Psychoanalytic Theory of Psychosexual Development; and the Assessment of Parental Attitudes in Relation to Child Adjustment, by Edward Joseph Shoben, Jr. Genetic Psychology Monographs, Vol. 39, 1st half. Provincetown, Mass.: Journal Press, 1949. 148 pp.

The first study is a thesis, Stanford University, the second, an abridgment of Shoben's thesis, University of Southern California.

BONAPARTE, MARIE, Princess, Female Sexuality. Tr. by John Rodker. New York: International Universities, 1953. 225 pp.

1962 edition, Grove, New York.

Translation of "De la Sexualité de la Femme."

BOOTH, MEYRICK. Youth and Sex: A Psychological Study. London, Eng.: Allen & Unwin, 1932. 224 pp.

1933 edition, Morrow, New York.

BOOTH, SYLVIA DACHSLAGER. Perceived Similarity of Sex-role Characteristics among Preadolescent and Adolescent Girls. New York: 1963. 125 pp.

Thesis, Columbia University.

BOUSFIELD, PAUL. Sex and Civilization. London, Eng.: Paul, 1925. 294 pp.

1925 New York edition published by Dutton.

"Argues that many of those characteristics which we consider masculine or feminine are not really fundamental, but are due to artificial differentiation, which is deleterious to the efficiency of the race. The disabilities of women are not nearly as great as are commonly supposed; they result from the prevailing male dominance and with different upbringing they might disappear."

BRADY, L. STRAYER. The Psychology of Sex Fascination: Or, How to Win the Right Kind of Husband. New York: Dove, 1925. 122 pp.

BREND, WILLIAM A. Sacrifice to Attis: A Study of Sex and Civilization. London, Eng.: Heinemann, 1937. 350 pp.

"Argues that man is profoundly influenced by irrational fear; fear of the religion he developed, fear of the civilization he created, fear of his emotions, fear of his sexuality. The birth-rate is diminishing and the race will die out unless our whole attitude towards sex is revised, substituting enlightenment and freedom for superstition and fear."

BRENTON, MYRON. The American Male. New York: Coward-McCann, 1966. 252 pp.

1970 edition published by Fawcett Crest, New York.

"States the need for a re-evaluation of what constitutes the masculine role, and points the way to reaching the goal of being male, though equal."

BRIDGES, JAMES WINFRED. Meaning and Varieties of Love: A Psychological Analysis and Interpretation. Cambridge, Mass.: Sci-Art, 1935. 240 pp.

BROWN, DANIEL G. Sex-role Preference in Young Children. Psychological Monographs: General and Applied, Vol. 70, No. 14; whole no. 421. Washington, D.C.: American Psychological Association, 1956. 19 pp.

"Based upon a dissertation submitted . . . to the University of Denver."

BROWNE, FRANCES WORSLEY STELLA. Sexual Variety and Variability among Women, and Their Bearing upon Social Reconstruction. British Society for the Study of Sex Psychology, Publication No. 3. London, Eng.: Beaumont, 1915. 14 pp.

BRUYS, FRANÇOIS. The Art of Knowing Women: Or, the Female Sex Dissected, in a Faithful Representation of Their Virtues and Vices . . . A Dissertation Concerning Adultery, and a Learned Treatise on Divorce . . . Written in French, by the Chevalier Plaute-Amour, pseud., and by Him Published at the Hague, 1729. Now Faithfully Made English with Improvements. London, Eng.: Printed in the year 1730. 237 pp.

"Added by the translator to the original work is 'A Treatise of Adultery and Divorce' written by Thomas Morer."

BUSH, DAVID Van. Practical Psychology and Sex Life. Chicago, Ill.: David Van Bush, 1922. 801 pp.

CALVERTON, VICTOR FRANCIS, and S. D. SCHMALHAUSEN, eds. Sex in Civilization. Intro. by Havelock Ellis. Garden City, N.Y.: Garden City Publishing, 1931 (?). 709 pp.

"Photocopy (positive) made by University Microfilms, Ann Arbor, Mich. in 1967."

Contents: Introduction; Sex through the Ages; The Role of Sex in Behavior; Sex and Psycho-Sociology; Sex and Psychoanalysis; The Clinical Aspects of Sex; Sex in Poetry and Fiction.

CAPRIO, FRANK SAMUEL. Facts and Fallacies about Sex. New York: Citadel, 1966. 63 pp.

CAPRIO, FRANK SAMUEL. The Sexually Adequate Female. North Hollywood, Calif.: Wilshire, 1972. 223 pp. Illus.

Reprint of 1953 edition, published by Citadel, New York.

CHAKRABERTY, CHANDRA. Pragmatic Philosophy: A Study in the Philosophy of Sex According to Modern Science. Calcutta, India: Krishna, 1942 (?) 109 pp.

CHAMBERLAIN, ALLAN B. Sex-role-identification, Self-acceptance and Manifest Anxiety in Adolescent Boys and Girls. Garden City, N.Y.: 1961. 57 pp.

"Thesis — Adelphi, Garden City, N.Y."

"Typewritten copy."

CHAMPION, RICHARD K. The Sweet Smell of Sex. London, Eng.: Canova, 1969. 181 pp. Illus.

Deals with the effects of odors on sexual feelings.

CHAPMAN, JOSEPH DUDLEY. The Feminine Mind and Body: The Psychosexual and Psychosomatic Reactions of Women. New York: Philosophical Library, 1967. 325 pp.

CHASSEGUET-SMIRGEL, JANINE, et al. Female Sexuality: New Psychoanalytic Views. Ann Arbor; Mich.: University of Michigan Press, 1970.
220 pp.

Translation of "Recherches Psychanalytiques Nouvelles sur la Sexualité
Féminine," published in 1964.

1970 French edition has the title "La Sexualité Féminine...."

CHESSER, EUSTACE. The Cost of Loving. New York: Citadel, 1965. 223 pp.

Published by Methuen, London, England in 1964.

CHRISTENSON, CORNELIA. Kinsey: A Biography. Bloomington, Ind.:
Indiana University Press, 1971. 241 pp. Illus.

CLEPHANE, IRENE. Towards Sex Freedom. London, Eng.: Lane, 1935.
243 pp.

"Traces the growth of the freedom of women since the end of the eighteenth
century. Suggests in the last chapter that, while a preference for complete
promiscuity is exceptional, in most men and women sexual desire goes out
to a few particular persons."

CLEUGH, JAMES. The Marquis and the Chevalier: A Study in the Psychology
of Sex as Illustrated by the Lives and Personalities of the Marquis de Sade,
1740-1814, and the Chevalier von Sacher-Masoch, 1836-1905. New York:
Duell, Sloane and Pearce. 1952. 295 pp. Illus.

First published in England in 1951.

Reprinted in 1970 by Greenwood Press, Westport, Conn.

COLE, LUELLA, and I. N. HALL. Psychology of Adolescence. 7th ed. New
York: Holt, Rinehart and Winston, 1970. 669 pp. Illus.

First edition published in 1936.

COLLINS, JOSEPH. The Doctor Looks at Love and Life. New York: New
Home Library, 1942. 279 pp.

Reprint of 1926 edition.

Contents: Love: The Sex Urge, Its Onset and Management; Sexual Frigidity
and Marital Incompatibility; Matrimony Wreckers; Homosexuality; Life:
Adult Infantilism....

CROOKSHANK, FRANCIS GRAHAM. Individual Sexual Problems. Psyche
Miniatures, Medical Series, No. 14. London, Eng.: Paul, 1932. 150 pp.

Contents: Sexual Problems of Adolescence and Marriage; Individual Psychology and the Sexual Problem.

DAVENPORT, FRANCES ISABEL. Adolescent Interests: A Study of the Sexual
Interests and Knowledge of Young Women. Archives of Psychology, No. 66.
New York: Columbia University, 1923. 62 pp.

Published also as doctoral thesis, Columbia University, with slightly
different title.

DAVIS, ELISABETH GOULD. The First Sex. New York: Putnam, 1971.
382 pp.

Deals with role of women in history.

DELEEUW, HENDRIK. Woman, the Dominant Sex. New York: Yoseloff, 1957. 240 pp.

English edition has the subtitle "From Bloomers to Bikinis."

DELL, FLOYD. Love in the Machine Age: A Psychological Study of the Transition from Patriarchal Society. New York: Farrar & Rinehart, 1930. 428 pp.

"Aims to bring to serious readers the fruits of modern psychological discoveries, to popularize modern and scientific views of sexual ethics and behaviour."

De MARTINO, MANFRED F., ed. Sexual Behavior and Personality Characteristics. New York: Grove, 1966. 412 pp.

Reprint of 1963 edition, published by Citadel, New York.

"An anthology of articles by 24 authorities."

DENES, GYULA. The Sex-conscious and the Love-shy. New York: Citadel, 1961. 213 pp.

DEUTSCH, HELENE. The Psychology of Women: A Psychoanalytic Interpretation. New York: Grune & Stratton, 1962-1963. 2 vols.

Vol. 1, "Girlhood." Vol. 2, "Motherhood."

Reprint of 1944-1945 edition.

De WIT, GERARD A. Symbolism of Masculinity and Femininity: An Empirical Phenomenological Approach to Developmental Aspects of Symbolic Thought in Word Associations and Symbolic Meanings of Words. New York: Springer, 1963. 107 pp.

DILLON, MICHAEL. Self: A Study in Ethics and Endocrinology. London, Eng.: Heinemann, 1946. 128 pp.

"The first part of the book describes the effects of the endocrine glands on the sexual and mental nature of man and woman. The second part follows with a discussion of personality, mind, and freewill."

DUYCKAERTS, FRANÇOIS. The Sexual Bond. Tr. by John A. Kay. New York: Dell, 1971. 225 pp.

Published by Delacorte, New York, in 1970.

Translation of "La Formation du Lien Sexuel."

EISNER, BETTY GROVER. The Unused Potential of Marriage and Sex. Boston, Mass.: Little, Brown, 1970. 243 pp.

ELLIOTT, GRACE LOUCKS. Understanding the Adolescent Girl. New York: Woman's Press, 1949. 134 pp.

Reprint of 1930 edition, published by Holt, New York.

ELLIS, ALBERT. The American Sexual Tragedy. 2nd ed., rev. New York: Stuart, 1962. 320 pp.

First published by Twayne, New York in 1954. Also published by Grove, New York in 1962. "A companion volume to 'The Folklore of Sex.' In a comparison of surveys of mass media in 1950 to those in 1960, the author traces the change in American attitudes toward love, courtship, marriage, family relations, and divorce."

ELLIS, ALBERT. The Art and Science of Love. New York: Stuart, 1960. 400 pp.

"Published in England under the title 'The Art and Practise of Love.' London, Souvenir Press, 1961. Also published by Dell, New York in 1965 and Bantam, New York in 1969."

"Lucid, comprehensive handbook integrating sex knowledge with a unique and effective psychological approach to sex-love relations."

ELLIS, ALBERT, and R. O. CONWAY. The Art of Erotic Seduction. New York: Stuart, 1967. 216 pp.

Also published by Ace, New York in 1969.

"Encyclopedic and amusing guide. Designed chiefly as a junior version of 'Sex and the Single Man,' but crammed with highly useful tidbits on mating and dating for Don Juans of all ages."

ELLIS, ALBERT. If This Be Sexual Heresy.... New York: Stuart, 1963. 253 pp.

Also published by Tower, New York in 1966. "An unexpurgated collection of essays on sex relations by the author, which were bowdlerized or entirely censored by the periodicals which originally commissioned them."

ELLIS, ALBERT. The Intelligent Woman's Guide to Man-Hunting. New York: Stuart, 1963. 320 pp.

Also published by Dell, New York in 1965. "Down-to-earth book that tells the single woman exactly how she can meet, attract, enchant, and maintain good sex-love relations with a suitable male partner."

ELLIS, ALBERT. The Sensuous Person: Critique and Corrections. New York: Stuart, 1972. 240 pp.

ELLIS, ALBERT. Sex and the Single Man. New York: Stuart, 1963. 318 pp.

Also published by Dell, New York in 1965. "Tells the bachelor, in unadulterated language, how to work at achieving maximum sex satisfaction and solving a host of other problems of bachelorhood."

ELLIS, ALBERT, ed. Sex Life of the American Woman and the Kinsey Report. New York: Greenberg, 1954. 214 pp.

ELLIS, ALBERT. Sex without Guilt. New York: Grove, 1965. 184 pp.

"A series of essays on various aspects of sex which present a highly permissive attitude toward sexual behavior."

First published by Stuart, New York, in 1958 and revised in 1966. Also published by Lancer, New York in 1969 and Wilshire, North Hollywood, California in 1970.

ELLIS, ALBERT. Suppressed: 7 Key Essays Publishers Dared Not Print. Chicago, Ill.: New Classics House, 1965. 124 pp.

"Includes a courageous and objective appraisal of wife-swapping; two philosophic essays, 'Intellectual Fascism' and 'Sex, Science, and Human Values'; an exploration of the relationship between sex ethics and personal worth."

ELLIS, ALBERT, and R. A. HARPER. Creative Marriage. New York: Stuart, 1961. 288 pp.

Also published under this title by Wilshire, North Hollywood, California in 1968. Published by Tower, New York, in 1966 under the title "The Marriage Bed."

ELLIS, ALBERT, and A. P. PILLAY, eds. Sex, Society and the Individual. Bombay, India: International Journal of Sexology, 1953. 448 pp. Illus.

"Selected papers, revised and brought up to date, from 'Marriage Hygiene' (1934-1937) and the 'International Journal of Sexology' (1947-1952)."

ELLIS, HAVELOCK. Analysis of the Sexual Impulse, Love and Pain, the Sexual Impulse in Women. 2nd ed., rev. and enl. Philadelphia, Pa.: Davis, 1931. 353 pp.

Reprint of 1913 edition.

First edition published in 1903; constitutes volume 3 of the author's "Studies in the Psychology of Sex."

ELLIS, HAVELOCK. The Erotic Rights of Women, and the Objects of Marriage: Two Essays. British Society for the Study of Sex Psychology, Publication No. 5. London, Eng.: Battley, 1918. 23 pp.

ELLIS, HAVELOCK. Erotic Symbolism: The Mechanism of Detumescence; The Psychic State in Pregnancy. Philadelphia, Pa.: Davis, 1930. 285 pp.

Reprint of 1906 edition.

Constitutes Vol. 5 of the author's "Studies in the Psychology of Sex."

ELLIS, HAVELOCK. Essays in War-time: Further Studies in the Task of Social Hygiene. Freeport, N.Y.: Books for Libraries Press, 1969. 252 pp.

Reprint of the 1917 edition.

Partial Contents: Feminism and Masculinism; The Mental Differences of Men and Women; The Conquest of Venereal Disease; Marriage and Divorce; Birth Control.

Second series, published in 1919, under the title "The Philosophy of Conflict, and Other Essays in War-time"; reprinted in 1970.

ELLIS, HAVELOCK. The Evolution of Modesty, the Phenomena of Sexual Periodicity, Auto-Erotism. 3rd ed., rev. and enl. Philadelphia, Pa.: Davis, 1920. 352 pp. Illus.

Reprint of 1910 edition.

First edition published in 1900.

Constitutes Vol. 1 of the author's "Studies in the Psychology of Sex."

ELLIS, HAVELOCK. Man and Woman: A Study of Secondary and Tertiary Sexual Characters. 8th ed., rev. London, Eng.: Heinemann, 1934. 469 pp. Illus. Diagrams.

"While the concept of equality of the two sexes has no biological foundation, and there can be no question of the superiority of either, the sexes are perfectly poised in complete equivalence and are compensatory in their unlikeness."

"Originally published in 1894. This edition has been largely rewritten and to a considerable extent brought up to date."

ELLIS, HAVELOCK. On Life and Sex. New York: New American Library, 1957. 236 pp.

Originally published separately in 1922 and 1931.

Contents: Little Essays of Love and Virtue; More Essays of Love and Virtue.

ELLIS, HAVELOCK. Psychology of Sex: A Manual for Students. 2nd ed. New York: Emerson, 1960. 377 pp.

Reprint of 1938 edition. First published in 1933.

Also published by New American Library, New York.

ELLIS, HAVELOCK. Sex in Relation to Society. New York: Random House, 1936. 750 pp.

First published in 1905 by Davis, Philadelphia, Pa.

Constitutes Vol. 6 of the author's "Studies in the Psychology of Sex."

ELLIS, HAVELOCK. Sexual Selection in Man: 1. Touch. 2. Smell. 3. Hearing. 4. Vision. Philadelphia, Pa.: Davis, 1928. 270 pp.

First published in 1905.

Constitutes Vol. 4 of the author's "Studies in the Psychology of Sex."

ELLIS, HAVELOCK. Studies in the Psychology of Sex. New York: Random House, 1942. 2 vols.

First published in seven volumes in 1900-1928.

Contents: Vol. 1, Pt. 1: The Evolution of Modesty; The Phenomena of Sexual Periodicity; Auto-Erotism. Vol. 1, Pt. 2: Analysis of the Sexual Impulse; Love and Pain; The Sexual Impulse in Women. Vol. 1, Pt. 3: Sexual Selection in Man. Vol. 1, Pt. 4: Sexual Inversion. Vol. 2, Pt. 1: Erotic Symbolism: The Mechanism of Detumescence; The Psychic State in Pregnancy. Vol. 2, Pt. 2: Eonism and Other Supplementary Studies. Vol. 2, Pt. 3: Sex in Relation to Society.

ELLIS, HAVELOCK. The Task of Social Hygiene. Boston, Mass.: Houghton, 1927. 414 pp.

First published in 1912.

Partial Contents: Introduction; The Changing Status of Women; The New Aspect of the Woman's Movement; The Emancipation of Women in Relation to Romantic Love.

EVOY, JOHN J., and M. O'KEEFE. The Man and the Woman: Psychology of Human Love. New York: Sheed, 1968. 143 pp.

FAITHFULL, THEODORE. The Future of Women, and Other Essays. London, Eng.: New Age, 1967. 183 pp.

FAITHFULL, THEODORE. Letters to Margaret: A Simple Introduction to Psychology. London, Eng.: Allen & Unwin, 1941. 160 pp.

FAST, JULIUS. The Incompatibility of Men and Women and How to Overcome It. New York: Evans, 1971. 173 pp. Illus.

FATHER AND SON WELFARE MOVEMENT OF AUSTRALIA. Understanding Psycho-sexual Development. Sydney, Australia: Father and Son Welfare Movement of Australia, 1960. 55 pp.

"Designed to assist clergy, social workers, teachers, etc., and oriented toward counseling."

FERENCZI, SANDOR. Further Contributions to the Theory and Technique of Psycho-analysis. Comp. by John Richman; authorized tr. by Jane Isabel Suttie and others. The International Psycho-analytical Library, No. 11. 2nd ed. London, Eng.: Hogarth, 1950. 480 pp.

Earlier edition, 1926.

FERENCZI, SANDOR. Sex in Psycho-analysis: Contributions to psycho-analysis. Authorized tr. by Ernest Jones. The Development of Psycho-analysis, by Sandor Ferenczi and Otto Rank. Authorized tr. by Caroline Newton. New York: Dover, 1960 (?). 2 vols. in 1.

"Earlier published as separates, the first under the title 'Contributions to Psycho-analysis,' 1916.

Translation from German of fifteen of the author's papers and of 'Entwicklungsziele der Psychoanalyse'."

FERENCZI, SANDOR. Thalassa: A Theory of Genitality. Tr. by Henry Alden Bunker. New York: Norton, 1968. 110 pp.

Translation of "Versuch Einer Genitaltheorie," first published in 1924 and reprint of English translation of 1938.

FIELDING, WILLIAM JOHN. Love and the Sex Emotions: Their Individual and Social Aspects. New York: Dodd, 1932. 357 pp.

FIELDING, WILLIAM JOHN. Sex and the Love-life. Rev. and enl. ed. New York: Dodd, 1959. 325 pp.

Earlier edition, 1927.

FIGES, EVA. Patriarchal Attitudes. New York: Stein and Day, 1970. 191 pp.

Reprinted by Fawcett, New York, in 1971.

FIRESTONE, SHULAMITH. The Dialectic of Sex: The Case for Feminist Revolution. New York: Morrow, 1970. 274 pp. Illus.

Reprinted by Bantam, New York, in 1971.

FLIESS, ROBERT. Erogeneity and Libido: Addenda to the Theory of the Psychosexual Development of the Human. His Psychoanalytic Series, vol. 1. New York: International Universities Press, 1957. 325 pp. Illus.

Reprinted in 1971.

FORBAT, SANDOR, ed. Love and Marriage. New York; Liveright, 1938. 432 pp.

"London edition (Pallos) with some variations in text, has the title 'Love, Marriage, Jealousy'."

"A symposium containing chapters by Julian Huxley, Stekel, Havelock Ellis and others."

FOREL, AUGUSTE HENRI. The Sexual Question: A Study of the Sexual Life in All Its Aspects: Physiology, Psychology, Sociology. English adaptation from the 2nd German ed., rev. and enl. by C. F. Marshall. Rev. ed. New York: Emerson, 1944. 536 pp. Illus.

Written in 1905 under the title "Die Sexuelle Frage."

FREUD, SIGMUND. Beyond the Pleasure Principle. Tr. and newly ed. by James Strachey. New York; Liveright, 1970. 68 pp.

"This monograph announces, as the result of twenty-five years of intensive work, a complete change in the aims of psycho-analytic technique. The theory of the death-instinct is enunciated and the development of the libido theory is reviewed."

Translation of "Jenseits Des Lust-Prinzips," published in 1920.

FREUD, SIGMUND. The Case of Dora, and Other Papers. Tr. by Joan Riviere and others. New York: Norton, 1952. 243 pp.

FREUD, SIGMUND. Freud: On Sex and Neurosis. Ed. by Sander Katz. Tr. by Joan Riviere et al. Garden City, N.Y.: Garden City Pub., 1949. 216 pp.

"Glossary and preface by Paul Goodman."

FREUD, SIGMUND. Modern Sexual Morality and Modern Nervousness. New York: Eugenics, 1938. 48 pp.

FREUD, SIGMUND. The Sexual Enlightenment of Children. His Collected Papers, 5. New York: Collier, 1963. 189 pp.

FREUD, SIGMUND. Sexuality and the Psychology of Love. New York: Collier, 1963. 223 pp.

"The author's papers on sexuality in approximate order of their first appearance."

FREUD, SIGMUND. Three Essays on the Theory of Sexuality. Tr. and newly ed. by James Strachey. New York: Basic Books, 1963. 130 pp.

Reprinted by Avon, New York, 1971.

First published in 1905 under the title "Drei Abhandlungen zur Sexual-theorie."

Several versions and translations in existence.

FRIED, EDRITA. The Ego in Love and Sexuality. New York: Grune & Stratton, 1960. 296 pp.

The 1962 edition, published by Grove, New York, has the title "On Love and Sexuality."

FRIEDAN, BETTY. The Feminine Mystique. New York: Dell, 1964. 384 pp.

Reprinted in 1970.

First published in 1963 by Norton, New York.

FRIEDMAN, LEONARD J. Virgin Wives: A Study of Unconsummated Marriages. London, Eng.: Tavistock, 1971. 161 pp.

First published in 1962.

FROMM, ERICH. The Art of Loving. New York: Harper, 1956. 133 pp.

Also published by Bantam, New York. Love is discussed in all its aspects, not only romantic love, but also the love of parents for children, brotherly love, erotic love, self-love, and love of God.

FROMME, ALLAN. The Ability to Love. New York: Farrar, Straus and Giroux, 1965. 366 pp.

Reprinted by Pocket Books, New York and Wilshire, Hollywood, Calif.

GALLICHAN, WALTER MATTHEW [Geoffrey Mortimer]. Chapters on Human Love. London, Eng.: University Press, 1900. 283 pp.

GALLICHAN, WALTER MATTHEW. Evolution, Theory, Physiology, Psychology and Ideal Practice of Human Love. New York: Walden, 1939. 283 pp.

GAMBLE, ELIZA BURT. The Sexes in Science and History: An Inquiry into the Dogma of Woman's Inferiority to Man. New York: Putnam, 1916. 407 pp.

Revised edition of "The Evolution of Woman," published in 1894.

GLASGOW, MAUDE. Problems of Sex. Boston, Mass.: Christopher, 1949. 199 pp.

GOLDMAN, GEORGE D., and D. S. MILMAN, eds. Modern Woman: Her Psychology and Sexuality. Springfield, Ill.: Thomas, 1969. 275 pp.

"A scholarly book that grew out of the postdoctoral program in psychotherapy at Adelphi University and its annual conference."

GORNICK, VIVIAN, and B. K. MORAN, eds. Woman in Sexist Society: Studies in Power and Powerlessness. New York: Basic, 1971. 515 pp.

GRANT, VERNON W. The Psychology of Sexual Emotion: The Basis of Selective Attraction. New York: Longmans, Green, 1957. 270 pp.

GREENE, THAYER A. Modern Man in Search of Manhood. New York: Association Press, 1967. 128 pp. Illus.

"A Jungian analysis of what it means to be a man in the world of changing values and sex roles."

GREER, GERMAINE. The Female Eunuch. New York: McGraw-Hill, 1971. 349 pp.

A discussion of woman's role in society, past and present, by a young British professor.

GRIMKE, SARAH MOORE. Letters on the Equality of the Sexes and the Condition of Woman. New York: Source Book Press, 1970. 128 pp.

Reprint of the 1838 edition.

GRODDECK, GEORG WALTHER. The Book of the It. Authorized tr. by V. M. E. Collins. New York: Vintage Books, 1961. 262 pp.

Translation of "Das Buch vom Es," published in 1928 (?).

"Psychoanalytic letters to a friend."

GRODDECK, GEORG WALTHER. The World of Man. Authorized tr. by
V. M. E. Collins. London, Eng.: Vision, 1951. 271 pp. Illus.

"Extracts from the writings of Groddeck, including the greater part of his
last work 'Der Mensch als Symbol' (1933) selected by the translator."

Reprint of 1934 edition.

GROUP FOR THE ADVANCEMENT OF PSYCHIATRY. Normal Adolescence:
Its Dynamics and Impact. New York: Scribner, 1968. 127 pp.

"This report represents the thinking of a group of leading psychiatrists and
contains a great deal of valuable information about the psychosexual development — of the average teenager."

GUITTON, JEAN. Feminine Fulfillment. Tr. by Paul J. Oligny. Chicago,
Ill.: Franciscan Herald, 1965. 116 pp.

Translation of "Une Femme dans la Maison."

GUITTON, JEAN. Human Love. Chicago, Ill.: Franciscan Herald, 1966.
245 pp.

Translation of "Essai sur l'Amour Humain."

Also published in 1951 under the title "Essay on Human Love."

HALE, NATHAN G. Freud and the Americans: The Beginnings of Psychoanalysis in the United States, 1876-1917. Freud in America, Vol. 1. New
York: Oxford, 1971. 574 pp.

Originally presented as the author's thesis, University of California at
Berkeley.

HARDING, MARY ESTHER. The Way of All Women: A Psychological Interpretation. New York: Longmans, 1946. 335 pp.

"Dr. Jung, in his introduction, describes it as 'an important contribution to
this striving of our time for a deeper knowledge of the human being and for
a clarification of the confusion existing in the relationship between the
sexes'."

Reprint of 1933 edition.

HARDING, MARY ESTHER. Woman's Mysteries, Ancient and Modern: A Psy-
chological Interpretation of the Feminine Principle as Portrayed in Myth,
Story, and Dreams. New and rev. ed. New York: Pantheon, 1955. 256 pp.
Illus.

"Companion volume to the author's Way of All Women."

Original edition published by Longmans, New York, 1935.

HARRINGTON, CHARLES CHRISTOPHER. Errors in Sex-role Behavior in
Teen-age Boys. New York: Teachers College, Columbia University, 1970.
109 pp.

HARRINGTON, JOHN, comp. Male and Female: Identity. Perception in Communication. New York: Wiley, 1972. 168 pp. Illus.

HARTLEY, CATHERINE GASQUOINE. The Truth about Woman. London, Eng.:
Nash, 1913. 404 pp.

"Rejects the common belief that in sex relations man is the dominant partner, but takes the converse view."

HARTOGS, RENATUS, and H. FANTEL. Four-letter Word Games: The Psychology of Obscenity. New York: Evans, 1967. 186 pp.

HAUGHTON, ROSEMARY. Love. Baltimore, Md.: Penguin, 1972. 202 pp.

Originally published in 1970 by Watts, London, England.

HEAPE, WALTER. Sex Antagonism. New York: Putnam, 1913. 217 pp.

Contents: Introductory; The Problems; Exogamy; Totemism; Maternal Impressing and Birth-marks; Biology and Dr. Frazer's Theory; Primitive and Modern Sex Antagonism.

HEATON, WALTER. Temperament and Sex in Life and Art. Boston, Mass.: Badger, 1919. 144 pp.

HELMAN, PATRICIA KENNEDY. Free to Be a Woman. Garden City, N.Y.: Doubleday, 1971. 140 pp.

HENNESSEY, CAROLINE. The Strategy of Sexual Struggle. New York: Lancer, 1971. 208 pp.

HERNTON, CALVIN C. Sex and Racism in America. New York: Grove, 1966. 180 pp. Illus.

First published in 1965.

HERSCHBERGER, RUTH. Adam's Rib. New York: Pellegrini & Cudahy, 1948. 221 pp.

"Analysis of the position of women in modern society."

HIRSCH, ARTHUR HENRY. The Love Elite: The Story of Woman's Emancipation and Her Drive for Sexual Fulfillment. New York: Julian, 1963. 281 pp.

HIRSCHFELD, MAGNUS. Sex in Human Relationships. Tr. by John Rodker. Intro. by Norman Haire. International Library of Sexology and Psychology, ed. by Norman Haire. London, Eng.: Lane, 1935. 218 pp.

"First published in French under the title 'L'Ame et l'Amour'."

HITZ, GERTRUDE. The Importance of Knowledge Concerning the Sexual Nature: A Suggestive Essay. Washington, D.C.: Washington Society for Moral Education, 1884. 32 pp.

HOBBS, LISA. Love and Liberation: Up Front with the Feminists. New York: McGraw-Hill, 1970. 161 pp.

HOCH, PAUL H., and J. Zubin, eds. Psychosexual Development in Health and Disease. New York: Grune & Stratton, 1949. 283 pp. Diagrams.

"Proceedings of the thirty-eighth annual meeting of the American Psychopathological Association, June, 1948."

HODGE, MARSHALL BRYANT. Your Fear of Love. Garden City, N.Y.: Doubleday, 1967. 270 pp. Illus.

HOLE, JUDITH, and E. LEVINE. Rebirth of Feminism. Chicago, Ill.: Quadrangle, 1971. 500 pp.

HOLLITSCHER, WALTER. Sigmund Freud, an Introduction: A Presentation of His Theory and Discussion of the Relationship between Psychoanalysis and Sociology. Freeport, N.Y.: Books for Libraries, 1970. 119 pp.

Reprint of 1947 edition.

HOLTER, HARRIET. Sex Roles and Social Structure. Oslo, Norway: Universitetsforlaget, 1970. 298 pp. Tables.

HORNEY, KAREN. Feminine Psychology: Papers. Ed. with Intro. by Harold Kelman. New York: Norton, 1967. 269 pp.

"Sponsored by the Association for the Advancement of Psychoanalysis."

HORTON, THOMAS D. What Men Don't Like about Women. New York: Greenfield, 1945. 144 pp.

HOWARD, WILLIAM LEE. Sex Problems in Worry and Work. New York: Clode, 1915. 204 pp.

HUDSON, KENNETH. Men and Women: Feminism and Anti-feminism Today. Levittown, N.Y.: Transatlantic Arts, 1969. 187 pp.

HUTTON, LAURA. The Single Woman: Her Adjustment to Life and Love. Rev. ed. New York: Roy, 1962. 132 pp.

Earlier editions, 1935 and 1937 have the title "The Single Woman and Her Emotional Problems."

JANEWAY, ELIZABETH. Man's World, Women's Place: A Study in Social Mythology. New York: Morrow, 1971. 319 pp.

JASTROW, JOSEPH. Freud: His Dream and Sex Theories. New York: Permabooks, 1959. 290 pp.

Original title, "The House That Freud Built," published in 1932 by Greenberg, New York.

JEANNIÈRE, ABEL. The Anthropology of Sex. Tr. by Julie Kernan. New York: Harper, 1967. 188 pp.

Translation of "Anthropologie Sexuelle," Paris, 1964.

JUNG, CARL GUSTAV. Psychology of the Unconscious: A Study of the Transformations and Symbolism of the Libido; A Contribution to the History of the Evolution of Thought. Authorized tr. with Intro. by Beatrice M. Hinkle. New York: Dodd, 1957. 566 pp. Illus.

Earlier edition, 1916.

Translation of "Wadlungen und Symbole der Libido."

JUNG, EMMA. Animus and Anima: Two Essays. New York: Analytical Psychology Club of New York, 1957. 94 pp.

"Translation of 'Ein Beitrag zum Problem des Animus,' by C. F. Baynes and of 'Die Anima als Naturwesen,' by H. Nagel."

KAHN, SAMUEL. The Psychology of Love. New York: Philosophical Library, 1968. 101 pp.

KENEALY, ARABELLA. Feminism and Sex-extinction. London, Eng.: Unwin, 1920. 313 pp.

"The purpose of this book is to dissuade women from exploiting a world's misfortunes for their own immediate profit, and to reconcile them, in their profounder interests and in those of the race, to surrender freely all the masculine employments into which mischance has cast them." — Foreword.

KEY, ELLEN KAROLINA SOFIA. The Renaissance of Motherhood. Tr. from the Swedish by A.E.B. Fries. New York: Source Book Press, 1970. 171 pp.

Reprint of the 1914 edition, published by Putnam, New York.

KEY, ELLEN KAROLINA SOFIA. The Woman Movement. Tr. by M. B. Borthwick. Intro. by Havelock Ellis. New York: Putnam, 1912. 224 pp.

"A discussion, by a notable pioneer of woman's freedom in Sweden, of the meaning of the woman movement, including its influence on the relations between men and women; on marriage; and on motherhood."

KING, BOSWELL. Sex and Human Nature [studies]. London, Eng.: Wales Publishing Co., 1933. 304 pp.

Contents: Sex; Love; Marriage and Divorce; Birth Control; Epilogue.

KLEIN, H. SYDNEY, ed. Sexuality and Aggression in Maturation: New Facets. London, Eng.: Bailliere, Tindall & Cassell for the Institute of Psycho-Analysis, 1969. 68 pp.

Consists of the 1969 winter lectures, delivered under the auspices of the British Psycho-Analytical Society. United States publisher: Williams & Wilkins Co., Baltimore, Md.

KLEIN, VIOLA. The Feminine Character: History of an Ideology. International Library of Sociology. London, Eng.: Paul, 1946. 228 pp.

"An attempt to clarify the idea of 'femininity' by a study and coordination of the theories developed by a number of the leading authorities during recent years."

KNOPF, OLGA. The Art of Being a Woman. Ed. by Alan Porter. Boston, Mass.: Little, Brown, 1932. 307 pp.

KOHLBERG, LAWRENCE, and E. ZIGLER. The Impact of Cognitive Maturity on the Development of Sex Role Attitudes in the Years 4 to 8. Provincetown, Mass.: 1967.

"In 'Genetic Psychology Monographs,' Vol. 75 (1967), pp. 89-165."

KOLLONTAĬ, ALEKSANDRA MIKHAĬLOVNA. The Autobiography of a Sexually Emancipated Communist Woman. Ed. with Afterword by Iring Fetscher. Tr. by Salvator Attanasio. New York: Herder, 1971. 137 pp.

KOMISAR, LUCY. The New Feminism. New York: Watts, 1971. 181 pp.

Recommended for young adults.

KRICH, ARON M., ed. The Sexual Revolution. New York: Dell, 1964-1969. 2 vols.

Vol. 1, "Pioneer Writings on Sex." Vol. 2, "Seminal Studies into 20th Century American Sexual Behavior."

KUHN, ALVIN BOYD. Sex as Symbol: The Ancient Light in Modern Psychology. Elizabeth, N.J.: Academy, 1945. 345 pp.

LANDIS, CARNEY, and M. M. BOLLES. Personality and Sexuality of the Physically Handicapped Woman. New York and London, Eng.: Hoeber, 1942. 171 pp.

LANDIS, CARNEY, et al. Sex in Development: A Study of the Growth and Development of the Emotional and Sexual Aspects of Personality, Together with Physiological, Anatomical, and Medical Information on a Group of 153 Normal Women and 142 Female Psychiatric Patients. College Park, Md.: McGrath, 1970. 329 pp.

Reprint of 1940 edition, published by Hoeber, New York.

LANG, THEO. The Difference between a Man and a Woman. New York: Day, 1971. 413 pp.

LAWRENCE, DAVID HERBERT. Psychoanalysis of the Unconscious, and Fantasia of the Unconscious. New York: Viking, 1960. 225 pp.

Originally published as separates in 1921 and 1922, respectively.

LAY, WILFRED. Man's Unconscious Passion. New York: Dodd, Mead, 1920. 246 pp.

LEDERER, WOLFGANG. The Fear of Women. New York: Grune & Stratton, 1968. 360 pp. Illus.

LEPP, IGNACE. The Psychology of Loving. Tr. by Bernard B. Gilligan. Baltimore, Md.: Helicon, 1963. 223 pp.

Translation of "Psychanalyse de l'Amour." Reprinted by New American Library, New York, 1971.

LOWEN, ALEXANDER. Love and Orgasm. New York: Macmillan, 1965. 303 pp.

Reprinted by New American Library, New York, 1971.

LUDOVICI, ANTHONY MARIO. The Future of Woman. London, Eng.: Paul, 1936. 152 pp.

"A supplement to 'Lysistrata' rather than a revised edition of it." — Preface.

LUDOVICI, ANTHONY MARIO. Lysistrata: Or Woman's Future and Future Woman. Fwd. by Norman Haire. New York: Dutton, 1925. 110 pp.

LUDOVICI, ANTHONY MARIO. Man: An Indictment. New York: Dutton, 1927. 374 pp.

"The author contends that woman is only gaining ground through the degeneration of man."

LUDOVICI, ANTHONY MARIO. Woman: A Vindication. New York: Knopf, 1923. 331 pp.

"The author works on the premise that the place of woman in the scheme of things is as mother of the race and that anything that tends to interfere with her physical vigor and constitutional bias in favor of life is evil."

LUDOVICI, LAURENCE JAMES. The Final Inequality: A Critical Assessment of Woman's Sexual Role in Society. New York: Norton, 1965. 271 pp.

Also published by Muller, London, England in 1965.

LUNDIN, JOHN PHILIP [pseud.]. Ghosts of Venery: A Psychoerotic Self-analysis. New York: Julian, 1965. 310 pp.

LUNDIN, JOHN PHILIP [pseud.]. Women: The Autobiographical Reflections of a Frustrated Male. Intro. by R. E. L. Masters. New York: Julian Press, 1963. 336 pp.

LYNN, DAVID BRANDON. Parental and Sex Role Identification: A Theoretical Formulation. Berkeley, Calif.: McCutchan, 1969. 131 pp. Illus.

MacCOBY, ELEANOR E., et al. The Development of Sex Diferences. Stanford Studies in Psychology, 5. Stanford, Calif.: Stanford University, 1966.

McDERMOTT, SANDRA. Female Sexuality: Its Nature and Conflicts. New York: Simon & Schuster, 1971. 223 pp.

First published under the title "Studies in Female Sexuality."

McINNES, EDITH. Bearing Human Fruit. London, Eng.: Regency, 1968. 302 pp.

McNEMAR, QUINN, and L. M. TERMAN. Sex Differences in Variational Tendency: From the Department of Psychology of Stanford University. Worcester, Mass.: Clark University, 1936. 65 pp.

"An examination of the available evidence on the relative variability of boys and girls and of men and women, in mental and physical traits."

MAILER, NORMAN. The Prisoner of Sex. New York: New American Library, 1971. 175 pp.

Also published by Little, Brown, Boston, Mass., 1971.

MARKE, SVEN, and I. GOTTFRIES. Measurement of Sex Role Perception and Its Relation to Psychological Masculinity-feminity. Psychological Research Bulletin, 10:5, 1970. Lund, Sweden: Lund University, 1970. 33 pp. Illus.

MASSERMAN, JULES HYMEN. Sexuality of Women: Scientific Proceedings of the Tenth Annual Spring Meetings of the American Academy of Psychoanalysis. Science and Psychoanalysis, Vol. 10. New York: Grune & Stratton, 1966. 168 pp.

MASTERS, ROY. Sex, Sin & Solution. Los Angeles, Calif.: Foundation of Human Understanding, 1970. Vol. 1.

MATTHEWS, EDWARD RUSSELL. Sex, Love and Society. London, Eng.: Gollancz, 1959. 199 pp.

MAY, ROLLO. Love and Will. New York: Norton, 1969. 352 pp.

MEAD, MARGARET. Male and Female: A Study of the Sexes in a Changing Society. New York: Morrow, 1949. 477 pp.

1968 edition, Dell, New York.

MENNINGER, KARL. Love against Hate. New York: Harcourt, 1964. 311 pp.

"Develops the concept of Freud that the innate nature of human beings is made up of death and a life instinct, the one expressing itself in hate, frustration, and destructiveness, the other in love supported by faith and hope."

Also published by Harcourt in 1942.

MENNINGER, WILLIAM CLAIRE, et al. How to Understand the Opposite Sex. New York: Sterling, 1956. 192 pp. Illus.

MILLETT, KATE. Sexual Politics. Garden City, N.Y.: Doubleday, 1970. 393 pp.

The author maintains that the relationship between the sexes is and always has been a political one— a continuing power struggle in which women have been sometimes idolized, other times patronized, always exploited.

MILNER, ESTHER. Effects of Sex Role and Social Status on the Early Adolescent Personality. Genetic Psychology Monographs No. 2, Vol. 49. Provincetown, Mass., 1949. pp. 231-325

MOLL, ALBERT. Libido Sexualis: Studies in the Psycho-sexual Laws of Love Verified by Clinical Sexual Case Histories. New York: American Ethnological Press, 1933. 384 pp.

"Untersuchungen über die Libido Sexualis"...has been translated into English by D. Berger."

1966 edition, Brandon, North Hollywood, Calif.

MONEY, JOHN, ed. Sex Research: New Developments. Contributors: Frank A. Beach et al. New York: Holt, 1965. 260 pp. Illus.

"A symposium...devoted to the frontiers of research in sex behavior."

MONEY-KYRLE, ROGER ERNIE. Development of the Sexual Impulses. International Library of Psychology, Philosophy and Scientific Method, No. 101. New York: Harcourt, 1932. 219 pp.

Reprinted in 1950.

MONTAGU, ASHLEY. The Natural Superiority of Women. Rev. ed. New York: Macmillan, 1968. 235 pp.

"A plea for more mutual love and understanding and complete social equality of the sexes."

First published in 1954.

Revised edition reprinted in 1970.

MORGAN, ELAINE. The Descent of Woman. New York: Stein and Day, 1972. 258 pp.

MORGAN, ROBIN. The Sisterhood Is Powerful: An Anthology of Writings from the Women's Liberation Movement. New York: Random, 1970. 602 pp. Illus.

MUKHERJI, SANTOSH KUMAR. Psychology of Love and Sex of the Hindus. Calcutta, India: Oriental Agency, 1960 (?). 119 pp. Illus.

NAGERA, HUMBERTO, et al. Basic Psychoanalytic Concepts on the Libido Theory. Hampstead Clinic Psychoanalytic Library, Vol. 1. London, Eng.: Allen & Unwin, 1969. 194 pp.

NEGRI, VITALI. Psychoanalysis of Sexual Life. Los Angeles, Calif.: Western Institute of Psychoanalysis, 1949. 274 pp.

NEWTON, NILES. Maternal Emotions: A Study of Women's Feelings toward Menstruation, Pregnancy, Childbirth, Breast Feeding, Infant Care, and Other Aspects of Their Femininity. A Psychosomatic Medicine Monograph. New York: Hoeber, 1955. 140 pp.

PARRISH, EDWARD. Sex and Love Problems. New York: Psychology Institute of America, 1935. 153 pp.

PAYETTE, GASTON C. How to Get and Hold a Woman. Montreal, Canada: Gaston C. Payette, 1968. 182 pp.

PETERSON, BRUCE HENRY. Understanding Psychosexual Development. Sydney, Australia: Family Life Movement of Australia, 1970. 126 pp.

PHILP, HOWARD LITTLETON. A Psychologist Looks at Sex. New York: Hutchinson, 1945. 110 pp.

Also London edition.

POMEROY, WARDELL BAXTER. Sexual Behavior Before and After Psychosurgery. New York: 1954. 41 leaves.

Thesis, Columbia University.

Published by University Microfilms, Ann Arbor, Michigan.

REICH, WILHELM. The Function of the Orgasm: Sex-economic Problems of Biological Energy. London, Eng.: Panther Books, 1968. 384 pp. Illus.

Translation from the manuscript of "Die Funktion des Orgasmus." First published in 1942 as Vol. 1 of "The Discovery of the Orgone."

1961 edition published by Noonday, New York.

REIK, THEODOR. The Many Faces of Sex. New York: Farrar, 1966. 202 pp.

REIK, THEODOR. The Need to Be Loved. New York: Farrar, 1963. 276 pp.

REIK, THEODOR. Of Love and Lust: On the Psychoanalysis of Romantic and Sexual Emotions. New York: Farrar, Strauss and Cudahy, 1957. 623 pp.

REIK, THEODOR. A Psychologist Looks at Love. New York: Farrar and Rinehart, 1944. 300 pp.

"Contrary to the libido theory of Freud, it is argued that love does not originate from the sexual urge but is essentially an attempt to escape from oneself in search of an ideal self."

REIK, THEODOR. Psychology of Sex Relations. New York: Grove, 1961. 243 pp.

1945 edition, Rinehart, New York.

REIK, THEODOR. Sex in Man and Woman: Its Emotional Variations. New York: Noonday, 1960. 249 pp.

1963 edition, Mayflower Books, London, England.

ROBBINS, JHAN, and J. ROBBINS. An Analysis of Human Sexual Inadequacy. New York: New American Library, 1971. 317 pp. Illus.

ROBERTIELLO, RICHARD C. Sexual Fulfillment and Self-affirmation. Larchmont, N.Y.: Argonaut, 1964. 156 pp.

ROBERTS, GWILYM O. The Road to Love: Avoiding the Neurotic Pattern. Prefatory note by William Brown. Fwd. by David R. Mace. London, Eng.: Allen & Unwin, 1950. 230 pp.

ROBINSON, MARIE NYSWANDER. The Power of Sexual Surrender. Garden City, N.Y.: Doubleday, 1959. 263 pp.

ROSENBERG, BENJAMIN GEORGE, and B. SUTTON-SMITH. Ordinal Position and Sex-role Identification. Worcester, Mass.: 1964. pp. 297-328

In "Genetic Psychology Monographs," Vol. 70, 1964.

ROSENBERG, BENJAMIN GEORGE, and B. SUTTON-SMITH. Sex and Identity. Person in Psychology Series. New York: Holt, 1972. 113 pp.

ROSENBERG, HENRIETTA [Walter S. Keating]. Sex Studies from Freud to Kinsey. New York; Stravon, 1949. 92 pp.

ROSENFELS, PAUL. Love and Power: The Psychology of Interpersonal Creativity. New York: Libra, 1966. 232 pp.

RUITENBEEK, HENDRIK MARINUS. The Male Myth. New York: Dell, 1967. 223 pp.

"Explores and debunks some of the myths, clichés, and stereotypes about the American male."

RUITENBEEK, HENDRIK MARINUS, ed. Psychoanalysis and Female Sexuality. New Haven, Conn.: College & University Press, 1966. 251 pp.

RUITENBEEK, HENDRIK MARINUS, ed. Psychoanalysis and Male Sexuality. New Haven, Conn.: College & University Press, 1966. 268 pp.

RUITENBEEK, HENDRIK MARINUS, ed. Sexuality and Identity. New York: Dell, 1971. 402 pp.

SAPIRSTEIN, MILTON RICHARD. Emotional Security. London, Eng. and New York: Rider, 1951. 291 pp. Illus.

SAXE, LOUIS P., and N. B. GERSON. Sex and the Mature Man. New York: Gilbert, 1964. 256 pp.

1970 edition published by Simon & Schuster, New York.

SCHAEFFER, DIRK L., ed. Sex Differences in Personality: Readings. Belmont, Calif.: Brooks/Cole, 1971. 186 pp.

SCHEINFELD, AMRAM. Women and Men. New York: Harcourt, 1944. 453 pp.

1947 edition, Chatto & Windus, London, England.

The author discusses fundamental differences between women and men in temperament and behavior.

SCHWAB, LAURENCE, and K. MARKHAM. Discover your Sexual Personality. Woodbridge, Conn.: Apollo, 1971. 138 pp.

SCHWARTZ, WILLIAM ALEXANDER [L. T. Woodward]. Sex and Hypnosis: A Doctor's Report on the Daring New Therapy for Emotional Problems and Sexual Conflicts. Derby, Conn.: Monarch, 1961. 138 pp.

SCHWARTZ, WILLIAM ALEXANDER [L. T. Woodward]. Sex and the Armed Services: A Doctor's Confidential Report on the Sexual Behavior of Men and Women in Military Life. Derby, Conn.: Monarch, 1960. 140 pp.

SCHWARZ, OSWALD. The Psychology of Sex. Harmondsworth, Middlesex, Eng.: Penguin, 1962. 288 pp.

Several editions published previously.

Also 1970 edition.

SCOTT-MAXWELL, FLORIDA PIER. Women and Sometimes Men. New York: Knopf, 1957. 207 pp.

"A study of the relationship of the feminine and masculine elements in present-day women."

SEWARD, GEORGENE HOFFMAN, and R. C. WILLIAMSON, eds. Sex Roles in Changing Society. New York: Random, 1970. 419 pp.

Some articles reprinted from other sources.

SHEPARD, MARTIN. The Love Treatment: Sexual Intimacy between Patients and Psychotherapists. New York: Wyden, 1971. 208 pp.

1972 edition, Paperback Library, New York.

SOLOMON, JOSEPH C. A Synthesis of Human Behavior: An Integration of Thought Processes and Ego Growth. New York: Grune & Stratton, 1954. 265 pp. Illus.

SPITZ, RICHARD H., and S. S. SCHUMACHER. Developmental Sexuality. Current Problems in Pediatrics, Vol. 1, No. 6. Chicago, Ill.: Year Book Medical Publishers, 1971. 34 pp.

STEKEL, WILHELM. Disguises of Love: Psychoanalytical Sketches. New York: Dodd, 1929. 171 pp.

1922 edition, Paul, London, England.

STEKEL, WILHELM. Sex and Dreams: The Language of Dreams. Boston, Mass.: Badger, 1922. 322 pp.

A translation of the first portion of "Die Sprache des Traumes."

STEKEL, WILHELM. Sex and Psychoanalysis: Twelve Essays. New York: Eugenics, 1932. 320 pp.

STERBA, RICHARD. Introduction to the Psychoanalytic Theory of the Libido. 3rd ed. New York: R. Brunner, 1968. 81 pp.

STERN, KARL. The Flight from Woman. New York: Farrar, 1965. 310 pp.

"The author sees a fundamental problem of man through the ages as a rejection of the acceptance of love simply because such acceptance is somehow equated with weakness."

SUTTIE, IAN DISHART. The Origins of Love and Hate. London, Eng.: Paul, 1939. 275 pp.

"Opposing the Freudian theory, the author argues that the source of love is not sex but the need for food, and that the original object of love is the mother."

1952 edition, Julian, New York.

SYMPOSIUM ON FEMININE PSYCHOLOGY. New York Medical College, Flower and Fifth Avenue Hospitals, 1950. Feminine Psychology: Its Implications for Psychoanalytic Medicine. New York: Dept. of Psychiatry, Psychoanalytic Division, 1950. 75 pp.

TABORI, PAUL. Dress and Undress: The Sexology of Fashion. London, Eng.: New English Library, 1969. 223 pp.

TALMEY, BERNARD SIMON. Woman: A Treatise on the Normal and Pathological Emotions of Feminine Love. New York: Stanley, 1904. 228 pp.

TENENBAUM, JOSEPH. The Riddle of Woman: A Study in the Social Psychology of Sex. New York: Furman, 1936. 477 pp.

1929 edition, Macaulay, New York.

TERMAN, LEWIS MADISON, and C. C. MILES. Sex and Personality: Studies in Masculinity and Femininity. Assisted by Jack W. Dunlap et al. New York: Russell & Russell, 1968. 600 pp.

Reprint of 1936 edition.

THOMAS, WILLIAM ISAAC. Sex and Society: Studies in the Social Psychology of Sex. Chicago, Ill.: University of Chicago, 1907. 325 pp.

"These studies have been published in various journals at different times."

THOMPSON, CLARA MABEL. On Women. Ed. by Maurice R. Green. Fwd. by Erich Fromm. New York: New American Library, 1971. pp. 17-192

Selected from "Interpersonal Psychoanalysis," by Clara M. Thompson, published by Basic in 1964.

THOMPSON, MARY LOU, ed. Voices of the New Feminism. Boston, Mass.: Beacon, 1970. 246 pp.

TREVETT, REGINALD FREDERICK. The Tree of Life: Sexuality and the Growth of Personality. New York: Kenedy, 1964. 191 pp.

TRIDON, ANDRÉ. Psychoanalysis and Love. New York: Permabooks, 1949. 239 pp.

1922 edition, Brentano's, New York.

VAËRTING, MATHILDE, and M. VAËRTING. The Dominant Sex. London, Eng.: Allen & Unwin, 1923. 240 pp.

"The fundamental theory of this book is that what we call 'masculine' qualities today are merely the qualities of a dominant sex, and what we call 'feminine' qualities are merely the qualities of a subordinate sex. Much of what we call 'masculinity' and 'femininity' is not congenital, but is the result of the prevailing sex-dominance, and is reacquired from generation to generation."

WAEHNER, TRUDE S. Interpretation of Spontaneous Drawings and Paintings. Preference for Sex Symbols and Their Personality Correlates, by Kate Franck. Genetic Psychology Monographs, Vol. 33. Provincetown, Mass.: Journal Press, 1946. 123 pp. Illus.

WALKER, KENNETH MacFARLANE, and P. PLETCHER [pseud.]. Sex and Society: A Psychological Study of Sexual Behaviour in a Competitive Culture. London, Eng.: Muller, 1955. 236 pp.

1970 edition, Penguin, London.

WALKER, KENNETH MacFARLANE. Sexual Behaviour, Creative and Destructive. London, Eng.: Kimber, 1966. 272 pp.

WALLACH, MICHAEL A., and C. GREENBERG. Personality Functions of Symbolic Sexual Arousal to Music. Psychological Monographs, General and Applied, Vol. 74, No. 7, whole no. 494. Washington, D.C.: American Psychological Association, 1960. 18 pp. Illus.

WALLIS, JACK HAROLD. Thinking about Love. London, Eng.: Routledge, 1969. 168 pp.

1970 edition, Roy, New York.

WEIGERT, EDITH. The Courage to Love: Selected Papers. New Haven, Conn.: Yale University, 1970. 421 pp.

WEININGER, OTTO. Sex and Character. New York: Putnam's Sons, 1906. 356 pp.

Also published by Heinemann, London, England.

Translation from German.

WEXBERG, ERWIN. Individual Psychology and Sex. Tr. from the German by W. Béran Wolfe. London, Eng.: Cape, 1931. 223 pp.

"An exposition, in clear, simple language of the sexuality of men, women, and children, according to Adlerian Individual Psychology."

WEXBERG, ERWIN. The Psychology of Sex: An Introduction. New York: Farrar, 1931. 215 pp.

Authorized translation into English by W. B. Wolfe.

WHITNEY, JAMES LYMAN. Love and Marriage in a Changing World. San Francisco, Calif.: Parker Printing, 1958. 477 pp.

WILSON, COLIN. Origins of the Sexual Impulse. New York: Putnam, 1963. 263 pp.

1966 edition, Panther, London, England.

WINICK, CHARLES. The New People: Desexualization in American Life. New York: Pegasus, 1968. 384 pp.

WITTELS, FRITZ. The Sex Habits of American Women. New York: Eton, 1951. 189 pp. Illus.

WOLLSTONECRAFT, MARY. A Vindication of the Rights of Woman: With Strictures on Political and Moral Subjects. New York: Collector's Editions, 1970. 452 pp.

Reprint of 1792 edition, published by Johnson, London, England. Several other editions in existence.

WOOLLEY, HELEN BRADFORD THOMPSON. The Mental Traits of Sex: An Experimental Investigation of the Normal Mind in Men and Women. Chicago, Ill.: University of Chicago, 1903. 188 pp.

Published also under the title "Psychological Norms in Men and Women."

Doctoral thesis, University of Chicago, 1901.

WORTIS, S. BERNARD, et al. Physiological and Psychological Factors in Sex Behavior. Annals of the New York Academy of Sciences, Vol. 47, Art. 5. New York: The Academy of Sciences, 1947. pp 603-664

YARROS, RACHELLE SKIDELSKI. Modern Woman and Sex: A Feminist Physician Speaks. New York: Vanguard, 1933. 218 pp.

5.
SEX AND RELIGION

AUER, ALFONS, et al. Celibacy and Virginity. Dublin, Ireland: Gill, 1968. 111 pp.

BABBAGE, STUART BARTON. Christianity and Sex. Chicago, Ill.: Inter-Varsity, 1963. 59 pp.

BABBAGE, STUART BARTON. Sex and Sanity: A Christian View of Sexual Morality. Philadelphia, Pa.: Westminster, 1967. 98 pp.

BAILEY, DERRICK SHERWIN. Sexual Ethics: A Christian View. New York: Macmillan, 1963. 159 pp.

"Traces the origins of our Western sexual tradition and discusses the moral and personal aspects of sex from a religious point of view." First published in 1962 under the title "Common Sense About Sexual Ethics."

BAILEY, DERRICK SHERWIN. Sexual Relation in Christian Thought. New York: Harper, 1959. 312 pp.

London edition, Longmans, has the title "The Man-woman Relation in Christian Thought."

BAYNE, JOHN SLOANE. Back to Eden: The Secret of the Temple. Philadelphia, Pa.: McKay, 1932. 220 pp.

BELGUM, DAVID RUDOLPH. The Church and Sex Education. Philadelphia, Pa.: Lutheran Church Press, 1967. 128 pp.

BLENKINSOPP, JOSEPH. Celibacy, Ministry, Church: An Enquiry into the Possibility of Reform in the Present Self-Understanding of the Roman Catholic Church and Its Practice of Ministry. New York: Herder, 1968. 252 pp.

BLENKINSOPP, JOSEPH. Sexuality and the Christian Tradition. Dayton, Ohio: Pflaum, 1969. 127 pp.

BRANDRETH, HENRY RENAUD TEVINER, and D. BAILEY. Celibacy and Marriage: A Study in Clerical Vocation. London, Eng.: S.P.C.K., 1944. 48 pp.

Publication of the Society for Promoting Christian Knowledge in London.

BRAV, STANLEY ROSENBAUM. Since Eve: A Bible-Inspired Sex Ethic for Today. New York: Pageant, 1959. 204 pp.

BRIFFAULT, ROBERT. Sin and Sex. New York: Macaulay, 1931. 253 pp.

British edition, Allen, London.

BRITISH COUNCIL OF CHURCHES. Sex and Morality: A Report to the British Council of Churches, October, 1966. Philadelphia, Pa.: Fortress, 1966. 77 pp.

British edition published by S.C.M. Press, London.

BUCKLEY, JOSEPH. Christian Design for Sex: Principles and Attitudes for Parents and Teachers. Chicago, Ill.: Fides, 1952. 216 pp.

BUSENBARK, ERNEST. Symbols, Sex and the Stars in Popular Beliefs: An Outline of the Origins of Moon and Sun Worship, Astrology, Sex Symbolism, Mystic Meaning of Numbers, the Cabala, and Many Popular Customs, Myths, Superstitions, and Religious Beliefs. New York: Truth Seeker Co., 1949. 396 pp.

CABOT, RICHARD CLARKE. The Christian Approach to Social Morality: Three Lectures on the Consecration of the Affections, and Report of the Commission on Social Morality. New York: National Board, Young Women's Christian Associations, United States of America, 1913. 99 pp.

CABOT, RICHARD CLARKE. Christianity and Sex. New York: Macmillan, 1937. 78 pp.

CALLAHAN, SIDNEY CORNELIA. Exiled to Eden: The Christian Experience of Sex. New York: Sheed, 1969. 248 pp.

1968 edition published under the title "Beyond Birth Control."

COLAIANNI, JAMES F., ed. Married Priests and Married Nuns. New York: McGraw, 1968. 230 pp.

Reprinted in 1969 by Ace, New York.

COLE, WILLIAM GRAHAM. Sex and Love in the Bible. New York: Association, 1959. 448 pp.

Reprinted by Brown, Deer Park, New York.

COLE, WILLIAM GRAHAM. Sex in Christianity and Psychoanalysis. New York: Oxford, 1955. 239 pp.

"Contrasts past and present Christian thinking about sex. Also contrasts the views of Jesus, Paul, Augustine, Calvin, and Freud."

"Issued also on microfilm as a thesis, Columbia University, with the title 'Interpretation of Sex in Christianity and Psychoanalysis'."

CRUMP, BASIL WOODWARD. The Secret Doctrine on the Problem and Evolution of Sex. Blavatsky Pamphlets, No. 2. Victoria, B.C., Canada: H.P.B. Library, 1890. 10 pp.

CUNNEEN, SALLY. Sex: Female; Religion: Catholic. New York: Holt, 1968. 171 pp.

Also published by Burns, London, England, 1968. Deals with the views of American Catholic women on contraception, confession, parochial education, the Church, and their responsibility to society.

DAVIDSON, ALEX. The Returns of Love: Letters of a Christian Homosexual. London, Eng.: Inter-Varsity, 1970. 93 pp.

DEMANT, VIGO AUGUSTE. Christian Sex Ethics: An Introduction. New York: Harper, 1963. 127 pp.

British edition, 1963, by Hodder, London.

DENS, PIERRE [Homo]. Extracts from Peter Dens' and Bishop Kenrick's Moral Theology. Tr. into English and German, for the use of fathers, husbands, and brothers. Chicago, Ill.: n.p., 1871. 73 pp.

Text in English, German, and Latin. Originally written circa 1770.

DIMOCK, EDWARD C. The Place of the Hidden Moon: Erotic Mysticism in the Vaisnavasahajiyā Cult of Bengal. Chicago, Ill.: University of Chicago, 1966. 299 pp.

"Much of this material was presented as part of the author's thesis at Harvard University, Cambridge, Massachusetts, 1959."

DOHERTY, DENNIS. The Sexual Doctrine of Cardinal Cajetan. Studien zur Geschichte der Katholischen Moraltheologie, Bd. 12. Regensburg, Germany: Pustet, 1966. 372 pp.

Inaugural dissertation, Würzburg, Germany.

DONIGER, SIMON, ed. Sex and Religion Today. New York: Association Press, 1953. 238 pp.

DOUGALL, JAMES W. C., ed. Christianity and the Sex-Education of the African. London, Eng.: Society for Promoting Christian Knowledge, 1937. 128 pp.

Papers by the editor and others.

EICKHOFF, ANDREW R. A Christian View of Sex and Marriage. New York: Free Press, 1966. 270 pp.

EPSTEIN, LOUIS M. Sex Laws and Customs in Judaism. New York: Ktav, 1968. 251 pp.

Reprint of 1948 edition, published by Bloch, New York.

"Companion to 1942 work, 'Marriage Laws in the Bible and the Talmud'."

FEIJÓ, DIOGO ANTÓNIO. Demonstration of the Necessity of Abolishing a Constrained Clerical Celibacy, Exhibiting the Evils of that Institution, and the Remedy. Tr. from the Portuguese, with Intro. and Appendix, by D. P. Kidder. Philadelphia, Pa.: Sorin, 1844. 128 pp.

Written in Portuguese, circa 1840.

FEUCHT, OSCAR E., ed. Sex and the Church: A Sociological, Historical, and Theological Investigation of Sex Attitudes. St. Louis, Mo.: Concordia, 1961. 277 pp.

"A review and examination of church teachings in the past in light of present problems. Issued by the Family Life Committee of the Lutheran Church, Missouri Synod."

FIELDING, WILLIAM JOHN. Sexual Obsessions of Saints and Mystics. Girard, Kans.: Haldeman-Julius, 1925. 64 pp.

FITCH, WILLIAM. Christian Perspectives on Sex and Marriage. Grand Rapids, Mich.: Eerdmans, 1971. 214 pp.

FORD, JOSEPHINE MASSINGBERD. A Trilogy on Wisdom and Celibacy. Notre Dame, Ind.: University of Notre Dame, 1967. 256 pp.

GAGERN, FRIEDRICH ERNST. New Views of Sex-Marriage-Love. Tr. by Erika Scavillo. Glen Rock, N.J.: Paulist Press, 1968. 102 pp.

Translation of "Das Neue Gesicht der Ehe."

GEIS, RUDOLPH. Principles of Catholic Sex Morality. Tr. and ed. by Charles Bruehl. New York: Wagner, 1930. 105 pp.

"Translation of 'Katholische Sexual-ethik'."

GENNÉ, ELIZABETH, and W. GENNÉ. Christians and the Crisis in Sex Morality: The Church Looks at the Facts about Sex and Marriage Today. New York: Association Press, 1962. 123 pp.

GOLDBERG, BEN ZION. Sex in Religion. New York: Liveright, 1970. 386 pp. Illus.

Originally published under the title "The Sacred Fire," 1930.

GRAY, ARTHUR HERBERT. Men, Women, and God. Rev. ed. London, Eng.: Student Christian Movement Press, 1957. 149 pp.

"A discussion of sex questions from the Christian point of view, dealing with the social, personal, and physical relations of the sexes." First published by Doran, New York, in 1923.

GREEN, ZELMA BELL. Christian Male-Female Relationship: A Three-Month Course Designed for Individual or Group Study. Grand Rapids, Mich.: Baker, 1967. 111 pp. Illus.

GREET, KENNETH G. The Mutual Society: Aspects of the Relationship of Men and Women. The Beckly Social Service Lecture, 1962. London, Eng.: Epworth, 1962. 170 pp.

GREGG, RICHARD BARTLETT. Spirit through Body. Boston, Mass.: University Press of Cambridge, 1956. 53 pp.

GRIMM, ROBERT. Love and Sexuality. Tr., with Fwd. by David R. Mace. New York: Association Press, 1964. 127 pp.

Translation of "Amour et Sexualité: Essai d'Éthique Théologique," published by DeLachaux, Neuchâtel, Switzerland. "Interpretation of human sexuality from the Protestant perspective, using an open dialogue approach."

HAFFERT, JOHN MATHIAS. Sex and the Mysteries. Washington, N.J.: Ave Maria Institute, 1970. 280 pp. Illus.

Deals with chastity.

HANNAY, JAMES BALLANTYNE. IHOH, Rome's Supreme Fraud. Aberdeen, Scotland: Albany. 1930. 39 pp. Illus.

"A postscript to my 'Rise, Decline, and Fall of the Roman Religion' founded upon our Rome-created Bible."—The Author.

HANNAY, JAMES BALLANTYNE. The Rise, Decline and Fall of the Roman Religion. London, Eng.: Religious Evolution Research Society, 1925. 257 pp. Illus.

HANNAY, JAMES BALLANTYNE. Sex Symbolism in Religion. London, Eng.: Religious Evolution Research Society, 1922. 2 vols.

Reprinted by Haskell, New York, 1971, as No. 35 of "Studies in Comparative Literature."

HAUGHTON, ROSEMARY. The Holiness of Sex. Rev. and enl. ed. St. Meinrad, Ind.: Abbey, 1969. 128 pp.

Originally published in 1965, by Abbey.

HEBERT, ALBERT J. Priestly Celibacy—Recurrent Battle and Lasting Values. Houston, Tex.: Lumen Christi, 1971. 198 pp.

HEFLEY, JAMES C. Sex, Sense, and Nonsense: What the Bible Does and Doesn't Say about Sex. Elgin, Ill.: David Cook, 1971. 96 pp.

HERON, ALASTAIR, ed. Towards a Quaker View of Sex: An Essay by a Group of Friends. Rev. ed. London, Eng.: Friends Home Service Committee, 1964. 84 pp.

Earlier edition, 1963.

HODGSON, LEONARD. Sex and Christian Freedom: An Enquiry. New York: Seabury, 1967. 127 pp.

London edition, 1967, by Student Christian Movement Press.

HOLMES, URBAN TIGNER. The Sexual Person: The Church's Role in Human Sexual Development. New York: Seabury, 1970. 163 pp.

"A revised form of a study prepared by the Department of Christian Education of the Diocese of Louisiana."

HOWARD, CLIFFORD. Sex and Religion: A Study of the Relationship and Its Bearing on Civilization. London, Eng.: Williams & Norgate, 1925. 201 pp.

"Argues that our civilization is the result of suppression and control of sex by the Christianity of Paul. Women were suppressed and a man's world created. Now women are coming into their own; the world would be immensely better and happier if governed by women, as it probably will be in the future."

HOWARD, CLIFFORD. Sex Worship: An Exposition of the Phallic Origin of Religion. 2nd ed. Washington, D.C.: Clifford Howard, 1898. 215 pp.

First edition, 1897.

HULME, WILLIAM EDWARD. God, Sex and Youth. St. Louis, Mo.: Concordia, 1968. 184 pp.

Originally published in 1959 by Prentice-Hall, Englewood Cliffs, N. J.

KEENAN, ALAN, and J. RYAN. Marriage: A Medical and Sacramental Study. New York: Sheed, 1955. 337 pp. Illus.

KRULJF, TH. C. De. The Bible on Sexuality. Tr. by F. Vander Heijden. De Pere, Wis.: St. Norbert Abbey, 1966. 108 pp.

Translation of "De Bijbel over Sexualiteit," Roermond, The Netherlands, 1963.

LEA, HENRY CHARLES. History of Sacerdotal Celibacy in the Christian Church. 4th ed., rev. London, Eng.: Watts, 1932. 629 pp.

Earlier edition, 1867, published under the title "An Historical Sketch of Sacerdotal Celibacy in the Christian Church."

LEE, ERNEST GEORGE [Edward Dodge]. Christianity and Sex Morality. London, Eng.: Lindsey, 1933. 67 pp.

Le GRAND, LUCIEN. The Biblical Doctrine of Virginity. New York: Sheed, 1963. 167 pp.

LEWIS, JOSEPH. The Bible Unmasked. New York: The Freethought Press Assn., 1963. 236 pp.

First published in 1926.

LIMNER, ROMAN RECHNITZ. Sex and the Unborn Child: Damage to the Fetus Resulting from Sexual Intercourse during Pregnancy. Fwds. by Alan F. Guttmacher and Theodor Reik. New York: Julian, 1969. 229 pp.

LOUKES, HAROLD. Christians and Sex: A Quaker Comment. London, Eng.: Friends Home Service Committee, 1962. 31 pp.

MACE, DAVID ROBERT. The Christian Response to the Sexual Revolution. Nashville, Tenn.: Abingdon, 1970. 142 pp.

MARR, GEORGE SIMPSON. Sex in Religion: An Historical Survey. London, Eng.: Allen, 1936. 285 pp.

MI-KEE [pseud.]. Unchastity Sanctioned by Religion and Mystic Fears. Allahabad, India: Social Research Institute, 1963. 64 pp.

NARRAMORE, CLYDE M. A Christian Answers Kinsey. Wheaton, Ill.: Van Kampen, 1954. 32 pp. Illus.

NORTHCOTE, HUGH. Christianity and Sex Problems. 2nd ed. Philadelphia, Pa.: Davis, 1923. 478 pp.

Previous edition published by David, Philadelphia, 1916.

PATAI, RAPHAEL. Sex and Family in the Bible and the Middle East. Garden City, N.Y.: Doubleday, 1959. 282 pp.

"Anthropological study of sex and the family in the Middle East which throws light on the world of the Bible." 1960 edition under the title "Family, Love, and the Bible" published by Macgibbon and Kee, London, England.

PEALE, NORMAN VINCENT. Sin, Sex and Self-Control. Garden City, N.Y.: Doubleday, 1965. 207 pp.

PERELLA, NICOLAS JAMES. The Kiss, Sacred and Profane: An Interpretative History of Kiss Symbolism and Related Religio-Erotic Themes. Berkeley, Calif.: University of California, 1969. 356 pp. Illus.

PERRIN, JOSEPH MARIE. Virginity. Tr. by Katherine Gordon. Westminster, Md.: Newman, 1956. 161 pp. Illus.

Translation of "La Virginité," Paris, 1952.

PHIPPS, WILLIAM E. Was Jesus Married? The Distortion of Sexuality in the Christian Tradition. New York: Harper, 1970. 239 pp.

PIPER, OTTO A. The Biblical View of Sex and Marriage. New York: Scribner, 1960. 239 pp.

"Complete revision of the 'Christian Interpretation of Sex,' published by Scribner in 1941."

PITTENGER, WILLIAM NORMAN. The Christian View of Sexual Behavior: A Reaction to the Kinsey Report. Greenwich, Conn.: Seabury, 1954. 71 pp.

PITTENGER, WILLIAM NORMAN. Making Sexuality Human. Philadelphia, Pa.: Pilgrim, 1970. 96 pp.

RHYMES, DOUGLAS. No New Morality: Christian Personal Values and Sexual Morality. Indianapolis, Ind.: Bobbs, 1964. 155 pp.

"A presentation of current sex concerns set in a framework of values and ethics that the author believes will work in contemporary society."

ROCK, AUGUSTINE, ed. Sex, Love and the Life of the Spirit. The Aquinas Institutes of Philosophy and Theology Special Lectures, Vol. 1, 1965. Chicago, Ill.: Priory, 1966. 236 pp.

RYAN, MARY PERKINS, and J. J. RYAN. Love and Sexuality: A Christian Approach. New York: Holt, 1967. 196 pp.

"Set in a religious framework, the role of love is examined for both the single individual and the married couple." 1969 edition, Garden City, New York, Image Books.

SCORER, CHARLES GORDON. The Bible and Sex Ethics Today. London, Eng.: Tyndale, 1966. 124 pp.

SHELDON, WILMON HENRY. Sex and Salvation. New York: Vantage, 1955. 169 pp.

SHEVILL, IAN W. A. Christian Chastity: Sex in the 1960's a Christian Viewpoint on Youth and Morals. Townsville, P. Q., Canada: Stanton, 1960. 16 pp. Illus.

SHROCK, CECIL C. A Christian Looks at Sex and the Home. Philadelphia, Pa.: Dorrance, 1971. 70 pp.

TAPP, SIDNEY CALHOUN. Sex, the Key to the Bible. Kansas City, Mo.: Sidney C. Tapp, 1918. 172 pp.

TAPP, SIDNEY CALHOUN. Sexology of the Bible: The Fall and Redemption of Man, a Matter of Sex. Kansas City, Mo.: Sidney C. Tapp, 1915. 179 pp.

Previous edition published in 1913.

TAYLOR, MICHAEL J., comp. Sex: Thoughts for Contemporary Christians. Garden City, N.Y.: Doubleday, 1972. 262 pp.

TREVETT, REGINALD FREDERICK. The Church and Sex. The Twentieth Century Encyclopedia of Catholicism, Vol. 103. Section 9: The Church and the Modern World. New York: Hawthorn, 1960. 126 pp.

"A Roman Catholic interpretation of sexuality."

TREVETT, REGINALD FREDERICK. Sex and the Christian. Faith and Fact Books. London, Eng.: Burns, 1960. 128 pp.

UNIUERSITIES of ITALY and FRAUNCE. English Experience: Its Record in Early Printed Books Published in Facsimile, No. 329. Amsterdam, Netherlands: Theatrum Orbis Terrarum; New York: Da Capo, 1971.

"At head of title: Italy and France. Original title page reads: 'The determinations of the moste famous and mooste excellent vniuersities of Italy and Fraunce, that it is so vnlefull for a man to marie his brothers wyfe/ that the Pope hath no power to dispence therwith.' S.T.C. No. 14287."

VALENTE, MICHAEL F. Sex: The Radical View of a Catholic Theologian. New York: Bruce, 1970. 158 pp.

"The author disputes the theory of intrinsic evil in birth control, nonprocreative intercourse, masturbation, homosexuality and bestiality."

Von HILDEBRAND, DIETRICH. Celibacy and the Crisis of Faith. Chicago, Ill.: Franciscan Herald, 1971. 116 pp.

Translation of "Zölibat und Glaubenskrise."

Von HILDEBRAND, DIETRICH. In Defense of Purity: An Analysis of the Catholic Ideals of Purity and Virginity. Chicago, Ill.: Franciscan Herald, 1970. 142 pp.

1931 edition published by Longmans, New York. Several other editions in existence. Translation of "Reinheit und Jungfraulichkeit."

Von HILDEBRAND, DIETRICH. Man and Woman. Chicago, Ill.: Franciscan Herald, 1966. 103 pp.

Addresses on the nature of sex. Based on lectures given over the past few years.

WADE, JOSEPH D. Chastity, Sexuality and Personal Hangups: A Guide to Celibacy for Religious and Laity. Staten Island, N.Y.: Alba House, 1971. 174 pp.

WALKER, BENJAMIN. Sex and the Supernatural: Sexuality in Religion and Magic. London, Eng.: Macdonald, 1970. 127 pp. Plates.

WALTON, ALAN HULL. New Vistas: Being a Contribution towards the Further Study of Some Problems Regarding Religion, Sex, and Morals. London, Eng.: Fortune, 1944. 218 pp.

WATTS, ALAN WILSON. Nature, Man, and Woman. New York: Pantheon, 1958. 209 pp. Illus.

English edition has the subtitle "A New Approach to Sexual Experience." Reprinted by New American Library, New York, 1960.

WEBER, LEONHARD MARIA. On Marriage, Sex, and Virginity. Tr. by Rosaleen Brennan. New York: Herder, 1966. 144 pp.

WESSLER, MARTIN F. Christian View of Sex Education: A Manual for Church Leaders. St. Louis, Mo.: Concordia, 1967. 87 pp.

WESTCOTT, GEORGE FOSS. Christianity, Free Thinking, and Sex. London, Eng.: Academy of Visual Arts, 1968. 39 pp.

WHITE, ERNEST. Marriage and the Bible. Nashville, Tenn.: Broadman, 1965. 149 pp.

WILKIN, VINCENT. The Image of God in Sex. New York: Sheed, 1955. 88 pp. Illus.

WYRTZEN, JACK. Sex and the Bible. Grand Rapids, Mich.: Zondervan, 1958. 63 pp.

WYRTZEN, JACK. Sex is not Sinful? A Biblical View of the Sex Revolution. Grand Rapids, Mich.: Zondervan, 1970. 64 pp.

YORK, RAYMOND. The Truth of Life Is Love. New York: Herder, 1968. 206 pp. Illus.

6.
SEX ATTITUDES, CUSTOMS, AND BEHAVIOR

ADULTERY

AMERASINGHE, A. RANJIT B. Adultery as Injuria in South African and Ceylon Law. Colombo, Ceylon: Times of Ceylon, 1966. 44 pp.

BELL, RALCY HUSTED. Some Aspects of Adultery: A Study. New York: Eugenics, 1933. 55 pp.

1921 edition, Critic and Guide Company, New York.

BERGER, EVELYN MILLER. Triangle: The Betrayed Wife. Chicago, Ill.: Nelson Hall, 1971. 210 pp.

BOYLAN, BRIAN RICHARD. Infidelity. New York: Dell, 1972. 228 pp.

1971 edition, Prentice-Hall, Englewood Cliffs, N.J.

CAPRIO, FRANK SAMUEL. Marital Infidelity. New York: Citadel, 1953. 272 pp.

DICKSON, RUTH. Married Men Make the Best Lovers. Los Angeles, Calif.: Sherbourne, 1967. 174 pp.

ELLIS, ALBERT. The Civilized Couple's Guide to Extramarital Adventure. New York: Wyden, 1972.

HUNT, MORTON M. The Affair: A Portrait of Extra-marital Love in Contemporary America. New York: World Publishing, 1970. 317 pp.

MORSE, BENJAMIN. The Sexually Promiscuous Female. Derby, Conn.: Monarch, 1963. 158 pp.

NEUBECK, GERHARD, ed. Extra-marital Relations. Englewood Cliffs, N.J.: Prentice-Hall, 1969. 205 pp. Illus.

"A series of papers by sociologists and psychologists analyzing infidelity in a nonjudgmental way."

PETERSON, JOYCE, and M. MERCER. Adultery for Adults: A Unique Guide to Self-development. New York: Coward-McCann, 1968. 126 pp.

1971 edition, Bantam, New York.

SAUNDERS, CRAIG L. The Unfaithful. New York: Award, 1971. 186 pp.

TABORI, PAUL. Taken in Adultery: A Short History of Woman's Infidelity throughout the Ages, Its Rewards and Its Punishments. London, Eng.: New English Library, 1967. 254 pp.

INCEST

CORMIER, BRUNO M., et al. Psychodynamics of Father-daughter Incest. Montreal, Canada: McGill University, 1962. 19 pp.

"Mimeographed."

DURKHEIM, EMILE, and ALBERT ELLIS. Incest: The Nature and Origin of the Taboo. Tr. with Intro. by Edward Sagarin. Together with The Origins and the Development of the Incest Taboo, by Albert Ellis. New York: Stuart, 1963. 186 pp.

MASTERS, ROBERT E. L. Patterns of Incest: A Psycho-social Study of Incest Based on Clinical and Historic Data. New York: Julian, 1963. 406 pp. Illus.

Reprinted by Ace, New York, 1970.

WEINBERG, SAMUEL KIRSON. Incest Behavior. New York: Citadel, 1963. 267 pp.

"A study of interfamily sexual relationships based on interviews with some 200 individuals who have been involved in an incestuous relationship. The author discusses the kind of family setting where incest is likely to occur, explores the effects upon the total family, and projects the effects of such behavior on society."

Earlier edition, 1955.

MASTURBATION

ALIBERT. Onanism. Paris, France: Medical Library, 1900(?) 95 pp.

Contents: Onanism amongst Men. Its Causes, Methods, and Disorders. Masturbation amongst Women. Its Causes. Different Methods of Masturbation. Symptoms. Consequences. Treatment.

BRODIE, R. J. & CO. The Secret Companion: A Medical Work on Onanism. London, Eng.: Brodie, 1845. 126 pp.

DODSON, VICTOR. Auto-erotic Acts and Devices. Los Angeles, Calif.: Medco, 1967. 160 pp. Illus.

ELLIS, HAVELOCK. Female Auto-erotic Practices. New ed. Inglewood, Calif.: Monogram, 1965. 96 pp. Illus.

GOGERN, FRIEDRICH ERNST. Problem of Onanism. Tr. from the German by Meyrick Booth. Westminster, Md.: Newman, 1955. 135 pp.

Translation of "Die Zeit der Geschlechtlichen Reife."

GOLD, MORRIS. The Non-libidinal Aspects of Masturbation. Altstätten, Switzerland: 1957. 39 pp. Illus.

Inaugural dissertation, Zürich.

GORDON, DAVID COLE. Self-love. New York: Macmillan, 1970. 96 pp.

First published in 1968 under the title "Self-love and a Theory of Unification."

KELLY, LOMBARD G., et al. Female Masturbation. New ed. Inglewood, Calif.: Banner, 1966. 192 pp. Illus.

MASTERS, ROBERT E. L., ed. Sexual Self-stimulation. Los Angeles, Calif.: Sherbourne, 1967. 352 pp.

"A collection of authoritative papers which examines history and technique of male and female masturbatory practices including physical aspect and the erotic fantasies employed."

Also 1971 edition by Tower, New York.

MEAGHER, JOHN FRANCIS WALLACE. A Study of Masturbation and the Psychosexual Life. 3rd ed. Baltimore, Md.: Wood, 1936. 149 pp.

Original edition published in 1924.

"A very complete summary of the subject in all its aspects."

MENZIES, K. Autoerotic Phenomena in Adolescence: An Analytical Study of the Psychology and Psychopathology of Onanism. Fwd. by Ernest Jones. 2nd ed. New York: Hoeber, 1921. 100 pp.

Earlier edition, 1919, published by Lewis, London, Eng.

"A psychological treatise from the Freudian viewpoint."

OAKLEY, ERIC GILBERT. Solo Sex: The Problems of the Sexually Lonely. London, Eng.: Canova, 1969. 184 pp.

STEKEL, WILHELM. Auto-eroticism: A Psychiatric Study of Onanism and Neurosis. Authorized tr. by James S. Van Teslaar. New York: Liveright, 1950. 289 pp.

Translation of Part 1 of "Onanie und Homosexualität."

Also published about 1938 by Humphries in Boston, Mass.

TISSOT, SAMUEL AUGUSTE ANDRÉ DAVID. A Treatise on the Diseases Produced by Onanism. New York: Collins, 1832. 114 pp.

3rd edition of the original "L'onanisme," published by Grasset in Lausanne, Switzerland, 1764.

WAKELY, R. T. Woman and Her Secret Passions. New York: n.p., 1846. 108 pp.

"Containing an Exact Description of the Female Organs of Generation; Their Uses and Abuses; Together with a Detailed Account of the Causes and the Cure of the Solitary Vice."

WIENHOLTZ, WILLIAM F. An Interpretation of the Fall of Man: Psychological Ramifications of Masturbation and the Concept of Original Sin. New York: William-Frederick, 1951. 15 pp.

ORAGENITAL RELATIONS

CAULDWELL, DAVID OLIVER. Questions and Answers about Cunnilingus: Light on Operation-third-sex. Ed. by E. Haldeman-Julius. Girard, Kans.: Haldeman-Julius, 1950. 31 pp.

HAGERMAN, R. J. Oral Love. Los Angeles: Medco, 1967. 160 pp.

LEGMAN, GERSHON. Oragenitalism: Oral Techniques in Genital Excitation. New York: Julian, 1969. 319 pp.

Reprinted in 1971 by Paperback Library, New York.

PHALLICISM

BERGER, CHARLES G. Our Phallic Heritage. New York: Greenwich Book Publishers, 1966. 216 pp. Illus.

BRECKENRIDGE, MRS. CHARLES. Land of the Lingam. London, Eng.: Hurst & Blackett, 1933. 288 pp. Illus.

BROWN, SANGER. Sex Worship and Symbolism of Primitive Races: An Interpretation. Boston, Mass.: Badger, 1922. 149 pp. Illus.

Earlier edition published in 1916.

BRYK, FELIX. Sex and Circumcision: A Study of Phallic Worship and Mutilation in Men and Women. North Hollywood, Calif.: Brandon, 1967. 342 pp. Illus.

1934 edition has the title "Circumcision in Man and Woman."

COLEMAN, STANLEY JACKSON, ed. Sex Symbols and Phallic Phantasies. Douglas, Isle of Man, Eng.: Folklore Academy, 1962. 12 pp.

DAUGHERTY, MASON. Sex Worship and Disease [Phallic Worship]: A Scientific Treatise on Sex Worship and Its Influence on Religion and Symbolism. Cleveland, Ohio: Mason Daugherty, 1935. 240 pp. Illus.

"With Special Reference to Disease of the Sexual Organs."

DULAURE, JACQUES ANTOINE. Gods of Generation: A History of Phallic Cults among Ancients and Moderns. Tr. from the French by A. F. N. New York: Panurge, 1933. 280 pp.

1805 French edition has the title "Des Divinités Génératrices, ou Du Culte du Phallus Chez les Anciens et les Modernes."

HUDSON, ABISHA S. [Sha Rocco]. The Masculine Cross and Ancient Sex Worship. New York: Commonwealth, 1904. 65 pp. Illus.

Preface dated 1874.

KNIGHT, RICHARD PAYNE, and T. WRIGHT. Sexual Symbolism: A History of Phallic Worship. Intro. by Ashley Montagu. New York: Julian, 1957. 2 vols. in 1.

Contents: Vol. 1, "A Discourse on the Worship of Priapus," by R. P. Knight, written circa 1800; Vol. 2, "The Worship of the Generative Powers during the Middle Ages of Western Europe," by Thomas Wright, written circa 1860.

LONGWORTH, T. CLIFTON. The Worship of Love: A Study of Nature Worship throughout the World. London, Eng.: Torchstream, 1954. 271 pp. Illus.

MULLA, FERIDUN. De Cultu Phalli: Being a History of the Rise, Progress and Decline of the Phallic Religions of the World [Advance Tabular Analysis]. Hyderabad, Deccan, India: India Publishing, 1938. 42 pp.

SCOTT, GEORGE RYLEY. Phallic Worship: A History of Sex and Sex Rites in Relation to the Religions of All Races from Antiquity to the Present Day. London, Eng.: Laurie, 1941. 299 pp.

Sex Mythology: Including an Account of the Masculine Cross. London, Eng.: n.p., 1898. 64 pp.

STONE, LEE ALEXANDER. The Story of Phallicism: With Other Essays on Related Subjects by Eminent Authors. Intro. by Frederick Starr. Chicago, Ill.: Covoci, 1927. 2 vols.

TALBOT, PERCY AMAURY. Some Nigerian Fertility Cults. New York: Oxford, 1927. 140 pp.

Reprinted by Barnes & Noble, New York, 1967.

WALL, OTTO AUGUSTUS. Sex and Sex Worship [Phallic Worship]: A Scientific Treatise on Sex, Its Nature and Function and Its Influence on Art, Science, Architecture, and Religion — with Special Reference to Sex Worship and Symbolism. College Park, Md.: McGrath, 1970. 608 pp. Illus.

Earlier edition, 1919, published by Mosby, St. Louis, Mo.

WESTROPP, HODDER MICHAEL. Primitive Symbolism: As Illustrated in Phallic Worship of the Reproductive Principle. Intro. by J. G. R. Forlong. New Delhi, India: Kumar, 1970. 68 pp.

First published in 1885 by Redway, London, England.

SEX CUSTOMS

ALLGROVE, GEORGE. Love in the East. London, Eng.: Gibbs & Phillips, 1962. 159 pp.

BAILEY, FLORA L. Some Sex Beliefs and Practices in a Navaho Community: With Comparative Material from Other Navaho Areas. Reports of the Ramah Project, Report No. 2. Cambridge, Mass.: The Museum, 1950. 108 pp.

BARDIS, PANOS D. The Family in Changing Civilizations. 2nd ed. New York: Simon & Schuster, 1969. 1 vol.

"A collection of scholarly articles on ancient sex and family customs."

BERNDT, RONALD MURRAY, and C. H. BERNDT. Sexual Behavior in Western Arnhem Land. Viking Fund Publications in Anthropology, No. 16. New York: 1951. 247 pp. Illus.

Reprinted by Johnson, New York, circa 1968.

BESTERMAN, THEODORE. Men against Women: A Study of Sexual Relations. London, Eng.: Methuen, 1934. 238 pp.

BETTELHEIM, BRUNO. Symbolic Wounds: Puberty Rites and the Envious Male. New rev. ed. New York: Collier, 1962. 194 pp.

1954 edition, Free Press, Glencoe, Ill.

BIGGS, ROBERT D. Sā zi ga: Ancient Mesopotamian Potency Incantations. Locust Valley, N.Y.: Augustin, 1967. 86 pp.

"Parts of the present study were included in the writer's Ph.D. dissertation."

BLACKWOOD, B. Both Sides of Buka Passage: An Ethnographic Study of Social, Sexual, and Economic Questions on the North-western Solomon Islands. Oxford, Eng.: Clarendon, 1935. 624 pp.

BLAKE, JUDITH. Family Structure in Jamaica: The Social Context of Reproduction. New York: Free Press, 1962. 262 pp.

BLOCH, IWAN. Ethnological and Cultural Studies of the Sex Life in England as Revealed in Its Erotic and Obscene Literature and Art. Tr. and ed. by R. Deniston. New York: Falstaff, 1934. 385 pp.

BLOCH, IWAN. The Sexual Extremities of the World. New York: Book Awards, 1964. 356 pp.

Deals with sex customs in Great Britain.

BLOCH, IWAN. Sexual Life in England. London, Eng.: Transworld, 1965. 542 pp.

Translation of "Das Geschlechtsleben in England," 1901. First published in 1938 in London by Aldor, with the title "Sexual Life in England Past and Present," and published in 1936 under the title "Sexual Life in England." Several other versions and translations are in existence.

BLOCH, IWAN. The Sexual Life of Our Time: A Complete Encyclopedia of the Sexual Sciences in Their Relation to Modern Civilization. Authorized tr. by M. E. Paul. New York: Falstaff, 1937. 790 pp.

Translation of "Das Sexualleben unserer Zeit," 1907.

Several other versions and translations are in existence.

"A comprehensive digest of the views and opinions of a large number of sexologists, investigators, and philosophers."

BRANDT, PAUL [Hans Licht]. Sexual Life in Ancient Greece. Tr. by J. H. Freese. Ed. by Lawrence H. Dawson. New York: Barnes & Noble, 1963. 556 pp. Illus.

Based on the author's "Sittengeschichte Griechenlands": Vol. 1, "Die Grieschische Gesellschaft" and Vol. 2, "Das Liebesleben der Griechen," 1923.

Several other versions and translations are in existence.

BRUSENDORFF, OVE, and P. HENNINGSEN. A History of Eroticism. New York: Stuart, 1963. 6 vols.

Vol. 1, "Antiquity"; Vol. 2, "Middle Ages"; Vol. 3, "From the Time of the Marquis de Sade"; Vol. 4, "Victorianism"; Vol. 5, "Twentieth Century"; Vol. 6, "In Our Time."

Also published in Copenhagen, Denmark by Veta.

BRYK, FELIX. Dark Rapture: The Sex Life of the African Negro. English version by Dr. A. J. Norton. Intro., Critique of Sexual Anthropology, by J. D. Unwin. New York: Walden, 1939. 167 pp.

Reprinted by Juno, Forest Hills, N.Y., in 1944.

BRYK, FELIX. Voodoo-Eros: Ethnological Studies in the Sex-life of the African Aborigines. Rev. ed. Tr. from the German by M. R. Sexton. New York: United Book Guild, 1964. 251 pp. Illus.

Translation of "Neger-eros," Berlin, Marcus & Weber, 1928.

1933 edition privately printed by Falstaff, New York.

BURTON, RICHARD FRANCIS. The Erotic Traveler. Ed. by Edward Leigh. New York: Putnam, 1967. 189 pp.

CHAKRABERTY, CHANDRA. Sex Life in Ancient India: An Explanatory & Comparative Study. Calcutta, India: Mukhopadhyay, 1963. 167 pp.

CHAKRABERTY, CHANDRA. Sexology of the Hindus: A Study in the Hindu Psychology of Sex with Modern Interpretations. Calcutta, India: Krishna, 1945 (?). 126 pp.

Another edition, Luzac, London, Eng., 1938.

CHOU, ERIC. The Dragon and the Phoenix. New York: Arbor, 1971. 222 pp.

London edition, published by Joseph in 1971, has the subtitle "Love, Sex and the Chinese."

CLEUGH, JAMES. A History of Oriental Orgies: An Account of Erotic Practices among the Peoples of the East and Near East. New York: Crown, 1968. 219 pp.

British edition has the title "Oriental Orgies: An Account of Some Erotic Practices among Non-Christians."

Another edition published by Dell, New York, 1971.

CLEUGH, JAMES. Love Locked Out: An Examination of the Irrepressible Sexuality of the Middle Ages. New York: Crown, 1964. 320 pp.

British edition, published in 1963 by Blond, London, has the subtitle "A Survey of Love, Licence and Restriction in the Middle Ages."

COLTON, HELEN. Our Sexual Evolution. New York: Watts, 1971. 180 pp.

Intended for use in Grade 7 and beyond.

COOKE, CHARLES EDWARD, and E. ROSS. Sex Can Be an Art! Los Angeles, Calif.: Sherbourne, 1964. 254 pp.

CRAWLEY, ALFRED ERNEST. Dress, Drinks, and Drums: Further Studies of Savages and Sex. Ed. by Theodore Besterman. London, Eng.: Methuen, 1931. 274 pp.

CRAWLEY, ALFRED ERNEST. Studies of Savages and Sex. Ed. by Theodore Besterman. Select Bibliographies Reprint Series. Freeport, N.Y.: Books for Libraries Press, 1969. 300 pp.

Reprint of 1929 edition, published by Dutton, New York.

Also reprinted in 1969 by Johnson, New York.

DADACHANJI, SEROZH [Sardi]. Erotic Love through the Ages. London, Eng.: Walton, 1962. 275 pp. Illus.

DAY, DONALD. The Evolution of Love. New York: Dial, 1954. 522 pp.

"Sketches the history of the relations between the sexes from Biblical times to the present."

De MENTE, BOYE. Bachelor's Hawaii. Rutland, Vt.: Tuttle, 1967. 176 pp. Map.

First published in 1964.

De MENTE, BOYE. Bachelor's Japan. Rutland, Vt.: Tuttle, 1966. 173 pp.

Reprinted in 1967.

De MENTE, BOYE. Bachelor's Mexico. Rutland, Vt.: Tuttle, 1967. 175 pp.

DENIS, ARMAND. Taboo. New York: Putnam, 1967. 201 pp. Illus.

First published by Allen, London, Eng., in 1966.

Deals with sex customs and the moral climate in Asian countries.

DEVEREUX, GEORGE. Sexual Life of the Mohave Indians: An Interpretation in Terms of Social Psychology. Berkeley, Calif.: University of California, 1936. 116 pp.

Doctoral thesis, University of California.

DINGWALL, ERIC JOHN. The Girdle of Chastity: A Medico-Historical Study. New York: Macaulay, 1960 (?). 164 pp. Illus.

First edition published in Paris, France, by Le Divan in 1923.

DINGWALL, ERIC JOHN. Male Infibulation. London, Eng.: Bale, 1925. 145 pp. Illus.

"Studies in the Sexual Life of Ancient and Mediaeval Peoples, Vol. 1."

Du BOIS, CORA ALICE. Girls' Adolescence Observances in North America. Berkeley, Calif.: University of California, 1932. 98 leaves. Tables.

Doctoral thesis, University of California, December, 1932.

ELLIS, ALBERT. The Folklore of Sex. New York: Grove, 1961. 255 pp.

"A survey of the attitudes expressed through 200 best-selling novels and leading newspapers in 1950 is contrasted with attitudes in 1960 in the same media plus radio, television, and stage plays. Presents a picture of American attitudes toward various forms of sexual behavior." First published by Boni, New York in 1951. British title, "Sex Beliefs and Customs."

EMRICH, DUNCAN, comp. The Folklore of Love and Courtship: The Charms and Divinations, Superstitions and Beliefs, Signs and Prospects of Love, Sweet Love. New York: American Heritage, 1970. 51 pp. Illus.

EMRICH, DUNCAN. The Folklore of Weddings and Marriage: The Traditional Beliefs, Customs, Superstitions, Charms and Omens of Marriage and Marriage Ceremonies. New York: American Heritage, 1970. 51 pp.

EPTON, NINA CONSUELO. Love and the English. Cleveland, Ohio: World, 1961. 390 pp. Illus.

First published by Cassell, London, England in 1960.

EPTON, NINA CONSUELO. Love and the French. Cleveland, Ohio: World, 1960. 368 pp. Illus.

First published by Cassell, London, England in 1959.

EPTON, NINA CONSUELO. Love and the Spanish. Cleveland, Ohio: World, 1962. 215 pp. Illus.

First published by Cassell, London, England in 1960.

FEHLINGER, HANS. Sexual Life of Primitive People. New York: United Book Guild, 1945. 133 pp.

Reprint of 1921 British edition which is a translation of "Das Geschlechtsleben der Naturvölker," published in 1921.

FIELDING, WILLIAM JOHN. Strange Customs of Courtship and Marriage. New York: Permabooks, 1949. 246 pp.

Earlier edition, New Home Library, New York, 1942.

FLACELIÈRE, ROBERT. Love in Ancient Greece. Tr. from the French by James Cleugh. New York: Crown, 1962. 224 pp. Illus.

Translation of "L'Amour en Grèce," published in Paris by Hachette in 1960.

FORBERG, FRIEDRICH KARL. The Manual of Exotica Sexualia. North Hollywood, Calif.: Brandon, 1965. 248 pp.

Originally written in the nineteenth century.

FRAZER, JAMES GEORGE. Totemica: A Supplement to Totemism and Exogamy. New York: Barnes & Noble, 1969. 518 pp.

Reprint of 1937 edition published by Macmillan, London, England.

FRAZER, JAMES GEORGE. Totemism and Exogamy: A Treatise on Certain Early Forms of Superstition and Society. New York: Barnes & Noble, 1969. 4 vols.

Reprint of 1910 edition published by Macmillan, London, England.

GICHNER, LAWRENCE ERNEST. Erotic Aspects of Chinese Culture. n.p., 1957. 130 pp. Illus.

GLOVER, JACK. The Sex Life of the American Indian. Wichita Falls, Tex.: 1968. 95 pp. Illus.

GOLDSTONE, SALO H. An Independent Course, Outstanding System of a Specialist Antiseptic Medical Mohel: Circumcision. New York: n.p., 1950. 18 pp. Illus.

"A New Method with the Latest Inventions and Improvements Strictly in Accordance with the Hebrew and Medical Sanitary Laws and Traditions."

GORDIS, ROBERT. Sex and the Family in the Jewish Tradition. New York: Burning Bush, 1967. 64 pp.

GRABOWSKI, ZBIGNIEW ANTHONY. The English Psycho-analysed. London, Eng.: Sidgwick & Jackson, 1967. 307 pp.

GRAHAM-MURRAY, JAMES. A History of Morals. London, Eng.: Library 33, 1966. 159 pp. Illus.

GRIMAL, PIERRE. Love in Ancient Rome. Tr. from the French by Arthur Train, Jr. New York: Crown, 1967. 306 pp.

Translation of "L'Amour à Rome."

GRUNWALD, HENRY ANATOLE, ed. Sex in America. New York: Bantam, 1964. 311 pp.

Also published by Transworld, London, England, 1965.

GULIK, ROBERT HANS Van. Sexual Life in Ancient China: A Preliminary Survey of Chinese Sex and Society from Circa 1500 B.C. till 1644 A.D. New York: Humanities, 1961. 392 pp. Illus.

Originally published by Brill, Leiden, The Netherlands in 1961.

HARRISON, LIETA. The Wantons. Tr. from the Italian by Diana Fussell. London, Eng.: Ortolan, 1966. 140 pp.

"Originally published as 'Le Svergognate,' in Rome, by Edizione de Novissima, 1963."

Deals with sex customs in Sicily.

HAYS, HOFFMAN REYNOLDS. The Dangerous Sex: The Myth of Feminine Evil. New York: Pocket Books, 1965. 307 pp.

First published in 1964 by Putnam, New York.

"The author's thesis is that man's fear of women has always distorted the relationship between the sexes."

HENRIQUES, FERNANDO. Love in Action: The Sociology of Sex. New York: Dutton, 1960. 432 pp.

First published by MacGibbon, London, England, 1959.

"A cross-cultural and anthropological survey of sexual behavior, courtship and marriage."

HENSLIN, JAMES M., ed. Studies in the Sociology of Sex. New York: Appleton, 1971. 410 pp.

HERNTON, CALVIN C. Coming Together: Black Power, White Hatred, and Sexual Hang-ups. New York: Random, 1971. 181 pp.

HIRSCH, EDWIN WALTER. Sex Life in Babylonia. Chicago, Ill.: Research Publications, 1941. 36 pp.

"First published in the 'Urologic and Cutaneous Review,' Sept. 1941."

HIRSCHFELD, MAGNUS. Men and Women: The World Journey of a Sexologist. New York: Putnam, 1935. 325 pp.

Translation of "Die Weltreise Eines Sexualforschers."

English title, "Women East and West."

HUMANA, CHARLES, and W. WU. The Ying Yang: The Chinese Way of Love. New York: Avon, 1971. 255 pp.

HUNT, MORTON M. Natural History of Love. New York: Funk & Wagnalls, 1967. 416 pp.

"A survey of love and its customs through history."

Reprint of 1959 edition, published by Knopf, New York.

IBERT, JEAN CLAUDE, and J. CHARLES. Love, the French Way. Tr. by Marguerite Barnett. London, Eng.: Heinemann, 1961. 206 pp. Illus.

Translation of "L'Amour et les Français," published in 1958 by Hachette, Paris, France.

IBN HAZM, 'ALI IBM AHMAD. The Ring of the Dove: A Treatise on the Art and Practice of Arab Love. Tr. by A. J. Arberry. London, Eng.: Luzac, 1953. 288 pp.

Translated from a manuscript of the eleventh century now in the University of Leiden, Netherlands.

Several other versions and translations are in existence.

KIEFER, OTTO. Sexual Life in Ancient Rome. Tr. by Gilbert and Helen Highet. New York: Barnes & Noble, 1952. 379 pp. Illus.

Translation of "Kulturgeschichte Roms unter Besonderer Berücksichtigung der Römischen Sitten," published in 1933.

Reprint of 1934 translation published by Routledge, London, England.

KINSLEY, D. A. [Allen Edwardes]. Erotica Judaica: A Sexual History of the Jews. New York: Julian, 1967. 238 pp.

KINSLEY, D. A. [Allen Edwardes]. The Jewel in the Lotus: A Historical Survey of the Sexual Culture of the East. Intro. by Albert Ellis. New York: Julian, 1959. 293 pp.

Reprinted in 1971 by Lancer, New York.

KINSLEY, D. A. [Allen Edwardes], and R. E. L. MASTERS. The Cradle of Erotica: A Study of Afro-Asian Sexual Expression and an Analysis of Erotic Freedom in Social Relationships. New York: Julian, 1963. 362 pp.

KLINE, MEREDITH G. By Oath Consigned: A Reinterpretation of the Covenant Signs of Circumcision and Baptism. Grand Rapids, Mich.: Eerdmans, 1968. 110 pp.

"Revised version of 2 articles first published in the 'Westminster Theological Journal,' Vol. 27:1, Nov. 1964, and Vol. 27:2, May 1965."

KOKKOKA. The Koka Shastra: Being the Ratirahasya of Kokkoka and Other Medieval Indian Writings on Love. Tr. with Intro. by Alex Comfort. New York: Stein and Day, 1965. 171 pp. Map.

Several other versions and translations of this eighth-century work are in existence.

LAUBSCHER, BAREND JACOB FREDERICK. Sex, Custom and Psychopathology: A Study of South African Pagan Natives. New York: McBride, 1938. 347 pp.

British edition published in 1937.

LAURENT, EMILE, and P. NAGOUR. Magica Sexualis: Mystic Love Books of Black Arts and Secret Sciences. Tr. by Raymond Sabatier. New York: Anthropological Press, 1934. 274 pp. Illus.

Translation of "L'Occultisme et L'Amour."

Reprinted by Brandon, North Hollywood, Calif., 1971.

LEVINE, ESAR, ed. Chastity Belts: An Illustrated History of the Bridling of Women, Containing Numerous Explanatory Excerpts from Curious, Facetious and Erotic Books. New York: Panurge, 1931. 288 pp. Illus.

LEVY, HOWARD SEYMOUR. Chinese Footbinding: The History of a Curious Erotic Custom. Fwd. by Arthur Waley. New York: Rawls, 1966. 352 pp. Illus.

Reprinted by Twayne, New York, 1970.

LEWINSOHN, RICHARD. A History of Sexual Customs. Tr. by Alexander Mayce. New York: Harper, 1959. 424 pp. Illus.

Reprinted in 1971.

Translation of "Eine Weltgeschichte der Sexualität," by Morus, pseud., published by Rowohlt, Hamburg, Germany, 1956.

LEWIS, JOSEPH. In the Name of Humanity! New York: Eugenics, 1949. 158 pp. Illus.

Deals with circumcision.

LINNER, BIRGITTA. Sex and Society in Sweden. In collaboration with Richard J. Litell. Pref. by Lester A. Kirkendall. New York: Pantheon, 1967. 204 pp. Illus.

Another edition, Harper, New York, 1972.

LONGMORE, LAURA. The Dispossessed: A Study of the Sex-life of Bantu Women in Urban Areas in and around Johannesburg. London, Eng.: Cape, 1959. 334 pp. Illus.

Another edition published by Transworld, London, England, 1966.

LONGWORTH, T. CLIFTON. The Gods of Love: The Creative Process in Early Religion. Westport, Conn.: Associated Booksellers, 1960. 273 pp. Illus.

LOUDAN, JACK. The Hell-rakes. London, Eng.: Books for You, 1967. 192 pp. Illus.

Deals with sex customs of eighteenth-century Great Britain and Ireland.

McPHARLIN, PAUL. Love and Courtship in America. New York: Hastings, 1946. 40 pp. Illus.

MALINOWSKI, BRONISLAW. Sex, Culture and Myth. New York: Harcourt, 1962. 346 pp.

British edition by Hart-Davis, London, 1963.

MALINOWSKI, BRONISLAW. Sex and Repression in Savage Society. International Library of Psychology, Philosophy & Scientific Method. New York: Harcourt, 1927. 285 pp.

Another edition published by Meridian, New York, 1955.

MALINOWSKI, BRONISLAW. The Sexual Life of Savages in North-western Melanesia: An Ethnographic Account of Courtship, Marriage, and Family Life among the Natives of the Trobriand Islands, British New Guinea. Pref. by Havelock Ellis. New York: Harcourt, 1962. 603 pp. Illus., maps.

Reprint of 1929 one-volume edition published by Halcyon House, New York. British edition, published by Routledge in 1929, also in two-volume edition.

MANTEGAZZA, PAOLO. The Sexual Relations of Mankind. North Hollywood, Calif.: Brandon, 1966. 364 pp. Plates.

1935 edition has the notation that "This work, with the two already published, 'Physiology of Love' and 'Hygiene of Love,' completes the Love Trilogy."

1932 edition has the title "Anthropological Studies of Sexual Relations of Mankind."

Translation of "Gli Amori Degli Uomini," published in 1885.

MARCHAND, HENRY L. Erotic History of France: Including a History of Its Erotic Literature. New York: Panurge, 1933. 287 pp.

MARSHALL, DONALD S., and R. C. SUGGS, eds. Human Sexual Behavior: Variations in the Ethnographic Spectrum. Studies in Sex & Society. New York: Basic, 1971. 302 pp.

MEAD, MARGARET. From the South Seas: Studies of Adolescence and Sex in Primitive Societies. New York: Morrow, 1939. 3 vols. in 1.

Contents: Coming of Age in Samoa; Growing up in New Guinea; Sex and Temperament in Three Primitive Societies.

These three works have also been published separately.

MEAD, MARGARET. Sex and Temperament in Three Primitive Societies. New York: Morrow, 1963. 335 pp. Illus.

"First published in 1935. This 1963 edition contains new preface and preface to the 1950 edition."

MEADOWS, ROBERT, comp. A Private Anthropological Cabinet of 500 Authentic Racial-esoteric Photographs and Illustrations after the Originals from Scientific Explorations, Field Studies and Museum Archives. New York: Falstaff, 1934. 104 pp. Illus.

"Portrays intimate rites and customs ... ethnic mutilations and many other curiosities of the erotic life of savage and civilized races of mankind."

MEHTA, RUSTAM JEHANGIR. 1001 Ways of Kissing: The Origin, History, and Technique of Kissing, based on Indian, Oriental and Western Works on Love, Sex and Romance. Bombay, India: Taraporevala, 1962. 116 pp. Illus.

MEHTA, RUSTAM JEHANGIR. Scientific Curiosities of Love-life and Marriage: A Survey of Sex Relations, Beliefs and Customs of Mankind in Different Countries and Ages. Bombay, India: Taraporevala, 1947. 270 pp.

MEREDITH, OSCAR. The Lure of Lust: The Saga of Man's Ceaseless Search for Sexual Excitement. London, Eng.: Tallis, 1969. 188 pp. Illus.

MEYER, JOHANN JAKOB. Sexual Life in Ancient India: A Study in the Comparative History of Indian Culture. New York: Dutton, 1930. 2 vols.

An account of the life of woman in ancient India, based upon material in the Mahābhārata and the Ramayana.

Translation of "Das Weib in Altindischen Epos."

MONTAGU, ASHLEY. Coming into Being among the Australian Aborigines: A Study of the Procreative Beliefs of the Native Tribes of Australia. Fwd. by B. Malinowski. New York: Dutton, 1938. 362 pp. Illus.

Issued also as a doctoral thesis, Columbia University.

MONTAGU, ASHLEY. Sex, Man, and Society. New York: Putnam, 1969. 287 pp.

MURDOCK, GEORGE PETER. Social Structure. New York: Free Press, 1965. 387 pp.

1949 edition published by Macmillan, New York.

"An anthropologist analyzes the sexual, marital, and family structures of 250 human societies."

MUSSER, JOSEPH W. Celestial or Plural Marriage: A Digest of the Mormon Marriage System as Established by God through the Prophet Joseph Smith. Salt Lake City, Utah: Musser, 1944. 154 pp. Illus.

"For the most part, a compilation and rearrangement of the information on the subject published in the 'Truth' magazine, volumes five to seven, inclusive."

NEMECEK, OTTOKAR. Virginity: Pre-nuptial Rites and Rituals. New York: Philosophical Library, 1958. 129 pp. Illus.

OAKLEY, ERIC GILBERT [Paul Gregson]. Orgies of Torture and Brutality: A Historical Study. London, Eng.: Walton, 1965. 264 pp.

ODENWALD, ROBERT PAUL. The Disappearing Sexes. New York: Random, 1965. 175 pp.

"Case histories illustrating the evolution of the female emancipation and the problems resulting from the sexual revolution."

PARTRIDGE, BURGO. History of Orgies. New York: Crown, 1960. 246 pp.

1958 edition, Blond, London, Eng.

"A scholarly commentary on orgies, both public and private, from the Greeks and Romans to the 20th-century rock-and-roll."

PAWLOWSKI, PAUL. Two Men Sharing One Wife. London, Eng.: P. Pawlowski, 1970. 60 pp. Illus.

"A Polyandry Study Group Report."

PEARSALL, RONALD. The Worm in the Bud: The World of Victorian Sexuality. New York: Macmillan, 1969. 560 pp.

British edition published by Weidenfeld & Nicolson.

PHADKE, NARAYAN SITARAM. Sex Problems in India: Or Scientific Study of Sex Life and Some Curious Marriage Customs Prevailing in India. 2nd ed. Bombay, India, Taraporevala, 1929. 350 pp.

PIKE, EDGAR ROYSTON. Love in Ancient Rome. London, Eng.: Muller, 1965. 285 pp. Illus.

RACHEWILTZ, BORIS De. Black Eros: Sexual Customs of Africa from Prehistory to the Present Day. Tr. by Peter Whigham. New York: Stuart, 1965. 329 pp. Illus.

Translation from the Italian of "Eros Nero."

"Sociological study and history of the role of eroticism in African life."

RUGOFF, MILTON ALLAN. Prudery and Passion. New York: Putnam, 1971. 413 pp.

SCOTT, GEORGE RYLEY. Curious Customs of Sex and Marriage: An Inquiry Relating to All Races and Nations from Antiquity to the Present Day. New York: Key, 1960. 312 pp. Illus.

SCOTT, GEORGE RYLEY. Far Eastern Sex Life: An Anthropological, Ethnological and Sociological Study of the Love Relations, Marriage Rites and Home Life of the Oriental Peoples. London, Eng.: Swan, 1943. 198 pp.

SIMONS, GEOFFREY LESLIE. A History of Sex. London, Eng.: New English Library, 1970. 188 pp.

SMITH, ELMER L. Bundling among the Amish. Witmer, Pa.: Applied Arts, 1968. 34 pp. Illus.

Reprint of 1961 edition.

STEPHENS, WILLIAM N. The Oedipus Complex Hypothesis: Cross Cultural Evidence. New York: Free Press, 1962. 273 pp.

"A study of anthropological reports of preliterate societies to test the Freudian hypothesis of the 'Oedipus Complex'."

STERN, BERNHARD. The Scented Garden: Anthropology of the Sex Life in the Levant. Tr. by D. Berger. New York: American Ethnological Press, 1934. 443 pp.

STEVENS, CHRISTOPHER. Secret and Forbidden: The Moral History of the Passions of Mankind. New York: Living Books, 1966. 300 pp. Illus.

STILES, HENRY REED. Bundling: Its Origin, Progress and Decline in America. New York: Book Collector Association, 1934. 146 pp.

Also 1869 edition.

SUGGS, ROBERT C. Marquesan Sexual Behavior. New York: Harcourt, 1966. 251 pp.

"A study of past and present practices among the Polynesian people."

TABORI, PAUL, Dress and Undress: The Sexology of Fashion. London, Eng.: New English Library, 1969. 223 pp.

TABORI, PAUL. A Pictorial History of Love. London, Eng.: Spring, 1966. 320 pp. Illus.

TAYLOR, G. RATTRAY. Sex in History. New York: Vanguard, 1970. 336 pp.

Reprint of 1954 edition.

1953 edition, Thames and Hudson, London, Eng.

"Traces the historical changes in attitude toward sex in Western culture and attempts to show how current attitudes and behavior are related to historical problems with sex."

WALDEMAR, CHARLES. The Mystery of Sex. Tr. by Laura and Andrew Tilburg. London, Eng.: Elek, 1960. 284 pp. Illus.

Translation of "Magie der Geschlechter," published in Munich, Germany, 1958.

WINDSOR, EDWARD. The Hindu Art of Love. New York: Panurge, 1932. 275 pp.

X, DR. JACOBUS [pseud.]. The Erogenous Zones of the World: Descriptions of the Intra-sexual Manners and Customs of the Semi-civilized Peoples of Africa, Asia, America and Oceania, the Whole Paraphernalia of Their Love, by a French Army surgeon. New York: Book Awards, 1964. 448 pp.

Taken from "Untrodden Fields of Anthropology" published before 1898, which is a translation of "L'Amour aux Colonies."

YOUNG, WAYLAND HILTON. Eros Denied: Sex in Western Society. New York: Grove, 1964. 415 pp.

"An historical account spanning 2,000 years of Western culture and analyzing the forces which both suppressed and perverted human sexual instincts. Compares the attitudes in our culture with those in other societies, past and present."

SEXUAL BEHAVIOR

ABERLE, SOPHIE BLEDSOE De, and G. W. CORNER. Twenty-five Years of Sex Research: History of the National Research Council, Committee for Research in Problems of Sex, 1922-1947. Philadelphia, Pa.: Saunders. 1953. 248 pp.

ADAMS, CLIFFORD ROSE. An Informal Preliminary Report on Some Factors Relating to Sexual Responsiveness of Certain College Wives. State College, Pa.: n. p., 1953. 651 pp.

ADAMS, OSCAR FAY. The Presumption of Sex, and Other Papers. Boston, Mass.: Lee & Shepard, 1892. 149 pp.

Contents: The Presumption of Sex; The Mannerless Sex; The Vulgar Sex; The Ruthless Sex; The Brutal Sex; Our Dreadful American Manners.

ALD, ROY. Sex Off-campus. New York: Grosset & Dunlap, 1969. 192 pp.

"Twelve college couples openly discuss their shared living quarters in off-campus housing and the motivations, events, and problems behind the new sexual freedom which has radically changed university life."

AMERICAN ACADEMY OF POLITICAL AND SOCIAL SCIENCE. Sex and the Contemporary American Scene. Philadelphia, Pa.: American Academy of Political and Social Science, 1968. 232 pp.

AMERICAN SOCIAL HYGIENE ASSOCIATION. Sexual Behavior: How Shall We Define and Motivate What is Acceptable? Publication No. A-796. New York: American Social Hygiene Assn., 1950. 32 pp.

"Papers and notes from a panel discussion at the thirty-seventh annual meeting, February 1, 1950."

"Reprinted from the 'Journal of Social Hygiene,' Vol. 36, April 1950."

AMERICAN SOCIAL HYGIENE ASSOCIATION. Problems of Sexual Behavior: Research, Education, Community Action. Publication No. A-732. Intro. by Charles Walter Clarke. New York: American Social Hygiene Assn., 1948. 138 pp.

"Proceedings of a symposium held by the American Social Hygiene Association during its annual conference of social hygiene executives, March 30-April 1, 1948, in New York City, to consider the first published report of a series of studies of sex phenomena by Prof. Alfred C. Kinsey, Wardell B. Pomeroy, and Clyde E. Martin, and its relation to the social hygiene program."

AMOROSO, HENRI. Sexual Behavior and Customs of the French. Tr. by Lowell Blair. New York: Macfadden, 1965. 143 pp.

Translation of "La Condition Sexuelle des Français," 1963.

BARTELL, GILBERT D. Group Sex: A Scientist's Eyewitness Report on the American Way of Swinging. New York: Wyden, 1971. 298 pp.

"Based on studies of more than 280 middle-class male and female 'swingers' in the South and Midwest."

BEDARD, MICHELLE [pseud.]. Canada in Bed. Toronto, Canada: Pagurian, 1969. 157 pp.

On the cover: "An Irreverent Study of Canadian Sexual Attitudes."

BEIGEL, HUGO G., ed. Advances in Sex Research. New York: Harper, 1963. 261 pp.

"Thirty-one experts present a wide range of new findings and reports on experiments in theoretical and clinical aspects of sexual problems. Deals with new knowledge on behavior and attitudes, artificial insemination, sex and aging, and various forms of deviation."

BELL, ROBERT R. Premarital Sex in a Changing Society. Englewood Cliffs, N.J.: Prentice-Hall, 1966. 182 pp.

"An analysis of the changing nature of premarital sex in American society, tracing social forces which have influenced sexual morality up to the present time. Also examines present day premarital sexual attitudes and behavior and discusses the influence of social class, race, and religion upon these."

BERGLER, EDMUND, and W. S. KROGER. Kinsey's Myth of Female Sexuality: The Medical Facts. New York: Grune & Stratton, 1954. 200 pp.

BRADLEY, MATT. New American Sexual Appetites. North Hollywood, Calif.: Brandon, 1966. 155 pp.

BRECHER, EDWARD M. The Sex Researchers. Boston, Mass.: Little, Brown, 1969. 354 pp.

1971 edition, New American Library, New York.

"The author devotes individual chapters to Havelock Ellis, Kraft-Ebing, Freud, van de Velde, Kinsey, Masters and Johnson, and sizeable chapter sections to other less widely known researchers."

BREEDLOVE, WILLIAM, and J. BREEDLOVE. Swap Clubs: A Study in Contemporary Sexual Mores. Los Angeles, Calif.: Sherbourne, 1964. 256 pp.

BREEDLOVE, WILLIAM, and J. BREEDLOVE. The Swinging Set. Los Angeles, Calif.: Sherbourne, 1965. 157 pp.

1967 edition, Ortolan Press, London, England.

"An investigation of the sexual habits of the freethinkers of today's society."

BROWN, JOE DAVID, ed. Sex in the '60s: A Candid Look at the Age of Mini-morals, by the Staff of Time. New York: Time-Life Books, 1968. 118 pp.

CAULDWELL, DAVID OLIVER. Questions and Answers on Sex and the American Attitude. Ed. by E. Haldeman-Julius. Girard, Kans.: Haldeman-Julius, 1950. 29 pp.

"Press reports, magazines, books, letters, and other sources have been combed for the data included in this book. Reflected are attitudes toward sex in its biological, legal, economic, social, and various other aspects."

CHARLES, DAVID, and R. A. CHEZ, eds. Sex on Campus. Amsterdam, The Netherlands: Excerpta Medica Foundation, 1969. 114 pp.

"Presents the results of a seminar which brought together educators, sociologists, churchmen, and physicians to discuss the campus milieu, contraception, virginity, and unwed pregnancy."

CHARTHAM, ROBERT. Sex Manners of the Young Generation. London, Eng.: New English Library, 1970. 125 pp.

CHESSER, EUSTACE. Sexual Behaviour. Rev. ed. London, Eng.: Transworld, 1964. 287 pp.

The 1949 edition has the subtitle "Normal and Abnormal."

CHESSER, EUSTACE, et al. The Sexual, Marital and Family Relationships of the English Woman. New York: Roy, 1957(?) 642 pp. Illus.

Earlier edition, Hutchinson, London, England, 1956.

This title is also known as "The Chesser Report."

CLARKE, EDWIN LEAVITT. Petting: Wise or Otherwise? New York: Association Press, 1938. 32 pp.

COCHRAN, WILLIAM GEMMELL, et al. Statistical Problems of the Kinsey Report on Sexual Behavior in the Human Male. Washington, D.C.: American Statistical Association, 1954. 338 pp. Tables.

"A report of the American Statistical Association Committee to advise the National Research Council, Committee for Research in Problems of Sex."

Reprinted by Greenwood, Westport, Conn.

COFFIN, TRISTRAM. The Sex Kick: Eroticism in Modern America. New York: Macmillan, 1966. 256 pp.

COLLIER, JAMES LINCOLN. The Hypocritical American: An Essay on Sex Attitudes in America. Indianapolis, Ind.: Bobbs, 1964. 210 pp.

COMFORT, ALEXANDER. Sex in Society. New York: Citadel, 1966. 172 pp.

First published in Britain in 1950 under the title "Sexual Behavior in Society."

COOPER, WENDY. Hair: Sex, Society, Symbolism. New York: Stein and Day, 1971. 233 pp.

CUBER, JOHN F., and P. B. HARROFF. Sex and the Significant Americans: A Study of Sexual Behavior among the Affluent. Baltimore, Md.: Penguin, 1966. 204 pp.

1965 edition, published by Appleton, New York, under the title "The Significant Americans."

DAVIS, KATHARINE BEMENT. Factors in the Sex Life of 2,200 Women. Publications of the Bureau of Social Hygiene. New York: Harper, 1929. 430 pp. Tables.

"A study, based on answers to questionnaires written by 1,000 married women of good standing and 1,200 unmarried college graduates, of the prevalence of various factors in the sex life of women, and their effects."

De MARTINO, MANFRED F. The New Female Sexuality: The Sexual Practices and Experiences of Social Nudists, Potential Nudists, and Lesbians. Fwd. by Albert Ellis. New York: Julian, 1969. 236 pp.

DEUTSCH, ALBERT, ed. Sex Habits of American Men: A Symposium on the Kinsey Report. New York: Prentice-Hall, 1948. 244 pp.

"Comments, by thirteen authorities, on various aspects of the Kinsey Report, including psychiatry, sociology, anthropology, statistics, law, religion, education."

DITZION, SIDNEY HERBERT. Marriage, Morals, and Sex in America: A History of Ideas. New York: Octagon, 1969. 460 pp.

Earlier edition, 1953.

"A history of the attitudes toward sex from colonial times to the present."

EHRMANN, WINSTON W. Premarital Dating Behavior. New York: Bantam, 1960. 396 pp.

"Deals with the post-World War II practices of a representative group of college students."

1959 edition published in two parts by Holt, New York.

ELLIOTT, NEIL. Sensuality in Scandinavia. New York: Weybright and Talley, 1970. 271 pp.

ERNST, MORRIS LEOPOLD, and D. G. LOTH. American Sexual Behavior and the Kinsey Report. Fwd. by Robert L. Dickinson. New York: Greystone, 1948. 191 pp.

English edition has the title "Sexual Behavior and the Kinsey Report."

EYLES, LEONORA. Unmarried but Happy. London, Eng.: Gollancz, 1947. 140 pp.

"Deals with physical, social, and psychological problems of unmarried women. Written by a journalist of wide experience."

FIELDING, WILLIAM JOHN. Sanity in Sex. New York: Dodd, 1922. 333 pp.

"Documentation of sex attitude changes on part of society."

FISCHER, H. C., and E. X. DUBOIS. Sexual Life during the World War. London, Eng.: Aldor, 1937. 485 pp.

Deals with the sexual and moral conditions during the First World War.

FORD, CLELLAN STEARNS, and F. A. BEACH. Patterns of Sexual Behavior. Fwd. by Robert Latou Dickinson. New York: Harper, 1951. 307 pp. Map. Diagrams.

British edition, published by Eyres, London, 1952.

Reprinted in 1970.

FRYER, PETER. Mrs. Grundy: Studies in English Prudery. New York: London House, 1964.

British edition, published by Dobson, London, 1963.

"A detailed study of the prudery, verbal taboos and euphemisms that the English language has produced."

GAGNON, JOHN H., and W. SIMON, eds. The Sexual Scene. Chicago, Ill.: Aldine, 1970. 150 pp.

"Originally appeared in 'Trans-action Magazine,' 1964-1969."

Partial Contents: Perspectives on the Sexual Scene, by J. H. Gagnon and W. Simon; Psycho-sexual Development, by W. Simon and J. H. Gagnon; How and Why America's Sex Standards are Changing, by I. L. Reiss; Hippie Morality: More Old than New, by B. M. Berger; Our Unlovable Sex Laws, by F. Rodell; Abortion Laws and Their Victims, by A. S. Rossi; Lesbian Liaisons, by D. A. Ward and G. G. Kassebaum.

GEBHARD, PAUL H., et al. Pregnancy, Birth and Abortion. New York: Harper, 1958. 282 pp. Diagrams. Tables.

A research study by the staff of the Institute for Sex Research, Indiana University.

GEBHARD, PAUL H., et al. The Sexuality of Women. Library of Sexual Behavior, Vol. 1. New York: Stein and Day, 1970. 144 pp.

Translation of "Die Sexualität der Frau."

GEDDES, DONALD PORTER, and E. CURIE, eds. About the Kinsey Report: Observations by 11 Experts on Sexual Behavior in the Human Male. New York: New American Library, 1948. 166 pp. Diagrams.

GEDDES, DONALD PORTER, ed. An Analysis of the Kinsey Reports on Sexual Behavior in the Human Male and Female. New York: Dutton, 1954. 319 pp.

"Sixteen experts from a wide variety of disciplines evaluate the Kinsey reports on both the male and the female. The last section of the book presents a record of the reactions of the press and the public to each volume."

GHURYE, GOVIND SADASHIV. Sexual Behaviour of the American Female. Bombay, India: Current Book House, 1956. 173 pp.

GITTELSON, NATALIE. The Erotic Life of the American Wife. New York: Delacorte, 1972. 380 pp.

A small portion of this was published originally in different form in 'Harpers Bazaar.'

GOLDBERG, ISAAC. The Sexual Life of Man, Woman and Child: Notes on a Changing Valuation of Behavior. Girard, Kans.: Haldeman-Julius, 1927. 63 pp.

GREENE, GAEL. Sex and the College Girl. New York: Dial, 1964. 256 pp.

GROUP FOR THE ADVANCEMENT OF PSYCHIATRY. COMMITTEE ON THE COLLEGE STUDENT. Sex and the College Student: A Developmental Perspective on Sexual Issues on the Campus. New York: Atheneum, 1966. 178 pp.

"Some Guidelines for Administrative Policy and Understanding of Sexual Issues."

HARRIS, SARA. The Puritan Jungle: America's Sexual Underground. New York: Putnam, 1969. 256 pp.

HARTMAN, WILLIAM E., et al. Nudist Society: An Authoritative, Complete Study of Nudism in America. New York: Crown, 1970. 432 pp. Illus.

Also published by Avon, New York, 1971.

Contains a list of nudist camps.

HIMELHOCH, JEROME, and S. F. FAVA, eds. Sexual Behavior in American Society: An Appraisal of the First Two Kinsey Reports. New York: Norton, 1955. 446 pp.

"Edited for the Society for the Study of Social Problems."

"An analysis by 39 sociologists, psychologists, anthropologists, statisticians, ministers and other professionals."

HIRSCH, ARTHUR HENRY. Sexual Misbehavior of the Upper Cultured: A Mid-century Study of Behavior Trends Outside Marriage in the United States since 1930. Human Relations Research, Chicago, Publications in Human Behavior Trends, Vol. 1. New York: Vantage, 1955. 512 pp.

"Limited to white persons."

HIRSCHFELD, MAGNUS, ed. Sexual History of the World War: Brought up-to-date by Edward Podolsky. Rev. ed. New York: Cadillac, 1946. 318 pp.

"From reports collected by the Institute for Sexual Science, Berlin, Germany."

Translation of "Sittengeschichte des Weltkrieges" published in 1930.

First published in English in 1941.

HOLT, SIMMA. Sex and the Teen-age Revolution. Toronto, Canada: McClelland and Stewart, 1967. 163 pp.

ILFELD, FRED, and R. LAUER. Social Nudism in America. New Haven, Conn.: College and University Press, 1964. 240 pp.

INGRAM, KENNETH. The Modern Attitude to the Sex Problem. New York: Stokes, 1930. 158 pp.

INSTITUT FRANÇAIS d'OPINION PUBLIQUE. Patterns of Sex and Love: A Study of the French Woman and Her Morals. Tr. by Lowell Blair. New York: Crown, 1961. 234 pp. Illus.

Translation of "La Française et L'Amour."

"A Study of the French Institute of Public Opinion, with comments by Michel Audiard, et al."

JAMES, DON. The Sexual Side of Life: The Truth about Love and Sex in Modern Society. Derby, Conn.: Monarch, 1959. 207 pp.

KARLEN, ARNO. Sexuality and Homosexuality: A New View. New York: Norton, 1971. 666 pp.

KINSEY, ALFRED CHARLES, et al. Sexual Behavior in the Human Female. Philadelphia, Pa.: Saunders, 1953. 842 pp. Diagrams.

Another edition, Pocket Books, New York, 1965.

A famous study of female sexual behavior by the staff of the Institute for Sex Research, Indiana University.

KINSEY, ALFRED CHARLES, et al. Sexual Behavior in the Human Male. Philadelphia, Pa.: Saunders, 1948.

"A pioneering study of male sexual behavior by the staff of the Institute for Sex Research, Indiana University. It demonstrated statistically for the first time how wide the gap had become between officially sanctioned and actual sexual behavior in our society."

KIRKENDALL, LESTER A., and R. N. WHITEHURST, eds. The New Sexual Revolution. New York: Brown, 1971. 236 pp.

KIRKENDALL, LESTER ALLEN. Premarital Intercourse and Interpersonal Relationships: A Research Study of Interpersonal Relationships Based on Case Histories of 668 Premarital Intercourse Experiences Reported by 200 College Level Males. New York: Julian, 1961. 302 pp. Illus.

Reprinted by Matrix House, New York, in 1966.

KIRKENDALL, LESTER ALLEN, and E. OGG. Sex and Our Society. Public Affairs Pamphlet No. 366. New York: Public Affairs Committee, 1964. 28 pp. Illus.

KRONHAUSEN, PHYLLIS, and E. KRONHAUSEN. Sex Histories of American College Men. New York: Ballantine, 1960. 313 pp.

LENZ, LUDWIG LEVY. Discretion and Indiscretion: Memoirs of a Sexologist. Tr. by B. Ross. Exclusive ed. for the Middle East. Cairo, Egypt: al-Maaref Press, 1949. 541 pp.

LEUBA, CLARENCE JAMES. The Sexual Nature of Man, and Its Management. Garden City, N.Y.: Doubleday, 1954. 40 pp. Illus.

LIEBERMAN, BERNHARDT, ed. Human Sexual Behavior: A Book of Readings. New York: Wiley, 1971. 444 pp. Illus.

LIPKE, JEAN CORYLLEL. Dating. Minneapolis, Minn.: Lerner, 1971. 69 pp. Illus.

Discusses dating conduct, asking for a date, double dating, blind dates, pick-ups, going steady, and the emotional and physical reactions of being close to another person.

McKNIGHT, GERALD. The English at Love. Illus. by R. Dewar. London, Eng.: New English Library, 1967. 174 pp. Illus.

MEAD, MARGARET. Male and Female: A Study of the Sexes in a Changing World. New York: Morrow, 1949. 477 pp.

"An analysis of male and female behavior with emphasis on the role of culture in contemporary society."

"The substance of this work was given as the Jacob Gimbel Lectures in sex psychology at the University of California, San Francisco, Nov. 1946."

MORSE, BENJAMIN. Adolescent Sexual Behavior: A Comprehensive Study of Our Teen-age Society, Its Morals, Its Codes and Its Taboos. Derby, Conn.: Monarch, 1964. 141 pp.

MORSE, BENJAMIN. Sexual Behavior of the American College Girl. New York: Lancer, 1963. 174 pp.

NEVILLE-ROLFE, SYBIL KATHERINE BURNEY, ed. Sex in Social Life. New York: Norton, 1950. 504 pp. Illus.

1949 edition, Allen & Unwin, London.

OTTO, HERBERT ARTHUR, ed. The New Sexuality. Palo Alto, Calif.: Science & Behavior Books, 1971. 289 pp.

PACKARD, VANCE OAKLEY. The Sexual Wilderness: The Contemporary Upheaval in Male-Female Relationships. New York: McKay, 1968. 553 pp.

"Analysis of the values governing sexual relations, and the resulting behavior in the United States and selected foreign countries today."

British edition, Longmans, 1968, has different subtitle.

PARCA, GABRIELLA, ed. Italian Women Confess. Tr. by Carolyn Gaiser. New York: Farrar, 1963. 267 pp.

Translation of "Le Italiane Si Confessano," 1959. "A selection of letters sent to Italian lovelorn columns by young Italian women seeking advice."

PARCA, GABRIELLA. Love Italian Style. Tr. by Allyn Moss and Romano Giachetti. Englewood Cliffs, N.J.: Prentice-Hall, 1966. 298 pp.

Translation of "I Sultani," 1965.

"This book is the result of interviews with more than one thousand Italian males, both married and bachelors, about their sexual behavior."

PARMELEE, MAURICE FARR. Nudism in Modern Life: The New Gymnosophy. Intro. by Havelock Ellis. 4th American rev. ed. Mays Landing, N.J.: Sunshine Book, 1941. 303 pp.

"Includes the Decision of the United States Court of Appeals for the District of Columbia Regarding the Alleged Obscenity of the Nudist Illustrations."

Original American Publication, 1927, issued under the title "The New Gymnosophy."

POMEROY, WARDELL BAXTER. Dr. Kinsey and the Institute for Sex Research. New York: Harper, 1972. 479 pp. Illus.

REICHE, REIMUT. Sexuality and Class Struggle. Tr. from German by S. Bennett. New York: Praeger, 1971. 175 pp.

Translation of "Sexualität und Klassenkampf."

1970 edition, London, England.

REISS, IRA L. Premarital Sexual Standards in America: A Sociological Investigation of the Relative Social and Cultural Integration of American Sexual Standards. Glencoe, Ill.: Free Press, 1960. 286 pp. Illus.

REISS, IRA L. The Social Context of Premarital Sexual Permissiveness. New York: Holt, 1967. 256 pp.

"Analyzes the results of surveys taken among white and black high school and college students and adults."

RICHARDSON, HERBERT WARREN. Nun, Witch, Playmate: The Americaniza-
tion of Sex. New York: Harper, 1971. 147 pp.

"The central idea is that human sexuality is as much a function of society
as of biology, and that changes in attitudes toward sex accompany other
social changes."

RUBENSTEIN, PAUL, and H. MARGOLIS. The Groupsex Tapes. New York:
McKay, 1971. 306 pp.

"98 participants in the newest, most revolutionary release of sexual in-
hibitions tell what they do, why they do it, and what it reveals about new
dimensions in male-female relationships."

SAGARIN, EDWARD, et al. Sex and the Contemporary American Scene. The
Annals of the American Academy of Political and Social Science, Vol. 376.
Philadelphia, Pa.: American Academy of Political and Social Science, 1968.
232 pp.

SCHUR, EDWIN M., ed. The Family and the Sexual Revolution. Bloomington,
Ind.: Indiana University, 1964. 427 pp.

"Selected readings on changing sex standards, the role of women, and
birth control."

1966 edition, Allen & Unwin, London, England.

SCOTT, JAMES FOSTER. The Sexual Instinct: Its Use and Dangers as Affecting Heredity and Morals; Essentials to the Welfare of the Individual and
the Future of the Race. Chicago, Ill.: n.p., 1930. 473 pp.

Issued also under the title "Heredity and Morals . . . ," Treat, New York,
1898.

SCOTT, GEORGE RYLEY. The Common Sense of Nudism, Including a Survey
of Sun-bathing and "Light Treatments." London, Eng.: Laurie, 1934. 165
pp. Plates.

"English nudist and sun-bathing societies: their policies and aims."

SHILOH, AILON, comp. Studies in Human Sexual Behavior: The American
Scene. Prefatory remarks by Paul H. Gebhard. Springfield, Ill.:
Thomas, 1970. 460 pp. Illus.

SHINOZAKI, NOBUO. Report on Sexual Life of Japanese. Tokyo, Japan:
The Institute of Population Problems, Welfare Ministry, 1957. 34 pp.
Illus.

Research-data of Jinko Mondai Kenkyusho, Tokyo

SOROKIN, PITIRIM A. The American Sex Revolution. Boston, Mass.:
Sargent, 1956. 186 pp.

"This well-known sociologist expresses deep concern for what is happening
to American morals. He sees the trend toward sexual permissiveness as
leading to the downfall of our society."

1965 edition, Sargent, Boston, Mass.

SPRAGUE, W. D. Sexual Behavior of American Nurses. New York: Lancer,
1963. 159 pp.

STAFFORD, PETER. Sexual Behavior in the Communist World: An Eyewitness Report of Life, Love, and the Human Condition behind the Iron Curtain. New York: Julian, 1967. 287 pp. Illus.

TRAINER, RUSSELL. Sex and Love among the Poor. New York: Ballantine, 1968. 314 pp.

UNWIN, JOSEPH DANIEL. Sex and Culture. London, Eng.: Oxford University, 1934. 676 pp.

"This book is based on the hypothesis that what we call 'civilization' has been built up by compulsory sacrifices in the gratification of innate desires."

WALKER, KENNETH MacFARLANE. Sex and a Changing Civilization. London, Eng.: Lane, 1935. 135 pp.

WELLS, JOHN WARREN. Eros and Capricorn: A Cross-cultural Survey of Sexual Attitudes and Techniques. New York: Lancer, 1968. 191 pp.

WHITMAN, HOWARD JAY. The Sex Age. Garden City, N.Y.: Doubleday, 1962. 247 pp.

"Concerns itself with the extensive but superficial preoccupation of Americans with sex."

Also published by Bobbs-Merrill, Indianapolis, Ind. in 1963.

WINOKUR, GEORGE, ed. Determinants of Human Sexual Behavior. Springfield, Ill.: Thomas, 1963. 230 pp. Illus.

"Proceedings of the Fourth Annual Conference on Community Mental Health Research, Social Science Institute, Washington University."

WORLD LEAGUE FOR SEXUAL REFORM. Sex Reform Congress, 1929: Reports of Addresses Delivered at the Third International Congress, by Bertrand Russell, Bernard Shaw, and others. Ed. by Norman Haire. London, Eng.: Routledge, 1930. 710 pp. Plates.

7.
SEX DEVIATION

HOMOSEXUALITY AND LESBIANISM

ACKERLEY, JOE RANDOLPH. My Father and Myself. New York: Coward-McCann, 1969. 219 pp.

Also 1968 edition. The author's memoirs.

ALBANY TRUST. Homosexuality: Some Questions and Answers. London, Eng.: Albany Trust, 1970. 20 pp.

ALEXANDER, MARSHA. Label My Love Lesbian. North Hollywood, Calif.: Brandon House, 1969. 174 pp.

ALIBERT. Tribadism and Saphism. Paris, France: Privately printed, 1926. 86 pp.

ALLEN, CLIFFORD. Homosexuality: Its Nature, Causation and Treatment. London, Eng.: Staples, 1958. 143 pp.

ALTMAN, DENNIS. Homosexual: Oppression and Liberation. New York: Outerbridge, 1971. 242 pp.

"A landmark book that discusses gay liberation, not as a political movement but as a change in individual perspective and the implications for the rest of society."

ANOMALY [pseud.]. The Invert and His Social Adjustment: To Which Is Added a Sequel by the Same Author. 2nd ed. Westminster, Md.: Christian Classics, 1969. 289 pp.

Reprint of the 1948 edition. 1929 edition published by Williams & Wilkins.

ARONSON, MARVIN LUCIUS. A Study of the Freudian Theory of Paranoia by Means of a Group of Psychological Tests. University Microfilms, Ann Arbor, Mich. Publication No. 2374. Ann Arbor, Mich.: University Microfilms, 1951. 169 leaves.

Thesis, University of Michigan. Abstracted in "Microfilm Abstracts," Vol. 11 (1951), No. 2, p. 443-444.

BAILEY, DERRICK SHERWIN. Homosexuality and the Western Christian Tradition. London, Eng.: Longmans, 1955. 181 pp.

BANIS, VICTOR J. Men and Their Boys: The Homosexual Relationship between Adult and Adolescent. Los Angeles, Calif.: Medco, 1966. 144 pp.

BECKER, RAYMOND De. The Other Face of Love. London, Eng.: Spearman, 1967. 203 pp. Illus.

Translation of "L'érotisme d'en face."

BELL, ARTHUR. Dancing the Gay Lib Blues: A Year in the Homosexual Liberation Movement. New York: Simon & Schuster, 1971. 191 pp.

BENSON, R. O. D. In Defense of Homosexuality, Male and Female: A Rational Evaluation of Social Prejudice. New York: Julian, 1965. 239 pp.

BERG, CHARLES. Fear, Punishment, Anxiety and the Wolfenden Report. London, Eng.: Allen & Unwin, 1959. 126 pp.

Partly reprinted from various medical journals.

BERG, CHARLES, ed. Homosexuality: A Subjective and Objective Investigation. London, Eng.: Allen & Unwin, 1958. 415 pp.

American edition, 1954, edited by A. M. Krich, has the title "The Homosexuals, as Seen by Themselves and Thirty Authorities."

BERG, CHARLES, and C. ALLEN. The Problem of Homosexuality. New York: Citadel, 1958. 221 pp.

Contents: Homosexuality; Its Nature, Causation and Treatment, by C. Allen; The Foundations of Homosexuality, by C. Berg; The Wolfenden Report: Discussion and criticism, by C. Berg; Report of the Committee on Homosexual Offences and Prostitution.

BERGLER, EDMUND. Homosexuality: Disease or Way of Life? New York: Hill and Wang, 1956. 302 pp.

BERGLER, EDMUND. One Thousand Homosexuals: Conspiracy of Silence, or Curing and Deglamorizing Homosexuals? Paterson, N.J.: Pageant, 1959. 249 pp.

BERNSTEIN, ALLEN. Millions of Queers: Our Homosexual America. n.p., 1940. 149 leaves.

BIEBER, IRVING, et al. Homosexuality. New York: Basic Books, 1962. 358 pp.

"A psychoanalytic study of male homosexuals based on research with heterosexual and homosexual individuals in treatment."

BRAATEN, LEIF JOHAN, and C. DOUGLAS DARLING. Overt and Covert Homosexual Problems among Male College Students. Genetic Psychology Monographs, Vol. 71. Provincetown, Mass., 1965. pp. 269-310.

BRANSON, HELEN P. Gay Bar. Intro. by Blanche M. Baker. San Francisco, Calif.: Pan-Graphic, 1957. 89 pp. Illus.

BRITISH MEDICAL ASSOCIATION. Homosexuality and Prostitution. London, Eng.: British Medical Assn., 1956. 94 pp. Illus.

"A memorandum of evidence prepared by a special committee of the Council of the British Medical Association for submission to the Departmental Committee on Homosexuality and Prostitution. First published, 1955."

BUCKLEY, MICHAEL J. Morality and the Homosexual: A Catholic Approach to a Moral Problem. Westminster, Md.: Newman, 1960. 214 pp.

CAPPON, DANIEL. Toward an Understanding of Homosexuality. Englewood Cliffs, N.J.: Prentice-Hall, 1965. 302 pp.

CAPRIO, FRANK SAMUEL. Female Homosexuality: A Psychodynamic Study of Lesbianism. New York: Citadel, 1967. 334 pp.

CARPENTER, EDWARD. The Intermediate Sex: A Study of Some Transitional Types of Men and Women. London, Eng.: Allen & Unwin, 1952. 175 pp.

"A sympathetic study of the problems and a plea for the enlightened understanding of men and women of intermediate or mixed temperament. The chapter 'The Intermediate Sex' was first published in 1897 under the title 'An Unknown People.' "

First published in 1908. Partial Contents: The Intermediate Sex; The Homogenic Attachment; Affection in Education; The Place of the Uranian in Society.

CAVANAGH, JOHN R. Counseling the Invert. Milwaukee, Wis.: Bruce, 1966. 306 pp.

CHESSER, EUSTACE. Live and Let Live: The Moral of the Wolfenden Report. Fwd. by John Wolfenden. London, Eng.: Heinemann, 1958. 126 pp.

CHESSER, EUSTACE. Odd Man Out: Homosexuality in Men and Women. London, Eng.: Gollancz, 1959. 192 pp.

CHIDECKEL, MAURICE. Female Sex Perversion: The Sexually Aberrated Woman as She Is. New York: Brown, 1963. 331 pp. Illus.

Reprint of 1935 edition.

CHURCHILL, WAINWRIGHT. Homosexual Behavior among Males: A Cross-Cultural and Cross-Species Investigation. Englewood Cliffs, N.J.: Prentice-Hall, 1971. 346 pp.

"This book argues that homosexual behavior should be viewed as a utilization of natural capacities rather than as distortion, crime, or disease." Earlier edition, 1967, published by Hawthorn, New York.

CORY, DONALD WEBSTER [pseud.], and J. P. LEROY. The Homosexual and His Society: A View from Within. New York: Citadel, 1963. 276 pp.

CORY, DONALD WEBSTER [pseud.] The Homosexual in America: A Subjective Approach. Intro. by Albert Ellis. 2nd ed. New York: Castle, 1960. 334 pp.

Earlier edition, 1951, by Greenberg, New York. Appendices: A. Government Documents Pertaining to Homosexuality. B. Extracts from the Statutes of the Forty-eight States. C. Bibliography of Technical Literature. D. Check List of Literary Works.

CORY, DONALD WEBSTER [pseud.], ed. Homosexuality: A Cross-Cultural Approach. New York: Julian, 1956. 440 pp.

Partial Contents: Homosexual Love, by E. Westmarck; The Perversions of Love, by P. Mantegazza; Male Homosexuality in Ancient Greece, by H. Licht; The Love called "Socrates," by Voltaire; Criteria for a Hormonal Explanation, by A. C. Kinsey; Homosexuality, Sodomy, and Crimes against Nature, by M. Ploscowe; Are Homosexuals Necessarily Neurotic? by A. Ellis; Influence of Heterosexual Culture, by A. Ellis; Changing Attitudes toward Homosexuals, by D. W. Cory [pseud.].

CORY, DONALD WEBSTER [pseud.]. The Lesbian in America. Intro. by Albert Ellis. New York: Citadel, 1964. 288 pp.

"This volume helps to delineate some of the major differences between lesbianism and male homosexuality and to dispel many of the misconceptions about lesbians."

CRISP, QUENTIN. The Naked Civil Servant. London, Eng.: Cape, 1968. 217 pp.

CUTLER, MARVIN. Homosexuals Today: A Handbook of Organizations and Publications. Los Angeles, Calif.: Publications Division of One, Inc., 1956. 188 pp. Illus.

DAVIDSON, ALEX. The Returns of Love: Letters of a Christian Homosexual. London, Eng.: Inter-Varsity, 1970. 93 pp.

DAVIDSON, MICHAEL. Some Boys. London, Eng.: Bruce, 1970. 199 pp.

A personal narrative.

DRAKEFORD, JOHN W. Forbidden Love: A Homosexual Looks for Understanding and Help. Waco, Tex.: Word Books, 1971. 149 pp.

EAST COAST HOMOPHILE ORGANIZATIONS. Homosexuality: Civil Liberties and Social Rights. New York: n.p., 1965. 144 leaves.

"Transcript of addresses delivered at the East Coast Homophile Organizations Conference, October 9, 10, and 11, 1964, Sheraton-Park Hotel, Washington, D. C."

EGLINTON, J. Z. Greek Love. New York: Layton, 1964. 504 pp.

ELLIS, ALBERT. Homosexuality: Its Causes and Cure. Intro. and a terminal essay, "Homosexuality and the Mystique of the Gigantic Penis," by Donald Webster Cory. New York: Stuart, 1965. 288 pp.

"Detailed application of the principles of rational psychotherapy to the relief of homosexual phobias and compulsions. Includes verbatim transcripts of interviews with homosexual patients."

ELLIS, HAVELOCK. A Note on the Bedborough Trial. London, Eng.: University Press, 1898. 23 pp.

"The author's account of his work, 'Sexual Inversion,' and the trial proceeding from Bedborough's sale of a copy."

ELLIS, HAVELOCK. Sexual Inversion. 3rd ed., rev. and enl. Philadelphia, Pa.: Davis, 1915. 391 pp.

Earlier edition, 1901. Constitutes Vol. 2 of the author's "Studies in the Psychology of Sex."

FAITHFULL, THEODORE JAMES. Bisexuality: An Essay on Extraversion and Introversion. London, Eng.: Bale, 1927. 96 pp. Diagrams.

FISHER, PETER. The Gay Mystique: The Myth and Reality of Male Homosexuality. New York: Stein and Day, 1972. 258 pp.

FLORIDA. LEGISLATIVE INVESTIGATION COMMITTEE. Homosexuality and Citizenship in Florida: A Report. Tallahassee, Fla.: n.p., 1964. 27 leaves.

FORD, LAURA MAY. Bittersweet: The Autobiography of a Lesbian. New York: Exposition, 1969. 144 pp.

FOSTER, JEANNETTE HOWARD. Sex Variant Women in Literature: A Historical and Quantitative Survey. New York: Vantage, 1956. 412 pp.

"An extended analysis and survey of the attitudes of peoples through the centuries toward lesbian relationships as mirrored in fiction, drama, and poetry."

FREEDMAN, MARK. Homosexuality and Psychological Functioning. Belmont, Calif.: Brooks/Cole, 1971. 124 pp.

GARDE, NOEL I. Jonathan to Gide: The Homosexual in History. New York: Vantage, 1964. 751 pp.

GERBER, ISRAEL JOSHUA. Man on a Pendulum: A Case History of an Invert. New York: American Press, 1955. 320 pp.

GIDE, ANDRÉ PAUL GUILLAUME. Corydon. With a comment on the second dialogue in Corydon, by Frank Beach. New York: Farrar, Straus, 1950. 220 pp.

First published in Paris in 1911. The English translation is based on the new edition of 1924. British translation has the subtitle "Four Socratic Dialogues." "A tract in defense of homosexuality, written in the form of four dialogues."

GLOVER, EDWARD, ed. The Problem of Homosexuality. London, Eng.: I.S.T.D., 1957. 39 pp.

Being a memorandum presented to the Departmental Committee on Homosexual Offences and Prostitution, by a joint committee representing the Institute for the Study and Treatment of Delinquency, and the Portman Clinic.

GRAHAM, JAMES. The Homosexual Kings of England. London, Eng.: Tandem, 1968. 92 pp. Illus.

Contents: William Rufus; Richard I; Edward II; Richard II; James I; William III.

GREAT BRITAIN. COMMITTEE ON HOMOSEXUAL OFFENSES AND PROSTITUTION. Wolfenden Report. New York: Stein and Day, 1963. 243 pp. Tables.

"The British report which recommended that 'homosexual behavior between consenting adults, in private, be no longer a criminal offense,' and was finally accepted as law. It also made proposals for dealing with prostitution." Published in London, England in 1957.

GROSS, ALFRED A. Strangers in Our Midst: Problems of the Homosexual in American Society. Washington, D.C.: Public Affairs Press, 1962. 182 pp.

GUNNISON, FOSTER. An Introduction to the Homophile Movement. Hartford, Conn.: Institute of Social Ethics, 1967- Vol. 1-

HAMILTON, GILBERT Van TASSEL, and G. LEGMAN. On the Cause of Homosexuality: Two Essays, the Second in Reply to the First. New York: n.p., 1950. 30 pp.

Contents: Homosexuals and Their Mothers, by G. V. Hamilton; Fathers and Sons, by G. Legman.

HARRIS, EDWARD F., and E. B. BUMBALOUGH. An Evaluation of the Legal, Medical and Psychological Attitudes of Homosexuality in Contemporary American Society. n.p., 1969. 109 leaves.

HASSELRODT, R. LEIGHTON. Twilight Women around the World. London, Eng.: Champion, 1965. 191 pp. Illus.

HATTERER, LAWRENCE J. Changing Homosexuality in the Male: Treatment for Men Troubled by Homosexuality. New York: McGraw-Hill, 1970. 492 pp.

HICKEY, OWEN. Law and Laxity. Issues of Today, 4. London, Eng.: Times Newspapers, 1970. 20 pp.

Deals with various issues such as homosexuality, abortion, divorce, and obscenity.

HOFFMAN, MARTIN. The Gay World: Male Homosexuality and the Social Creation of Evil. New York: Basic Books, 1968. 212 pp.

"A study by a social psychiatrist of the homosexual as he exists in his 'natural milieu' rather than in the psychiatric consulting room or the court of law."

HUDSON, BILLY. Christian Homosexuality. North Hollywood, Calif.: Aware Press, 1971. 240 pp.

HUMPHREYS, LAUD. Tearoom Trade: Impersonal Sex in Public Places. Chicago, Ill.: Aldine, 1970. 180 pp.

HUTTON, ROBERT. Of Those Alone. London, Eng.: Sidgwick, 1958. 235 pp.

"Autobiography."

HYDE, HARFORD MONTGOMERY. The Love That Dared Not Speak Its Name: A Candid History of Homosexuality in Britain. Boston, Mass.: Little, 1970. 323 pp.

"First published in England, by Heinemann, London in 1970 under the title 'The Other Love.' "

JERSILD, JENS. Boy Prostitution. Tr. by Oscar Bojesen. Copenhagen, Denmark: Gad, 1956. 101 pp.

JERSILD, JENS. The Normal Homosexual Male versus the Boy Molester. Copenhagen, Denmark: Nyt Nordisk, 1967. 112 pp.

JONES, H. KIMBALL. Toward a Christian Understanding of the Homosexual. New York: Association Press, 1966. 160 pp.

British edition, 1967, published by S.C.M. Press, London.

JONES, RHODA. Left-Handed in Love: As Told by Rhoda Jones to John Ringrose. London, Eng.: Panther, 1970. 127 pp.

KAHN, SAMUEL. Mentality and Homosexuality. Boston, Mass.: Meador, 1937. 249 pp.

KARLEN, ARNO. Sexuality and Homosexuality: A New View. New York: Norton, 1971. 666 pp.

KRANZ, SHELDON, comp. The H Persuasion: How Persons Have Permanently Changed from Homosexuality through the Study of Aesthetics Realism with Eli Siegel. Intro. by Ten van Griethuysen. New York: Definition, 1971. 136 pp.

KUHN, DONALD. The Church and the Homosexual: A Report on a Consultation. San Francisco, Calif.: Glide Urban Center, 1965. 38 pp.

"Sponsored by the Methodist Older Youth/Young Adult Project, the Division of Alcohol Problems and General Welfare of the Methodist Board of Christian Social Concerns, and the Glide Urban Center."

McCAFFREY, JOSEPH ANTHONY. Homosexuality: Toward a Moral Synthesis. Rome, Italy: Catholic Book Agency, 1969. 93 pp.

Thesis, University of St. Thomas Aquinas, Rome.

MAGEE, BRYAN. One in Twenty: A Study of Homosexuality in Men and Women. New ed. London, Eng.: Secker and Warburg, 1968. 191 pp.

Earlier edition, 1966.

MARLOWE, KENNETH. The Male Homosexual. Los Angeles, Calif.: Sherbourne, 1965. 158 pp.

MARLOWE, KENNETH. Mr. Madam: Confessions of a Male Madam. London, Eng.: Mayflower, 1967. 319 pp.

1964 edition published by Shelbourne in Los Angeles, California.

"Autobiography of an active homosexual, a female impersonator, the 'madam' of a homosexual house of prostitution, catering to an exclusive Hollywood clientele."

MARMOR, JUDD., ed. Sexual Inversion: The Multiple Roots of Homosexuality. New York: Basic Books, 1965. 358 pp.

"Seventeen authorities in the fields of biological, social, medical, and behavioral science discuss the multiple roots of homosexuality and suggest new treatment approaches."

MARTIN, HAROLD. Men and Cupid: A Reassessment of Homosexuality and of Man's Sexual Life in General. London, Eng.: Fortune, 1965. 159 pp.

MASTERS, ROBERT E. L. Eros and Evil: The Sexual Psychopathology of Witchcraft. New York: Julian, 1962. 322 pp.

Several other editions are in existence.

MASTERS, ROBERT E. L. The Homosexual Revolution: A Challenging Exposé of the Social and Political Directions of a Minority Group. New York: Julian, 1962. 230 pp.

Other editions are in existence.

MATHEWS, ARTHUR GUY. Is Homosexuality a Menace? New York: McBride, 1957. 302 pp.

MERCER, JESSIE DECAMARRON. They Walk in Shadow: A Study of Sexual Variations with Emphasis on the Ambisexual and Homosexual Components and Our Contemporary Sex Laws. New York: Comet, 1959. 573 pp. Illus.

MILLER, MERLE. On Being Different: What it Means to Be a Homosexual. New York: Random, 1971. 65 pp.

MITCHELL, ROGER S. The Homosexual and the Law. New York: Arco, 1969. 96 pp.

MORSE, BENJAMIN. The Homosexual: A Frank Study of Abnormal Sex Life among Males. Derby, Conn.: Monarch, 1962. 158 pp.

MORSE, BENJAMIN. The Lesbian: A Frank, Revealing Study of Women Who Turn to Their Own Sex for Love. Derby, Conn.: Monarch, 1961. 142 pp.

MURPHY, JOHN. Homosexual Liberation: A Personal View. New York: Praeger, 1971. 182 pp.

OBERHOLTZER, W. DWIGHT, ed. Is Gay Good? Ethics, Theology, and Homosexuality. Philadelphia, Pa.: Westminster, 1971. 287 pp.

OLLENDORFF, ROBERT HERRMANN VIKTOR. The Juvenile Homosexual Experience and Its Effect on Adult Sexuality. New York: Julian, 1966. 245 pp.

OVESEY, LIONEL. Homosexuality and Pseudohomosexuality. New York: Science House, 1969. 157 pp.

PITTENGER, WILLIAM NORMAN. Time for Consent. 2nd ed., rev. and enl. London, Eng.: S.C.M. Press, 1970. 124 pp.

1967 edition has the subtitle "A Christian's Approach to Homosexuality."

PLUMMER, DOUGLAS [pseud.]. Queer People. Intro. by Donald Webster
Cory. New York: Citadel, 1965. 122 pp.

1963 edition, W. H. Allen, London, England.

POMEROY, WARDELL B., et al. The Same Sex: An Appraisal of Homosexuality. Ed. by Ralph Weltge. Philadelphia, Pa.: Pilgrim, 1969. 164 pp.

PRISONER X [pseud.]. Prison Confidential. Los Angeles, Calif.: Medco,
1969. 202 pp.

QUERLIN, MARISE. Women without Men. New York: Dell, 1965. 174 pp.

Translation of "Femmes sans Hommes."

READE, BRIAN, comp. Sexual Heretics: Male Homosexuality in English
Literature from 1850 to 1900. Selected anthology with Intro. by B. Reade.
New York: Coward-McCann, 1971. 459 pp. Illus.

Previously published in 1970.

REES, TUDOR, and H. V. USILL, eds. They Stand Apart: A Critical Survey of
the Problems of Homosexuality. London, Eng.: Heinemann, 1955. 220 pp.

ROBERTIELLO, RICHARD C. Voyage from Lesbos: The Psychoanalysis of a
Female Homosexual. New York: Citadel, 1959. 253 pp.

ROBERTS, AYMER. Forbidden Freedom. London, Eng.: Linden, 1960. 112 pp.

ROSENFELS, PAUL. Homosexuality: The Psychology of the Creative Process.
Roslyn Heights, N.Y.: Libra, 1971. 169 pp.

RUBIN, ISADORE, ed. The "Third Sex": New York: New Book Co., 1961.
112 pp. Illus.

"Articles by Clifford Allen and Others."

A compilation on homosexuality, written by leading authorities.

RUITENBEEK, HENDRIK MARINUS. Homosexuality and Creative Genius.
New York: Obolensky, 1967. 330 pp.

RUITENBEEK, HENDRIK MARINUS. The New Homosexuality: Including the
Author's Essays, The Dutch Situation and The Myth of Bisexuality. To be
published by Souvenir Press, London, Eng., 1973.

RUITENBEEK, HENDRIK MARINUS, ed. The Problem of Homosexuality in
Modern Society. New York: Dutton, 1963. 304 pp.

"An anthology of articles by sixteen experts discusses the origins and
treatment of homosexuality from many differing points of view. It contains several papers which deal with homosexuality from the newer sociological frame of reference as well as traditional psychoanalytic views. It
includes the author's essay, 'Men Alone: The Male Homosexual and the
Disintegrated Family.' "

SAVITSCH, EUGÈNE De. Homosexuality, Transvestism and Change of Sex.
London, Eng.: Heinemann, 1958. 120 pp.

SCHOFIELD, MICHAEL GEORGE [Gordon Westwood]. A Minority: A Report
on the Life of the Male Homosexual in Great Britain. London, Eng.: Longmans, 1960 216 pp.

SCHOFIELD, MICHAEL GEORGE [Gordon Westwood]. Society and the Homosexual. London, Eng.: Gollancz, 1952. 191 pp.

American edition, Dutton, 1953.

SCHOFIELD, MICHAEL GEORGE. Sociological Aspects of Homosexuality: A Comparative Study of Three Types of Homosexuals. Boston, Mass.: Little, Brown, 1965. 244 pp.

SCHWARTZ, WILLIAM ALEXANDER [L. T. Woodward]. Twilight Women. New York: Lancer, 1963. 157 pp.

Explores lesbianism through six case histories.

SMITH, TIMOTHY D'ARCH. Love in Earnest: Some Notes on the Lives and Writings of English "Uranian" Poets from 1889 to 1930. London, Eng.: Routledge, 1970. 280 pp.

SOCARIDES, CHARLES W. The Overt Homosexual. New York: Grune, 1968. 245 pp.

STEARN, JESS. The Sixth Man. Garden City, N.Y.: Doubleday, 1961. 286 pp.

"An intensive study of homosexuality in America, including some attention to psychological and physiological implications."

STEKEL, WILHELM. Bi-Sexual Love: The Homosexual Neurosis. Boston, Mass.: Badger, 1922. 359 pp.

Reissued by Emerson, New York, 1944. Translation of a part of one volume of the author's "Störungen des Trieb-und Affektleben."

STEKEL, WILHELM. The Homosexual Neurosis. Tr. by J. S. Van Teslaar. Rev. ed. Brooklyn, N.Y.: Physicians and Surgeons Book Co., 1934. 322 pp.

"The present volume completes my English version of the 'Homosexualität' portion of the author's 'Onanie und Homosexualität.' The first portion has been issued...under the title 'Bisexual Love.'— Translator's Preface."

STERLING, DAVID LYN. Sex in the Basic Personality. Wichita, Kans.: Hubbard Dianetic Foundation, 1952. 180 pp.

SYMONDS, JOHN ADDINGTON. A Problem in Greek Ethics: Being an Inquiry into the Phenomenon of Sexual Inversion, Addressed especially to Medical Psychologists and Jurists. New York: Haskell, 1971. 73 pp.

"Reprint of the 1901 edition."

TEAL, DONN. The Gay Militants. New York: Stein and Day, 1971. 355 pp.

TOBIN, WILLIAM J. Homosexuality and Marriage: A Canonical Evaluation of the Relationship of Homosexuality to the Validity of Marriage in the Light of Recent Rotal Jurisprudence. Rome, Italy: Catholic Book Agency, 1964. 378 pp.

TYLER, PARKER. Screening the Sexes: Homosexuality in the Movies. New York: Holt, 1972. 367 pp. Illus.

VEDDER, CLYDE BENNETT, and P. G. KING. Problems of Homosexuality in Corrections. Springfield, Ill.: Thomas, 1967. 63 pp.

WEINBERG, GEORGE H. Society and the Healthy Homosexual. New York: St. Martin's, 1972. 150 pp.

WELTGE, RALPH W., ed. The Same Sex: An Appraisal of Homosexuality. Philadelphia, Pa.: Pilgrim, 1969. 164 pp.

"This volume, intended as a resource for individual or group study, grew out of a United Church of Christ staff consultation on homosexuality. A number of the papers are reprints of articles by well-known authorities; others are original papers, some written by spokesmen for the homosexual community."

WEST, DONALD JAMES. Homosexuality. Rev. ed. Chicago, Ill.: Aldine, 1968. 304 pp.

1955 British edition published by Duckworth in London. 1955 American edition published under the title "The Other Man, a Study of the Social, Legal, and Clinical Aspects of Homosexuality."

"Brings the problems of male homosexuality out into the open and discusses them in the light of modern knowledge. Reviews the historical facts about homosexual behavior in preliterate cultures and gives evidence about what causes homosexuality and offers suggestions for treatment and prevention."

WHITE, ERNEST. The Homosexual Condition: A Study of Fifty Cases in Man. Derby, Eng.: Smith, 1963. 41 pp.

WILDEBLOOD, PETER. Against the Law. London, Eng.: Weidenfeld and Nicolson, 1956. 189 pp.

First published in 1955, by Messner, New York.

WILDEBLOOD, PETER. A Way of Life. London, Eng.: Weidenfeld and Nicolson, 1956. 191 pp.

WILLIAMS, COLIN J., and M. S. WEINBERG. Homosexuals and the Military: A Study of Less than Honorable Discharge. New York: Harper, 1971. 221 pp.

WILLIS, STANLEY E. Understanding and Counseling the Male Homosexual. Boston, Mass.: Little, Brown, 1967. 225 pp.

"For any therapist and for anyone who works with homosexuals, a practicing psychiatrist and professor of law in forensic psychiatry has written a carefully tentative and objective book on the complicated subject of homosexuality."

WOLFF, CHARLOTTE. Love between Women. New York: St. Martin's, 1971. 230 pp.

WOOD, ROBERT WATSON. Christ and the Homosexual: Some Observations. Intro. by Albert Ellis. New York: Vantage, 1960. 221 pp.

WYDEN, PETER, and B. WYDEN. Growing Up Straight: What Every Thoughtful Parent Should Know about Homosexuality. New York: Stein and Day, 1968. 256 pp.

"The purpose of this book is to tell parents what they can do to prevent their children from becoming homosexual."

SADISM AND MASOCHISM

BERG, KARL. The Sadist. Authorized tr. by Olga Illner and George Godwin. Library of Abnormal Psychological Types, No. 1. London, Eng.: Heinemann, 1945. 177 pp. Illus.

COULTERAY, GEORGE De. Sadism in the Movies. Tr. by Steve Hult. New York: Medical Press, 1965. 191 pp. Illus.

Translation of "Le Sadisme au Cinéma," published in Paris in 1964.

DELEUZE, GILLES. Masochism: An Interpretation of Coldness and Cruelty. New York: Braziller, 1971. 248 pp.

"Together with the entire text of 'Venus In Furs,' by Leopold von Sacher-Masoch. Translation of 'Présentation de Sacher-Masoch.'"

EISLER, ROBERT. Man into Wolf: An Anthropological Interpretation of Sadism, Masochism, and Lycanthropy. New York: Philosophical Library, 1952. 286 pp.

"A lecture delivered at a meeting of the Royal Society of Medicine." 1951 edition published by Routledge, London, England.

GODWIN, GEORGE STANLEY. Peter Kürten: A Study in Sadism. London, Eng.: Heinemann, 1945. 60 pp.

"First published in 1938."

GREGSON, PAUL. Orgies of Torture and Brutality: A Historical Study. London, Eng.: Walton, 1965. 264 pp. Illus.

MEIBOM, JOHANN HEINRICH. On the Use of Flogging in Venereal Affairs ... Chester, Pa.: Import Publishing Co., 1961. 31 pp.

"Translation of 'De Flagrorum Usu,' written in the seventeenth century. Reprint of the English translation, published in Paris in 1801."

OAKLEY, ERIC GILBERT. Sex and Sadism throughout the Ages. London, Eng.: Walton, 1965. 286 pp. Illus.

"Sociological study of the sadist and masochist compulsions throughout the ages, and in the contemporary scene; translates historical and modern research into narrative form for the lay-reader."

REIK, THEODOR. Masochism in Sex and Society. Tr. by M. H. Beigel and G. M. Kurth. New York: Grove, 1962. 439 pp.

Translation of "Aus Leiden Freuden." Originally published as "Masochism in Modern Man."

STEKEL, WILHELM. Sadism and Masochism: The Psychology of Hatred and Cruelty. Authorized English version by Louise Brink. New York: Liveright, 1955. 2 vols.

Also published in 1929 by Liveright and reprinted in 1968 by W.S.P. Translation of "Sadismus und Masochismus." Other editions are in existence.

SEX DEVIATION IN GENERAL

ALLEN, CLIFFORD. A Textbook of Psychosexual Disorders. New York: Oxford University Press, 1962. 408 pp. Illus.

1940 edition under the title "The Sexual Perversions and Abnormalities." "A scientific treatise, dealing with the biological aspects of sexual aberrations from the psychological point of view. It is stated, as the result of clinical experience, that sexual perversions are commoner, and successful therapeutic treatment more hopeful, than is generally realized."

ARTHUR, CHESTER ALAN. The Circle of Sex, by Gavin Arthur [pseud.?] New Hyde Park, N.Y.: University Books, 1966. 151 pp. Illus.

Discusses a new method of sexual classification.

BLEDSOE, ROBERT J. Female Sexual Deviations and Bizarre Practices. Los Angeles, Calif.: Sherbourne, 1964. 138 pp.

BLEDSOE, ROBERT J. Male Sexual Deviations and Bizarre Practices. Los Angeles, Calif.: Sherbourne, 1964. 157 pp.

BLOCH, IWAN. Anthropological Studies in the Strange Sexual Practises of All Races in All Ages, Ancient and Modern, Oriental and Occidental, Primitive and Civilized. Tr. from the German by Keene Wallis. New York: Anthropological Press, 1933. 246 pp.

"Translation of Vol. 1 of 'Beiträge zur Aetiologie der Psychopathia sexualis.' "

BLOCH, IWAN. The Marquis de Sade's 120 Days of Sodom: His Anthropologia Sexualis of the 600 Perversions Practised in the School for Libertinage, the Whole French Age of Debauchery, Derived from the Private Archives of the French Government. New York: Book Awards, 1966. 237 pp. Illus.

Translation of "Neue Forschungen Über den Marquis de Sade und seine Zeit." 1934 edition published by Falstaff Press in New York.

BLOCH, IWAN. Marquis de Sade, the Man and His Age: Studies in the History of the Culture and Morals of the Eighteenth Century. Tr. by J. Bruce. Newark, N.J.: Julian, 1931. 290 pp.

Translated from Marquis de Sade, "Der Mann Und Seine Zeit."

BOSS, MEDARD. Meaning and Content of Sexual Perversions: A Daseinsanalytic Approach to the Psychopathology of the Phenomenon of Love. Tr. by Liese Lewis Abell. 2nd ed. New York: Grune and Stratton, 1949. 153 pp.

Translation of "Sinn und Gehalt der sexuellen Perversionen."

BRAND, CLAVEL. Fetish. London, Eng.: Luxor, 1970. 189 pp.

BRAND, CLAVEL. The Rubber Devotee and the Leather Lover. London, Eng.: Luxor, 1970. 189 pp. Illus.

BRIAULT, MAURICE. Polytheism and Fetishism. Tr. by Patrick Browne. St. Louis, Mo.: Herder, 1931. 185 pp. Illus.

BUCHEN, IRVING H., comp. The Perverse Imagination: Sexuality and Literary Culture. New York: New York University Press, 1970. 296 pp.

CABANÈS, AUGUSTIN. The Erotikon: Being an Illustrated Treasury of Scientific Marvels of Human Sexuality. Tr. from the French by Robert Meadows. New York: Book Awards, 1966. 248 pp. Illus.

"A cabinet of unusual illustrations depicting curiosities described in the text of this work." 16 pages inserted.

CAPRIO, FRANK SAMUEL. Variations in Sexual Behavior: A Psychodynamic Study of Deviations in Various Expressions of Sexual Behavior. Fwd. by George W. Henry. New York: Citadel, 1967. 344 pp.

Reprint of 1955 edition.

CAPRIO, FRANK SAMUEL, and D. R. BRENNER. Deviations of Sexual Behavior. New York: Paperback Library, 1969. 364 pp.

Originally published in 1961 by Citadel, New York under the title "Sexual Behavior: Psycho-Legal Aspects."

CAULDWELL, DAVID OLIVER. Perverted Haters of Sex.... Ed. by E. Haldeman-Julius. Girard, Kans.: Haldeman-Julius, 1947. 32 pp.

CAULDWELL, DAVID OLIVER. Questions and Answers on Undinism, an Eccentric, although Natural, Sexual Interest in Urine, Seeing others Micturate and Related Behavior. Ed. by E. Haldeman-Julius. Girard, Kans.: Haldeman-Julius, 1950. 29 pp.

CAULDWELL, DAVID OLIVER, ed. Transvestism: Men in Female Dress. New York: Sexology Corp., 1956. 128 pp. Illus.

CAULDWELL, DAVID OLIVER. Unusual Female Sex Practices. New ed. Inglewood, Calif.: Banner, 1966. 215 pp. Illus.

CHESSER, EUSTACE. Sexual Behaviour. Rev. ed. London, Eng.: Transworld, 1964. 287 pp.

1949 edition has the subtitle "Normal and Abnormal."

CHESSER, EUSTACE. Strange Loves: The Human Aspects of Sexual Deviation. New York: Morrow, 1971. 255 pp.

London edition has the title "The Human Aspects of Sexual Deviation," published by Jarrolds, 1971.

CLECKLEY, HERVEY MILTON. The Caricature of Love: A Discussion of Social, Psychiatric, and Literary Manifestations of Pathologic Sexuality. New York: Ronald, 1957. 319 pp.

CREW, FRANCIS ALBERT ELEY. Sexuality and Intersexuality. British Society for the Study of Sex Psychology, Publication No. 14. London, Eng.: British Sexological Society, 1925. 23 pp.

DOUGLAS, JACK D., comp. Observations of Deviance. New York: Random, 1970. 340 pp.

Contents: An Abortion Clinic Ethnography, by D. W. Ball; Sexual Modesty, Social Meanings, and the Nudist Camp, by M. S. Weinberg; Breakfast with Topless Barmaids, by R. G. Ames, S. W. Brown, and N. L. Weiner; B-Girls and Prostitutes, by S. Cavan; Prostitution, by W. Young; The Dynamics of Prison Homosexuality: The Character of the Love Affair, by D. A. Ward and G. G. Kassebaum; On Becoming a Lesbian, by W. Simon and J. H. Gagnon; On Being in the "Community," by W. Simon and J. H. Gagnon.

DUBOIS-DESAULLE, GASTON. Bestiality: An Historical, Medical, Legal, and Literary Study. Tr. from the French, with addenda, by A. F. N. New York: Panurge, 1933. 299 pp.

Translation of "Étude Sur La Bestialité Au Point de Vue Historique, Médical et Juridique," published in Paris, France, 1905.

ELLIS, HAVELOCK. Eonism and Other Supplementary Studies. Philadelphia, Pa.: Davis, 1928. 539 pp. Diagrams.

Constitutes Vol. 7 of the author's "Studies In the Psychology of Sex."

FARLEY-GRAY, ROGER, ed. The Leather Scene: A Guide in Photographs to the Sexual World of Leather and Latex. London, Eng.: Canova, 1970. 187 pp. Illus.

FÉRÉ, CHARLES SAMSON. The Evolution and Dissolution of the Sexual Instinct. Completely authorized tr. of the 2nd ed., rev. Paris, France: Carrington, 1904. 358 pp.

Translation of "L'Instinct Sexuel: Évolution et Dissolution."

1932 edition published by Anthropological Press, New York, has the title "Scientific and Esoteric Studies in Sexual Degeneration in Mankind."

FREEMAN, GILLIAN. The Undergrowth of Literature. London, Eng.: Nelson, 1967. 196 pp. Illus.

Deals with the treatment of sex deviation in recent American prose writings.

GAGNON, JOHN H., and W. SIMON, eds. Sexual Deviance. New York: Harper, 1967. 310 pp.

"This collection of articles, dealing with sexual deviance from a sociological point of view, treats the subjects of homosexuality and prostitution most extensively."

GILBERT, MICHAEL M., and R. S. TRALINS. 21 Abnormal Sex Cases. New York: Paperback Library, 1966. 285 pp.

GILLETTE, PAUL J. Psychodynamics of Unconventional Sex Behavior and Unusual Practices. Los Angeles, Calif.: Holloway House, 1966. 317 pp.

GLOVER, EDWARD. The Social and Legal Aspects of Sexual Abnormality. London, Eng.: Institute for the Study and Treatment of Delinquency, 1956. 20 pp.

GREAT BRITAIN. LAWS, STATUTES, ETC. Indecency with Children Act, 1960. London, Eng.: 1960. 3 pp.

HARTWELL, SAMUEL WILLARD. A Citizen's Handbook of Sexual Abnormalities and the Mental Hygiene Approach to Their Prevention: A Report of the Governor's Study Commission on Sex Deviates. Washington, D.C.: Public Affairs Press, 1951. 71 pp.

"A report to the Committee on Education of the Governor's Study Commission on the Deviated Criminal Sex Offender, State of Michigan." First published by the State of Michigan in 1950.

HENRY, GEORGE WILLIAM. All the Sexes: A Study of Masculinity and Femininity. New York: Rinehart, 1955. 599 pp.

Deals with the psychological and sociological factors producing sex variants. Case histories support the findings of the author.

HENRY, GEORGE WILLIAM. Masculinity and Femininity. New York: Collier, 1964. 320 pp.

"Originally published as Parts I and II of "All the Sexes.' "

HENRY, GEORGE WILLIAM. Sex Variants: A Study of Homosexual Patterns. New York: Hoeber, 1941. 2 vols. Illus.

"With sections contributed by specialists in particular fields and sponsored by the Committee for the Study of Sex Variants, Inc."

HENRY, GEORGE WILLIAM. Society and the Sex Variant. New York: Collier, 1965. 382 pp.

"Originally published as Parts III, IV, and V of 'All the Sexes.' "

KRAFFT-EBING, RICHARD Von. Aberrations of Sexual Life, after the Psychopathia Sexualis: A Medico-Legal Study for Doctors and Lawyers, brought Up to Date and Issued by Alexander Hartwich. Tr. from the German by Arthur Vivan Burbury. Springfield, Ill.: Thomas, 1959. 345 pp. Diagrams.

Reprint of 1951 edition published by Staples, New York.

KRAFFT-EBING, RICHARD Von. Psychopathia Sexualis, with Especial Reference to the Antipathic Sexual Instinct: A Medico-Forensic Study. Tr. from the 12th German ed. and with Intro. by Franklin S. Klaf. New York: Stein and Day, 1965. 434 pp.

Translation of "Psychopathia Sexualis, Mit Besonderer Berücksichtigung der Conträren Sexualempfindung," first published in the nineteenth century. Several other versions and translations are in existence.

LONDON, LOUIS SAMUEL. Abnormal Sexual Behavior: Twenty-three Detailed Case Studies. New York: Julian, 1957. 427 pp. Illus.

Reprinted by Wehman, Hackensack, New Jersey.

LONDON, LOUIS SAMUEL. Sexual Deviations in the Female: Case Histories of Frustrated Women. Rev. ed. New York: Julian, 1957. 172 pp.

First published in 1952.

LONDON, LOUIS SAMUEL, and F. S. CAPRIO. Sexual Deviations. Washington, D.C.: Linacre, 1950. 702 pp.

Written by two doctors, this work deals with all types of deviations.

LORAND, SÁNDOR, and M. BALINT, eds. Perversions, Psychodynamics and Therapy. New York: Random, 1956. 308 pp.

British edition, Ortolan, London, 1965.

MASSERMAN, JULES HYMEN, ed. Dynamics of Deviant Sexuality. American Academy of Psychoanalysis. Science and Psychoanalysis, Vol. 15. New York: Grune and Stratton, 1969. 106 pp.

"Scientific proceedings."

MASTERS, ROBERT E. L. Forbidden Sexual Behavior and Morality: An Objective Re-examination of Perverse Sex Practices in Different Cultures. Intro. by Harry Benjamin. New York: Julian, 1962. 431 pp.

"Explains behavior prohibited in all cases by general social custom and in most cases by law. The fact and legend of human-animal sex contacts are explored and analyzed. The physiology and psychology of homosexual acts, male and female, are discussed from fresh perspectives. The effect on sexual behavior of various narcotic drugs is discussed. Interracial sex relationships are dealt with in the light of recent writings and scientific data."

MASTERS, ROBERT E. L. Sex-Driven People: An Autobiographical Approach to the Problem of the Sex-Dominated Personality. Intro. by Allen Edwardes. Los Angeles, Calif.: Sherbourne, 1966. 287 pp.

"Case histories of nymphophiles, bestiality and others driven to unusual needs for erotic release. Prepared by a noted authority in the field of sexual psychopathology."

Reprinted in 1969 by Paperback Library, New York, under the title "Sexual Obsession."

MICHIGAN. DEPARTMENT OF MENTAL HEALTH. Crucial Issues in the Treatment and Control of Sexual Deviation in the Community. Lansing, Mich.: Dept. of Mental Health, 1951. 58 pp. Illus.

" A report of the State Psychiatric Research Clinic in Detroit, with recommendations as formulated by H. Warren Dunham. A condensation of the original report of the Clinic."

MICHIGAN. GOVERNOR'S STUDY COMMISSION ON SEX DEVIATES. Report. Lansing, Mich.: State of Michigan, 1951. 245 pp. Maps.

MOHR, JOHANN W., et al. Pedophilia and Exhibitionism: A Handbook. Toronto, Canada: University of Toronto, 1964. 204 pp. Illus.

MOLL, ALBERT. Perversions of the Sex Instinct: A Study of Sexual Inversion Based on Clinical Data and Official Documents. Tr. by Maurice Popkin. Newark, N.J.: Julian, 1931. 237 pp.

First published in German.

MUNDINGER, GERDA. Corporal Punishment. New York: Grove, 1971. 146 pp.

OLIVER, BERNARD J. Sexual Deviation in American Society: A Social-Psychological Study of Sexual Non-Conformity. New Haven, Conn.: College and University Press, 1967. 256 pp.

PAITICH, DANIEL. Parent-Child Relations and Sexual Deviations. Toronto, Canada: Toronto Psychiatric Hospital, 1960. 28 pp.

"Mimeographed."

PODOLSKY, EDWARD, and C. WADE. Erotic Symbolism: A Study of Fetishism in Relation to Sex. New York: Epic, 1960. 127 pp. Illus.

PODOLSKY, EDWARD, and C. WADE. Exhibitionism. New York: Epic, 1961. 64 pp.

PODOLSKY, EDWARD, and C. WADE Voyeurism. New York: Epic, 1961. 64 pp.

POTTER, La FOREST. Strange Loves: A Study in Sexual Abnormalities. New York: Dodsley, 1935. 243 pp.

RICKLES, NATHAN KING. Exhibitionism. Philadelphia, Pa.: Lippincott, 1950. 198 pp.

ROSEN, ISMOND, ed. The Pathology and Treatment of Sexual Deviation: A Methodological Approach. Oxford Medical Publications. New York: Oxford University Press, 1964. 510 pp. Illus.

RUITENBEEK, HENDRIK MARINUS, comp. The Psychotherapy of Perversions. New York: Citadel, 1967. 474 pp.

SAGARIN, EDWARD, and D. E. J. MacNAMARA, eds. Problems of Sex Behavior. New York: Crowell, 1968. 288 pp.

"Part of a series of selected studies in social problems, this volume contains selections from books on such subjects as contemporary attitudes towards sexual behavior, illegitimacy, prostitution, homosexuality, incest, rape, child molestation, and pornography."

SCHINDLER, GORDON WENCZEL [Porter Davis]. Sex Perversion and the Law. El Segundo, Calif.: Banner Books, 1950- Vol. 1-

SCHUR, EDWIN M. Crimes without Victims; Deviant Behavior and Public Policy: Abortion, Homosexuality, Drug Addiction. Englewood Cliffs, N.J.: Prentice-Hall, 1965. 180 pp.

"Discussion from a sociological point of view of such areas as abortion, homosexuality, and drug addiction."

SCHWARTZ, WILLIAM ALEXANDER [L. T. Woodward]. Sex Fiend: A Doctor's Realistic Report on the Darker Side of Love and Sexual Impulses Gone Wild. Derby, Conn.: Monarch, 1961. 139 pp.

SCOTT, GEORGE RYLEY, and C. WADE. Sex Pleasures and Perversions: A Book of Practical Sexual Advice for Males and Females. Westport, Conn.: Associated Booksellers, 1963. 114 pp.

STEINBACHER, JOHN A. The Child Seducers. Fullerton, Calif.: Educator Publications, 1971. 402 pp.

STEKEL, WILHELM. Sexual Aberrations: The Phenomena of Fetishism in Relation to Sex. Authorized English version tr. from the first German ed. by S. Parker. New York: Liveright, 1971. 2 vols. in 1.

Translation of "Der Fetischismus." Several other versions and translations of this work are in existence.

TRAINER, RUSSELL. The Lolita Complex. New York: Citadel, 1966. 315 pp.

TRIMBLE, JOHN F. Pedophilia. Torrance, Calif.: Monogram, 1968. 207 pp. Illus.

ULLERSTAM, LARS. The Erotic Minorities. New York: Grove, 1966. 172 pp.

Translation of "De erotiska minoriteterna."

WEDECK, HARRY EZEKIEL, ed. Pictorial History of Morals. New York: Philosophical Library, 1963. 314 pp. Illus.

"Text and art reproductions demonstrate changes in sexual attitudes and conduct from ancient times to the present."

WOLFGANG, MICHAEL S. Male and Female Sexual Deviations. Los Angeles, Calif.: Sherbourne, 1964. 141 pp.

8.
SEX DISEASES AND DISORDERS

FRIGIDITY AND IMPOTENCE

ABBOT, GEORGE. The Case of Impotency, as Debated in England, in That Remarkable Tryal anno 1613, between Robert, Earl of Essex, and the Lady Frances Howard, Who, after Eight Years of Marriage Commenc'd a Suit against Him for Impotency . . . . London, Eng.: Curll, 1715. 2 vols. in 1.

Vol. 2 contains: I. The Tryal of Mervin, Lord Audley, Earl of Castlebaven for Sodomy and a Rape, Anno 1631. II. The Proceedings upon the Bill of Divorce, between His Grace Henry, Duke of Norfolke and Lady Mary Mordant . . . 1699.

Third edition, London, England, Curll, 1719. The author, Archbishop of Canterbury, born in 1562, was one of those who prepared the King James Version of the Bible.

BERGER, STANLEY. The Role of Sexual Impotence in the Concept of Self in Male Paraplegics. Ann Arbor, Mich.: University Microfilms, 1952. 172 leaves as determined from the film.

Thesis, New York University. Abstracted in "Dissertation Abstracts." Vol. 2 (1952, No. 4, p. 533). Microfilm copy of typescript. Positive.

BIEZIN, J. The Torments of a Frigid Woman: A Case History of a Sexual Difficulty. New York: Cadillac, 1953. 313 pp.

Translation of "Les Tourments d'Une Femme Frigide."

BRENKLE, JOHN JOSEPH. The Impediment of Male Impotence with Special Application to Paraplegia. Catholic University of America, Canon Law Studies, No. 423. Washington, D.C.: Catholic University of America, 1963. 185 pp.

Thesis, Catholic University of America.

CAPRIO, FRANK SAMUEL. The Sexually Adequate Male. North Hollywood, Calif.: Wilshire, 1972. 224 pp. Illus.

Earlier edition, 1952 by Citadel, New York.

DEVENSKY, I. How to Overcome Sex Frigidity in Women: A Guide to Proper Sex Behavior. New York: William-Frederick, 1952. 36 pp. Illus.

DOUBLAS, G. ARCHIBALD. The Nature and Causes of Impotence in Man and Barrenness in Women Explained... and Compleat Directions for a Lady's Managing Herself in the Nicest Article of Her Health, with Innocent and Effectual Medicines for All the Complaints Incident to That Sex. London, Eng.: Brett, 1758. 54 pp.

FRATTIN, PETER LOUIS. The Matrimonial Impediment of Impotence: Occlusion of Spermatic Ducts and Vaginismus: A Historical Synopsis and a Commentary. Catholic University of America, Canon Law Studies, No. 381. Washington, D.C.: Catholic University of America, 1958. 117 pp.

Thesis, Catholic University of America.

GLOVER, LELAND ELLIS. The Impotent Male. Derby, Conn.: Monarch, 1963. 155 pp.

HAMMOND, WILLIAM ALEXANDER. Sexual Impotence in the Male and Female. Detroit, Mich.: Davis, 1887. 305 pp.

"First edition published in 1883, under the title 'Sexual Impotence in the Male'."

HASTINGS, DONALD W. Impotence and Frigidity. Boston, Mass.: Little, Brown, 1963. 144 pp.

"Presents the known medical information about impotence and frigidity, discussing in nontechnical language the various types of these problems and their possible causes." Also published by Dell, New York in 1966.

HIRSCH, EDWIN WALTER. Impotence and Frigidity. New York: Citadel, 1966. 284 pp.

JOHNSON, JOHN. Disorders of Sexual Potency in the Male. New York: Pergamon, 1968. 116 pp. Illus.

"This concise book grew out of an M.D. thesis, which studied seventy-six patients referred for potency problems to Maudsley Hospital, London."

KANT, FRITZ. Frigidity: Dynamics and Treatment. Springfield, Ill.: Thomas, 1969. 61 pp.

KELLY, GEORGE LOMBARD. So You Think You're Impotent! Sexual Science. Augusta, Ga.: Southern Medical Supply Co., 1957. 80 pp. Illus.

LEVINE, LENA, and D. LOTH. The Frigid Wife: Her Way to Sexual Fulfillment. New York: Messner, 1962. 256 pp.

McCARTHY, JOHN. The Matrimonial Impediment of Impotence with Special Reference to the Physical Capacity for Marriage of an "Excised Woman" and of a "Doubly Vasectomised Man." Rome, Italy: Officium Libri Catholici, 1948. 83 pp.

MORSE, BENJAMIN. Sexual Surrender in Women: A Penetrating Inquiry into Frigidity, Its Causes, Manifestations and Cures. Derby, Conn.: Monarch, 1962. 155 pp.

MURPHY, H. C. Sexual Decline: Its Cause and Cure. Kansas City, Mo.: Hudson-Kimberly, 1900. 120 pp. Illus.

PODOLSKY, EDWARD. What You Should Know about Sexual Frigidity. New York: Cadillac, 1953. 160 pp. Illus.

PODOLSKY, EDWARD. What You Should Know about Sexual Impotence. New York: Cadillac, 1953. 157 pp. Illus.

POPENOE, PAUL BOWMAN. Sexual Inadequacy of the Male: A Manual for Counselors. Los Angeles, Calif.: American Institute of Family Relations, 1946. 41 pp.

ROBINSON, MARIE NYSWANDER. Power of Sexual Surrender. New York: Doubleday, 1959. 263 pp.

"Deals with the problem of sexual frigidity in women. The author believes frigidity to be an expression of neurosis."

ROBINSON, WILLIAM JOSEPHUS. Sexual Impotence: A Practical Treatise on the Causes, Symptoms, and Treatment of Sexual Impotence and Other Sexual Disorders in Men and Women. New York: Eugenics, 1934. 542 pp.

Also 1913 edition.

SMALL, ALVAN EDMOND. Causes That Operate to Produce the Premature Decline of Manhood, and the Best Means of Obviating Their Effects and of Bringing about a Restoration of Health. Chicago, Ill.: Clindinning, 1873. 59 pp.

STEKEL, WILHELM. Frigidity in Woman, in Relation to Her Love Life. Authorized English version by James S. Van Teslaar. New York: Washington Square Press, 1967. 627 pp.

Translation of "Die Geschlechtskälte der Frau," published in 1927 by Wien, in Berlin. Several translations and versions are in existence.

STEKEL, WILHELM. Impotence in the Male: The Psychic Disorders of Sexual Functions in the Male. New York: Liveright, 1971. 2 vols.

Reprint of 1927 edition. "Classic clinical study of the relationship between male psychological disorders and the ability to achieve orgasm." Translation of "Die Impotenz des Mannes." Several translations and versions are in existence.

WERSHUB, LEONARD PAUL. Sexual Impotence in the Male. Springfield, Ill.: Thomas, 1959. 126 pp. Illus.

SEX DISEASES AND DISORDERS IN GENERAL

ACTON, WILLIAM. The Functions and Disorders of the Reproductive Organs in Childhood, Youth, Adult Age, and Advanced Life, Considered in Their Physiological, Social, and Moral Relations. 4th American ed. Philadelphia, Pa.: Lindsay and Blakiston, 1875. 348 pp.

Several other editions are in existence. First edition published in 1857, Blakiston, Philadelphia, Pa.

ALLEN, CLIFFORD. A Textbook of Psychosexual Disorders. 2nd ed. New York: Oxford University Press, 1969. 478 pp. Illus.

Previous edition published in 1962 by Oxford.

ASHLEY, DAVID J. B. Human Intersex. Fwd. by R. W. Evans. Baltimore, Md.: Williams & Wilkins, 1962. 357 pp. Illus.

BEARD, GEORGE MILLER. Sexual Neurasthenia, Nervous Exhaustion: Its Hygiene, Causes, Symptoms, and Treatment. With a Chapter on Diet for the Nervous. Ed. by A. D. Rockwell. 6th ed. with formulas. New York: Treat and Co., 1905. 316 pp.

Posthumous manuscript. First edition published in 1884 by Treat, New York.

BELLIVEAU, FRED B., and L. RICHTER. Understanding Human Sexual Inadequacy. Fwd. by William H. Masters and Virginia E. Johnson. Boston, Mass.: Little, Brown, 1970. 242 pp. Illus.

BENJAMIN, HARRY. The Transsexual Phenomenon. New York: Julian, 1966. 286 pp. Illus.

"An analysis of persons desiring to change their sex, together with personal case histories of transsexuals."

BERNARD, BERNARD. Sex Weaknesses: Their Cause and Remedy, by a Physical Culture Consultant. 2nd ed. Sausalito, Calif.: Physical Culture Consultants, 1927. 173 pp.

Other editions are in existence.

BIGELOW, C. Sexual Pathology: A Practical and Popular Review of the Principal Diseases of the Reproductive Organs. Chicago, Ill.: Ottaway, 1875. 194 pp.

BROSTER, LENNOX ROSS, et al. The Adrenal Cortex and Intersexuality. Fwd. by Sir Walter Langdon-Brown. London, Eng.: Chapman, 1938. 245 pp.

CALIFORNIA. DEPARTMENT OF PUBLIC HEALTH. Summary of Requirements for Premarital Examinations in the States and Territories of the United States and the Provinces of Canada. Sacramento, Calif.: State Printing Office, 1957. 18 pp.

CAULDWELL, DAVID OLIVER. Hypersexuality . . . Is Anyone Oversexed? Viewpoints of Physiologists, Psychiatrists, and Sociologists on Precocious Sexuality and Nymphomania. Girard, Kans.: Haldemann-Julius, 1947. 32 pp.

CAULDWELL, DAVID OLIVER. Sex and Psycho-Somatology: A Study of the Various Aspects of the Relation of Psycho-Somatic Medicine to Sexuality and Sexual Disorders, Including Important Endocrine Data. Girard, Kans.: Haldemann-Julius, 1947. 32 pp.

CAULDWELL, DAVID OLIVER. What Is a Hermaphrodite? Ed. by E. Haldemann-Julius. Girard, Kans.: Haldemann-Julius, 1947. 32 pp.

CAULDWELL, DAVID OLIVER. Why There Are Orgastic and Other Sexual Cripples: Conditions Most Likely to Respond to Intelligent Treatment. Ed. by E. Haldemann-Julius. Girard, Kans.: Haldemann-Julius, 1948. 31 pp.

CAWADIAS, ALEXANDER PANAGIOTI. Hermaphroditos: The Human Intersex. 2nd ed. London, Eng.: Heinemann, 1946. 81 pp. Illus.

COURT-BROWN, WILLIAM MICHAEL. Abnormalities of the Sex Chromosome Complement in Man. Medical Research Council, Special Report Series, No. 305. London, Eng.: H.M. Stationery Office, 1964. 239 pp. Illus.

COURTENAY, FRANCIS BURDETT. On Spermatorrhoea and Certain Functional Derangements and Debilities of the Generative System: Their Nature, Treatment, and Cure. 11th ed. London, Eng.: Baillière, 1878. 123 pp.

Earlier editions published under the title "On Spermatorrhoea and the Professional Fallacies and Popular Delusions Which Prevail in Relation to Its Nature, Consequences, and Treatment."

COURTENAY, MICHAEL. Sexual Discord in Marriage: A Field for Brief Psychotherapy. Fwd. by Michael Balint. Mind and Medicine Monographs, No. 16. Philadelphia, Pa.: Lippincott, 1968. 137 pp.

"Report of a research project undertaken by a team of doctors working in a Family Planning Association marital problem clinic." Also published by Tavistock, London, England in 1968.

COWELL, ROBERTA ELIZABETH. Roberta Cowell's Story. London, Eng.: Heinemann, 1954. 154 pp. Illus.

Also published by British Book Centre, New York in 1954.

A personal narrative of a change from male to female.

DEWHURST, CHRISTOPHER JOHN, and R. R. GORDON. The Intersexual Disorders. Baltimore, Md.: Williams, 1969. 154 pp. Illus.

Also published by Baillière, London, England, 1969.

DIXON, EDWARD HENRY. A Treatise on Diseases of the Sexual System: Adapted to Popular Instruction. 10th ed., with Appendix. New York: De Witt, 1867. 312 pp. Illus.

First published in 1845. Titles vary slightly.

DIXON, EDWARD HENRY. Woman and Her Diseases, From the Cradle to the Grave: Adapted Exclusively to Her Instruction in the Physiology of Her System and All the Diseases of Her Critical Periods. 10th ed. Philadelphia, Pa.: Bradley, 1860. 318 pp.

Earlier edition published in 1847.

ELLIS, ALBERT, and E. SAGARIN. Nymphomania: A Study of the Oversexed Woman. New York: Gilbert, 1964. 255 pp.

Also published by Macfadden, New York and by Ortolan, London, England in 1965.

FEDERMAN, DANIEL D. Abnormal Sexual Development: A Genetic and Endocrine Approach to Differential Diagnosis. Philadelphia, Pa.: Saunders, 1967. 206 pp. Illus.

FRIEDMAN, ALFRED S., et al. Therapy with Families of Sexually Acting-Out Girls. New York: Springer, 1971. 214 pp.

GHERTLER, MONTE, and A. PALCA, eds. The Couple: A Sexual Profile by Mr. and Mrs. K. New York: Coward, 1971. 181 pp.

"A husband and wife's frank account of their experience in the Masters and Johnson Sex Clinic."

GILLETTE, PAUL J., comp. The Layman's Explanation of Human Sexual Inadequacy. New York: Award Books, 1970. 284 pp.

GREEN, RICHARD, and J. MONEY, eds. Transsexualism and Sex Reassignment. Baltimore, Md.: Johns Hopkins, 1969. 512 pp. Illus.

"An encyclopedic text bringing together over thirty contributors representing different disciplines in the United States and Europe."

GREENBLATT, ROBERT BENJAMIN, ed. The Hirsute Female. Intro. by M. F. Ashley Montagu. Springfield, Ill.: Thomas, 1963. 313 pp. Illus.

HAYES, ALBERT HAMILTON. The Science of Life, Or Self-Preservation: A Medical Treatise on Nervous and Physical Debility, Spermatorrhoea, Impotence, and Sterility. Boston, Mass.: Peabody Institute (?), 1868. 278 pp.

HIRSCHFELD, MAGNUS. Sexual Anomalies: The Origins, Nature and Treatment of Sexual Disorders. Rev. ed. New York: Emerson, 1948. 538 pp.

"A summary of the author's works, compiled as a humble memorial by his pupils. A textbook for the medical and legal professions, ministers, educators, psychologists, biologists, sociologists, and social workers, criminologists and students in these fields." Originally published in 1936 by Aldor, London, England, under the title "Sexual Anomalies and Perversions."

HIRSCHFELD, MAGNUS. Sexual Pathology: A Study of Derangements of the Sexual Instinct. Authorized tr. by J. Gibbs. Rev. ed. New York: Emerson, 1940. 368 pp.

Earlier edition, 1932.

JACOBSON, ERNST LUDWIG HARTHERN [Niels Hoyer], ed. Man Into Woman: An Authentic Record of a Change of Sex. Tr. from the German by H. J. Stenning. Intro. by Norman Haire. New York: Dutton, 1933. 288 pp. Illus.

"The true story of the miraculous transformation of the Danish painter, Einar Wegener (Andreas Sparre)." Translation of "Ein Mensch Wechselt Sein Geschlecht."

JIRÁSEK, JAN E. Development of the Genital System and Male Pseudohermaphroditism. Ed. by M. M. Cohen. Baltimore, Md.: Johns Hopkins, 1971. 136 pp. Illus.

JONES, GEORGEANNA SEEGAR. The Management of Endocrine Disorders of Menstruation and Fertility. American Lecture Series, No. 206. American Lectures in Endocrinology. Bannerstone Division. Springfield, Ill.: Thomas, 1954. 198 pp. Illus.

JONES, HOWARD WILBUR, and W. W. SCOTT. Hermaphroditism, Genital Anomalies and Related Endocrine Disorders. 2nd ed. Baltimore, Md.: Williams & Wilkins, 1971. 564 pp. Illus.

Earlier edition, 1958.

JORGENSEN, CHRISTINE. Christine Jorgensen: A Personal Autobiography. Intro. by Harry Benjamin. New York: Eriksson, 1967. 332 pp.

KLAF, FRANKLIN SIMON, and B. J. HURWOOD. Nymphomania: A Psychiatrist's View. New York: Lancer, 1964. 159 pp.

KLAF, FRANKLIN SIMON. Satyriasis: A Study of Male Nymphomania. New York: Lancer, 1966. 158 pp.

MacFADDEN, BERNARR ADOLPHUS. Superb Virility of Manhood: Giving the Causes and Simple Home Methods of Curing the Weaknesses of Men. New York: Physical Culture Publishing Co., 1904. 390 pp.

MacFADDEN, BERNARR ADOLPHUS. The Virile Powers of Superb Manhood: How Developed, How Lost, How Regained. New York: Physical Culture Publishing Co., 1900. 237 pp.

MASTERS, WILLIAM HOWELL, and V. E. JOHNSON. Human Sexual Inadequacy. Boston, Mass.: Little, Brown, 1970. 467 pp. Illus.

"On the basis of eleven years of careful clinical research, Masters and Johnson present findings for the treatment of impotency, ejaculatory disorders, inadequate female response, vaginismus, dyspareunia and problems of aging. The book is a basic and essential resource for all counselors, as well as those seriously interested in human sexuality."

MEAKER, SAMUEL RAYNOR. A Doctor Talks to Women: What They Should Know about the Normal Functions and Common Disorders of the Female Organs. New York: Simon and Schuster, 1954. 231 pp. Illus.

MONEY, JOHN. Sex Errors of the Body: Dilemmas, Education, Counseling. Baltimore, Md.: Johns Hopkins, 1968. 145 pp. Illus.

"Discusses various types of anomalies in development explaining their causes, their psychosexual effects, and the necessary sex education to help the individual achieve successful sexual attitudes and functioning or to provide supportive counseling."

NUNBERG, HERMANN. Problems of Bisexuality as Reflected in Circumcision. London, Eng.: Imago, 1949. 83 pp.

"Originally printed in the 'International Journal of Psycho-Analysis,' Vol. 28, 1947, under the title 'Circumcision and Problems of Bisexuality.' "

OVERZIER, CALUS, ed. Intersexuality. New York: Academic Press, 1963. 563 pp. Illus. Diagrams.

Translation of "Die Intersexualität."

PILLAY, AYAPPEN PADMANABLAN. Disorders of Sex and Reproduction: Aetiology, Diagnosis and Treatment. London, Eng.: Lewis, 1948. 300 pp.

PODOLSKY, EDWARD, and C. WADE. Nymphomania. New York: Epic, 1961. 64 pp.

PRICE, DOROTHY, ed. A Historical Review of Embryology and Intersexuality: Fact and Fancy. Leiden, Netherlands: Brill, 1967. 20 pp. Illus.

Psycho-Dynamics of Change of Sex Through Surgery. Baltimore, Md.: Williams & Wilkins, 1969. 108 pp

Reprint of "Journal of Nervous and Mental Diseases," Vol. 147, November, 1968.

RASHAD, M. NABIL, and W. R. M. MORTON, eds. Selected Topics on Genital Anomalies and Related Subjects. Springfield, Ill.: Thomas, 1969. 931 pp. Illus.

RICHMOND, SAMUEL A. Manhood, Womanhood: A Treatise on Secret Indulgence and Excessive Venery, Showing How Virility Is Destroyed, and How Restored, with a Word of Warning to Both Sexes. St. Joseph, Mo.: Richmond Nervine, 1885. 208 pp.

SAFIER, BENNO, et al. A Psychiatric Approach to the Treatment of Promiscuity. American Social Hygiene Assn., Publication No. A-741. New York: n.p., 1949. 81 pp.

"A further report of a psychiatric study made under the auspices of the Venereal Disease Division, United States Public Health Service, the California State Department of Public Health, and the San Francisco Department of Public Health, January, 1943, to July, 1947. An expansion of an earlier study, 'An Experiment in the Psychiatric Treatment of Promiscuous Girls, by E. G. Lion and others.'"

SCHRENCK Von NOTZING, ALBERT PHILIBERT FRANZ. The Use of Hypnosis in Psychopathia Sexualis, with Especial Reference to Contrary Sexual Instinct. Authorized tr. from the German by Charles Gilbert Chaddock. New York: Institute for Research in Hypnosis Publication Society, 1956. 320 pp.

SCHWARTZ, WILLIAM ALEXANDER [L. T. Woodward]. Sex and Hypnosis: A Doctor's Report on the Daring New Therapy for Emotional Problems and Sexual Conflicts. Derby, Conn.: Monarch, 1961. 138 pp.

SCOTT, VALERIE X. [pseud.]. Surrogate Wife, as Told to Herbert d'H. Lee. New York: Dell, 1971. 320 pp.

SHEPARD, MARTIN. The Love Treatment: Sexual Intimacy between Patients and Psychotherapists. New York: Wyden, 1971. 208 pp.

1971 edition, Paperback Library, New York.

SHIFF, NATHAN ALLEN. Diary of a Nymph. New York: Stuart, 1961. 192 pp.

SIMMERS, HANS H., et al. Testicular Feminization: Endocrine Function of Feminizing Testes, Comparison with Normal Testes. Springfield, Ill.: Thomas, 1965. 108 pp. Illus.

"Provides the physician with information on normal and abnormal testicular endocrine function and target organ response."

SIMMONS, DAWN LANGLEY. Man into Woman: A Transsexual Autobiography. New York: Macfadden, 1971. 192 pp.

Also 1970 edition.

SOPCHAK, ANDREW L. Changes in Sexual Behavior, Desire and Fantasy in Breast Cancer Patients under Androgen and Estrogen Therapy. Garden City, N.Y.: n.p., 1957. 113 leaves. Illus.

Doctoral thesis, Adelphi College. Typewritten copy.

STEVENS, BARBARA C. Marriage and Fertility of Women Suffering from Schizophrenia or Affective Disorders. New York: Oxford University Press, 1969. 188 pp. Illus.

STOLLER, ROBERT J. Sex and Gender: On the Development of Masculinity and Feminity. New York: Science House, 1968. 383 pp.

"Comprehensive discussion of the development of masculinity and femininity, primarily on the basis of observation of patients with marked aberrations in their masculinity and femininity."

STRAKOSCH, FRANCES MARIE. Factors in the Sex Life of Seven Hundred Psychopathic Women. Utica, N.Y.: State Hospitals Press, 1934. 102 pp.

Doctoral thesis, Columbia University.

STURGIS, FREDERIC RUSSELL. Sexual Debility in Man. 2nd ed. Chicago, Ill.: Login, 1930. 434 pp.

1900 edition published by Treat in New York.

TARNOVSKY, VENYAMIN MILHAILOVICH. The Sexual Instinct and Its Morbid Manifestations from the Double Standpoint of Jurisprudence and Psychiatry. Paris, France: Carnington, 1898. 239 pp.

THOMSON, WILLIAM ARCHIBALD ROBSON, ed. Sex and Its Problems. Edinburgh, Scotland: Livingstone, 1968. 90 pp.

Appeared originally as a series of articles in the "Practitioner," 1967.

U. S. PUBLIC HEALTH SERVICE. DIVISION OF SPECIAL HEALTH SERVICES. Premarital Health Examination Legislation: Analysis and Compilation of State Laws. U. S. Public Health Service, Publication No. 383. Washington, D.C.: n.p., 1954. 114 pp.

WAHL, CHARLES WILLIAM, ed. Sexual Problems: Diagnosis and Treatment in Medical Practice. New York: Free Press, 1967. 300 pp.

"This volume for physicians who have had no psychiatric training includes such topics as the taking of a sexual history, sexual problems that relate to physical conditions, obstetrics and gynecology, marriage, chronic illness, conception control, abortion surgery and such psychological problems as anxiety. Also covers such specifically sexual problems as homosexuality, deviations, potency disturbances, and promiscuity."

WALINDER, JAN. Transsexualism: A Study of Forty-Three Cases. Göteborg University, Psychiatric Research Centre, Report 2. New York: Humanities, 1969. 125 pp.

Originally a thesis at the University of Göteborg, Sweden, 1967.

WALKER, KENNETH MacFARLANE, and E. B. STRAUSS. Sexual Disorders in the Male. 4th rev. ed. London, Eng.: Cassell, 1954. 260 pp. Illus.

"A practical manual on how to deal with the various forms of sexual disability intended for the general practitioner and student rather than the expert specialist. The collaboration between a surgeon and a psychologist has secured a balanced presentation of the whole subject in both its psychic and its somatic aspects."

Several other editions under different titles.

WALLACE, IRVING. The Nympho and Other Maniacs. New York: Simon and Schuster, 1971. 475 pp.

YOUNG, HUGH. Genital Abnormalities, Hermaphroditism and Related Adrenal Diseases. Baltimore, Md.: Williams & Wilkins, 1937. 649 pp. Illus.

STERILITY

AMELAR, RICHARD D. Infertility in Men: Diagnosis and Treatment. Philadelphia, Pa.: Davis, 1966. 150 pp. Illus.

ASZMANN, PAUL E. Tubal Tests in the Diagnosis of Sterility. Milwaukee, Wis.: n.p., 1929. 18 pp.

BASSETT, WILLIAM T. Counseling the Childless Couple. Englewood Cliffs, N.J.: Prentice-Hall, 1963. 139 pp.

BEHRMAN, SAMUEL J., and R. W. KISTNER, eds. Progress in Infertility, by 50 Authors. Boston, Mass.: Little, Brown, 1968. 1,033 pp. Illus.

BERKOW, SAMUEL GORDON. Childless: A Study of Sterility, Its Causes and Treatment. New York: Furman, 1937. 307 pp. Illus.

BIGELOW, HORATIO RIPLEY. The Moral Significance of Sterility. Cincinnati, Ohio: n.p., 1883. 24 pp.

Reprinted from "Obstetric Gazette," Cincinnati, Ohio, 1883, Vol. 1... and other related reprints.

BRAZ, JORGE. The Infertile Marriage: Methods of Diagnosis and Treatment. Haarlem, The Netherlands: Bohn, 1963. 263 pp. Illus.

Translation of "Esterilidade Conjugal."

BUXTON, CHARLES LEE, and A. L. SOUTHAM. Human Infertility. New York: Hoeber-Harper, 1958. 229 pp. Illus.

DAVIS, MAXINE. Hope for the Childless Couple. New York: McGraw-Hill, 1965. 197 pp.

ELLIOT, ANDREW GEORGE [Rennie Macandrew]. Wanted—A Child! A Book to Help Couples to Have Children. London, Eng.: Wales, 1945. 120 pp. Illus.

American edition, 1958, by Associated Booksellers, New York.

FAMILY PLANNING ASSOCIATION. For Childless Wives: A Doctor Advises. 2nd ed. rev. London, Eng.: Family Planning Assn., 1952. 18 pp.

Earlier edition, 1950.

FARRIS, EDMOND JOHN. Human Fertility and Problems of the Male. White Plains, N.Y.: Author's Press, 1950. 211 pp.

FERGUSON, JAMES HENRY. Why Can't We Have a Baby? New York: Pyramid, 1957. 127 pp. Illus.

FISHBEIN, MORRIS, ed. Children for the Childless: A Concise Explanation of the Medical, Scientific, and Legal Facts about Conception, Fertility, Sterility, Heredity, and Adoption. With chapters by Sidonie Matsner Gruenberg and others. Garden City, N.Y.: Doubleday, 1954. 223 pp. Illus.

FJÄLLBRANT, BO. Sperm Antibodies and Sterility in Men. Acta obstetrica et gynecologica Scandinavica, Vol. 47, Suppl. 4. Lund, Sweden: Lasarettet, 1968. 37 pp. Illus.

GALTON, LAWRENCE. New Facts for the Childless. Intro. by Alan F. Guttmacher. New York: Crowell, 1953. 184 pp. Illus.

GARDNER, AUGUSTUS KINSLEY. The Causes and Curative Treatment of Sterility, with a Preliminary Statement of the Physiology of Generation. New York: De Witt, 1856. 170 pp. Illus.

HAMBLEN, EDWIN CROWELL. Facts for Childless Couples. 2nd ed. Springfield, Ill.: Thomas, 1960. 130 pp. Illus.

HOTCHKISS, ROBERT SHERMAN. Etiology and Diagnosis in the Treatment of Infertility in Men. American Lecture Series, No. 53. American Lectures in Endocrinology. Springfield, Ill.: Thomas, 1952. 73 pp. Illus.

HUMPHREY, MICHAEL. The Hostage Seekers: A Study of Childless and Adopting Couples. Studies in Child Development. New York: Humanities, 1970. 162 pp. Illus.

Originally published by Longmans, London, England, 1969.

Case studies in sterility.

ISRAEL, SPENCER LEON. Diagnosis and Treatment of Menstrual Disorders and Sterility. 5th ed. New York: Hoeber, 1967. 638 pp.

First through fourth editions written by Mazer and Israel.

JOËL, CHARLES AKIBA. Fertility Disturbances in Men and Women: A Textbook with Special Reference to Etiology, Diagnosis and Treatment. New York: Karger, 1971. 617 pp. Illus.

JOHANSSON, CARL JOHAN. Clinical Studies on Sterile Couples, with Special Reference to the Diagnosis, Etiology and Prognosis of Infertility. Tr. by Nils Erik Enkvist. Acta obstetrica et gynecologica Scandinavica, Vol. 36, Suppl. 5. Helsinki, Finland: Mercator, 1957. 168 pp. Illus.

KAUFMAN, SHERWIN ALLEN. New Hope for the Childless Couple: The Causes and Treatment of Infertility. New York: Simon and Schuster, 1970. 159 pp.

KLEEGMAN, SOPHIA J., and S. A. KAUFMAN. Infertility in Women: Diagnosis and Treatment. Philadelphia, Pa.: Davis, 1966. 340 pp. Illus.

LEIKKOLA, AIRI. Seminal Fluids, Composition in Barren Marriages. Tr. by Hilkka Kontiopaa and L. A. Keyworth. Acta obstetrica et gynecologica Scandinavica, Vol. 34, Suppl. 3. Turku, Finland: n.p., 1955. 105 pp. Illus.

McLANE, CHARLES MORDECAI, and R. N. CREADICK, eds. Infertility: Psychophysiology. Clinical Obstetrics and Gynecology, Vol. 8, No. 1. New York: Hoeber, 1965. 248 pp. Illus.

MONTAGU, ASHLEY. The Reproductive Development of the Female, with Especial Reference to the Period of Adolescent Sterility: A Study in the Comparative Physiology of the Infecundity of the Adolescent Organism. 2nd ed. New York: Julian, 1957. 234 pp. Illus.

First edition, published in 1946 has the title "Adolescent Sterility."

ROLAND, MAXWELL. Management of the Infertile Couple. Springfield, Ill.: Thomas, 1968. 234 pp. Illus.

Chapters on "Semen Analysis" and "Male Infertility" by Matthew Freund and Joseph E. Davis.

ROMMER, JACK JAY. Sterility: Its Cause and Its Treatment. Springfield, Ill.: Thomas, 1952. 424 pp. Illus.

RUBIN, ISIDOR CLINTON. Uterotubal Insufflation: A Clinical Diagnostic Method of Determining the Tubal Factor in Sterility Including Therapeutic Aspects and Comparative Notes on Hysterosalpingography. St. Louis, Mo.: Mosby, 1947. 453 pp.

SIMMONS, FRED ALBERT. The Diagnosis and Treatment of the Infertile Female. American Lecture Series, No. 220. American Lectures in Endocrinology. Springfield, Ill.: Thomas, 1954. 83 pp. Illus.

SIMS, JAMES MARION. Clinical Notes on Uterine Surgery, with Special Reference to the Management of the Sterile Condition. New York: Wood, 1869. 401 pp.

SUGIHARA, CLARENCE YOSHIO. Male and Female Sterility. St. Paul, Minn.: n.p., 1941. 26 leaves.

SWYER, GERALD ISAAC MacDONALD. We Want a Baby. London, Eng.: Foyle, 1959. 70 pp. Illus.

TYLER, EDWARD TITLEBAUM. Sterility Office Management of the Infertile Couple. New York: McGraw-Hill, 1961. 425 pp. Illus.

University of California at Los Angeles, School of Medicine.

VEHASKARI, ALLAN. On Sterility in Finnish Women with Special Reference to Its Causes and Prognosis. Acta obstetrica et gynecologica Scandinavica, Vol. 28, Suppl. 5. Helsinki, Finland, n.p.: 1948. 123 pp.

VELDE, THEODOOR HENDRIK Van De. Fertility and Sterility in Marriage: Their Voluntary Promotion and Limitation. Tr. by Stella Browne. New York: Random, 1948. 401 pp.

"The third and last volume of . . . [the author's] trilogy on marital problems." Translation of "Die Fruchtbarkeit in der Ehe und ihre Wunschgemässe Beeinflüssung." 1931 edition published by Covici in New York.

WALL, ROSCOE L. Evaluation and Management of Infertility. Clinical Obstetrics and Gynecology, Vol. 12, No. 4. New York: Hoeber, 1969. pp. 845-1093. Illus.

Includes "Ovarian Tumors, ed. by Hugh R. K. Barber."

WARNER, MARIE PICHEL. Modern Fertility Guide: Practical Advice for the Childless Couple. New York: Funk & Wagnalls, 1969. 244 pp. Illus.

1961 edition published under the title "The Couple Who Want a Baby."

WHITEHEAD, JAMES. On the Causes and Treatment of Abortion and Sterility. 2nd ed. Philadelphia, Pa.: Lea, 1854. 320 pp.

"Being the Result of an Extended Practical Inquiry into the Physiological and Morbid Conditions of the Uterus, with Reference especially to Leucorrhal Affections, and the Diseases of Menstruation." Earlier edition, 1848.

WILLIAMS, WALTER WILKINSON. Sterility: The Diagnostic Survey of the Infertile Couple. 3rd ed. Baltimore, Md.: Williams & Wilkins, 1964. 515 pp. Illus.

VENEREAL DISEASE

ACTON, WILLIAM. A Practical Treatise on Diseases of the Urinary and Generative Organs (in Both Sexes). Part I. Non-Specific Diseases. Part II. Syphilis. 2nd ed. London, Eng.: Churchill, 1851. 693 pp.

First edition published in 1841 by Renshaw, London, England, has the title "A Complete Practical Treatise on Venereal Diseases."

Several other editions are in existence.

AMERICAN SOCIAL HEALTH ASSOCIATION.

This organization issues many publications on venereal diseases.

AMERICAN SOCIAL HEALTH ASSOCIATION. Today's VD Control Problem— 1971. New York: n.p., 1971. 58 pp. Illus.

A joint statement cosponsored by the American Public Health Association and the American Venereal Disease Association.

ASSOCIATION OF BRITISH PHARMACEUTICAL INDUSTRY. The Venereal Diseases. London, Eng.: Assn. of British Pharmaceutical Industry, 1963. 31 pp. Illus.

BATCHELOR, RALPH CAMPBELL LINDSAY, and M. MURRELL. A Short Manual of Venereal Diseases and Treponematosis. 2nd ed. Edinburgh, Scotland: Livingstone, 1961. 316 pp. Illus.

First edition has the title "Venereal Diseases Described for Nurses...." Edinburgh, Scotland, Livingstone, 1951.

BENDER, STEPHEN J. Venereal Disease. Contemporary Topics in Health Science Series. Dubuque, Iowa: Brown, 1971. 53 pp. Illus.

BOWEN, CARROL T. Handbook on VD. Coral Gables, Fla.: University of Miami, 1952. 66 pp.

BRITISH COLUMBIA. DIVISION OF VENEREAL DISEASE CONTROL. Nurses Manual of Venereal Diseases. Victoria, Canada: n.p., 1958. 39 pp.

BRITISH COLUMBIA. DIVISION OF VENEREAL DISEASE CONTROL. Physicians Manual of Venereal Diseases. Victoria, Canada: Division of Public Health Education, Health Branch, Department of Health and Welfare, 1958. 35 pp.

BRITISH MEDICAL ASSOCIATION. Venereal Disease and Young People: Report. London, Eng.: British Medical Assn., 1964. 160 pp.

BROOKS, STEWART M. The V. D. Story. South Brunswick, N.J.: Barnes, 1971. 162 pp. Illus.

BROWN, ABE A., and S. PEDAIR. Venereal Disease, a Renewed Challenge. Public Affairs Pamphlet, No. 292 A. New York: Public Affairs Committee, 1964. 20 pp.

BROWN, WILLIAM J., et al. Syphilis and Other Venereal Diseases. Cambridge, Mass.: Harvard University Press, 1970. 241 pp. Illus.

CALIFORNIA. DEPARTMENT OF PUBLIC HEALTH. Venereal Diseases: Information for Educators. Berkeley, Calif.: n.p., 1965. 46 pp.

CALIFORNIA. LAWS, STATUTES, ETC. Laws and Regulations Relating to Venereal Disease Control: Excerpts from the California Health and Safety Code, California Civil Code, California Business and Professions Code and California Administrative Code. Berkeley, Calif.: Department of Public Health, 1968. 29 pp.

CANADA. DEPARTMENT OF NATIONAL HEALTH AND WELFARE. Venereal Disease: What You Should Know. Rev. ed. Ottawa, Canada: n.p., 1957. 59 pp. Illus.

Earlier edition 1948.

CANIZARES, ORLANDO. Modern Diagnosis and Treatment of the Minor Venereal Diseases: The Management of Chancroid, Granuloma Inguinale and Lymphogranuloma Venereum in General Practice. American Lecture Series, No. 228. American Lectures in Dermatology. Springfield, Ill.: Thomas, 1954. 131 pp. Illus.

CATTERALL, ROBERT DUNCAN. A Short Textbook of Venereology: The Sexually Transmitted Diseases. Philadelphia, Pa.: Lippincott, 1965. 198 pp. Illus.

CATTERALL, ROBERT DUNCAN. The Venereal Diseases: A Book About Sexually Transmitted Infections. London, Eng.: Evans, 1967. 160 pp. Illus.

CATTERALL, ROBERT DUNCAN. Venereology for Nurses: A Textbook of the Sexually Transmitted Diseases. London, Eng.: English Universities Press, 1964. 146 pp. Illus.

CLARKE, CHARLES WALTER. Taboo: The Story of the Pioneers of Social Hygiene. Washington, D.C.: Public Affairs, 1961. 109 pp.

CURTIS, LINDSAY R. V. D.: America's Growing Threat. Rev. ed. Dallas, Tex.: Alcohol Narcotics Education, 1969. 84 pp. Illus.

DREW, JOHN. Human Reproduction and Venereal Disease. London, Eng.: Faber, 1944. 124 pp.

"Describes briefly the process of reproduction so as to show how venereal infection is caused. Summarizes the nature of syphilis and gonorrhoea and their treatment. Discusses sterility in men and women."

FRANKL, PAUL. Venereal Diseases: A Guide for African Students and Medical Assistants. Nairobi, Kenya: Eagle Press, East African Literature Bureau, 1958. 43 pp. Illus.

FREED, LOUIS FRANKLIN. The Social Aspect of Venereal Disease. Johannesburg, South Africa: n.p., 1951. 237 pp.

Thesis, University of the Witwatersrand, Johannesburg.

GROVER, JOHN W. V.D.: The ABC's. Englewood Cliffs, N.J.: Prentice-Hall, 1971. 148 pp. Illus.

HOLLICK, FREDERICK. A Popular Treatise on Venereal Diseases, in All Their Forms, Embracing Their History and Probable Origin, Their Consequences, Both to Individuals and to Society, and the Best Modes of Treating Them. New York: Strong, 1852. 413 pp. Illus.

"Adapted for general use."

INTERNATIONAL UNION AGAINST THE VENEREAL DISEASES AND THE TREPONEMATOSES.

This organization issues many publications on venereal diseases.

JOHNSON, BASCOM, comp. Digest of Laws and Regulations Relating to the Prevention and Control of Syphilis and Gonorrhea in the Forty-Eight States and the District of Columbia. American Social Hygiene Assn., Publication No. A-274. New York: The American Social Hygiene Assn., 1940. 438 pp.

"Published with the cooperation of the United States Public Health Service."

KING, AMBROSE JOHN. Recent Advances in Venereology. London, Eng.: Churchill, 1964. 496 pp. Illus.

KING, AMBROSE JOHN, and C. NICOL. Venereal Diseases. 2nd ed. Philadelphia, Pa.: Davis, 1969. 319 pp. Illus.

Earlier edition, 1964. 1969 edition also published by Baillière, London, England.

LOBB, HENRY W. Treatise on the Errors of Youth and Diseases of the Sexes. Philadelphia, Pa.: n.p., 1894. 191 pp.

McLACHLAN, ANGUS ELRICK WILLIAM. McLachlan's Handbook of Diagnosis and Treatment of Venereal Diseases. Ed. by A. S. Grimble. 5th ed. Edinburgh, Scotland: Livingstone, 1969. 222 pp. Illus.

First edition published in 1944.

MARSHALL, JAMES. The Venereal Diseases: A Manual for Practitioners and Students. New York: Macmillan, 1944. 348 pp.

"Describes the basis of diagnosis of venereal disease and methods of treatment which can easily be carried out in private practice. A complete description of all the manifestations of the venereal and allied diseases is attempted."

MORTON, ROBERT STEEL. So Now You Know About V. D. and Diseases Transmitted Sexually. London, Eng.: British Medical Association, 1968. 31 pp.

MORTON, ROBERT STEEL. Venereal Diseases. Baltimore, Md.: Penguin Books, 1966. 185 pp. Illus.

"Discusses treatment not only from a medical standpoint but as an application of social policy based on the science of human behavior."

NEW YORK SOCIETY FOR THE PREVENTION OF CONTAGIOUS DISEASES.

This organization issues many publications on venereal diseases.

NORONHA, SOCRATES De. The Organisation of Venereal Diseases Clinics. Bombay, India: Bombay Social Hygiene Council, 1962. 190 pp. Illus.

ROSEBURY, THEODOR. Microbes and Morals: The Strange Story of Venereal Disease. New York: Viking, 1971. 361 pp. Illus.

SCHNEIDER, ROBERT E. Handbook on Venereal Disease. Boston, Mass.: Allyn and Bacon, 1968. 70 pp. Illus.

SHEVLIN, JULIUS B., and I. H. GOLDBERG. A Programmed Unit on Venereal Disease. Boston, Mass.: Allyn and Bacon, 1969. 44 pp. Illus.

SILVER, PHILIP S. Venereal Disease, A Simple Explanation: Facts for Everyone to Know in a Language for Everyone to Understand by a V.D. Specialist. Edinburgh, Scotland: Livingstone, 1966. 15 pp. Illus.

STOPES, MARIE C. Prevention of Venereal Disease. 3rd ed. New York: Putnam, 1939. 62 pp.

"A revised and enlarged edition of the book originally published in 1921 as 'The Truth about Venereal Disease.' A practical account of methods of disinfection which may be adopted by persons who run a risk of contracting V. D."

U. S. COMMUNICABLE DISEASE CENTER, ATLANTA. Venereal Disease in Children and Youth. Atlanta, Ga.: n.p., 1961. 30 pp.

U. S. PUBLIC ADVISORY COMMITTEE ON VENEREAL DISEASE CONTROL. Venereal Disease Education: A Report of the Special Subcommittee of the Public Advisory Committee on Venereal Disease Control. Public Health Service Publication, No. 1190. Atlanta, Ga.: U. S. Communicable Disease Center, Venereal Disease Branch, 1964. 31 pp.

U. S. PUBLIC HEALTH SERVICE. DIVISION OF VENEREAL DISEASES.

This organization issues many publications on venereal diseases.

WARWICK, W. TURNER. Handbook on Venereal Diseases: For Nurses and Others Engaged in the Routine Treatment of These Diseases. London, Eng.: Faber, 1941. 233 pp.

"Gives a complete survey of general principles of treatment, with details of recognized procedures. More suitable than the larger textbooks for nurses and similar readers."

WILLCOX, RICHARD ROBERT. Textbook of Venereal Diseases and Treponematoses. 2nd ed. London, Eng.: Heinemann, 1964. 492 pp. Illus.

First edition has the title "A Text-Book of Venereal Diseases."

WILSON, JOHN MICHAEL. Sickness and Society: The Problem of Venereal Disease. London, Eng.: Sheldon, 1961. 51 pp.

WYKES, ALAN. The Doctor and His Enemy. New York: Dutton, 1966. 213 pp.

"Combines the biography of an anonymous British specialist in venereal diseases with a discussion of studies in sexual abnormalities and the chief venereal diseases."

YALE UNIVERSITY. SCHOOL OF MEDICINE. DEPARTMENT OF PUBLIC HEALTH. Cooperative Studies in the Social and Educational Aspects of Venereal Disease Control. New Haven, Conn.: n.p., 1948. 3 vols.

Sponsored by the Department of Public Health, Yale University, and the Venereal Disease Division of the United States Public Health Service.

9.
SEX EDUCATION

ACHILLES, PAUL STRONG. The Effectiveness of Certain Social Hygiene Literature. New York: American Social Hygiene Assn., 1923. 117 pp.

Doctoral thesis, Columbia University, 1923. "A study made under the auspices of the Committee on Evaluation of Social Hygiene Literature of the American Social Hygiene Association."

ADKINS, GRACE REESE. The Sex Life of Girls and Young Women. Cincinnati, Ohio: Standard Publishing Co., 1919. 191 pp.

ALASKA. DEPARTMENT OF EDUCATION. Guidelines to Human Sexuality Education. Juneau, Alaska: Dept. of Education, 1967. 46 pp.

ALLAN, DOROTHEEN. How the Baby Came. London, Eng.: Heinemann, 1963. 32 pp. Illus.

ALLEN, MARY WOOD. Teaching Truth. Teaching Truth Series. Ann Arbor, Mich.: Wood-Allen, 1903. 97 pp.

First published, 1892.

ALLENDY, RENE F., and H. LOBSTEIN. Sex Problems in School. Tr. by Egon Larsen. New York: Staples, 1948. 182 pp.

ALLERS, RUDOLPH. Sex Psychology in Education. St. Louis, Mo.: Herder, 1937. 287 pp.

Translation of "Sexual Pädagogik."

ALLISON, SAMUEL DUDLESTON. VD Manual for Teachers. New York: Emerson, 1946. 149 pp.

"A modification and amplification of a VD manual for teachers, prepared by the Venereal Disease Division of the Board of Health ... and the Division of Health Education, Department of Public Instruction, territory of Hawaii."—Preface.

AMERICAN ASSOCIATION FOR HEALTH, PHYSICAL EDUCATION AND RECREATION. A Resource Guide in Sex Education for the Mentally Retarded. Washington, D.C.: 1971. 55 pp.

A joint project of the Sex Information and Education Council of the United States and AAHPER.

AMERICAN ASSOCIATION FOR HEALTH, PHYSICAL EDUCATION AND RECREATION. Sex Education Series. Washington, D.C.: National Education Assn., 1961-.

AMERICAN FEDERATION FOR SEX HYGIENE. Report of the Sex Education Sessions of the Fourth International Congress on School Hygiene and of the Annual Meeting of the Federation at Buffalo, New York, August 27th and 29th, 1913. New York: American Federation for Sex Hygiene, 1913. 151 pp.

AMERICAN FEDERATION FOR SEX HYGIENE. Report of the Special Committee on the Matter and Methods of Sex Education. New York: The American Federation for Sex Hygiene, 1913. 32 pp.

Presented before the subsection of sex hygiene of the fifteenth International Congress on Hygiene and Demography held in Washington, D. C., September 23-28, 1912.

AMERICAN SOCIAL HYGIENE ASSOCIATION. Boy Meets Girl in Wartime. New York: American Social Hygiene Assn., 1943. 32 pp. Illus.

"The American Social Hygiene Association brought together a group of experienced leaders to develop this pamphlet."

AMERICAN SOCIAL HYGIENE ASSOCIATION. The Boy Problem. New York: American Social Hygiene Assn., 1920. 32 pp.

AMERICAN SOCIAL HYGIENE ASSOCIATION. Child Questions and Their Answers. New York: American Social Hygiene Assn., 1920. 18 pp.

AMERICAN SOCIAL HYGIENE ASSOCIATION. Education for Family Living: General Trends and Work in Various Communities and School Systems. New York: American Social Hygiene Assn., 1949. 40 pp.

A symposium by Adolf Weinzirl and others.

AMERICAN SOCIAL HYGIENE ASSOCIATION. From Boy to Man. New York: American Social Hygiene Assn., 1944. 16 pp.

Earlier edition, 1930.

AMERICAN SOCIAL HYGIENE ASSOCIATION. Health for Girls. New York: American Social Hygiene Assn., 1933. 16 pp.

AMERICAN SOCIAL HYGIENE ASSOCIATION. Opinions on Sex Education. New York: American Social Hygiene Assn., 1915. 16 pp.

AMERICAN SOCIAL HYGIENE ASSOCIATION. Publications not listed are available from:

American Social Health Association
1740 Broadway
New York, New York 10019

AMSTUTZ, H. CLAIR. Growing Up to Love: A Guide to Sex Education for Parents. Scottdale, Pa.: Herald Press, 1956. 103 pp. Illus.

Revised edition, 1966.

ANCHELL, MELVIN. Sex and Sanity. New York: Macmillan, 1971. 310 pp. Illus.

ANDERSON, JACOB GRANT. Sex Life and Home Problems. Anderson, Ind.: Gospel Trumpet, 1921. 216 pp.

ANDERSON, WAYNE J. How to Discuss Sex with Teen-Agers: A Handbook for Parents, Teachers, and Counselors. Minneapolis, Minn.: Denison, 1969. 259 pp. Illus.

ANDERSON, WAYNE J. How to Explain Sex to Children. Minneapolis, Minn.: Denison, 1971. 176 pp. Illus.

ANDERSON, WAYNE J. How to Understand Sex: Guidelines for Students. Minneapolis, Minn.: Denison, 1966. 271 pp.

ANZER, RICHARD C. [Dixie Anner]. Girl Chasers, Sex Life in Hudson County: A Sociological Study of, But not for, Teenagers and a Strange Cult of Raptores. New York: Frederick, 1951. 180 pp.

ARNSTEIN, HELENE S. Your Growing Child and Sex: A Parent's Guide to the Sexual Development, Education Attitudes, and Behavior of the Child, from Infancy through Adolescence. Indianapolis, Ind.: Bobbs, 1967. 188 pp.

In consultation with the Child Study Association of America.

AUBURN UNIVERSITY, EDUCATION INTERPRETATION SERVICE. Education for Responsible Parenthood. Raleigh, N.C.: Health Publications Institute, 1950. 80 pp. Illus.

AVERY, CURTIS E., and L. F. BECK. Sex Education and Human Heredity. Eugene, Oreg.: Oregon Dept. of Education, 1957. 6 pp.

AVERY, CURTIS E., and L. F. KIRKENDALL. The Oregon Developmental Center Project in Family Life Education. Portland, Oreg.: Brown Trust, 1955. 60 pp.

BACHELOR, EVELYN N., et al. Teen Conflicts: Readings in Family Life and Sex Education. Berkeley, Calif.: Diablo Press, 1968. 240 pp.

"A text for high school students made up primarily of selections from articles which have appeared in the popular press and are relevant to student interests and needs."

BAILEY, JAMES ROSS. Sexuality Explained. Ashland, Wis.: Home Hygiene Health Club, 1901. 120 pp.

BAKER, JOHN NEWTON. Sex Education in High Schools. New York: Emerson, 1942. 155 pp.

BALL, S. B. Female Sexual Science and Hygiene Designed Especially for Girls and Women. Nicklow, W.Va.: 1908. 154 pp.

BAMFORD, EMMA JOSEPHINE. Growing and Knowing: A Simple Story of Life for Girls and Boys. Greensborough, Australia: All Saints' Vicarage, 1939. 48 pp.

BARBER, GEOFFREY OSBORN. School Education in Hygiene and Sex: Lectures Given at Felsted School. Cambridge, Eng.: Heffer, 1936. 71 pp.

BARNES, KENNETH CHARLES. 15+ Facts of Life. London, Eng.: British Medical Assn., 1961. 32 pp.

BARNES, KENNETH CHARLES. He and She. Rev. ed. Harmondsworth, Eng.: Penguin Books, 1970. 207 pp. Illus.

Earlier edition, London, 1958.

BARNES, KENNETH CHARLES, and F. BARNES. Sex, Friendship and Marriage. London, Eng.: Allen & Unwin, 1948. 205 pp.

Earlier edition 1938. "For older boys and girls approaching adulthood, teachers, and parents. Discusses the physical, mental, and emotional aspects of friendship, courtship, marriage, and child-rearing."

BARUCH, DOROTHY WALTER. New Ways in Sex Education: A Guide for Parents and Teachers. New York: McGraw-Hill, 1959. 256 pp.

BASTID, JANE, and D. HUISMAN. Where Do Babies Come From? London, Eng.: Dobson, 1963. 26 pp.

Translation of "D'où Viennent les Enfants?"

BATTEN, CHARLES EDWARD, and D. E. McLEAN. Fit To Be Tied: An Approach to Sex Education and Christian Marriage. Greenwich, Conn.: Seabury, 1960. 124 pp.

BAUER, WILLIAM WALDO. Moving into Manhood. Garden City, N.Y.: Doubleday, 1963. 107 pp. Illus.

BAUER, WILLIAM WALDO, and F. M. BAUER. Way to Womanhood. Garden City, N.Y.: Doubleday, 1965. 112 pp.

BAUSCH, WILLIAM J. A Boy's Sex Life: A Handbook of Basic Information and Moral Guidance. Notre Dame, Ind.: Fides, 1969. 189 pp. Illus.

BECK, LESTER FRED. Human Growth: The Story of How Life Begins and Goes On, Based on the Educational Film of the Same Title. Rev. ed. New York: Harcourt, 1969. 120 pp.

Also 1949 edition.

BEE, LAWRENCE STEPHEN. The Social Scientist's Stake in Teaching Marriage and Family Relations. New York: American Social Hygiene Assn., 1959. 16 pp.

BEELER, MAXWELL NEWTON. The Garden of Babies: An Answer to Children's Queries about their Origin. New York: Exposition, 1958. 122 pp. Illus.

BEERY, RAY COPPOCK. The Wonderful Story of Life. Pleasant Hill, Ohio: Parents Assn., 1951. 3 vols.

Contents: Pt. 1. For Pre-school Children; Pt. 2. For Pre-adolescent Children; Pt. 3. For the Adolescent.

BELGUM, DAVID RUDOLPH. The Church and Sex Education. Philadelphia, Pa.: Lutheran Church Press, 1967. 128 pp.

BELL, EVELYN S., and E. FARAGOH. The New Baby. Philadelphia, Pa.: Lippincott, 1939. 64 pp.

"Suggestions to parents for letting the preschool child participate in getting ready for the arrival and caring for the new baby after birth."

BELNAP, W. DEAN, and G. C. GRIFFIN. About Life and Love: Facts of Life, for LDS Teens. Salt Lake City, Utah: Deseret, 1968. 276 pp.

BENELL, FLORENCE B. Educational Approach to Venereal Disease Control: A VD Education Guide for Grades 7 through 12. Palo Alto, Calif.: National Press, 1965. 26 pp. Illus.

BENNER, RALPH, and S. BENNER. Sex and the Teenager. New York: Macfadden-Bartell, 1964. 160 pp.

BENSON, LEONARD G. The Family Bond: Marriage, Love, and Sex in America. New York: Random, 1971. 431 pp.

BERENSTAIN, STANLEY, and J. BERENSTAIN. How to Teach Your Children about Sex...without Making a Complete Fool of Yourself. New York: McCall, 1970. 64 pp. Illus.

BERGE, ANDRÉ. The Sexual Instruction of Children. London, Eng.: Sheed, 1963. 150 pp.

Translation of "L'éducation Sexuelle chez L'Enfant."

BERNARD, BERNARD. Sex Development, or, Sex Evolution: Love, Birth, and Development. 2nd ed. Chicago, Ill.: Health and Life Publishing, 1942. 95 pp.

Also, 1922 edition.

BERRILL, NORMAN JOHN. Sex and the Nature of Things. New York: Dodd, 1953. 256 pp. Illus.

Columbia University Press, 1967. "A discussion of the biological aspects of sex."

BIBBY, HAROLD CYRIL. How Life Is Handed On. Rev. ed. New York: Collier, 1964. 95 pp. Illus.

Earlier edition, 1947. "Suitable for children of 10 years and up."

BIBBY, HAROLD CYRIL. Sex Education: A Guide for Parents, Teachers, and Youth Leaders. Ed. by L. J. F. Brimble. New York: Emerson, 1947. 311 pp.

BIESTER, LILLIAN L. Units in Personal Health and Human Relations: By the Educational Services of the Minnesota Department of Health. Minneapolis, Minn.: University of Minnesota, 1947. 267 pp.

BIGELOW, MAURICE ALPHEUS. Adolescence, Education and Hygienic Problems. The National Health Series. Ed. by the National Health Council. New York: Funk & Wagnalls, 1937. 99 pp.

Earlier edition, 1924.

BIGELOW, MAURICE ALPHEUS. Sex Education: A Series of Lectures Concerning Knowledge of Sex in its Relation to Human Life. New York: American Social Hygiene Assn., 1936. 307 pp.

Earlier edition, 1916.

BLANZACO, ANDRÉ, et al. VD: Facts You Should Know. New York: Lothrop, Lee and Shepard, 1970. 63 pp. Illus.

BLOUNT, RALPH EARL. Health as a Heritage. Boston, Mass.: Allyn and Bacon, 1924. 44 pp.

BLOUNT, RALPH EARL. The Origin of Life. Oak Park, Ill.: Blount, 1917. 31 pp.

Earlier edition, 1913.

BLUM, SAM. What Every Nice Boy Knew about Sex. New York: Geis Associates, 1967. 94 pp. Illus.

"Nostalgic commentary on the passing of the Sex Myth—looking back to pre-Spock days when facts were for grownups and boys were steeped in marvelous misinformation and technicolor ignorance."

BOHANNAN, PAUL. Love, Sex, and Being Human: A Book About the Human Condition for Young People. Garden City, N.Y.: Doubleday, 1969. 144 pp.

BONNAR, ALPHONSUS. The Catholic Doctor. London, Eng.: Burns, 1951. 179 pp.

"This book is intended to provide Roman Catholic doctors with a reasoned and readable exposition of the teaching of the Roman Catholic Church on medico-moral questions of practical importance, such as sex and marriage, birth control, abortion, artificial insemination, euthanasia, sterilization, sexual excesses, and aberrations." Several editions published since 1937 edition.

BOROWITZ, EUGENE B. Choosing a Sex Ethic: A Jewish Inquiry. New York: Published by Schocken Books for B'nai B'rith Hillel Foundations, 1969. 182 pp.

"Examines the ambiguities of the new morality and situation ethics to establish a personal, nonprescriptive guide based on the recognition of the independent value of each man's conscience."

BRACHER, MARJORY LOUISE. Love, Sex, and Life. Rev. ed. Philadelphia, Pa.: Fortress, 1966. 151 pp.

"Originally published as a text to the Parish education and curriculum of the Lutheran Church in America."

BRACHER, MARJORY LOUISE. SRO, Overpopulation and You. Philadelphia, Pa.: Fortress, 1966. 216 pp.

Designed for grades 9 and up.

BRAGG, PAUL C. Truth about Sex. Hollywood, Calif.: National Diet and Health Association, 1929. 267 pp.

BREASTED, MARY. Oh! Sex Education! New York: Praeger, 1970. 343 pp.

BREWER, LESLIE. The Good News: Some Sidelights on the Strange Story of Sex Education. London, Eng.: Putnam, 1962. 142 pp.

BRITISH SOCIAL HYGIENE COUNCIL, LONDON. Preparation for Marriage: A Handbook. New York: Norton, 1933. 175 pp.

BRODERICK, CARLFRED B., and J. BERNARD, eds. The Individual, Sex and Society: A SIECUS Handbook for Teachers and Counselors. Baltimore, Md.: Johns Hopkins, 1969. 406 pp. Illus.

"Contains a series of papers dealing with the practical and programmatic aspects of sex education, the cultural and value context of sexuality, norms of sexual functioning, and special educational problems posed by sexual anomalies and aberrant sexual behavior."

BROWN, BRIAN. Making Sense of Loving. Illus. by Ken Brown. Redhill, Eng.: Denholm House, 1969. 63 pp.

BROWN, FREDERICK ROBERT, and R. T. KEMPTON. Sex Questions and Answers. 2nd ed. New York: McGraw-Hill, 1970. 278 pp. Illus.

Earlier edition, 1950.

BROWN, H. W. Sex Education in the Home. New York: American Social Hygiene Assn., 1933. 16 pp.

BROWN, THOMAS EDWARDS. A Guide for Christian Sex Education of Youth. New York: Association Press, 1968. 348 pp.

BROWNELL, CLIFFORD LEE. Youth Faces Maturity and Health Problems. New York: American Book Co., 1942. 30 pp.

BRUCKNER, PAUL JOHN. How to Give Sex Instructions. St. Louis, Mo.: The Queens' Work, 1946. 64 pp.

"A guide for parents, teachers, and others responsible for the training of young people." Earlier edition, 1937.

BUCKINGHAM, JAMIE. Coming Alive (Grades 5 and 6). Plainfield, N.J.: Logos International, 1970. 71 pp. Illus.

Describes, in a Christian context, the reproductive process, birth, growth, sexual development, and the function of various sexual organs.

BUCKINGHAM, JAMIE, and J. BUCKINGHAM. Your New Look: Junior High Age. Plainfield, N.J.: Logos International, 1970. 112 pp. Illus.

Stresses Christian values in viewing sex, reproduction, human anatomy, and physical and spiritual growth.

BUELTMANN, A. J. Take the High Road. Concordia Sex Education Series. St. Louis, Mo.: Concordia, 1967. 86 pp. Illus.

BUNDESEN, HERMAN NIELS. Toward Manhood. Philadelphia, Pa.: Lippincott, 1951. 175 pp.

English edition, 1952.

BURN, HELEN JEAN. Better than the Birds, Smarter than the Bees: No-Nonsense Answers to Honest Questions About Sex and Growing up. Nashville, Tenn.: Abingdon, 1969. 112 pp.

Questions and answers about the physical and ethical aspects of sex as they relate to individual maturity and interpersonal relationships.

BURNETT, WILL. Life Goes On. 2nd ed. Harcourt Brace Science Program. New York: Harcourt, 1959. 64 pp.

BURNITE, ALVENA. Tips for Teens on Love, Sex, and Marriage. Milwaukee, Wis.: Bruce, 1968. 96 pp.

Earlier edition, 1955.

BURT, JOHN J., and L. BROWER. Education for Sexuality: Concepts and Programs for Teaching. Philadelphia, Pa.: Saunders, 1970. 508 pp. Illus.

BUSCH, PHYLLIS S. Venereal Disease: A Teaching Reference Guide. Rev. ed. Trenton, N.J.: Division of Curriculum and Instruction, State of New Jersey, in cooperation with the New Jersey State Dept. of Health, 1968. 85 pp. Illus.

"A report of a survey of 5,000 Connecticut school children, K-12, who were studied to find out their interests, concerns, and problems relating to various areas of health including sex education."

BUTLER, GEORGE FRANK. Every Boy's Book. Chicago, Ill.: Abbott, 1912. 81 pp.

BUTTERFIELD, OLIVER McKINLEY. Love Problems of Adolescence. New York: Teachers College, Columbia University, 1939. 212 pp.

Teachers College, Columbia University. Contributions to Education, No. 768. Issued also as a doctoral thesis, Columbia University.

CADY, BERTHA LOUIS CHAPMAN. The Way Life Begins: An Introduction to Sex Education. New York: The American Social Hygiene Assn., 1939. 80 pp.

CAIN, ARTHUR H. Young People and Sex. Pref. by Elisabeth K. Hoyt. New York: Day, 1967. 126 pp.

A clear, factual discussion by a medical doctor. English title, "Sex for Young People." London, Foulsham, 1968.

Designed for grades 7 and up.

CALL, ALICE L. Toward Adulthood: Sex Education. Philadelphia, Pa.: Lippincott, 1969. 74 pp.

Earlier edition, 1964.

CALLAHAN, SIDNEY CORNELIA. Christian Family Planning and Sex Education. Notre Dame, Ind.: Ave Maria, 1969. 72 pp. Illus.

CAMMERON, KEITH [pseud.] You've Got to Have Love: A Book for Young Adults. Letchworth, Eng.: Daily Mirror, 1960. 128 pp.

CANDY, ROBERT. Please Tell Me. Sanbornville, N.H.: Wake-Brook House, 1958. 61 pp. Illus.

CARTLAND, BARBARA. Sex and the Teenager. London, Eng.: Muller, 1964. 126 pp.

CASSON, FREDERICK RONALD CHRISTOPHER. Sex and Adolescence. Foyle's Health Handbooks. London: Foyle, 1964. 76 pp.

CAULDWELL, DAVID O. Questions and Answers on the Life and Sexual Problems of Adolescents: A Booklet for Parents, Teachers and Those Whose Sex Nature is Maturing. Girard, Kans.: Haldeman-Julius, 1950. 31 pp. Illus.

CERVANTES, LUCIUS FERDINAND. And God Made Man and Woman: A Factual Discussion of Sex Differences. Chicago, Ill.: Regnery, 1959. 275 pp. Illus.

"Father Cervantes, S.J., a sociologist and marriage and family life counselor, offers teachers, parents, and couples the factual information that they need on the complex pattern of masculinity and femininity that enters into human behavior from infancy through adulthood."

CHADWICK, MARA LOUISE PRATT. Blossom Babies: How to Tell the Life Story to Little Children. New York: Eaton and Mains, 1913. 169 pp.

CHANG, CHING-SHENG. Sex Histories: China's First Modern Treatise on Sex Education. Tr. by Howard S. Levy. Yokohama, Japan: n.p., 1967. 117 pp.

CHANTER, ALBERT GEORGE. Sex Education in the Primary School. New York: St. Martin's, 1966. 100 pp.

CHESSER, EUSTACE. Grow Up and Live. Harmondsworth, Eng.: Penguin, 1949. 245 pp.

CHESSER, EUSTACE, and Z. DAWE. The Practice of Sex Education: A Plain Guide for Parents and Teachers. New York: Roy, 1946. 227 pp. Illus.

CHICAGO. MUSEUM OF SCIENCE AND INDUSTRY. The Miracle of Growth. Urbana, Ill.: University of Illinois, 1950. 73 pp. Illus.

"A simple but comprehensive account of conception, birth, and development from infancy to adolescence giving special attention to the consideration of heredity." "Text by Arnold Sundgaard in collaboration with the University Committee on Medical Sciences. Based on an exhibit developed by the University of Illinois."

CHILD STUDY ASSOCIATION OF AMERICA. Sex Education: Facts and Attitudes. Rev. ed. New York: Child Study Assn., 1940. 64 pp.

CHILD STUDY ASSOCIATION OF AMERICA. Sex Education and the New Morality: A Search for the Meaningful Social Ethics. New York: Child Study Assn., 1967. 90 pp.

Proceedings of the 42nd annual Conference of the Child Study Association of America, March 7, 1966.

CHILD STUDY ASSOCIATION OF AMERICA. What to Tell Your Children about Sex. Rev. ed. New York: Meredith, 1968. 118 pp. Illus.

"A revised edition of 'Facts of Life for Children,' published in 1954. Sex questions asked at different age levels are presented with simply worded useful answers."

CHILD STUDY ASSOCIATION OF AMERICA. When Children Ask about Sex. Rev. ed. New York: 1969. 40 pp.

Earlier edition, 1943.

CHURCH OF ENGLAND. NATIONAL ASSEMBLY, BOARD OF EDUCATION. Sex Education in Schools. London, Eng.: Church Information Office, 1964. 32 pp.

CITIZENS FOR IMPROVED EDUCATION. Sex Family Life Education and Sensitivity Training: Indoctrination or Education? San Mateo, Calif.: n.p., 1969. 55 pp. Illus.

CLAPP, EMILY VEAZIE. Growing Up in the World Today: For Boys and Girls in the Teens. Boston, Mass.: Massachusetts Society for Social Hygiene, 1951. 29 pp.

Earlier edition, 1932.

CLARK, Le MON. Sex and You. Indianapolis, Ind.: Bobbs, 1949. 203 pp.

CLARK, PERCY L. Sex Education: Why? Where? When? By Whom? Ithaca, N.Y.: Rational Life Pub. Co., 1928. 104 pp.

CLOSSON, ETHEL YOUNG. Family Living and Sex Education in the Elementary School. New York: Vantage, 1969. 133 pp.

CLYMER, REUBEN SWINBURNE. Higher Race Development: A Course of Instructions on the Right Use of Sex. Quakertown, Pa.: n.p., 1909. 168 pp.

COLE, WILLIAM GRAHAM. Sex and Selfhood. Philadelphia, Pa.: Geneva Press, 1968. 126 pp.

COLTON, HELEN. Adults Need Sex Education Too. Los Angeles, Calif.: Family Forum, 1970. 127 pp.

CORINA, FRANCIS JOSEPH. We Are Sixteen: The Tangled Skein of Youth and Sex, Unravelled in a Doctor's Study; a Book for All Young People. Bradford, Eng.: Clegg, 1944. 144 pp.

CORNER, GEORGE WASHINGTON. Attaining Manhood: A Doctor Talks to Boys About Sex. 2nd ed. New York: Harper, 1952. 97 pp. Illus.

Earlier edition, 1938.

CORNER, GEORGE WASHINGTON. Attaining Womanhood: A Doctor Talks to Girls About Sex. 2nd ed. New York: Harper, 1952. 112 pp. Illus.

Earlier edition, 1939.

COSGROVE, MARGARET. Seeds, Embryos, and Sex. New York: Dodd, 1970. 62 pp. Illus.

COURTNEY, PHOEBE. The Sex Education Racket. New Orleans, La.: Free Men Speak, Inc., 1969. 148 pp.

COX, FRANK D. Youth, Marriage, and the Seductive Society. Rev. ed. Dubuque, Iowa: Brown, 1968. 131 pp.

"Deals with dating patterns, premarital sex, problems of the young marriage and the economic influences on marriage."

COX, GLADYS MAY WATKINSON. Youth, Sex and Life. London, Eng.: Newnes, 1943. 233 pp. Illus.

First published in 1938.

CRAWFORD, NORMAN. Let's Be Frank about Sex. Sydney, Australia: N.S.W. Bookstall, 1943. 123 pp.

CRAWLEY, LAWRENCE Q. Reproduction, Sex, and Preparation for Marriage. Englewood Cliffs, N.J.: Prentice-Hall, 1964. 231 pp. Illus.

CREW, F. A. E. An Introduction to the Study of Sex. London, Eng.: Gollancz, 1932. 160 pp.

"The nature of sex, the origin of sex in the individual organism, the sex hormones, psychological aspects of sex, sex determination, and control of the sex ratio."

CROW, LESTER DONALD. Our Teen-Age Boys and Girls: Suggestions for Parents, Teachers, and Other Youth Leaders. New York: McGraw-Hill, 1945. 366 pp.

CROW, LESTER DONALD, and A. CROW. Sex Education for the Growing Family: Growing Up with the Emersons. Boston, Mass.: Christopher, 1959. 189 pp. Illus.

CURMAN, HANS, et al. What Shall I Tell My Child. Intro. by Theodor Reik. New York: Crown, 1966. 177 pp. Illus.

"Offers advice to parents, guidelines for teachers, and a description of sex instruction in Swedish schools."

DALRYMPLE, WILLARD. Sex Is for Real: Human Sexuality and Sexual Responsibility. McGraw-Hill Series in Health Education. New York: McGraw-Hill, 1969. 162 pp. Illus.

DARROW, FRANK M. Life Styles and Sex. Trona, Calif.: Frank M. Darrow, 1971. 68 pp.

DAVIES, EDMUND. Tell Us Now: Open Answers to the Actual Questions of the Young on Sex and Marriage. London, Eng.: Tandem, 1966. 155 pp.

DAVIS, MAXINE. Sex and the Adolescent. New York: Dial, 1958. 317 pp.

"Discusses male and female anatomy, sexual feeling and expression, homosexuality, reproduction, dating, premarital intercourse, and early marriage."

DAWKINS, JULIA. Teach Your Child about Sex. London, Eng.: Pearson, 1964. 94 pp. Illus.

DAWKINS, JULIA. A Textbook of Sex Education. Oxford, Eng.: Blackwell, 1967. 98 pp. Illus.

DELARGE, BERNADETTE, and T. EMIN. Girls Growing Up. London, Eng.: Chapman, 1968. 88 pp. Illus.

DENNETT, MARY WARE. Sex Education of Children: A Book for Parents. New York: Vanguard, 1931. 195 pp.

Designed to awaken in parents the meaning, nature, and possibilities of sex education as a factor for unifying and stabilizing the psychic life rather than a mode of approach isolated from life.

DENNETT, MARY WARE. The Sex Side of Life: An Explanation for Young People. Astoria, N.Y.: Mary W. Dennett, 1928. 27 pp.

DERSTINE, CLAYTON F. Manual of Sex Education for Parents, Teachers and Students. Grand Rapids, Mich.: Zondervan, 1943. 120 pp.

DESCHIN, CELIA S. The Teenager and VD: A Social Symptom of Our Times. New York: Rosen, 1969. 130 pp.

De SCHWEINITZ, KARL. Growing Up: How We Become Alive, Are Born, and Grow. 4th ed. New York: Macmillan, 1965. 54 pp. Illus.

Originally published in 1928. British title, "How a Baby Is Born." "A first book for the youngest group, for reading aloud by parents and for early self-readers."

DEYER, K. Sex and the Girl of 18: Or, The Frank Description as to How a Girl of Youth Should Behave. Amritsar, Punjab, India: Steno Pub. House, 1932. 225 pp.

De YONKER, JOHN F. From Teething Rings to Wedding Rings. Detroit, Mich.: Harlo, 1965. 142 pp.

DICKERSON, ROY ERNEST. Growing into Manhood. New York: Association Press, 1933. 100 pp. Illus.

DICKERSON, ROY ERNEST. Into Manhood. New York: Association Press, 1954. 116 pp. Illus.

DICKERSON, ROY ERNEST. So Youth May Know: New Viewpoints on Sex and Love. Rev. ed. New York: Association Press, 1948. 261 pp. Illus.

First published in 1930.

DIEHL, HAROLD SHEELY, and A. D. LATON. Families and Children. New York: McGraw-Hill, 1955. 15 pp. Illus.

DILLON, VALERIE VANCE, and W. J. IMBIORSKI. Your Child's Sex Life. Chicago, Ill.: Delaney, 1966. 120 pp. Illus.

DOUGALL, JAMES W. C., ed. Christianity and the Sex-Education of the African. London, Eng.: Society for Promoting Christian Knowledge, 1937. 128 pp.

Papers by the editor and others.

DRAKE, EMMA FRANCES ANGELL. The Daughter's Danger: Prize Paper to Girls of Sixteen and Upwards. Philadelphia, Pa.: Vir, 1905. 51 pp.

DRIVER, HELEN IRENE, ed. Sex Guidance for Your Child: A Parent Handbook. Madison, Wis.: Monoma, 1960. 192 pp. Illus.

DUVALL, EVELYN RUTH MILLIS. About Sex and Growing Up. New York: Association Press, 1968.

DUVALL, EVELYN RUTH MILLIS. Facts of Life and Love, for Teenagers. New York: Association Press, 1950. 360 pp. Illus.

1963 edition published under the title "Love and the Facts of Life."

DUVALL, EVELYN RUTH MILLIS. Love and the Facts of Life. New York: Association Press, 1963. 352 pp. Illus.

"Replacing her 'Facts of Life and Love for Teenagers.' "

DUVALL, EVELYN RUTH MILLIS. Why Wait till Marriage? New York: Association Press, 1965. 128 pp.

"This guidebook which deals one by one with popular arguments for premarital sex will give youth leaders and parents some insights into today's changing sex patterns. Written within a broadly religious framework." Several other versions of this work are available.

DUVALL, EVELYN RUTH MILLIS, and S. M. DUVALL. Sense and Nonsense about Sex. New York: Association Press, 1962. 124 pp.

DUVALL, EVELYN RUTH MILLIS, and S. M. DUVALL. Sex Ways in Fact and Faith: Bases for Christian Family Policy. New York: Association Press, 1961. 253 pp.

"Issued in connection with the North American Conference on Church and Family, this book is a compilation of authoritative information on many aspects of human sexual behavior."

EBERHARD, ERNEST. Sacred or Secret? Salt Lake City, Utah: Bookcraft, 1967. 123 pp.

ECKERT, RALPH GLENN. Sex Attitudes in the Home. New York: Association Press, 1956. 242 pp.

ECKERT, RALPH GLENN. So You Think It's Love! Dating, Necking, Petting, Going Steady. Public Affairs Committee, 1950. 32 pp. Illus.

EDDY, GEORGE SHERWOOD. Sex and Youth. Garden City, N.Y.: Doubleday, 1928. 338 pp.

EDDY, WALTER HOLLIS. Reproduction and Sex Hygiene: A Text and a Method. New York: American Social Hygiene Assn., 1916. 79 pp.

EDELSTON, HARRY. Problems of Adolescents. New York: Philosophical Library, 1956. 174 pp.

EDENS, DAVID. Teen Sense: A Guide to the Turbulent Teens. Anderson, Ind.: Warner, 1971. 112 pp.

EDWARDS, I. S., et al. Sex for Modern Teenagers. Adelaide, Australia: Rigby, 1969. 77 pp. Illus.

ELGIN, KATHLEEN. The Human Body: The Female Reproductive System. New York: Watts, 1969. 62 pp. Illus.

"Describes the female reproductive organs and their function in protecting, nourishing, and housing the fetus before birth."

ELGIN, KATHLEEN. The Human Body: The Male Reproductive System. New York: Watts, 1969. 54 pp. Illus.

"Describes the functions of the male reproductive organs, the production of sperm, and how it fertilizes the egg."

ELLIOTT, ANDREW GEORGE. Rennie Macandrew on Sex Education. London, Eng.: Wales, 1945. 110 pp.

ELLIOTT, GRACE LOUCKS, and H. BONE. The Sex Life of Youth. New York: Association Press, 1948. 142 pp.

"1929 edition has the subtitle 'Based on the Work of the Commission on Relations Between College Men and Women of the Council of Christian Associations.' "

ELLIS, HAVELOCK. On Life and Sex. New York: New American Library, 1957. 236 pp.

Earlier edition, 1931.

EMERSON, RITA MARIE. The Wonder of Growing Up. Dayton, Ohio: Pflaum, 1969. 46 pp.

"A Detailed and Concrete Exposition of a Sex-education Program for Grades One through Eight."

ESHLEMAN, MERLE W., and N. K. MACK. Christian Manhood for Adolescents and Young Men. Scottdale, Pa.: Herald Press, 1949. 110 pp. Illus.

ETS, MARIE HALL. The Story of a Baby. New York: Viking, 1939. 63 pp. Illus.

Also 1969 revised edition.

EVANS, EVA KNOX. The Beginning of Life: How Babies are Born. New York: Crowell-Collier, 1969. 63 pp. Illus.

EXNER, MAX JOSEPH. Problems and Principles of Sex Education. New York: Association Press, 1915. 39 pp.

A study of 948 college men.

FAEGRE, MARION ELLISON LYON. Understanding Ourselves. Minneapolis, Minn.: University of Minnesota Press, 1943. 43 pp. Illus.

On the cover: "A Discussion of Social Hygiene for Older Boys and Girls." "Originally prepared and published by the Minnesota Department of Health for distribution in Minnesota."

FAEGRE, MARION ELLISON LYON. Your Own Story. Minneapolis, Minn.: University of Minnesota Press, 1943. 52 pp.

FAITHFULL, THEODORE. Sex Education: A Handbook for Parents and Teachers. London, Eng.: New Age Publishers, 1970. 134 pp. Illus.

Previous edition published as "A Handbook of Sex Education," London, England, Rylee, 1951.

FARBER, SEYMOUR M., and R. H. L. WILSON, eds. Sex Education and the Teenager. Berkeley, Calif.: Diablo, 1967. 151 pp.

"Nontechnical papers delivered at a public symposium held at the University of California Medical School."

FARRELL, DAVID JOHN. Sex Education in Pictures. Sydney, Australia: n.p., 1946. 112 pp.

FATHER AND SON WELFARE MOVEMENT OF AUSTRALIA. A Guide to Manhood. Guide Series. Sydney, Australia: n.p., 1959. 33 pp. Illus.

FILAS, FRANCIS LAD. Sex Education in the Family. Englewood Cliffs, N.J.:
Prentice-Hall, 1966. 112 pp. Illus.

FIRKEL, EVA. The Mature Woman. Tr. by Elisabeth Reinecke and Paul C.
Bailey. Notre Dame, Ind.: Fides, 1968. 128 pp.

Translation of "Lebensreife." Intended for girls, grades 11 and beyond.

FISHER, ARTHUR STANLEY THEODORE. Happy Families: The Meaning of
Sex for Young Teenagers. Rev. ed. London, Eng.: Delisle, 1961. 27 pp.
Illus.

FOERSTER, FRIEDRICH WILHELM. Marriage and the Sex Problem. Tr. by
Meyrick Booth. Fwd. by Right Reverend Monsignor Fulton J. Sheen. New
York: Stokes, 1936. 228 pp.

Translation of the third edition of "Sexualethik und Sexualpädagogik,"
published in 1910.

FORBUSH, WILLIAM BYRON. The Sex-Education of Children. New York:
Funk & Wagnalls, 1919. 224 pp.

FOSTER, WILLIAM TRUFANT, ed. The Social Emergency: Studies in Sex
Hygiene and Morals. Intro. by Charles W. Eliot. Boston, Mass.: Houghton,
1914. 224 pp.

Essays by various authorities in the fields of education and sociology.

FRANK, LAWRENCE KELSO. The Conduct of Sex: Biology and Ethics of
Sex and Parenthood in Modern Life. New York: Morrow, 1961. 192 pp.

"Discusses the need for a new sex ethic as well as for sex education on a
broad basis."

FREUD, SIGMUND. The Sexual Enlightenment of Children. New York: Collier,
1963. 189 pp.

Vol. 5 of the author's "The Collected Papers."

FREY, MARGUERITE KURTH. I Wonder, I Wonder. St. Louis, Mo.: Concordia, 1967. 1 vol. Illus.

FRIBOURG, ARLETTE. Every Girl's Book of Sex. New York: Arc Books,
1967. 138 pp.

For teenage readers.

GAGERN, FRIEDRICH VON. Difficulties in Sex Education. Ed. and tr. by
Meyrick Booth. Cork, Ireland: Mercier, 1961. 48 pp.

Translation of "Harmonie von Seele und Leib."

GAIR, J. P. Sexual Knowledge for the Young Man. London, Eng.: Camden,
1945. 160 pp.

GAIR, J. P. Sexual Knowledge for the Young Woman. London, Eng.: Camden,
1945. 160 pp.

GALLICHAN, WALTER MATTHEW. Letters to a Young Man on Love and Health. New York: Stokes, 1920. 119 pp.

GALLICHAN, WALTER MATTHEW. The Poison of Prudery: An Historical Survey. Boston, Mass.; Stratford, 1929. 235 pp.

"The history of prudery, prejudice, and taboo in regard to matters of sex and sex-instruction."

GALLICHAN, WALTER MATTHEW. A Textbook of Sex Education for Parents and Teachers. Boston, Mass.: Small, Maynard, 1921. 294 pp.

GALLOWAY, THOMAS WALTON. Biology of Sex for Parents and Teachers. New York: Heath, 1922. 149 pp. Illus.

Earlier edition, 1913.

GALLOWAY, THOMAS WALTON. The Colleges and Sex Education. New York: American Social Hygiene Assn., 1928-29. 9 pts.

A Joint Study by the American Social Hygiene Association and Social Hygiene Committees in 202 Universities and Colleges, 1928-29.

GALLOWAY, THOMAS WALTON. The Father and His Boy: The Place of Sex in Manhood Making. New York: Association Press, 1921. 99 pp.

GALLOWAY, THOMAS WALTON. Human Nature Studies for the Early Grades, Supplementing the Usual Nature Studies. New York: American Social Hygiene Assn., 1929. 22 pp.

GALLOWAY, THOMAS WALTON. Parent-Teacher Guidance in Social Hygiene Education for Family Life. New York: American Social Hygiene Assn., 1950. 35 pp.

Excerpts from the book "Biology of Sex."

GALLOWAY, THOMAS WALTON. Sex and Life: A Message to Undergraduate Men. New York: Association Press, 1919. 84 pp.

GALLOWAY, THOMAS WALTON. Sex and Social Health: A Manual for the Study of Social Hygiene. New York: American Social Hygiene Assn., 1924. 360 pp.

GALLOWAY, THOMAS WALTON. Sex-Character Education in Junior High Schools. New York: American Social Hygiene Assn., 1929. 94 pp.

GALLOWAY, THOMAS WALTON. The Sex Factor in Human Life: A Study Outline for College Men. New York: American Social Hygiene Assn., 1921. 142 pp.

GALLOWAY, THOMAS WALTON. Social Hygiene in Health Education for Junior High Schools. New York: American Social Hygiene Assn., 1929. 31 pp.

GARLE, HENRY ERNEST. Social Hygiene Today. London, Eng.: G. Allen, 1936. 387 pp.

GEE, ARTHUR CECIL. So You're Grown Up Now! Bristol, Eng.: Wright, 1944. 31 pp.

GILDERHUS, GRANT, and E. M. LARSON, eds. Sex Education: Approach/
Program/Resources for the Parish. Minneapolis, Minn.: Sacred Design,
1968. 96 pp. Illus.

"A guide for churches to use in developing sex education programs for upper elementary, junior high, senior high and adult groups. Contains a bibliography, visual-aid list, glossary of both technical-scientific and slang
terms, a frank list of sample questions, and an outline of age level growth
patterns to assist teachers in their work with youth."

GILLMORE, EMMA WHEAT. The How and Why of Life. New York: Liveright,
1932. 196 pp.

GILMAN, CATHERYNE COOKE. A Vocabulary for Family Use in the Early
Sex Education of Children. 2nd ed., rev. Minneapolis, Minn.: Women's
Co-operative Alliance, 1931. 31 pp.

GITTELSOHN, ROLAND B. Consecrated unto Me: A Jewish View of Love and
Marriage. New York: Union of American Hebrew Congregations, 1965.
232 pp. Illus.

"A guide for the teenager by a prominent rabbi with a plea for marital
chastity made on the basis of quoting selected findings from several authors.
Problems for discussion are at the end of each chapter."

GLASSBERG, BERTRAND YOUNKER. Barron's Teen-Age Sex Counselor.
Woodbury, N.Y.: Barron, 1970. 182 pp. Illus.

Earlier edition, 1965. "Discusses differences between the sexes, individual
and joint expression of sexual feelings and the integration of sex into personality."

GOCHROS, HARVEY L., and L. G. SCHULTZ. Human Sexuality and Social
Work. New York: Association Press, 1972. 384 pp.

GOODLAD, SINCLAIR. Your Children's Questions: A Survey of Questions
about Personal Relationships asked by 1,000 Secondary School Children in
Lincolnshire. Lincoln, Eng.: Lincoln Diocesan Board of Moral Welfare,
1961. 32 pp.

GORDON, HENRY LAING. The Modern Mother: A Guide to Girlhood, Motherhood and Infancy. New York: Fenno, 1909. 277 pp.

GORDON, SOL. Facts about Sex: A Basic Guide. New York: Day, 1970. 48 pp.
Illus.

Grade 6 and up.

GORDON, SOL. Facts about Sex for Exceptional Youth. Plainview, N.Y.:
Charles Brown, 1969. 39 pp. Illus.

"A brief and simple book for handicapped adolescents written on a sixth-
grade reading comprehension level."

GOTTLIEB, BERNHARDT STANLEY. What a Boy Should Know about Sex.
Indianapolis, Ind.: Bobbs-Merrill, 1960. 192 pp.

"In a series of casual chats, the author takes up the various realistic
questions that are likely to be asked by boys of 11 to 14 years of age."

GOTTLIEB, BERNHARDT STANLEY. What a Girl Should Know about Sex. Indianapolis, Ind.: Bobbs-Merrill, 1961. 190 pp.

"Using simple case histories, the author emphasizes insights into the process of growth rather than facts. Designed for girls from 12 to 18 years of age."

GOULD, FREDERICK JAMES. On the Threshold of Sex: A Book for Readers Aged 14 to 21. London, Eng.: Daniel, 1909. 92 pp.

GOULD, WILLIAM LAWRENCE. Know Thyself. Albany, N.Y.: Research Supplier, 1948. 233 pp.

GRAMS, ARMIN. Sex Education: A Guide for Teachers and Parents. 2nd ed. Danville, Ill.: Interstate Printers and Publishers, 1970. 128 pp. Illus.

GRANT, EDWARD MILTON. Coming of Age: A Frank Study of The Problems of Adolescence. New York: Revell, 1939. 91 pp.

GREAT BRITAIN. BOARD OF EDUCATION. Sex Education in Schools and Youth Organisations. Education Pamphlet No. 119. London, Eng.: Great Britain, Board of Education, 1945. 22 pp.

GREAT BRITAIN. NATIONAL BIRTH-RATE COMMISSION. Youth and the Race: The Development and Education of Young Citizens for Worthy Parenthood. London, Eng.: Great Britain, National Birth-rate Commission, 1923. 378 pp.

GRIFFIN, MARY D. Manual on Sex Education. Boston, Mass.: Division of Communicable and Venereal Diseases, 1970. 89 pp. Illus.

Teacher's manual: a curriculum guide on sex education for elementary grades 5-6.

GRIFFITH, EDWARD FYFE. The Truth about the Stork. London, Eng.: Lewis, 1948. 137 pp.

GROVES, ERNEST RUTHERFORD, and G. H. GROVES. Sex in Childhood. New York: Macaulay, 1933. 247 pp.

"Written for parents, discussing the development of wholesome sex attitudes in children."

GRUBER, MAX VON. Hygiene of Sex: Authorized English Translation. Baltimore, Md.: Williams & Wilkins, 1926. 174 pp.

GRUENBERG, BENJAMIN CHARLES, ed. Parents and Sex Education. 3rd ed. New York: Viking, 1932. 112 pp.

Earlier edition, 1923. Intended for parents of children under school age.

GRUENBERG, BENJAMIN CHARLES, and J. L. KAUKONEN. High Schools and Sex Education. Washington, D.C.: U. S. Public Health Service, 1940. 110 pp.

Earlier edition, 1922.

GRUENBERG, SIDONIE MATSNER. The Wonderful Story of How You Were Born. Garden City, N.Y.: Doubleday, 1970. 41 pp. Illus.

First edition, 1952. "An explanation for young children of how life begins and develops from the union of a sperm and an egg."

GUARNERO, LUISA. The Wonder of Growing Up: A Book For The Modern Girl in Her Early Teens. London, Eng.: Campion, 1959. 165 pp. Illus.

GUDRIDGE, BEATRICE M. Sex Education in Schools. Washington, D.C.: National School Public Relations Association, 1969. 48 pp.

"A review of current policies and programs for the guidance of school board members, administrators, teachers, and parents."

GUIDANCE ASSOCIATES OF PLEASANTVILLE, NEW YORK. Sex Education U.S.A.: A Community Approach. Pleasantville, N.Y.: Guidance Associates of Pleasantville, 1968. 22 pp. Illus.

GUTTMACHER, ALAN FRANK. Human Sex Life: Life in the Making. New York: Sun Dial Press, 1940. 297 pp.

1933 edition under the title "Life in the Making."

GUTTMACHER, ALAN FRANK. The Story of Human Birth. New York: Penguin, 1947. 214 pp.

Revised and condensed edition of his "Into This Universe."

GUTTMACHER, ALAN FRANK. Understanding Sex: A Young Person's Guide. New York: Harper, 1970. 140 pp.

Original title, "Teenagers and Sex."

HACKER, ROSE. Telling the Teenagers: A Guide for Parents, Teachers and Youth Leaders. London, Eng.: Deutsch, 1966. 254 pp.

1961 edition under the title "The Opposite Sex."

HALEY, JOSEPH EDMUND. Accent on Purity: Guide for Sex Education. Chicago, Ill.: Fides, 1957. 130 pp.

Earlier edition, 1948.

HALL, WINFIELD SCOTT. From Youth into Manhood. New York: Association Press, 1909. 106 pp.

HALL, WINFIELD SCOTT. Girlhood and Its Problems: The Sex Life of Woman. Philadelphia, Pa.: Winston, 1919. 233 pp.

HALL, WINFIELD SCOTT. Instead of "Wild Oats": A Little Book for the Youth of Eighteen and Over. New York: Revell, 1912. 62 pp.

HALL, WINFIELD SCOTT. Sex Training in the Home. Chicago, Ill.: Midland, 1920. 128 pp.

HALL, WINFIELD SCOTT. Sexual Knowledge: The Knowledge of Self and Sex in Simple Language, for the Instruction of Young People. Philadelphia, Pa.: Winston, 1916. 320 pp.

Earlier edition, 1913.

HALL, WINFIELD SCOTT. Youth and Its Problems: The Sex Life of a Man. Philadelphia, Pa.: Winston, 1919. 266 pp.

HAMILTON, COSMO. A Plea for the Younger Generation. New York: Doran 1913. 74 pp.

HAMILTON, ELEANOR. Sex before Marriage: Guidance for Young Adults, Ages 16 to 20. New York: Meredith, 1969. 180 pp. Illus.

HANSEL, ROBERT R. Male/Female: A Junior-High Course in Sex Education. New York: Seabury, 1971. 64 pp. Illus.

Prepared by the Executive Council of the Episcopal Church.

HARRIS, ALAN EDWARD. Questions about Sex. London, Eng.: Hutchinson, 1968. 64 pp. Illus.

HEAD, JOHN JUAN. How Human Life Begins. London, Eng.: Murray, 1970. 46 pp. Illus.

HEGELER, STEN. Peter and Caroline: A Child Asks About Childbirth and Sex. London, Eng.: Tavistock, 1966. 30 pp. Illus.

Earlier edition Abelard-Schuman, Ltd., 1957. For children of four years and up.

HENDRICKS, WILLIAM CORNELIUS. God's Temples. Grand Rapids, Mich.: Eerdmans, 1966. 63 pp. Illus.

"Published for the National Union of Christian Schools."

HERSEY, HAROLD BRAINERD [H. Kincaid Murray]. Coercion and Perversion, or Primeval Degenerates: A Serious Sexual Study. New York: n.p., 1934. 125 pp.

HETTLINGER, RICHARD FREDERICK. Growing Up with Sex. New York: Seabury, 1971. 162 pp. Illus.

Ages 12 and up; grades 7 and up.

HETTLINGER, RICHARD FREDERICK. Living with Sex: The Student's Dilemma. New York: Seabury, 1966. 185 pp.

"Recommended for older youngsters."

HETTLINGER, RICHARD FREDERICK. Sexual Maturity. Basic Concepts in Health Science Series. Belmont, Calif.: Wadsworth, 1970. 66 pp.

HILU, VIRGINIA, ed. Sex Education and the Schools. New York: Harper, 1967. 153 pp.

Contains the proceedings of an Institute on Sex Education held by the National Association of Independent Schools in Princeton, New Jersey, 1966.

HINTON, GERTRUDE D. M. Teaching Sex Education: A Guide for Teachers. Palo Alto, Calif.: Fearon, 1969. 90 pp. Illus.

HODGES, BRUCE E. How Babies Are Born: The Story of Birth for Children. New York: Essandess, 1967. 62 pp. Illus.

HOFSTEIN, SADIE. The Human Story: Facts on Birth, Growth and Reproduction. Glenview, Ill.: Scott, Foresman, 1967. 46 pp. Illus.

HOMEL, STEVEN R., ed. The Physician and Sex Education. Pediatric Clinics of North America, Vol. 16, No. 2. Philadelphia, Pa.: Saunders, 1969. Pp. 327-528.

"A symposium."

HOUDEK, P. K. A Sourcebook for Adult Sex Education. Kansas City, Mo.: n.p., 1967. 52 pp. Illus.

Prepared for ministers, doctors, counselors, parent educators, college professors, speakers, writers, researchers.

HOWARD, WILLIAM LEE. Confidential Chats with Girls. New York: Clade, 1911. 162 pp.

HOWELL, JOHN C. Teaching about Sex: A Christian Approach. Nashville, Tenn.: Broadman, 1966. 149 pp.

HOWES, EDITH. The Enchanted Road. New York: Morrow, 1927. 246 pp. Illus.

HUBBARD, SUSAN DANA. Sex Knowledge for the Entire Family. New York: Independent Book Co., 1938. 120 pp.

HULME, WILLIAM EDWARD. Youth Considers Sex. New York: Nelson, 1965. 95 pp.

HUMMEL, RUTH STEVENSON. Wonderfully Made. Concordia Sex Education Series. St. Louis, Mo.: Concordia, 1967. 1 vol. Illus.

HUTCHIN, KENNETH CHARLES. Health and Sex. London, Eng.: Longmans, 1969. 87 pp. Illus.

ILLINOIS. SEX EDUCATION ADVISORY BOARD. Steps toward Implementing Family Life and Sex Education Programs in Illinois Schools. Springfield, Ill.: Office of the Superintendent of Public Instruction, 1968. 22 pp.

ILLINOIS. SEX EDUCATION ADVISORY BOARD. Policy Statement on Family Life and Sex Education. Springfield, Ill.: Office of the Superintendent of Public Instruction, 1967. 24 pp.

INGLEMAN-SUNDBERG, AXEL GUSTAF ISIDOR, and C. WIRSEN. A Child Is Born: The Drama of Life Before Birth in Unprecedented Photographs. New York: Dial, 1967. 156 pp.

London edition under the title "The Everyday Miracle." "A practical guide for the expectant mother."

INGLEBY, ALAN HENRY BELL. Learning to Love: A Wider View of Sex Education. 2nd rev. ed. London, Eng.: Hale, 1962. 142 pp. Illus.

Earlier edition, 1961.

INNES, RALPH H. Sex from the Standpoint of Youth. London, Eng.: Golden Eagle, 1933. 16 pp.

JACOBS, LEN, and B. JACOBS. The Family and Family Planning in the West Indies. London, Eng.: Allen & Unwin, 1967. 87 pp. Illus.

JAMES, JOHN. The Facts of Sex: A Revolutionary Approach to Sex Instruction for Teenagers. Princeton, N.J.: Brandon/Systems, 1970. 161 pp. Illus.

The author believes the female will soon dominate the male and supports the theory that the female is more highly sexed.

JOHNSON, ERIC W. Love and Sex in Plain Language. Philadelphia, Pa.: Lippincott, 1967. 68 pp. Illus.

Earlier edition, 1965. For grades 7-9. "Discusses male and female anatomy and sex roles as well as such subjects as masturbation, homosexuality, and contraception."

JOHNSON, ERIC W. Sex: Telling It Straight. Philadelphia, Pa.: Lippincott, 1970. 96 pp. Illus.

"Discusses such biological and social aspects of sex as the male and female reproductive systems, intercourse, pregnancy, birth control, venereal disease, and homosexuality."

JOHNSON, ERIC W., and C. B. JOHNSON. Love and Sex and Growing Up. Philadelphia, Pa.: Lippincott, 1970. 126 pp. Illus.

For grades 5-7.

JOHNSON, WARREN RUSSELL. Human Sexual Behavior and Sex Education: Perspectives and Problems. Health Education, Physical Education, and Recreation Series. 2nd ed. Philadelphia, Pa.: Lea and Febiger, 1968. 235 pp.

1963 edition under the title "Human Sex and Sex Education." "Discusses various theories of sex education."

JOHNSTON, DOROTHY GRUNBOCK. All about Babies: A Book To Teach Young Boys and Girls About Life. Grand Rapids, Mich.: Zondervan, 1962. 1 vol. Illus.

JONES, KENNETH LESTER, et al. Sex. New York: Harper, 1969. 168 pp. Illus.

An open and straightforward discussion, ranging from premarital sex to sexual response.

JONES, SCOTT N. Sex and the Now Generation. Richmond, Va.: Knox, 1970. 108 pp.

JUHASZ, ANNE McCREARY PHILLIPS, and G. SZASZ. Adolescents in Society: Selected Sources in Personal and Social Relationships. Curriculum Resources Books Series, 13. Toronto, Canada: McClelland, 1969. 88 pp. Illus. Maps.

KAHN, FRITZ. Our Sex Life: A Guide and Counsellor For Everyone. Tr. by George Rosen. New York: Knopf, 1942. 459 pp.

Earlier edition, 1939.

KALT, WILLIAM J., and R. J. WILKINS. Man and Woman. Chicago, Ill.: Regnery, 1967. 90 pp. Illus.

A manual for the discussion leader is included with this discussion booklet for young people.

KEATING, LESLIE E. Sex Education in the Club. Wallington, Eng.: Religious Education Press, 1945. 80 pp.

"Concluding Chapter by Evelyn Frost."

KELLER, DAVID HENRY. Sexual Education Series. New York: Popular Book Corp., 1928. 10 vols.

KELLOGG, JOHN HARVEY. Plain Facts. Battle Creek, Mich.: Good Health Pub. Co., 1917. 4 vols. Illus.

Previously published under the titles "Plain Facts About Sexual Life" (1877), and "Plain Facts For Old and Young" (1886).

KELLY, AUDREY. A Catholic Parent's Guide to Sex Education. New York: Hawthorn, 1962. 160 pp.

KELLY, AUDREY. Life and Our Children: A Parents' Guide to Sex Instruction. London, Eng.: Burns and Oates, 1961. 160 pp.

KELLY, GEORGE ANTHONY. The Catholic Youth's Guide to Life and Love. New York: Random, 1960. 209 pp.

For students in grades 10 and up.

KELLY, GEORGE ANTHONY. Your Child and Sex: A Guide for Catholic Parents. New York: Random, 1964. 236 pp.

London edition, 1966.

KENNER, JILL. Where Do Babies Come From? London, Eng.: National Marriage Guidance Council, 1969. 40 pp. Illus.

The story of human reproduction for primary and younger secondary school children and their parents.

KILANDER, HOLGER FREDERICK. Sex Education in the Schools: A Study of Objectives, Content, Methods, Materials, and Evaluation. New York: Macmillan, 1970. 435 pp. Illus.

KIND, ANNE, and J. LEEDHAM. Babies and Families. Programmes in Social Education. London, Eng.: Longmans, 1968. 31 pp. Illus.

Programmed sex information.

KIND, ROBERT WILLIAM, and J. LEEDHAM. Sex and Your Responsibility. Programmes in Social Education. London, Eng.: Longmans, 1969. 31 pp. Illus.

Programmed sex information.

KIND, ROBERT WILLIAM, and J. LEEDHAM. You Begin Life. London, Eng.: Longmans, 1968. 31 pp. Illus.

KIND, ROBERT WILLIAM, and J. LEEDHAM. You Grow Up. London, Eng.: Longmans, 1968. 31 pp. Illus.

KING, JOHN EDWARD LEYCESTER. Sex Enlightenment and the Catholic. Bellarmine Series, 10. London, Eng.: Burns, 1944. 65 pp.

KIRKENDALL, LESTER ALLEN. Helping Children Understand Sex. Chicago, Ill.: Science Research Associates, 1952. 49 pp. Illus.

KIRKENDALL, LESTER ALLEN. Sex Adjustments of Young Men. College Park, Md.: McGrath, 1970. 215 pp.

Reprint of 1940 edition published by Harper, New York.

KIRKENDALL, LESTER ALLEN. Sex Education as Human Relations. New York: Inor, 1950. 351 pp.

A guidebook on content and methods for school authorities and teachers.

KIRKENDALL, LESTER ALLEN, Understanding Sex. Chicago, Ill.: Science Research Associates, 1957. 48 pp. Illus.

KIRKENDALL, LESTER ALLEN. You're Maturing Now. Chicago, Ill.: Science Research Associates, 1968. 40 pp. Illus.

Original version published under the title "Finding Out About Ourselves" (1956).

KIRKENDALL, LESTER ALLEN, and R. F. OSBORNE. Teacher's Question and Answer Book on Sex Education. New London, Conn.: Croft, 1969. 112 pp.

"Two family life education experts discuss teaching methods and materials, curriculum content, teacher attitudes, student counseling, and the relationship between sex education and sexual morality. Written in question-answer format, this valuable book answers the basic questions common to teachers of sex education. It is especially helpful to the teacher embarking on an initial sex education assignment."

KIRSCH, FELIX MARIE. Sex Education and Training in Chastity. New York: Benziger, 1930. 540 pp.

KLEMER, DORA HUDSON. The Other Sex. New York: Association Press, 1944. 42 pp.

"A frank statement, addressed to both boys and girls, of the essential facts that young people want and need to know about sex."

KLEMER, DORA HUDSON. When Young People Ask about Sex. New York: Association Press, 1950. 62 pp. Illus.

KNEPP, THOMAS H. Human Reproduction, Health and Hygiene. New ed. Carbondale, Ill.: Southern Illinois University Press, 1967. 102 pp. Illus.

"Previous editions have the title 'The Human Reproductive System.' " Intended for use in grade 7 and up.

KOLB, ERWIN J. Parents Guide to Christian Conversation about Sex. Ed. by W. J. Fields. Concordia Sex Education Series, Book 5. St. Louis, Mo.: Concordia, 1967. 127 pp.

KONOPKA, GISELA. The Adolescent Girl in Conflict. Englewood Cliffs, N.J.: Prentice-Hall, 1966. 177 pp.

LADELL, ROBERT GEORGE MacDONALD. The Parents' Problem, Or How to Tell Children about Sex. London, Eng.: The Psychologist, 1941. 48 pp.

"Seeks to help the parent in the difficult problem of passing on sex knowledge to children in an honest and satisfactory manner. Shows how this can be done plainly and simply."

LADER, LAWRENCE, and M. MELTZER. Margaret Sanger: Pioneer of Birth Control. New York: Crowell, 1969. 174 pp. Illus.

"A biography of the woman who sacrificed her marriage, family life, and health to pioneer birth control education in the United States and abroad." Intended for use in grades 5-9.

LANDIS, PAUL H. Your Dating Days: Looking Forward to Happy Marriage. New York: Whittlesey House, 1954. 155 pp.

LARSEN, NILS PAUL. Facing Life. Honolulu, Hawaii: n.p., 1943. 57 pp.

A compilation of questions asked by a group of teenage girls and boys and the answers given.

LATON, ANITA DUNCAN, and E. W. BAILEY. Suggestions for Teaching Selected Material from the Field of Sex Responsiveness, Mating and Reproduction. Science in Modern Living Series, Monograph No. 2, Teachers College, Bureau of Educational Research in Science. New York: Teachers College, Columbia University, 1940. 118 pp.

LAWTON, SHAILER UPTON, and J. ARCHER. Sexual Conduct of the Teenager. New York: Greenberg, 1951. 180 pp.

LAYCOCK, SAMUEL RALPH. Family Living and Sex Education: A Guide for Parents and Youth Leaders. New York: Baxter, 1967. 144 pp.

"Published for Canadian Health Education Specialists Society."

LEDERER, ESTHER PAULINE [Ann Landers]. Ann Landers Talks to Teen-Agers about Sex. Englewood Cliffs, N.J.: Prentice-Hall, 1963. 131 pp.

Another edition by Fawcett, New York, 1970.

LEGGE, CECILIA MIREIO, and F. F. RIGBY. Life and Growth. London, Eng.: Faber, 1950. 79 pp. Illus.

"A supplementary reader on sex education suitable for use in the top class of a primary school and the lower forms in a secondary school."

LEHMAN, EDNA S. Talking to Children about Sex. New York: Harper, 1970. 235 pp.

A step-by-step handbook. Useful from kindergarten to grade 8.

LERRIGO, MARION OLIVE. A Doctor Talks to 9-12-Year-Olds. Chicago, Ill.: Budlong, 1965. 75 pp. Illus.

"Your Child from 9-12" (27 pages), inserted at end.

LERRIGO, MARION OLIVE, and H. SOUTHARD. Learning about Love: Sound Facts and Healthy Attitudes toward Sex and Marriage. The Dutton Series on Sex Education. New York: Dutton, 1956. 64 pp. Illus.

LERRIGO, MARION OLIVE, and H. SOUTHARD. Parents' Privilege: How, When, and What to Tell Your Child about Sex. The Dutton Series on Sex Education. New York: Dutton, 1956. 64 pp. Illus.

LERRIGO, MARION OLIVE, and H. SOUTHARD. Sex Education Series. Washington, D.C.: n.p., 1955. 5 vols. Illus.

LERRIGO, MARION OLIVE, and H. SOUTHARD. Sex Facts and Attitudes. The Dutton Series on Sex Education. New York: Dutton, 1956. 88 pp. Illus.

LERRIGO, MARION OLIVE, and H. SOUTHARD. A Story about You. New York: Dutton, 1969. 45 pp. Illus.

First published in 1955 as Vol. 2 of her Sex Education Series. For children between the ages of nine and twelve.

LERRIGO, MARION OLIVE, and H. SOUTHARD. What's Happening to Me? New York: Dutton, 1969. 48 pp. Illus.

First published in 1955 as part of her Sex Education Series. For grades 7-10.

Le SHAN, EDA J. Sex and Your Teen-Ager: A Guide for Parents. New York: McKay, 1969. 239 pp.

LEVINE, MILTON ISRA, and J. H. SELIGMANN. A Baby Is Born: The Story of How Life Begins. New York: Simon and Schuster, 1949. 54 pp.

Revised edition, Golden Press, 1966. For grades 1-4.

LEVINE, MILTON ISRA, and J. H. SELIGMANN. Helping Boys and Girls Understand Their Sex Roles. Chicago, Ill.: Science Research Association, 1953. 48 pp. Illus.

LEVINE, MILTON ISRA, and J. H. SELIGMANN. The Wonder of Life: How We are Born and How We Grow Up. New York: Simon and Schuster, 1952. 116 pp. Illus.

Earlier edition, 1944. For grades 5-9. A frank, lucid and scientific explanation of sex and reproduction.

LEWIS, DENSLOW. The Gynecologic Consideration of the Sexual Act. Weston, Mass.: M&S Press, 1970. 49 pp. Illus.

At the head of the title: "Pioneer Publication in American Medical Education Reform." An 11-page Appendix "with an account of Denslow Lewis, pioneer advocate of public sexual education and venereal prophylaxis, by Marc H. Hollender" has been added to this reprint of a work originally written in 1900.

LEWIS, WADE V. Sex: In Defence of Teen-Agers. Boston, Mass.: Christopher, 1967. 77 pp.

LIEBERMAN, BERNHARDT. Human Sexual Behavior: A Book of Readings. New York: Wiley, 1971. 444 pp. Illus.

LIEDERMAN, EARLE EDWIN. Sexual Guidance. New York: E. E. Liederman, 1926. 172 pp.

LINNER, BIRGITTA, and R. J. LITELL. Sex and Society in Sweden. New York: Pantheon, 1967. 204 pp. Illus.

"Describes the successes and failures of the state program of sex education in Sweden."

LIPKE, JEAN CORYLLEL. Birth. Minneapolis, Minn.: Lerner, 1971. 55 pp. Illus.

Describes the birth process and the care of the newborn baby.

LIPKE, JEAN CORYLLEL. Conception and Contraception. Minneapolis, Minn.: Lerner, 1971. 54 pp. Illus.

Discusses the male and female reproductive systems, contraception, and the effectiveness of various methods of contraception.

LIPKE, JEAN CORYLLEL. Dating. Minneapolis, Minn.: Lerner, 1971. 69 pp. Illus.

Discusses dating conduct, asking for a date, double dating, blind dates, pick-ups, going steady, and the emotional and physical reactions of being close to another person.

LIPKE, JEAN CORYLLEL. Heredity. Minneapolis, Minn.: Lerner, 1971. 61 pp. Illus.

Explains the biological factors of heredity that make each person unique.

LIPKE, JEAN CORYLLEL. Loving. Minneapolis, Minn.: Lerner, 1971. 56 pp. Illus.

Discusses the various kinds of love and their influence on an individual's growth, maturity, choice of a mate.

LIPKE, JEAN CORYLLEL. Marriage. Minneapolis, Minn.: Lerner, 1971. 61 pp. Illus.

Discusses the important considerations of marriage including housing, in-laws, sexual adjustment, and children.

LIPKE, JEAN CORYLLEL. Pregnancy. Minneapolis, Minn.: Lerner, 1971. 61 pp. Illus.

Describes the prenatal growth and development of a baby and the changes in the mother during the nine months of pregnancy.

LIPKE, JEAN CORYLLEL. Puberty and Adolescence. Minneapolis, Minn.: Lerner, 1971. 53 pp. Illus.

Describes the emotional and sexual developments in boys and girls entering puberty.

LIPKE, JEAN CORYLLEL. Sex Outside of Marriage. Minneapolis, Minn.: Lerner, 1971. 54 pp. Illus.

Discusses pregnancy as a result of premarital sex and the psychological and social ramifications of having an illegitimate child. Also examines legalities of adoption, homes for unwed mothers, alternatives to intercourse, and homosexuality.

Listen, Son: A Father's Talks on the Facts of Life and Catholic Ideals of Social Conduct. Chicago, Ill.: Franciscan Herald, 1957. 72 pp.

LOEB, ROBERT H. His and Hers: Dating Manners. New York: Association Press, 1970. 140 pp. Illus.

General guide to modern dating manners with specific suggestions for both boys and girls on how to get a date and be successful enough to win a repeat performance.

LONDON, COUNTY COUNCIL. Some Notes on Sex Education. Rev. ed. London, Eng.: London, County Council, 1964. 31 pp.

"A booklet explaining the policy of the L. C. C. with regard to sex education and notes for the guidance of teachers."

LONDON (COUNTY), EDUCATION COMMITTEE. Report ... on the Teaching of Sex Hygiene Together ... Information for Parents, Teachers and Ministers of Religion for the Purpose of Safeguarding Girls Seeking Employment. London, Eng.: Odhams, 1914. 36 pp.

LORAND, RHODA L. Love, Sex and the Teenager. New York: Macmillan, 1965. 243 pp.

LOSONCY, MARY JAN, and L. J. LOSONCY. Sex and the Adolescent. Notre Dame, Ind.: Ave Maria, 1971. 111 pp. Illus.

Introduces the physical and emotional aspects of sex with an emphases on Christian ethics.

LOWERY, DANIEL L. Life and Love: The Commandments for Teenagers. Glen Rock, N.J.: Paulist Press, 1964. 224 pp.

LUTES, DELLA THOMPSON. The Story of Life for Children. Cooperstown, N.Y.: Crist, 1914. 60 pp.

LYTTELTON, EDWARD. Training of the Young in Laws of Sex. New York: Longmans, 1900. 117 pp.

McKEEVER, WILLIAM ARCH. Instructing the Young in Regard to Sex. Manhattan, Kans.: n.p., 1912. 15 pp.

MALCHOW, CHARLES WILLIAM. Sexual Life: Embracing the Natural Sexual Impulse, Normal Sexual Habits, and Propagation, Together with Sexual Physiology and Hygiene. 7th ed. St. Louis, Mo.: Mosby, 1928. 317 pp.

Earlier edition, 1904, has the subtitle "A Scientific Treatise Designed For Advanced Students and The Professions."

MANLEY, HELEN. A Curriculum Guide in Sex Education. Rev. ed. St. Louis, Mo.: State Pub. Co., 1967. 72 pp.

Earlier edition 1964.

MARCH, NORAH HELENA. Sex Knowledge. New York: Dutton, 1922. 104 pp.

MARCH, NORAH HELENA. Toward Racial Health: A Handbook for Parents, Teachers and Social Workers on the Training of Boys and Girls. London, Eng.: Routledge, 1915. 326 pp.

A biological approach is adopted in sex instruction.

MARDEN, ORISON SWET. The Crime of Silence. New York: Physical Culture Pub. Co., 1915. 328 pp.

Shows necessity of teaching youth what they must know about sexual conduct.

MATTHEWS, EDWARD RUSSELL. Right from the Start: How a Baby Comes Into the World. London, Eng.: Rockliff, 1956. 60 pp. Illus.

MAY, JULIAN. How We Are Born. Titan ed. Chicago, Ill.: Follett, 1969. 48 pp. Illus.

MAY, JULIAN. Man and Woman. Chicago, Ill.: Follett, 1969. 46 pp. Illus.

For grades 3-7.

MAY, JULIAN. A New Baby Comes. Mankato, Minn.: Creative Education Press, 1970. 1 vol. Illus.

MAZUR, RONALD MICHAEL. Commonsense Sex: A Basis for Discussion and Reappraisal. Boston, Mass.: Beacon, 1968. 109 pp.

Deals with sexual ethics for youth.

MEILACH, DONA Z., and E. MANDEL. A Doctor Talks to 5 to 8 Year Olds. Chicago, Ill.: Budlong, 1966.

MELOCHE, ROMÉO ARTHUR. Tell Your Children: A Guide to Proper Sex Instruction for Children and Adolescents, Addressed to Catholic Parents, Teachers and Priests. Tr. by Gerald O'Connel. Montreal, Canada: Youth Welfare Publishers, 1957. 140 pp. Illus.

MEYER, FULGENCE. Helps to Purity: A Frank, yet Reverent, Instruction on the Intimate Matters of Personal Life for Adolescent Girls. Cincinnati, Ohio: St. Francis Book Shop, 1929. 90 pp.

MEYER, FULGENCE. Safeguards of Chastity: A Frank, yet Reverent, Instruction on the Intimate Matters of Personal Life for Young Men. Cincinnati, Ohio: St. Francis Book Shop, 1929. 84 pp.

MIDDLEWOOD, ESTHER LOUISE. Sex Education within the Family. Lansing, Mich.: Michigan Dept. of Health, 1954. 16 pp. Illus.

MILES, ELIZABETH ANN. How Life Begins: The Wonderful Story of Birth and Growth. Wellington, New Zealand: Reed, 1944. 36 pp. Illus.

MILES, HERBERT JACKSON. Sexual Understanding Before Marriage. Intro. by Paul Popenoe. Grand Rapids, Mich.: Zondervan, 1971. 222 pp. Illus.

MILLER, BENJAMIN FRANK, et al. Masculinity and Feminity. Boston, Mass.: Houghton, 1971. 120 pp. Illus.

MINNESOTA. DEPARTMENT OF EDUCATION. Guidelines for Family Life and Sex Education, Grades K-12. Curriculum Bulletin No. 32. St. Paul, Minn.: n.p., 1970. 96 pp.

MINNESOTA. DIVISION OF PUBLIC HEALTH EDUCATION. Venereal Disease Education: A Teaching Guide. Minneapolis, Minn.: n.p., 1966. 35 pp. Illus.

MOLL, ALBERT. The Sexual Life of the Child. Tr. from the German by Dr. Eden Paul. Intro. by Edward L. Thorndike. New York: Macmillan, 1912. 339 pp.

"An authoritative treatise on the sexuality of children, including physiology, psychology, pathology, and sex education."

MOONEY, BELLE STULL. How Shall I Tell My Child? A Parents' Guide to Sex Education for Children. New York: Cadillac, 1944. 192 pp.

MORLEY, MARGARET WARNER. The Renewal of Life: How and When to Tell the Story to the Young. Chicago, Ill.: McClurg, 1906. 200 pp.

MORLEY, MARGARET WARNER. The Spark of Life: The Story of How Living Things Come into the World, As Told for Girls and Boys. Chicago, Ill.: Revell, 1913. 62 pp.

Mother's Little Helper: Twelve Heart-to-Heart Talks of a Mother to Her Daughter. Chicago, Ill.: Franciscan Herald Press, 1955. 77 pp.

MOZES, EUGENE B. Sex Facts and Fiction for Teen-Agers. Baltimore, Md.: Ottenheimer, 1957. 169 pp. Illus.

MULLOWNEY, JOHN JAMES. The Hygiene of the Home, and Responsibility for Sex Education. Boston, Mass.: Christopher, 1926. 195 pp.

MUNCIE, ELIZABETH HAMILTON. Four Epochs of Life. New York: Gospel Publishing House, 1910. 272 pp.

MURPHY, CHARLES, and L. DAY. Sex: A Book for Teenagers. New York: Herder, 1970. 63 pp.

NAIS INSTITUTE ON SEX EDUCATION, PRINCETON, NEW JERSEY. A Summary Report. Boston, Mass.: National Assn. of Independent Schools, 1966. 24 pp.

NAISMITH, GRACE. Private and personal. New York: McKay, 1966. 272 pp.

"A guide to every feminine problem concerning sexual health, knowledge, and a happy marriage."

NARRAMORE, CLYDE MAURICE. How to Tell Your Children about Sex. Grand Rapids, Mich.: Zondervan, 1958. 97 pp. Illus.

NEUGARTEN, BERNICE LEVIN. Becoming Men and Women. Chicago, Ill.: Science Research Associates, 1955. 48 pp. Illus.

NEW JERSEY. LEGISLATURE. SENATE. COMMITTEE ON EDUCATION. Public Hearing before Senate and General Assembly Committees of Education: Re Sex Education in Public Schools: Assembly Concurrent Resolution No. 69. Trenton, N.J.: n.p., 1969.

NOBLE, GRANT. Growing Adult. Methuen's Clearway Programmed Books. London, Eng.: Methuen, 1967. 38 pp. Illus.

O'BRIEN, JOHN ANTHONY. Sex-Character Education: Explaining the Facts of Life to the Young. New York: Macmillan, 1952. 212 pp.

ODENWALD, ROBERT PAUL. How You Were Born. New York: Kenedy, 1963. 64 pp.

For grades 4-7.

OLIVEN, JOHN FREDERICK. Sexual Hygiene and Pathology: A Manual for the Physician and the Professions. 2nd ed. Philadelphia, Pa.: Lippincott, 1965. 621 pp.

Earlier edition, 1955.

ORAISON, MARC. Learning to Love: Frank Advice for Young Catholics. Tr. by André Humbert. New York: Hawthorn, 1965. 143 pp. Illus.

ORLICK, EMANUEL. Sex and Your Body. Montreal, Canada: Your Physique Publishing, 1944. 70 pp.

PARKER, VALERIA HOPKINS. For Daughters and Mothers. Indianapolis, Ind.: Bobbs, 1940. 138 pp.

PARSONS, LYDIA DOROTHY. Life: How It Comes. New York: McBride, 1922. 174 pp.

A child's book of elementary biology.

PATTON, EDWIN FRITZ. Introduction to Motherhood. South Pasadena, Calif.: Commercial Textbook Co., 1938. 137 pp.

Companion volume to the author's "Introduction to Manhood."

PATTULLO, ANN. Puberty in the Girl Who Is Retarded. New York: National Assn. for Retarded Children, 1969. 37 pp. Illus.

PECK, ELLEN. How to Get a Teen-Age Boy, and What to Do with Him When You Get Him. New York: Geis, 1969. 293 pp.

PEMBERTON, LOIS LOYD. The Stork Didn't Bring You: The Facts of Life for Teenagers. Edinburgh, Scotland: Nelson, 1957. 236 pp. Illus.

New York edition published in 1948.

PEMBERTON, PRENTISS L. Dialogue in Romantic Love: Promise and Communication. Valley Forge, Pa.: Judson, 1961. 64 pp.

Deals with sexual ethics. Designed for grades 9 and up.

PERRIN, MARK, and T. E. SMITH. Ideas and Learning Activities for Family Life and Sex Education. Dubuque, Iowa: W.C. Brown, 1972. 264 pp. Illus.

PERRY, PAULINE. Your Guide to the Opposite Sex: For the Under Twenties. London, Eng.: Pitman, 1969. 111 pp. Illus.

PIERSON, ELAINE C. Sex Is Never an Emergency: A Candid Guide for College Students. 2nd ed. Philadelphia, Pa.: Lippincott, 1971.

First edition has the title "A Guide for University of Pennsylvania Students, 1970-71."

PIKE, JAMES ALBERT. Teen-Agers and Sex. Englewood Cliffs, N.J.: Prentice-Hall, 1965. 146 pp.

PILKINGTON, ROGER. The Facts of Life: A Family Doctor Book. Sydney, Australia: Horwitz, 1957. 66 pp. Illus.

For children.

PILKINGTON, ROGER. Human Sex and Heredity: Who's Who—and Why. New York: Watts, 1963. 110 pp. Illus.

First published in 1961 under the title "Who's Who—and Why." Information about genetics for ages 12 and up.

PILKINGTON, ROGER. Parents' Guidance for Children's Sex Education. Encyclopaedia Britannica. Advisory Guides for Parents. London, Eng.: Encyclopaedia Brittanica, 1963. 30 pp. Illus.

PILKINGTON, ROGER. Sons and Daughters. London, Eng.: Allen & Unwin, 1951. 214 pp.

"Tells the story of the development of the human embryo from conception to birth, in simple language and with a lively humour."

PLACZEK, SIEGFRIED. Sexual Life of Man. Tr. by L. S. Morgan. 2nd ed. London, Eng.: Bale, 1931. 314 pp.

An Outline for Students, Doctors, and Lawyers. First English edition published in 1923. Translation of "Das Geschlechtsleben des Menschen."

POLE, MARY TUDOR. The Wonder of Life: A Talk with Children about Sex. New York: Fowler and Wells, 1905. 30 pp. Illus.

POMEROY, WARDELL BAXTER. Boys and Sex. New York: Delacorte, 1968. 157 pp.

POMEROY, WARDELL BAXTER. Girls and Sex. New York: Delacorte, 1970. 159 pp.

POPENOE, PAUL BOWMAN. Social Life for High School Girls and Boys. New York: American Social Hygiene Assn., 1941. 8 pp.

POWER, JULES. How Life Begins. New York: Simon and Schuster, 1965. 95 pp. Illus.

"The basis for a recent television program, this book tells with the aid of photographs and drawings, the story of where babies come from and how they develop."

POWERS, GRADY PAT, and W. BASKIN. Sex Education: Issues and Directives. New York: Philosophical Library, 1969. 532 pp.

"Interdisciplinary readings reflecting the best contemporary thinking and practice throughout all aspects of sex education: role of family, moral and ethical implications of permissiveness, positive aspects in existing programs, more."

PUNER, HELEN WALKER. Not While You're a Freshman: A Chapter in the Life of Monologue. New York: Coward-McCann, 1965. 191 pp.

"A mother's attempts to communicate with her college-going daughter on morality and sex."

RAINWATER, LEE. Family Design: Marital Sexuality, Family Size and Contraception. Social Research Studies in Contemporary Life. Chicago, Ill.: Aldine, 1965. 349 pp.

Sponsored by the Planned Parenthood Federation of America, Inc., World Population Campaign.

RAYNER, CLAIRE. Parent's Guide to Sex Education. Garden City, N.Y.: Dolphin, 1969. 110 pp. Illus.

Also London edition, 1968.

REED COLLEGE, PORTLAND, OREGON. Syllabus of a Course in Sexual Hygiene and Morals. Portland, Oreg.: Reed College, 1913. 37 pp.

REUSS, JOSEF MARIA. Modern Catholic Sex Instruction: A Practical Study of Sexuality and Love. Tr. by Theodore H. Zink. Baltimore, Md.: Helicon, 1964. 144 pp.

RICE, THURMAN BROOKS. How Life Goes On and On: A Story for Girls of High School Age. Chicago, Ill.: American Medical Assn., 1933. 39 pp.

RICE, THURMAN BROOKS. In Training, for Boys of High School Age. Chicago, Ill.: American Medical Assn., 1933. 48 pp.

RICE, THURMAN BROOKS. Sex, Marriage, and Family. Philadelphia, Pa.: Lippincott, 1946. 272 pp.

RICE, THURMAN BROOKS. The Story of Life, for Boys and Girls of Ten Years. Chicago, Ill.: American Medical Assn., 1933. 36 pp. Illus.

RICE, THURMAN BROOKS. The Venereal Diseases. American Medical Association, Bureau of Health and Public Instruction. Sex education pamphlet. Chicago, Ill.: American Medical Assn., 1933. 39 pp.

RICH, JOHN. Catching Up with Our Children: New Perspectives in Sex Instruction. Toronto, Canada: McClelland and Stewart, 1968. 96 pp.

RICHARDSON, FRANK HOWARD. For Boys Only: The Doctor Discusses the Mysteries of Manhood. Atlanta, Ga.: Tupper and Love, 1952. 91 pp.

For grades 5-11.

RICHMOND, WINIFRED VANDERBILT. An Introduction to Sex Education. New York: Farrar and Rinehart, 1934. 312 pp.

Also London edition, 1936. "Aims to set forth a summary of our present knowledge of the biology, history, psychology, and social aspects of sex, for classroom use and for the general reader."

RIEMER, YEHUDA. Sex Education and Moral Standards in the Youth Movement. Tel Aviv, Israel: Ichud Habonim, 1963. 70 pp.

RIESS, WALTER. The Teen-Ager You're Dating: A Christian View of Sex, About Boys for Girls, About Girls for Boys. St. Louis, Mo.: Concordia, 1964. 127 pp. Illus.

ROCHESTER, NEW YORK (DIOCESE), COMMITTEE ON SEX EDUCATION. Education in Love: Handbook for Parents. New York: Paulist Press, 1971. 31 pp. Illus.

A program in sex education and family life for grades 1 to 8.

ROGERS, KEITH FORRESTER. A Doctor's Advice to His Son: A Discussion of the Problems Peculiar to Youths and Men, with a Presentation of the Established Scientific Facts Underlying These Problems. Toronto, Canada: Ryerson, 1931. 71 pp.

RUBIN, ISADORE, and L. A. KIRKENDALL, eds. Sex in the Adolescent Years: New Directions in Guiding and Teaching Youth. New York: Association Press, 1968. 223 pp.

"A comprehensive selection of thirty-eight articles by various authorities on teenage sex guidance."

RUBIN, ISADORE, and L. A. KIRKENDALL, eds. Sex in the Childhood Years: Expert Guidance for Parents, Counselors, and Teachers. New York: Association Press, 1970. 190 pp.

RUNDEN, CHARITY EVA, comp. Selected Readings for Sex Education. Berkeley, Calif.: McCutchan, 1968. 324 pp.

RUPP, FREDERICK AUGUSTINE. Purity and Truth: Letters of a Physician to His Daughters on the Great Black Plague. Philadelphia, Pa.: Vir, 1910. 96 pp.

RUTLEDGE, AARON L. Premarital Counseling. Cambridge, Mass.: Schenkman, 1966. 366 pp.

SADLER, WILLIAM SAMUEL. A Doctor Talks to Teen-Agers: A Psychiatrist's Advice to Youth. St. Louis, Mo.: Mosby, 1948. 379 pp.

SALTMAN, JULES, ed. Teen Love, Teen Marriage. New York: Grosset, 1966. 156 pp.

Edited for the Public Affairs Committee.

SAND, RICHARD E. Things Your Mother Never Told You. Los Angeles, Calif.: Nash, 1970. 302 pp. Illus.

SANDS, SIDNEY L. Growing Up to Love, Sex, and Marriage. Boston, Mass.: Christopher, 1960. 131 pp.

SANGER, MARGARET. What Every Boy and Girl Should Know. Elmsford, N.Y.: Maxwell, 1969. 140 pp.

Reprint of 1927 edition.

SANGER, MARGARET. What Every Mother Should Know, Or, How Six Little Children Were Taught the Truth. 3rd ed. New York: Maisel, 1916. 63 pp.

SATTLER, HENRY V. Parents, Children, and the Facts of Life: A Text on Sex Education for Christian Parents and for Those Concerned with Helping Parents. Paterson, N.J.: St. Anthony Guild, 1952. 270 pp.

SCHAUFFLER, GOODRICH CAPEN. Guiding Your Daughter to Confident Womanhood. Englewood Cliffs, N.J.: Prentice-Hall, 1964. 208 pp. Illus.

SCHEINFELD, AMRAM. The Basic Facts of Human Heredity. New York: Washington Square Press, 1961. 273 pp. Illus.

First edition has the title "The Human Heredity Handbook."

SCHEINFELD, AMRAM. Why You Are You. London, Eng.: Abelard-Schuman, 1958. 171 pp. Illus.

SCHIFFERES, JUSTUS JULIUS. Healthier Living: A College Textbook in Personal and Community Health. 2nd ed. New York: Wiley, 1965. 502 pp. Illus.

Earlier edition, 1954.

SCHMIEDING, ALFRED. Sex in Childhood and Youth: A Guide for Christian Parents, Teachers, and Counselors. St. Louis, Mo.: Concordia, 1953. 158 pp. Illus.

SCHNEIDERS, ALEXANDER ALOYSIUS. A Curriculum Guide on Venereal Disease, for Junior High School Teachers. Boston, Mass.: Division of Communicable and Venereal Diseases, 1968. 88 pp. Illus.

SCHOFIELD, MICHAEL GEORGE. The Sexual Behaviour of Young People. Boston, Mass.: Little, Brown, 1965. 316 pp. Illus.

Studies the sexual attitudes and knowledge of 1,800 young people in Great Britain.

SCHULZ, ESTHER D., and S. R. WILLIAMS. Family Life and Sex Education: Curriculum and Instruction. New York: Harcourt, 1969. 281 pp.

"Useful in teacher-training and curriculum planning. Discusses the philosophy underlying sex education programs, teacher preparation, and methods of program evaluation. The bulk of the book is devoted to specific suggestions for program content at every grade level in an hypothetical school."

SCHWARTZ, WILLIAM A. [L.T. Woodward]. Sex in Our Schools, a Revealing Report on the Emotional Conflicts that Beset Our Younger Generation, Derby, Conn.: Monarch, 1962. 155 pp.

SCHWARTZ, WILLIAM F. Student's Manual of Venereal Disease: Facts about Syphilis and Gonorrhea. Washington, D.C.: American Assn. of Health, Physical Education, and Recreation Dept. of the National Education Assn., 1965. 152 pp. Illus.

Intended for grades 7 and up.

SCHWEIZER, EDSEL K. The Christian Parent Teaches about Sex. Minneapolis, Minn.: Augsburg, 1966. 102 pp.

SCOTTISH EDUCATION DEPARTMENT. The Needs of Youth in These Times. A Report of the Scottish Youth Advisory Committee. Edinburgh, Scotland: H.M. Stationery Office, 1945. 97 pp.

Suggests that more direct methods of sex instruction are necessary.

SEELEY, BOUDINOT. Christian Social Hygiene: A Guide for Youth. Portland, Oreg.: Seeley, 1919. 152 pp.

SEMMENS, JAMES, and K. E. KRANTZ, eds. The Adolescent Experience: A Counseling Guide to Social and Sexual Behavior. New York: Macmillan, 1970. 384 pp. Illus.

SEMMENS, JAMES, and W. M. LAIMERS. Teen-Age Pregnancy: Including Management of Emotional and Constitutional Problems. Springfield, Ill.: Thomas, 1968. 118 pp.

Sex Education: A Guide for Parents and Educators. Washington, D.C.: 1969. 35 pp.

Published by the Family Life Division, United States Catholic Conference and National Catholic Education Association.

Sex Education and the Parent. Pref. by the Countess Limerick. London, Eng.: Gollancz, 1932. 110 pp.

Sex Education: Approach, Program, Resources for the Parish. Minneapolis, Minn.: Sacred Design, 1968. 96 pp. Illus.

Sex Education Programs for Public Schools. Cambridge, Mass.: New England School Development Council, 1968. 47 pp.

SEX INFORMATION AND EDUCATION COUNCIL OF THE UNITED STATES.
Publications not listed are available from:
SIECUS Publication Office
1855 Broadway
New York, New York 10023

SEX INFORMATION AND EDUCATION COUNCIL OF THE UNITED STATES.
Sexuality and Man. New York: Scribner, 1970. 239 pp.

SHANNON, THOMAS WASHINGTON. Guide to Sex Instruction: A Comprehensive Guide to Parents. Marietta, Ohio: Mullikin, 1913. 266 pp.

SHANNON, THOMAS WASHINGTON. Self Knowledge and Guide to Sex Instruction: Vital Facts of Life for All Ages. Marietta, Ohio: Mullikin, 1913.
629 pp.

SHAPP, MARTHA, et al. Let's Find Out about Babies. New York: Watts, 1969.
47 pp. Illus.

Grades K-3.

SHARMAN, ALBERT. From Girlhood to Womanhood. Edinburgh, Scotland:
Livingstone, 1960. 72 pp. Illus.

SHEDD, CHARLIE W. The Stork Is Dead. Waco, Tex.: Word Books, 1968.
127 pp.

Grades 9 and up.

SHEPHERD, E. R. For Girls, a Special Physiology: Being a Supplement to the
Study of General Physiology. 12th ed. New York: Fowler and Wells, 1886.
225 pp.

SHULTZ, GLADYS DENNY. It's Time You Knew. Philadelphia, Pa.: Lippincott, 1955. 221 pp. Illus.

Revised edition, 1964.

SHULTZ, GLADYS DENNY. Letters to a New Generation: For Today's Inquiring Teenage Girl. Philadelphia, Pa.: Lippincott, 1971. 226 pp.

SHULTZ, GLADYS DENNY. Letters to Jane. Rev. ed. Philadelphia, Pa.:
Lippincott, 1960. 222 pp.

British edition, 1949.

SMART, ISABELLE THOMPSON. What a Father Should Tell His Little Boy.
New York: Funk & Wagnalls, 1911. 116 pp.

SMART, ISABELLE THOMPSON. What a Mother Should Tell Her Little
Girl. New York: Funk & Wagnalls, 1911. 105 pp.

SOUTHALL, K. H. Lectures to Youth Clubs on Growing Up, Sex Relationships, and Marriage. London, Eng.: Heinemann, 1965. 56 pp. Illus.

SOUTHARD, HELEN ELIZABETH FAIRBAIRN. Planning for Sex Education.
New York: Woman's Press, 1943. 20 pp.

With particular reference to Y. W. C. A. work with junior and senior high
school students.

SOUTHARD, HELEN ELIZABETH FAIRBAIRN. Sex before Twenty: New Answers for Young People. Fwd. by Mary S. Calderone. Rev. ed. New York: Dutton, 1971. 121 pp.

Examines the importance of sex in the life of a teen-ager discussing possible outlets and fulfillments for sexual needs.

SPERBER, PERRY A. Sex and the Dinosaur. St. Louis, Mo.: Fireside Books, 1970. 205 pp.

"Where, when, why, and how was sex created? How did it develop into what it is now? This is the complete story of sexual development. We see the era of the first proteins, the first cells, the first asexual plants and animals, proto-sex, bacteria, viruses, protozoans, ending with modern man. This is a fascinating and enchanting complete sexual education in one volume."

SPERRY, LYMAN BEECHER. Confidential Talks with Young Men. Chicago, Ill.: Revell, 1893. 179 pp.

SPERRY, LYMAN BEECHER. Confidential Talks with Young Women. Chicago, Ill.: Revell, 1893. 137 pp.

SPOCK, BENJAMIN McLANE. A Teenager's Guide to Life and Love. New York: Simon and Schuster, 1970. 190 pp.

Discusses various aspects of sexual behavior and the problems encountered by young people in sexual, emotional, and social involvements.

STAHL, JOSEF, et al. Straight Answers to Children's Questions. Tr. by J. Mendelssohn. Oxford, Eng.: Religious Education Press, 1968. 89 pp.

STALL, SYLVANUS. What a Young Boy Ought to Know. Philadelphia, Pa.: Winston, 1936. 191 pp.

On the cover: "Self and Sex Series for Men." Also 1897 edition.

STEINHARDT, IRVING DAVID. Sex Talks to Girls, Twelve Years and Older. Philadelphia, Pa.: Lippincott, 1939. 221 pp.

STEINHARDT, IRVING DAVID. Ten Sex Talks to Boys (10 Years and Older). Philadelphia, Pa.: Lippincott, 1914. 187 pp.

STEINKE, PETER L. Right, Wrong, or What? St. Louis, Mo.: Concordia, 1970. 85 pp. Illus.

A compilation of the opinions of young people between the ages of fifteen and twenty on sexual ethics.

STEINMETZ, URBAN G. Let's Talk about Sex. Notre Dame, Ind.: Fides, 1968. 248 pp.

STEWART, ORA PATE. A Letter to My Son. 3rd ed. Salt Lake City, Utah: Bookcraft, 1951. 109 pp.

STOKES, JOHN HINCHMAN. Sex Education and the Schools: A Discussion of the Basis for School Programs, with an Outline of a Course in Health and Human Relations, Including Faculty and Recommendations. New York: American Social Hygiene Assn., 1945. 18 pp.

STONE, LEE ALEXANDER. It Is Sex O'Clock. Fwd. by W. A. Evans. Chicago, Ill.: Lee A. Stone, 1928. 77 pp.

STONE, LEE ALEXANDER. An Open Talk with Mothers and Fathers: Presenting Some Present-Day Problems in Social Hygiene. Kansas City, Mo.: Burton, 1920. 117 pp.

STOPES, MARIE CHARLOTTE CARMICHAEL. Sex and the Young. New York: Putnam, 1926. 248 pp.

STORER, ROBERT VIVIAN. Adolescence and Marriage: A Survey of Sex in Modern Life. London, Eng.: Lane, 1934. 325 pp.

STORER, ROBERT VIVIAN. Sex and Disease: A Scientific Contribution to Sex Education and the Control of Venereal Disease. Sydney, Australia: Butterworth, 1929. 131 pp. Illus.

"Containing information for medical practitioners, parents, social workers, teachers, students, chemists, patients, and all young men."

STOWELL, WILLIAM LELAND. Sex, for Parents and Teachers. New York: Macmillan, 1930. 204 pp.

STRAIN, FRANCES BRUCE. Being Born. 3rd ed. New York: Hawthorn, 1970. 134 pp. Illus.

Originally published in 1936. Written for children. "Scientific presentation of the facts of human reproduction, well-illustrated diagrams and photographs. Also contains complete glossary for children."

STRAIN, FRANCES BRUCE. Love at the Threshold: A Book on Dating, Romance, and Marriage. New York: Appleton-Century, 1940. 349 pp.

STRAIN, FRANCES BRUCE. New Patterns in Sex Teaching: A Guide to Answering Children's Questions on Human Reproduction. New York: Appleton-Century, 1951. 261 pp.

Also 1934 edition.

STRAIN, FRANCES BRUCE. Sex Guidance in Family Life Education: A Handbook for the Schools. New York: Macmillan, 1942. 340 pp.

STRAIN, FRANCES BRUCE. Teen Days: A Book for Boys and Girls. New York: Appleton-Century, 1946. 183 pp.

STRAIN, FRANCES BRUCE, and C. L. EGGERT, Framework for Family Life Education: A Survey of Present Day Activities in Sex Education. Washington, D.C.: American Assn. for Health, Physical Education, and Recreation, 1956. 117 pp. Illus.

SWAROOP, R. Answers to Confidential Sex Questions. Lucknow, India: Madhuri, 1959. 117 pp. Illus.

SWEDEN. BEFOLKNINGSKOMMISSIONEN. Report on the Sex Question, by the Swedish Population Commission. Tr. and ed. by Virginia Clay Hamilton. Baltimore, Md.: Williams & Wilkins, 1940. 182 pp.

Published for the National Commission on Maternal Health.

SWEDEN. SKOLOVERSTYRELSEN. Handbook on Sex Instruction in Swedish Schools. Tr. by Norman Parsons. Stockholm, Sweden: n.p., 1957. 93 pp. Illus.

SWIFT, EDITH HALE. Step by Step in Sex Education. New York: Macmillan, 1938. 207 pp.

TALMEY, BERNARD SIMON. Genesis: A Manual for the Instruction of Children in Matters Sexual, for the Use of Parents, Teachers, Physicians, and Ministers. New York: The Practitioners' Publishing Co., 1910. 194 pp. Illus.

TAME, H. W. Time to Grow Up. London, Eng.: Macmillan, 1966. 96 pp. Illus.

1960 edition under the title "Peter and Pamela Grow Up."

TAYLOR, DONALD LAVOR, comp. Human Sexual Development: Perspectives in Sex Education. Philadelphia, Pa.: Davis, 1970. 407 pp. Illus.

TAYLOR, GERALD J. Adolescent Freedom and Responsibility: A Guide to Sexual Maturity. New York: Exposition, 1965. 68 pp. Illus.

TORREY, HARRY BEAL. Biology in the Elementary Schools and Its Contribution to Sex Education. New York: American Social Hygiene Assn., 1928. 34 pp.

TREVETT, REGINALD FREDERICK. Sex and Personal Growth. Saint Meinrad, Ind.: Abbey, 1967. 191 pp.

Published in 1964 under the title "The Tree of Life: Sexuality and the Growth of Personality."

TROBISCH, WALTER. Love is a Feeling to be Learned. Baden-Baden, Germany: Trobisch, 1969. 39 pp.

TUCKER, THEODORE F. Parents' Problems and Sex Education. London, Eng.: Lane, 1948. 144 pp.

Suggests how all the essential facts can be given to children briefly and safely.

TUCKER, THEODORE F. Sex Problems and Youth. London, Eng.: Allen & Unwin, 1941. 125 pp.

"A discussion of the conditions under which sex relationships are justified, primarily intended for young men, but of equal value to young women."

TUCKER, THEODORE F., and M. POUT. Answers to Awkward Questions of Childhood. New York: Kendall, 1935. 160 pp.

English title, "Awkward Questions of Childhood." "Gives simple, truthful, unsentimental answers to questions about birth and sex. Very suitable for mothers and young teachers."

TUCKER, THEODORE F., and M. POUT. Growing and Growing Up: A Booklet for Younger Girls. London, Eng.: Delisle, 1961. 40 pp. Illus.

TUCKER, THEODORE F., and M. POUT. How You Grow: A Book for Boys. London, Eng.: The Alliance, 1946. 40 pp.

"These are companion booklets, the one for girls, the other for boys. Both books cover pregnancy, birth, growing bigger, glands, menstruation, semen, mating, development of character, factually and simply, so that they could be understood by children of 8 years or more."

TUCKER, THEODORE F., and M. POUT. Sex Education in Schools. London, Eng.: Lane, 1937. 156 pp.

An account by two pioneers, of an extensive experiment in sex education in elementary schools in Wales. Deals with the normal child and not with abnormal cases.

UNITED STATES PUBLIC ADVISORY COMMITTEE ON VENEREAL DISEASE CONTROL. Venereal Disease Education: A Report of the Special Subcommittee of the Public Advisory Committee on Venereal Disease Control. Public Health Service Publication, No. 1190. Atlanta, Ga.: U.S. Communicable Disease Center, Venereal Disease Branch, 1964. 31 pp.

UNITED STATES. PUBLIC HEALTH SERVICE. Sex Education: A Symposium for Educators. Washington, D.C.: Government Printing Office, 1927. 58 pp.

VINCENT, CLARK E., comp. Human Sexuality in Medical Education and Practice. Springfield, Ill.: Thomas, 1968. 595 pp.

VIRGINIA. DEPARTMENT OF HEALTH. The Wonderful Story of Life: A Father's Talks with His Little Son Regarding Life and Its Reproduction. Richmond, Va.: Virginia State Dept. of Health, 1951. 16 pp.

1924 edition published by U. S. Public Health Service.

WALKER, ALAN. Love, Courtship, and Marriage: One of the Addresses Given to Young People during the Mission to the Nation. 3rd ed. Melbourne, Australia: General Conference Literature and Publications Committee of the Methodist Church of Australasia, 1953. 16 pp.

WALKER, EDWIN C. What the Young Need to Know: A Primer of Sex Rationalism. New York: E.C. Walker, 1905. 50 pp.

WARE, JOHN. Hints to Young Men, on the True Relation of Sexes. Boston, Mass.: Tappan, Whittemore and Mason, 1850. 64 pp.

WARNER, HUGH COMPTON. Puzzled Parents. Sex Education Booklets, No. 1. London, Eng.: SCM Press, 1952. 27 pp. Illus.

WARNER, HUGH COMPTON. The Start of a Family: The Story of Reproduction for Boys. Sex Education Booklets, No. 4. London, Eng.: SCM Press, 1952. 15 pp. Illus.

WARNER, HUGH COMPTON. Where Did I Come From? The Story of Reproduction for Children of Eight and Over. Sex Education Booklets, No. 2. London, Eng.: S.C.M. Press, 1952. 9 pp. Illus.

WARREN, MORTIMER A. Almost Fourteen: A Book Designed to be Used by Parents In the Training of Their Sons and Daughters. New York: Dodd, 1900. 131 pp.

Subtitle varies in 1892 edition.

WEATHERALL, R. A Scheme of Work in Sex Education and Social Biology. London, Eng.: British Social Hygiene Council, 1947. 17 pp.

These suggestions and schemes have arisen out of the pioneer efforts of officials and teachers of the Nottinghamshire Education Committee. Suggested syllabuses are given for children of various ages and in various types of schools.

WEATHERHEAD, LESLIE DIXON, et al. The Mastery of Sex, through Psychology and Religion. Garden City, N.Y.: Blue Ribbon, 1947. 246 pp.

"Deals with the sex problems and difficulties of young people from a psychological as well as a Christian standpoint." Earlier edition, 1932.

WELSH, MARY M. Parent, Child and Sex. Parent Education Series, No. 4. Dayton, Ohio: Pflaum, 1970. 120 pp. Illus.

WERNER, VIVIAN L. Margaret Sanger: Woman Rebel. New York: Hawthorn, 1970. 128 pp. Ports.

"The life of one of the first women to champion birth control and family planning. Intended for grades 6 and up."

WESSLER, MARTIN F. Christian View of Sex Education: A Manual for Church Leaders. Concordia Sex Education Series, Book 6. St. Louis, Mo.: Concordia, 1967. 87 pp.

WETHERILL, GLOYD GAGE. Sharing Sex Education with Children: A Guide for Parents. San Diego, Calif.: Heath, 1951. 45 pp. Illus.

WHITE HOUSE CONFERENCE ON CHILD HEALTH AND PROTECTION, 1930. SUBCOMMITTEE ON SOCIAL HYGIENE IN SCHOOLS. Social Hygiene in Schools: Report. New York: Century, 1932. 59 pp.

WHITING, ELLIS WILBUR. The Story of Life. Chicago, Ill.: Wilcox and Follett, 1949. 48 pp.

WHITMAN, HOWARD JAY. Let's Tell the Truth about Sex. New York: Pellegrini, 1948. 242 pp.

WIER, FRANK E. Sex and the Whole Person: A Christian View. New York: Abingdon, 1962. 64 pp.

"Teacher's book." A pupils' edition is also available.

WILE, IRA SOLOMON. Sex in Terms of Personal and Social Hygiene. n.p. National Interfraternity Conference, 1941. 33 pp.

"Prepared for college students."

WILLIAMS, MARY McGEE, and I. KANE. On Becoming a Woman. New York: Dell, 1959. 159 pp.

"Written to help the adolescent girl understand the physical, psychological, and emotional changes she is experiencing as well as the social pressures she faces. Also includes a good deal of practical information and suggestions on dress, make-up, and advice concerning dating."

WILLIAMS-ELLIS, AMABEL STRACHEY. How You Began: A Child's Introduction to Biology. Pref. by J. B. S. Haldane. New York: Coward-McCann, 1929. 96 pp. Illus.

London edition, 1928.

WILLKE, JACK C., and B. WILLKE. Sex Education: The How-to for Teachers. Cincinnati, Ohio: Hiltz, 1971. 189 pp.

WILLKE, JACK C., and B. WILLKE. The Wonder of Sex: How to Teach Children. Cincinnati, Ohio: Hiltz, 1969. 132 pp.

Earlier edition, 1964. "A guide for parents and teachers."

WILLOUGHBY, RAYMOND ROYCE. Sexuality in the Second Decade. Monographs for Research in Child Development, Vol. 2, No. 3. Washington, D.C.: Society for Research in Child Development, National Research Council, 1937. 57 pp. Tables.

Reprinted by Kraus, New York, 1966.

WILLSON, ROBERT NEWTON. The Social Evil in University Life. Philadelphia, Pa.: Vir, 1905. 58 pp.

"A talk with the students of the University of Pennsylvania."

WILSON, COLIN. Sex and the Intelligent Teenager. London, Eng.: Arrow, 1966. 192 pp.

WILSON, JOHN BOYD. Logic and Sexual Morality. Baltimore, Md.: Pelican, 1965. 281 pp.

"Discussion of morality and sex education by a former professor of religion who is now head of a research group in moral education at Oxford University."

WITMER, HELEN LELAND. Attitudes of Mothers toward Sex Education. Reports of Minnesota Joint Commission on Social Hygiene, No. 1. Minneapolis, Minn.: University of Minnesota Press, 1929. 112 pp.

WITT, ELMER N. Life Can Be Sexual. Concordia Sex Education Series. St. Louis, Mo.: Concordia, 1967. 110 pp. Illus.

For grades 9-12.

WOLF, LEONARD, ed. Voices from the Love Generation. Boston, Mass.: Little, Brown, 1968. 283 pp. Illus.

WOOD, THOMAS DENISON, et al. Sex Education, A Guide for Teachers and Parents. New York: Nelson, 1937. 41 pp.

WORCESTER, ALFRED. Sex-Hygiene: What to Teach and How to Teach It. Springfield, Ill.: Thomas, 1934. 134 pp.

WRIGHT, HELENA. Sex: An Outline for Young People. 3rd ed., rev. and reset. London, Eng.: Williams and Norgate, 1956. 116 pp. Illus.

First published, 1932, under the title "What is Sex?"

WYRTZEN, JACK. Sex is Not Sinful? A Biblical View of the Sex Revolution. Grand Rapids, Mich.: Zondervan, 1970. 64 pp.

10.
SEX IN LITERATURE

CENSORSHIP

Censorship For and Against. Intro. by Harold H. Hart. New York: Hart, 1971. 255 pp.

CLOR, HARRY M., ed. Censorship and Freedom of Expression: Essays on Obscenity and the Law, by Jerome Frank and Others. Chicago, Ill.: Rand McNally, 1971. 175 pp.

"Essays prepared for a conference held under the auspices of the Public Affairs Conference Center of Kenyon College."

CLOR, HARRY M. Obscenity and Public Morality: Censorship in a Liberal Society. Chicago, Ill,: University of Chicago Press, 1969. 315 pp.

"Examines the problem of censorship in a democracy, concluding that a carefully defined and strictly limited censorship is both desirable and possible."

CRAIG, ALEC. Above All Liberties. London, Eng.: Allen & Unwin, 1942. 205 pp.

"Essays on the suppression of erotic literature in England, U. S. A., and France, and the problem of pornography. Includes a sketch of the life of Havelock Ellis."

CRAIG, ALEC. The Banned Books of England. London, Eng.: Allen & Unwin, 1937. 207 pp.

"Describes the suppression of books alleged to be immoral or obscene, and explains the law on the subject. Compares the situation in England with that in Ireland and in America. Discusses the question of reform."

CRAIG, ALEC. Suppressed Books: A History of the Conception of Literary Obscenity. Fwd. by Morris L. Ernst. Cleveland, Ohio: World, 1963. 285 pp.

"First published in London, Eng. in 1962 under the title 'The Banned Books of England and Other Countries.'"

DAVIS, PHILIP RICHARD. Obscene Literature and the Constitution. Chicago, Ill.: Philip R. Davis, 1944. 14 pp.

De GRAZIA, EDWARD. Censorship Landmarks. New York: Bowker, 1969. 657 pp.

Cites and describes law cases and trials involving censorship and obscenity dating from 1600 to the present.

DENNETT, MARY WARE. Who's Obscene? New York: Vanguard, 1930. 281 pp. Illus.

"Trial of Mrs. Mary Ware Dennett, April, 1929, in the U. S. District Court, Eastern District of New York, for the distribution through the U. S. mail of the defendant's pamphlet entitled 'The Sex Side of Life'; verdict guilty. On appeal to the U. S. Circuit Court of Appeals for the Second Circuit, the decision of the lower court was reversed."

Contents: "The Sex Side of Life" Case; Other Cases of Post Office Suppression; Shall the Post Office Censorship Power Continue?

ERNST, MORRIS LEOPOLD, and A. LINDEY. The Censor Marches On: Recent Milestones in the Administration of the Obscenity Law in the United States. New York: Da Capo, 1971. 346 pp.

Reprint of 1940 edition, published by Doubleday, New York.

ERNST, MORRIS LEOPOLD, and W. SEAGLE. To the Pure: A Study of Obscenity and the Censor. New York: Viking, 1928. 336 pp.

Reprinted by Kraus, New York in 1969.

ERNST, MORRIS LEOPOLD, and A. U. SCHWARTZ. Censorship: The Search for the Obscene. New York: Macmillan, 1964. 288 pp.

FRIEDMAN, LEON, ed. Obscenity: The Complete Oral Arguments before the Supreme Court in the Major Obscenity Cases. New York: Chelsea House, 1970.

"Deals with cases of the past two decades, from 'Roth' to 'Eros Magazine,' from the movie 'The Lovers' to private ownership in Stanley vs. Georgia."

GERBER, ALBERT BENJAMIN. Sex, Pornography, and Justice. New York: Stuart, 1965. 349 pp. Illus.
"A study of pornography and the law from the Middle Ages to the present day. Includes many excerpts from questionable material."

GILLETTE, PAUL J. An Uncensored History of Pornography. Los Angeles, Calif.: Holloway, 1965. 224 pp.

GILMORE, DONALD H. Sex, Censorship, and Pornography. San Diego, Calif.: Greenleaf, 1969. 2 vols.

Contents: Vol. 1. The Past; Vol. 2. The Present.

GINZBURG, RALPH. Eros on Trial. New York: Fact Magazine, Book Division, 1966. 62 pp. Illus.

Deals with trials of 'Eros Magazine.'

HALLIS, FREDERICK. The Law of Obscenity. London, Eng.: Harmsworth, 1932. 40 pp.

HEWITT, CECIL ROLPH. Books in the Dock. London, Eng.: Deutsch, 1969. 144 pp.

Deals with obscenity laws and censorship in Great Britain.

HOYT, OLGA, and E. P. HOYT. Censorship in America. New York: Seabury, 1970. 127 pp.

Suitable for grades 6 and up.

HYDE, HARFORD MONTGOMERY. A History of Pornography. Intro. by Morris L. Ernst. New York: Farrar, 1965. 246 pp.

First published by Heinemann, London, England in 1964. Also published by Dell, New York in 1966. "An objective examination of the problem of pornography."

KILPATRICK, JAMES JACKSON. The Smut Peddlers. Garden City, N.Y.: Doubleday, 1960. 323 pp.

"Attempts by the various states to cope with obscenity through the mails and through vendors are reviewed by the author and court decisions on questions involving the First and Fourteenth Amendments are outlined."

KLAUSLER, ALFRED P. Censorship, Obscenity, and Sex. St. Louis, Mo.: Concordia, 1967. 104 pp.

Suitable for young adults from grade 9 on.

KRONHAUSEN, EBERHARD, and P. KRONHAUSEN. Pornography and the Law: The Psychology of Erotic Realism and Pornography. 2nd ed. New York: Ballantine, 1964. 416 pp.

"Through excerpts from literature ('Lady Chatterley's Lover' to 'Candy') and excerpts from various pornographic works, the authors make a distinction between 'erotic realism' and 'hard core pornography.'" First edition, 1959.

KUH, RICHARD H. Foolish Figleaves? Pornography In and Out of Court. New York: Macmillan, 1967. 368 pp.

KUTSCHINSKY, BERL. Studies on Pornography and Sex Crimes in Denmark. Copenhagen, Denmark: DBK, 1970. 197 pp.

"A report to the U. S. Presidential Commission on Obscenity and Pornography."

KYLE-KEITH, RICHARD. The High Price of Pornography. Washington, D.C.: Public Affairs Press, 1961. 230 pp.

"Examines in detail the nature and history of pornography and immorality in Western society and the reasons for the upsurge in pornography since World War II."

LAWRENCE, DAVID HERBERT. Pornography and Obscenity. New York: Knopf, 1930. 40 pp.

LAWRENCE, DAVID HERBERT. Sex, Literature, and Censorship: Essays. Ed. by Harry T. Moore. New York: Viking, 1959. 128 pp.

Also published by Twayne, New York, in 1953 and Heinemann, London, England, in 1955. A compilation of eight essays ranging from the author's "Making Love to Music" to "Pornography and Obscenity."

McCONNELL, JOHN LITHGOW CHANDOS [John Chandos], ed. To Deprave and Corrupt: Original Studies in the Nature and Definition of Obscenity. New York: Association Press, 1962. 207 pp.

MARCUSE, LUDWIG. Obscene: The History of an Indignation. Tr. from the German by K. Gershon. New York: Fernhill, 1965. 327 pp.

Published in London, England, by MacGibbon. Tr. from "Obszön: Geschichte einer Entrüstung." Munich, 1962.

MICHELSON, PETER. The Aesthetics of Pornography. New York: Herder, 1971. 247 pp.

"The author sees contemporary pornography as a natural product of the modern moral aesthetic imagination, considering it as a poetic genre, moral rhetoric and a form of tragedy in successive chapters."

MILLER, HENRY. Obscenity and the Law of Reflection. Yonkers, N.Y.: Alicat Book Shop, 1945. 24 pp.

NEW JERSEY. COMMISSION TO STUDY OBSCENITY AND DEPRAVITY IN PUBLIC MEDIA. Public Hearing. Trenton, N.J.: State of New Jersey: 1969-1970. 5 vols. in 6.

The Obscenity Laws: A Report by the Working Party Set up by a Conference Convened by the Chairman of the Arts Council of Great Britain. Fwd. by John Montgomerie, Chairman of the Working Party. London, Eng.: Deutsch, 1969. 123 pp.

Draft of the working party's Obscene Publications (repeals and amendments) Bill: Appendix a, pp. 38-41.

The Obscenity Report: The Report to the Task Force on Pornography and Obscenity. New York: Stein and Day, 1970. 130 pp. Illus.

Deals with United States laws on obscenity.

PAUL, JAMES C., and M. L. SCHWARTZ. Federal Censorship: Obscenity in the Mail. New York: Free Press, 1961. 368 pp.

"An objective analysis by two legal experts of censorship of the U. S. mail, with suggestions for various reforms."

PERRY, JOHN W. Recent Developments in the Law of Censorship of Literature. Melbourne, Australia: Victorian Council for Civil Liberties?, 1968. 4 pp.

At the head of the title: "First Australian Convention, Councils for Civil Liberties, Sydney, 1968."

QUINN, ALEXANDER JAMES. Censorship of Obscenity: A Comparison of Canon Law and American Constitutional Law. Rome, Italy: Officium Libri-Catholic Book Agency, 1963. 134 pp.

"An excerpt of a dissertation submitted in partial fulfillment of the requirements for the degree of doctor of canon law."

At the head of the title: "Pontificia Universitas Lateranensis. Theses ad Lauream in Jure Canonico."

REMBAR, CHARLES. The End of Obscenity: The Trials of Lady Chatterley, Tropic of Cancer and Fanny Hill. Fwd. by Norman Mailer. New York: Random, 1968. 528 pp.

1969 edition published by Deutsch, London, England.

RINGEL, WILLIAM E. Obscenity Law Today. Jamaica, N.Y.: Gould, 1970. 245 pp.

ST. JOHN-STEVAS, NORMAN. Obscenity and the Law. London, Eng.: Secker, 1956. 289 pp.

SCHINDLER, GORDON WENCZEL, comp. A Report on Denmark's Legalized Pornography. Torrance, Calif.: Banner, 1969. Vol. 1. Illus.

SCHROEDER, THEODORE ALBERT. A Challenge to Sex Censors. New York: Privately printed to promote the aims of the Free Speech League, 1938. 159 pp.

SCHROEDER, THEODORE ALBERT. Legal Obscenity and Sexual Psychology. New York: n.p., 1908. 35 pp.

SCHROEDER, THEODORE ALBERT [Amicus Curiae]. May it Please the Court: One Experienced with "Obscenity" now Portrays the Difficulties that Beset the Accused and his Attorney. Mays Landing, N.J.: Sunshine Book, 1945. 35 pp.

SCHROEDER, THEODORE ALBERT. "Obscene" Literature and Constitutional Law: A Forensic Defense of Freedom of the Press. New York: Privately printed for forensic uses, 1911. 439 pp.

SCHROEDER, THEODORE ALBERT. Our Prudish Censorship Unveiled. New York: The Free Speech League, 1915. Pp. 87-99.

"Reprinted from the 'Forum,' January 1914 [i.e., 1915] Vol. 53, No. 1." Published also in the 'Pacific Medical Journal,' Vol. 53, June, 1915.

SCOTT, GEORGE RYLEY. Into Whose Hands: An Examination of Obscene Libel in Its Legal, Sociological and Literary Aspects. London, Eng.: Swan, 1945. 236 pp.

SHARP, DONALD B., comp. Commentaries on Obscenity. Metuchen, N.J.: Scarecrow, 1970. 333 pp.

Partial contents: The Intransigent Threat of Ginzburg, by D. Sharp; Obscenity Censorship, by W. B. Lockhart and R. C. McClure; Sex Censorship, by R. B. Cairns and others.

UNITED STATES CONGRESS. SENATE. COMMITTEE ON POST OFFICE AND CIVIL SERVICE. Obscenity. Hearings, Ninety-first Congress, Second Session, on S. 3220 ... September 1, 1970. Washington, D.C.: U. S. Government Printing Office, 1970. 60 pp.

UNITED STATES CONGRESS. HOUSE. COMMITTEE ON POST OFFICE AND CIVIL SERVICE. Protection of Minors and of Right of Privacy from Sexually Oriented Mail: Report, Together with Individual Views, to Accompany H. R. 15693. Washington, D.C.: U.S. Government Printing Office, 1970. 18 pp.

Ninety-first Congress, Second Session. House of Representatives. Report No. 91-908.

UNITED STATES CONGRESS. HOUSE. COMMITTEE ON THE JUDICIARY. SUBCOMMITTEE No. 3. Antiobscenity Legislation Hearings. Ninety-first Congress. Washington, D.C.: U. S. Government Printing Office, 1970. 1,222 pp.

WIDMER, ELEANOR JOAN RACKOW, comp. Freedom and Culture: Literary Censorship in the 70's. Belmont, Calif.: Wadsworth, 1970. 216 pp.

SEX IN LITERATURE AND THE ARTS

ANAND, MULK RAJ. Kama Kala: Some Notes on the Philosophical Basis of Hindu Erotic Sculpture. New York: Nagel, 1958. 45 pp.

58 pages of plates.

ATKINS, JOHN ALFRED. Sex in Literature: The Erotic Impulse in Literature. New York: Grove, 1972. 411 pp.

Previous edition published in 1970.

BACON, JACK. Eros in Art. Los Angeles, Calif.: Elysium, 1969. 49 pp. Illus.

BASLER, ROY PRENTICE. Sex, Symbolism, and Psychology in Literature. New Brunswick, N.J.: Rutgers University, 1948. 226 pp.

Includes psychological interpretations of Coleridge's "Christabel," Tennyson's "Maud," Poe's "Ligeia," six of Poe's shorter poems and tales, and Eliot's "The Love Song of Alfred Prufrock." 1967 edition, Octagon Books, New York.

BATAILLE, GEORGES. Death and Sensuality: A Study of Eroticism and Taboo. New York: Walker, 1962. 276 pp.

"A discussion of eroticism in literature, anthropology, and depth psychology." 1969 edition, Ballantine Books, New York.

BATAILLE, GEORGES. Eroticism. Tr. from the French by M. Dalwood. London, Eng.: Calder, 1962. 276 pp. Illus.

Translation of L'Érotisme published by Éditions de Minuit, Paris, 1957.

BEURDELEY, MICHEL, et al. Chinese Erotic Art. Tr. from the French by D. Imber. Rutland, Vt.: Tuttle, 1969. 209 pp. Illus.

BOWIE, THEODORE, et al. Studies in Erotic Art. Studies in Sex and Society, 3. New York: Basic Books, 1970. 395 pp. Illus.

BROWN, ARTHUR WASHBURN. Sexual Analysis of Dickens' Props. New York: Emerson, 1971. 255 pp. Illus.

Analyzes the props in Dickens' novels in a manner akin to that employed by Sigmund Freud in interpreting dreams.

BROWN, NATHANIEL HAPGOOD. Shelley's Theory of Erotic Love. New York, 1964. 405 leaves.

Thesis, Columbia University. Typescript. Also, Microfilm (positive) of typescript. Ann Arbor, Mich. University Microfilms, 1964. One reel. Publication No. 5537.

Abstracted in "Dissertation Abstracts," Vol. 24, No. 11, May 1964, p. 4676.

BRUSENDORFF, OVE, and P. HENNINGSEN. Erotica for the Millions: Love in the Movies. Los Angeles, Calif.: Book Mart, 1960. 147 pp.

British edition published by Rodney, London, 1960. Translated from the Danish by E. Gress.

BRUSENDORFF, OVE, and P. HENNINGSEN. Love's Picture Book: The History of Pleasure and Moral Indignation. Tr. by H. B. Ward. Copenhagen, Denmark: Veta, 1960-1961. 4 vols. Illus.

BUCHEN, IRVING H., comp. The Perverse Imagination: Sexuality and Literary Culture. New York: New York University Press, 1970. 296 pp.

CALVERTON, VICTOR FRANCIS. Sex Expression in Literature. New York: Boni, 1926. 337 pp.

CORY, DONALD WEBSTER [pseud.], and R. E. L. MASTERS, eds. Violation of Taboo: Incest in the Great Literature of the Past and Present. New York: Julian, 1963. 422 pp.

DAHLBERG, EDWARD. The Carnal Myth: A Search into Classical Sensuality. New York: Weybright and Talley, 1968. 121 pp.

DURGNAT, RAYMOND. Eros in the Cinema. London, Eng.: Calder, 1966. 207 pp. Illus.

Deals with sex as treated in moving pictures.

ELISOFON, ELIOT. Erotic Spirituality: The Vision of Konarak. Comment by Alan Watts. New York: Macmillan, 1971. 125 pp. Illus.

Deals with the sexual aspects of the sculptures in the Temple of Konarak in India.

ELLMANN, MARY. Thinking about Women. New York: Harcourt, 1968. 240 pp.

"A study of stereotyped attitudes about women in literature, ranging from Jane Austen to Norman Mailer and Anthony Burgess."

ENSCOE, GERALD E. Eros and the Romantics: Sexual Love as a Theme in Coleridge, Shelley and Keats. Studies in English Literature, Vol. 45. The Hague, The Netherlands: Mouton, 1967. 180 pp.

U. S. edition has label on the title page: "Humanities, New York, 1967."

EWART, ANDREW. The Great Lovers. New York: Hart, 1968. 412 pp. Illus.

First published under the title "The World's Greatest Love Affairs." Partial Contents: Antony and Cleopatra; Robert and Elizabeth Browning; William Randolph Hearst and Marion Davies; The Duke of Windsor and Wallis Simpson.

FAGAN, JIM. Sex at the Cinema. London, Eng.: Scripts, 1967. 129 pp. Illus.

FITCH, ROBERT ELLIOT. The Decline and Fall of Sex, with Some Curious Digressions on the Subject of True Love. New York: Harcourt, 1957. 114 pp.

"A study of sex, using the works of contemporary novelists and scientists, by the Dean of the Pacific School of Religion in Berkeley, California."

FORBERG, FRIEDRICH KARL. Manual of Classical Erotology (De Figuris Veneris). New York: Grove, 1966. 2 vols. in 1.

Facsimile reprint of 1884 editon. Originally published in Latin with the title "Apophoreta" as a supplement to author's edition of Antonio Becca-delli's "Hermaphroditus," 1824.

FOUCHET, MAX POL. The Erotic Sculpture of India. Tr. by B. Rhys. New York: Criterion, 1959. 95 pp. Illus.

Translation of "L'Art Amoureux des Indes," published in Lausanne, Switz-erland in 1957.

FRYER, PETER, comp. The Man of Pleasure's Companion: A Nineteenth Cen-tury Anthology of Amorous Entertainment. London, Eng.: Barker, 1968. 208 pp. Illus.

FRYER, PETER. Secrets of the British Museum. New York: Citadel, 1968. 160 pp.

First published in 1966 by Secher, London, England under the title "Private Case—Public Scandal."

GERHARD, POUL. Pornography in Fine Art from Ancient Times up to the Present. Los Angeles, Calif.: Elysium, 1969. 187 pp. Illus.

GICHNER, LAWRENCE ERNEST. Erotic Aspects of Hindu Sculpture. Washing-ton, D.C., n.p., 1949. 56 pp. Illus.

GINZBURG, RALPH. An Unhurried View of Erotica. Intro. by Theodor Reik. New York: Helmsman, 1958. 128 pp.

Reprinted by Ace, New York.

GLICKSBERG, CHARLES IRVING. The Sexual Revolution in Modern American Literature. The Hague, The Netherlands: Nijoff, 1971. 257 pp.

American edition has a pasted label on the title page, "Humanities, New York, 1971."

GOLDFARB, RUSSELL M. Sexual Repression and Victorian Literature. Lewisburg, Pa.: Bucknell University Press, 1970. 222 pp.

GROSBOIS, CHARLES. Shunga, Images of Spring: Essay on Erotic Elements in Japanese Art. New York: Nagel, 1964. 157 pp. Illus.

GULIK, ROBERT HANS Van., ed. Erotic Colour Prints of the Ming Period, with an Essay on Chinese Sex Life from the Han to the Ch'ing Dynasty, B.C. 206-A.D. 1644. Tokyo, Japan: Privately published, 1951. 3 vols. Illus.

Contents: 1. English Text. Pt. 1: Historical Survey of Erotic Literature. Pt. 2: Historical Survey of Erotic Pictures. Pt. 3: Hua-ying-chin-chen, Annotated Translation. Appendix: Chinese Terminology of Sex. 2. Chinese Texts. 3. Reprint of the Hua-ying-chin-chen.

HANSON, GILLIAN. Original Skin: Nudity and Sex in Cinema and Theatre. London, Eng.: Stacey, 1970. 192 pp. Illus.

HUGHES, DOUGLAS A., ed. Perspectives on Pornography. New York: St. Martin, 1970. 223 pp.

Professor Hughes presents fourteen essays, all previously published between 1961 and 1969 in such magazines as "Atlantic Monthly," "New Republic," and "Esquire." They summarize current views on pornography.

KNIGHT, ARTHUR, and H. ALPERT. Playboy's Sex in Cinema. Chicago, Ill.: Playboy, 1971. 144 pp. Illus.

KRONHAUSEN, EBERHARD, and P. KRONHAUSEN. More Walter: Being a Further Examination of "My Secret Life." London, Eng.: Morntide, 1970. 192 pp.

"Volume three of Walter."

KRONHAUSEN, EBERHARD, and P. KRONHAUSEN. Walter, the English Casanova: A Presentation of his Unique Memoirs "My Secret Life." London, Eng.: Polybooks, 1967. 326 pp. Illus.

"My Secret Life' was published anonymously in Amsterdam about 1890. It has also been published by Grove, New York in 1966."

KRONHAUSEN, PHYLLIS, and E. KRONHAUSEN. Erotic Art: A Survey of Erotic Fact and Fancy in the Fine Arts. New York: Grove, 1968. 312 pp. Illus.

"A special report on the authors' First International Exhibition of Erotic Art which took place in the museums of Lund, Sweden, and Aarhus, Denmark, in 1968."

KRONHAUSEN, PHYLLIS, and E. KRONHAUSEN. Erotic Art 2. New York: Grove, 1970. 270 pp. Illus.

"Companion volume to the authors' 'Erotic Art.' "

KRONHAUSEN, PHYLLIS, and E. KRONHAUSEN. Erotic Fantasies: A Study of the Sexual Imagination. New York: Grove, 1970. 429 pp.

LAL, KANWAR. The Cult of Desire. Delhi, India: Asia Press, 1966. 104 pp. Illus.

Subtitle on the cover "An Interpretation of Erotic Sculpture in India."

LAL, KANWAR. Erotic Sculpture of Khajuraho. Delhi, India: Asia Press, 1970. 75 pp. 104 plates.

Discusses the art in the Temple at Khajuraho, India.

LAWRENCE, DAVID HERBERT. Apropos of Lady Chatterley's Lover. New ed. London, Eng.: Secker, 1931. 99 pp.

LEESON, FRANCIS. Kama Shilpa: A Study of Indian Sculptures Depicting Love in Action. Bombay, India: Taraporevala, 1962. 132 pp. Illus.

LEGMAN, GERSHON. The Horn Book: Studies in Erotic Folklore and Bibliography. New Hyde Park, N.Y.: University Books, 1964. 565 pp.

LEGMAN, GERSHON. Love and Death: A Study in Censorship. New York: Hacker, 1963. 95 pp.

Reprint of 1949 edition.

LOTH, DAVID GOLDSMITH. The Erotic in Literature: A Historical Survey of Pornography as Delightful as It Is Indiscreet. New York: Messner, 1961. 256 pp.

Love and Marriage. Man through His Art, Vol. 5. Greenwich, Conn.: New York Graphic Society, 1968. 64 pp. Illus.

"Endorsed by the World Confederation of Organizations of the Teaching Professions."

McCONNELL, JOHN LITHGOW CHANDOS [John Chandos]. A Guide to Seduction: Notes Towards the Study of Eros in the Western Tradition. London, Eng.: Muller, 1953. 263 pp. Illus.

McDERMOTT, JOHN FRANCIS, and K. B. TAFT, eds. Sex in the Arts: A Symposium. New York: Harper, 1932. 328 pp.

MARCADÉ, JEAN. Eros Kalos: Essay on Erotic Elements in Greek Art. New York: Nagel, 1962. 167 pp. Illus.

MARCADÉ, JEAN. Roma Amor: Essay on Erotic Elements in Etruscan and Roman Art. New York: Nagel, 1961. 129 pp. Illus.

MARCUS, STEVEN. The Other Victorians: A Study of Sexuality and Pornography in Mid-Nineteenth-Century England. Studies in Sex and Society, 1. New York: Basic Books, 1966. 292 pp.

MASTERS, R. E. L., and E. LEA, eds. The Anti-Sex: The Belief in the Natural Inferiority of Women: Studies in Male Frustration and Sexual Conflict. New York: Julian, 1964. 492 pp.

MILNER, MICHAEL. Sex on Celluloid. New York: Macfadden, 1964. 224 pp. Illus.

Deals with sex in moving pictures.

MORDELL, ALBERT. The Erotic Motive in Literature. New rev. ed. New York: Collier, 1962. 202 pp.

First published in 1919 by Boni, New York.

NOBILE, PHILIP, comp. The New Eroticism: Theories, Vogues and Canons. New York: Random, 1970. 238 pp.

Compilation of articles about erotica.

NØRGAARD, ERIK. With Love to You: A History of the Erotic Postcard. New York: Potter, 1969. 120 pp. Illus.

British edition published by MacGibbon in London.

ORTEGA Y GASSET, JOSÉ. On Love: Aspects of a Single Theme. Tr. by T. Talbot. New York: Meridian, 1957. 204 pp.

PARTRIDGE, ERIC. Shakespeare's Bawdy: A Literary and Psychological Essay and a Comprehensive Glossary. Rev. and enl. ed. London, Eng.: Routledge, 1968. 223 pp.

New York edition published by Dutton in 1948 and 1955.

PECKHAM, MORSE. Art and Pornography: An Experiment in Explanation. Studies in Sex and Society. New York: Basic Books, 1969. 306 pp.

1971 edition, Harper, New York.

PRAZ, MARIO. The Romantic Agony. Tr. from the Italian by A. Davidson. 2nd ed. New York: Meridian, 1956. 502 pp. Illus.

Translation of "La Carne, La Morte e Il Diavolo Nella Letteratura Romantica." Reprinted by Oxford University Press, New York, 1971.

RAWSON, PHILIP S. Erotic Art of the East: The Sexual Theme in Oriental Painting and Sculpture. Intro. by Alex Comfort. New York: Putnam, 1968. 380 pp. Illus.

"Textual appraisal of human love as practiced and visualized in the Orient with nearly three-hundred illustrations, thirty-two full color, each a graphic hymn to the splendor of love throughout all its varied manifestations, and representative of every Oriental tradition from Kama Sutra and Perfumed Garden to Sino-Japanese pillow book."

READE, BRIAN, comp. Sexual Heretics: Male Homosexuality in English Literature from 1850-1900. Selected anthology with Intro. by B. Reade. New York: Coward-McCann, 1971. 459 pp.

RICHMOND, HUGH M. Shakespeare's Sexual Comedy: A Mirror for Lovers. Indianapolis, Ind.: Bobbs, 1971. 210 pp.

SAGARIN, EDWARD. The Anatomy of Dirty Words. New York: Stuart, 1962. 220 pp.

"A study of the use of obscene and taboo language and its effect on our sexual attitudes." 1969 edition published by Paperback Library, New York.

SETH, B. R. Khajuraho in Pictures. Delhi, India: Asia Press, 1970. 22 pp. Illus.

Deals with sex in Indian art. Contains 147 plates.

SOLOMON, MARGARET C. Eternal Geomater: The Sexual Universe of "Finnegans Wake." Carbondale, Ill.: Southern Illinois University Press, 1969. 164 pp. Illus.

SURIEU, ROBERT. Sarv-é Naz: An Essay on Love and the Representation of Erotic Themes in Ancient Iran. English tr. by J. Hogarth. Unknown Treasures, Vol. 6. New York: Nagel, 1967. 185 pp. Illus.

URTEAGA BALLÓN, OSCAR. Interpretation of Sexuality in the Ceramic Art of Ancient Peru: Atlas of Paleopathology. Lima, Peru: Museo de Paleo-Patología, 1968. Vol. 1. Illus.

WALDBERG, PATRICK. Eros in La Belle Epoque. Tr. by H. R. Lane. New York: Grove, 1969. 191 pp. Illus.

Translation of "Éros Modern Style," published by Pauvert, Paris in 1964.

WALKER, ALEXANDER. Sex in the Movies: The Celluloid Sacrifice. Baltimore, Md.: Penguin, 1968. 284 pp. Illus.

First published as "The Celluloid Sacrifice" by Joseph, London, England, 1966.

11.
SEX, LOVE, COURTSHIP AND MARRIAGE TECHNIQUES

AGINS, JACK. Mates and Mismates: A Manual on Sex and Marriage Relations. Los Angeles, Calif.: Economy Press, 1952. 122 pp. Illus.

ALCOTT, WILLIAM ANDRUS. The Physiology of Marriage: By an Old Physician. Boston, Mass.: Jewett, 1856. 259 pp.

ALLEN, GINA, and C. G. MARTIN. Intimacy: Sensitivity, Sex, and the Art of Love. Chicago, Ill.: Cowles, 1971. 260 pp.

ANDERSON, CARL LEONARD. Physical and Emotional Aspects of Marriage. St. Louis, Mo.: Mosby, 1953. 234 pp. Illus.

ANDREWS, ALLEN. Sex and Marriage. London, Eng.: Newnes, 1964. 128 pp. Illus.

ANTHONY, REY [pseud.]. The Housewife's Handbook on Selective Promiscuity. New York: Documentary Books, 1962. 240 pp.

Aphrodisiac Remedies and Their Therapeutic Applications in Impotence and Sexual Weakness: Compiled from Standard Works and Articles of Eminent Physicians and Surgeons Contributed to Medical Journals, by the Editorial Staff of the 'Practical Medicine.' Delhi, India: Medical Science Press, 1905(?) 82 pp.

ARDEN, THEODORE Z. A Handbook for Husbands and Wives. Rev. by Ralph G. Eckert. Family Life Library. New York: Association Press. 1965. 125 pp. Illus.

ARMITAGE, ROBERT B. Private Lessons in the Cultivation of Sex Force: The Vital Power of Attraction between the Sexes ... the Most Advanced Teachings on Physical and Spiritual Regeneration. Library of Sexual Knowledge, Vol. 3. Chicago, Ill.: Franklin, 1932. 202 pp.

ARMSTRONG, S. R. Sexual Vitality: A Key to Health and Vigor. New York: Vim, 1904. 246 pp.

"A compendium of special information gathered from the most authoritative sources."

AUSTIN, G. LOWELL. A Doctor's Talk with Maiden, Wife, and Mother. With Recommendatory Letters from Mrs. Mary A. Livermore and Miss Frances E. Willard. Boston, Mass.: Lothrop, Lee & Shepard, 1907. 240 pp.

1883 edition has the title "Perils of American Women: Or a Doctor's Talk with Maiden, Wife, and Mother."

BAILEY, DERRICK SHERWIN. The Mystery of Love and Marriage: A Study in the Theology of Sexual Relations. New York: Harper, 1952. 145 pp.

BARUCH, DOROTHY WALTER, and H. MILLER. Sex in Marriage: New Understandings. New York: Harper, 1962. 277 pp.

1970 edition published by Hart, New York.

BASU, NRIPENDRA KUMER. The Art of Love in the Orient. 2nd ed. Calcutta, India: Medical Book, 1947. 266 pp.

BAUER, BERNHARD A. Women and Love. New York: Liveright, 1971. 2 vols.

Reprint of 1949 edition.

BECKLARD, EUGENE. Physiological Mysteries and Revelations in Love, Courtship, and Marriage: An Infallible Guidebook for Married and Single Persons, in Matters of the Utmost Importance to the Human Race. Tr. from the 3rd Paris ed. by Phillip M. Howard. New York: 1842. 192 pp.

BECKLARD, EUGENE. The Physiologist: An Infallible Guide to Health and Happiness for Both Sexes ... Being Physiological Information Concerning Love, Courtship, Marriage, and Many Other Things, Which Were Treated by the Famous Philosopher Aristotle .... Tr. from the 4th Paris ed., with corrections and additions by M. Sherman Wharton. 2nd ed. Boston: 1844. 108 pp.

BELHAM, GEORGE. The Virility Diet. Oxford, Eng.: Wolfe, 1965. 202 pp.

American edition, Lyle Stuart, New York, 1965.

BENSON, HOLGER. 100 Love Positions. Photos by Thomas Bergh. Los Angeles, Calif.: Guideways, 1969. 279 pp. Illus.

In English, French, German, and Swedish.

BERG, LOUIS, and R. STREET [pseud.]. The Basis of Happy Marriage: The Art of Sexual Relationship. New and enl. ed. London, Eng.: Mayflower, 1969. 160 pp. Illus.

Earlier edition, 1955.

BERG, LOUIS, and R. STREET [pseud.]. Sex: Methods and Manners. New York: McBride, 1953. 249 pp. Illus.

Revised edition, published by Archer, New York, in 1959.

BERNE, ERIC. Sex in Human Loving. New York: Simon and Schuster, 1970. 288 pp. Illus.

"Based on the 1966 Jake Gimbel Sex Psychology Lectures under the auspices of the Committee for Arts and Lectures, University of California, San Francisco Medical Center."

Also published by Pocket Books, New York, in 1971.

BERNSTIEN, ABRAHAM EMMANUEL [Jonathan Rodney]. A Handbook of Sex Knowledge. London, Eng.: Elek, 1960. 160 pp. Illus.

BIRCHALL, ELLEN F., and N. B. GERSON. Sex and the Adult Woman. New York: Gilbert, 1965. 237 pp.

BIRD, JOSEPH W., and L. F. BIRD. The Freedom of Sexual Love. New York: Doubleday, 1967. 189 pp.

Also 1970 Doubleday reprint.

BIRD, LOIS F. How to Be a Happily Married Mistress. Garden City, N.Y.: Doubleday, 1970. 189 pp.

BLOCH, IWAN. Odoratus Sexualis. New York: Panurge, 1933. 273 pp.

At the head of the title: "A Scientific and Literary Study of Sexual Scents and Erotic Perfumes."

BOIGELOT, RENE [Pierre Dufoyer]. Building a Happy Marriage. New York: Kenedy, 1962. 160 pp.

Translation of "Pour Toi, Fiancée et Jeune Épouse."

BRAGG, PAUL CHAPPUIS. Truth about Sex. Hollywood, Calif.: National Diet & Health Assn., 1929. 267 pp.

BRENTON, MYRON. Sex and Your Heart. New York: Award, 1971. 189 pp.

Earlier edition, Coward-McCann, New York, 1968.

"A discussion of the problems of sexual activity for the man or woman who has had a heart attack."

BRIGGMAN, HAROLD. Your Husband's Love. London, Eng.: Tandem, 1967. 158 pp.

BROSS, BARBARA. The Pleasures of Love. London, Eng.: Corgi, 1968. 220 pp.

Originally published in 1967, by Rapp & Carroll, London.

BROSS, BARBARA, and J. GILBEY. Complete Sexual Fulfillment. Los Angeles, Calif.: Sherbourne, 1967. 287 pp.

Also published in 1968 in New York by New American Library.

BROWN, HELEN GURLEY. Sex and the New Single Girl. Greenwich, Conn.: Fawcett, 1972. 224 pp.

1962 edition published under the title "Sex and the Single Girl."

BROWN, HELEN GURLEY. Sex and the Office. New York: Geis, 1964. 309 pp.

BURGESS, ERNEST WATSON, and P. WALLIN. Courtship, Engagement, and Marriage. Philadelphia, Pa.: Lippincott, 1954. 444 pp.

"First published in 1953 in an educational edition entitled 'Engagement and Marriage.'"

BURNS, JOHN HENRY. Sex and the Love Impulse: An Outspoken Guide to Happy Marriage. New York: Emerson, 1936. 61 pp.

Reissue, with minor alterations, of a work written under the pseudonym, X-Ray, and published in London, 1932, with the title "Love: An Outspoken Guide to Happy Marriage."

BUTTERFIELD, OLIVER McKINLEY. Sex Life in Marriage. Fwd. by S. J. Kleegman. New York: Emerson, 1962. 192 pp. Illus.

"The present material includes all the essential features of the booklet, 'Marriage and Sexual Harmony,' first published in 1929."

CALDERONE, MARY STEICHEN, et al. Release from Sexual Tensions: Toward an Understanding of Their Causes and Effects in Marriage. New York: Random, 1960. 238 pp.

CAPRIO, FRANK SAMUEL. The Art of Sexual Lovemaking: A Guide to a Happier Sex-Love Life for Married Couples. New York: Fairview, 1967. 192 pp. Illus.

Includes a 64-page section of male/female positional photographs intended only for self-instruction by adults.

CAPRIO, FRANK SAMUEL. How to Solve Your Sex Problems with Self-Hypnosis. New York: Citadel, 1964. 223 pp.

CAPRIO, FRANK SAMUEL. The Power of Sex. New York: Citadel, 1953. 229 pp.

CAPRIO, FRANK SAMUEL. Sex and Love: A Guide to Sex Health and Love Happiness. New York: Parker, 1959. 229 pp.

CAPRIO, FRANK SAMUEL. Variations in Lovemaking: A Modern Guide to What is Normal and Abnormal in Sex. New York: Richlee, 1968. 190 pp. Illus.

"Advanced Techniques for Achieving Maximum Gratification through Sexual Experimentation with Case Histories."

CAPRIO, FRANK SAMUEL. Your Right to Sex Happiness. New York: Citadel, 1966. 154 pp.

CAULDWELL, DAVID O. Premature Ejaculation—What to Do about It. Ed. by E. Haldeman-Julius. Girard, Kans.: Haldeman-Julius, 1948. 29 pp.

"Study of a Condition Common among Men of All Ages, with Corrective Methods and Reasons Why They Work."

CAULDWELL, DAVID O. Questions and Answers on the Sex Life and Sexual Problems of Unmarried Adults: Help for the Unmarried Adults, Who Usually Find Sexual Problems Far More Poignant Than Do Those Who Are Married. Ed. by E. Haldeman-Julius. Girard, Kans.: Haldeman-Julius, 1949. 29 pp.

CHARTHAM, ROBERT. Husband and Lover: The Art of Sex for Men. Fwd. by Ralph M. Crowley. New York: New American Library, 1967. 144 pp. Illus.

CHARTHAM, ROBERT. Mainly for Wives: The Art of Sex for Women. Fwd. by Le Mon Clark. Rev. ed. New York: New American Library, 1969. 128 pp.

Earlier edition published in England in 1964 has the subtitle "Practical Love-making."

CHARTHAM, ROBERT. The Sensuous Couple. New York: Ballantine, 1971. 189 pp.

CHARTHAM, ROBERT. Sex and the Over-Fifties. Chatsworth, Calif.: Brandon, 1972. 223 pp.

Earlier edition, 1970 published by Frewin, London, England.

CHARTHAM, ROBERT. Sex for Advanced Lovers. New York: New American Library, 1970. 126 pp. Illus.

English edition, published in 1969, has the title "Sex Manners for Advanced Lovers."

CHARTHAM, ROBERT. Sex Manners for Men. London, Eng.: Frewin, 1967. 240 pp.

CHESSER, ELIZABETH MacFARLANE SLOAN. Five Phases of Love. London, Eng.: Jenkins, 1939. 252 pp.

CHESSER, EUSTACE. Love and the Married Woman. New York: New American Library, 1970. 286 pp. Illus.

Reprint of 1969 edition, published by Putnam.

English edition, published in 1968 has the title "Sex and the Married Woman."

CHESSER, EUSTACE. Love without Fear: How to Achieve Sex Happiness in Marriage. New York: New American Library, 1971. 192 pp.

"Appeared originally in England as two separate books: 'Marriage and Freedom' (1946) and 'Love without Fear' (1946)."

CHESSER, EUSTACE. Unmarried Love. New York: McKay, 1965. 177 pp.

Also published by Jarrolds, London, England, in 1965. Emphasis of this work is upon honesty rather than chastity.

CHESSER, EUSTACE. Woman and Love. New York: Citadel, 1963. 175 pp.

First published in England in 1962.

CLARK, Le MON. The Enjoyment of Love in Marriage. Rev. and updated. New York: New American Library, 1969. 160 pp.

Earlier edition published in 1949 by Bobbs-Merrill, Indianapolis, Ind., under the title "Sex and You."

CLARK, Le MON. 101 Intimate Sexual Problems Answered. New York: New American Library, 1967. 191 pp.

"Includes material previously published in 'Sexology Magazine.'"

CLARK, Le MON, and I. RUBIN, eds. 150 Sex Questions and Answers. New York: Health Publications, 1960. 128 pp. Illus.

"Contains 34 anatomical illustrations."

CLINTON, CHARLES ALEXANDER. Sex Behavior in Marriage. New York: Pioneer, 1947. 159 pp. Illus.

Reprint of 1935 edition.

COX, BETTY J. The New Sexuality: How to Satisfy Your Mate. New York: Medical Press, 1969. 258 pp. Illus.

"On the spine, 'How to Please Your Mate.'"

Also published in Britain under this title.

CULLING, LOUIS T. A Manual of Sex Magick. St. Paul, Minn.: Llewellyn, 1971. 147 pp. Illus.

CURTIS, LINDSAY R. Sensible Sex: A Guide for Newlyweds. Salt Lake City, Utah: Publishers Press, 1968. 72 pp.

"Also published under the title 'And They Shall Be One Flesh.'"

DAVENPORT, JOHN. Aphrodisiacs and Love Stimulants, with Other Chapters on the Secrets of Venus: Being the Two Books Entitled Aphrodisiacs and Anti-Aphrodisiacs, and Curiositates Eroticae Physiologiae, or, Tabooed Subjects Freely Treated. Ed. with Intro. and notes by Alan Hull Walton. London, Eng.: Champion, 1965. 254 pp. Illus.

Reprint of the two works published separately in 1869 and 1875, respectively.

DAVIES, FREDERICK DENIS [D. I. Methuen]. Bride and Groom: The Sexual Side of Marriage. London, Eng.: Ben's Books, 1966. 151 pp. Diagrams.

DAVIS, MAXINE. Sexual Responsibility in Marriage. New York: Dial, 1963. 380 pp.

DAVIS, OLIVER BENNETT. Sex, Love, Longevity, and Health. New York: Vantage, 1959. 66 pp.

DEMING, JOHN EDMUND. Sex Primer for George's Wife. New York: Pageant 1961. 32 pp.

DEUTSCH, RONALD M. The Key to Feminine Response in Marriage. New York: Random, 1968. 172 pp. Illus.

Reprinted by Ballantine, New York, in 1969.

DICKINSON, ROBERT LATOU, and L. BEAM. A Thousand Marriages: A Medical Study of Sex Adjustment. Fwd. by Havelock Ellis. Westport, Conn.: Greenwood, 1970. 482 pp. Illus.

Reprint of 1931 edition, published by Williams & Wilkins.

DOW, JOSEPH. Mated. Torrance, Calif.: Banner Books, 1968. 303 pp. Illus.

DRAKE, EMMA FRANCES ANGELL. What a Young Wife Ought to Know. Self and Sex Series for Women. Philadelphia, Pa.: Vir, 1928. 286 pp.

"New up-to-date edition."

Earlier edition, 1901.

DRAKE, EMMA FRANCES ANGELL. What a Woman of Forty-Five Ought to Know. Self and Sex Series for Women. Philadelphia, Pa.: Vir, 1928. 211 pp.

"New up-to-date edition."

Earlier edition, 1902.

DRURY, MICHAEL. Advice to a Young Wife from an Old Mistress: As Told to the Author. Garden City, N.Y.: Doubleday, 1968. 125 pp.

DUFFEY, ELIZA BISBEE. The Relations of the Sexes. New York: Wood & Holbrook, 1876. 320 pp.

Reprinted in 1898.

DUFFEY, ELIZA BISBEE. What Women Should Know: A Woman's Book about Women, Containing Practical Information for Wives and Mothers. Philadelphia, Pa.: Altemus, 1893. 320 pp.

Earlier edition, 1873.

EARL, PAUL R. The Sex Guide. Philadelphia, Pa.: Literary Division, Biological & Medical Services, 1965. 54 pp. Illus.

EDENS, B. DAVID. Sexual Understanding among Young Married Adults. Durham, N.C.: Family Life Publications, 1955. 75 pp.

EICHENLAUB, JOHN ELLIS. The Marriage Art. New York: Dell, 1962. 223 pp.

Earlier edition 1961, published by L. Stuart, New York.

EICHENLAUB, JOHN ELLIS. New Approaches to Sex in Marriage. North Hollywood, Calif.: Wilshire, 1971. 205 pp.

Reprint of 1967 edition published by Delacorte, New York.

EICHENLAUB, JOHN ELLIS. The Troubled Bed: The Obstacles to Sexual Happiness in Marriage and What You Can Do about Them. New York: Delacorte, 1971. 172 pp.

ELLIS, HAVELOCK. Sex and Marriage: Eros in Contemporary Life. Ed. with a note by John Gawsworth. New York: Random, 1952. 219 pp.

1961 edition published by Pyramid, New York.

ENGLISH, MARY. How to Marry a Married Man. New York: Pinnacle, 1971. 187 pp.

EVANS, CHARLES BENJAMIN SHAFFER. Man and Woman in Marriage. Chicago, Ill.: Bruce-Roberts, 1931. 113 pp.

"A practical book on the question of sex in marriage, dealing with the problems that actually come up in everyday married life."

EVANS, CHARLES BENJAMIN SHAFFER. Sex Practice in Marriage. Intro. by Rudolph W. Holmes. Prefatory and other notes by Norman Haire. Rev. ed. New York: Emerson, 1951. 128 pp. Illus.

"Illustrative Diagrams Based on Actual Measurements of Normal Human Beings by Robert L. Dickinson."

Published in 1931 under the title "Man and Woman in Marriage."

EVERETT, MILLARD SPENCER. The Hygiene of Marriage: A Detailed Consideration of Sex and Marriage. New rev. ed. Cleveland, Ohio: World Publishing, 1943. 232 pp.

EXNER, MAX JOSEPH. The Rational Sex Life for Men. New York: Association Press, 1918. 95 pp.

Reprint of 1914 edition.

EXNER, MAX JOSEPH. The Sexual Side of Marriage. London, Eng.: Allen & Unwin, 1964. 127 pp. Illus.

Earlier edition, 1932 by Norton, New York.

"Dr. Exner has made skilful use of the researches of such recent writers as Van de Velde, Katherine Davis, and Hamilton and Beam."

EYLES, MARGARET LEONORA. Commonsense about Sex. Completely rewritten ed. London, Eng.: Gollancz, 1949. 94 pp. Illus.

"An interesting book on sexual behaviour giving a great deal of very useful advice."

Earlier edition, 1933. 1956 edition under the title "The New Commonsense about Sex."

EYLES, MARGARET LEONORA. Sex for the Engaged. New and rev. ed. London, Eng.: Hale, 1960. 93 pp.

Earlier edition, 1952.

FARMER, ARTHUR. Love on $5 a Day: An Indispensable Handbook for Those Who Use Both Hands. Hollywood, Calif.: Stanyan, 1971. 61 pp. Illus.

FELSTEIN, IVOR. Sex and the Longer Life. London, Eng.: Lane, 1970. 143 pp.

FRANK, STANLEY BERNARD. The Sexually Active Man Past Forty. New York: Macmillan, 1968. 240 pp.

"Sex instruction for men."

FRANZBLAU, ABRAHAM NORMAN. The Road to Sexual Maturity. New York: Simon and Schuster, 1954. 279 pp.

FRYEFIELD, MAURICE P. [William Allan Brooks]. Love and Sex. New York: Morris, 1922. 80 pp.

GABOR, ZSA ZSA. How to Catch a Man, How to Keep a Man, How to Get Rid of a Man. New York: Pocket Books, 1971. 158 pp.

Earlier edition, Doubleday, 1970.

GALLOWAY, THOMAS WALTON. Love and Marriage: Foundations of Social Health. National Health Council, National Health Series, No. 8. New York: Funk & Wagnalls, 1937. 102 pp.

1924 edition has the title "Love and Marriage: Normal Sex Relations."

GAMBERS, H. Ideal Marriage: Being a Complete Solution to the Sex Difficulties Confronting a Man during His Younger Days and Married Life. Bombay, India: Brijmohan, 1951. 250 pp. Illus.

Earlier edition, 1930.

GARRITY, JOAN TERRY [J.]. The Sensuous Woman: The First How-to Book for the Female Who Yearns to Be All Woman. New York: Stuart, 1969. 192 pp.

GELDENHUYS, JOHANNES NORVAL. The Intimate Life: Or, The Christian's Sex-Life. New York: Philosophical Library, 1952. 96 pp. Illus.

"A Practical, Up-to-Date Handbook Intended for Engaged or Newly Married Christians."

Reprinted by Attic, Greenwood, S.C.

"Abridged edition of 'Marriage and Legitimate Birth Control,' published, 1943, in Johannesburg, South Africa."

GIBERT, HENRI. Love in Marriage: The Meaning and Practice of Sexual Love in Christian Marriages. Tr. from the French by André Humbert. New York: Hawthorn, 1964. 224 pp.

Translation of "La Conduite de l'Amour."

GIFFORD, EDWARD S. The Charms of Love. London, Eng.: Faber, 1962. 277 pp.

GILL, JOHN THOMAS. How to Hold Your Husband: A Frank Psychoanalysis for Happy Marriage. Philadelphia, Pa.: Dorrance, 1951. 64 pp.

GREENBLAT, BERNARD R. A Doctor's Marital Guide for Patients. Chicago, Ill.: Budlong, 1957. 88 pp. Illus.

Periodically reprinted. Latest reprint, 1969.

GREENGROSS, WENDY. Sex in the Middle Years. London, Eng.: National Marriage Guidance Council, 1969. 25 pp.

GREER, REBECCA E. Why Isn't a Nice Girl like You Married? Or, How to Get the Most out of Life While You're Single. New York: Macmillan, 1969. 184 pp.

GREGORY, LEE. Win Him If You Want Him. New York: Hillman-Curl, 1937. 144 pp.

GREGORY, STEPHAN. How to Achieve Sexual Ecstasy. London, Eng.: Running Man Press, 1969. 224 pp. Illus.

GRIFFITH, EDWARD FYFE. A Sex Guide to Happy Marriage. Intro. by Robert Latou Dickinson. New York: Emerson, 1952. 352 pp. Illus.

First published in 1935 under the title "Modern Marriage and Birth Control."

London edition, 1963 published by Methuen, under the title "Modern Marriage."

GROVES, ERNEST RUTHERFORD, et al. Sex Fulfillment in Marriage. Illus. by Robert L. Dickinson. Rev. ed. New York: Emerson, 1943. 319 pp.

Also 1971 edition.

GROVES, ERNEST RUTHERFORD, and G. H. GROVES. Sex in Marriage. 3rd ed., rev. and expanded. New York: Emerson, 1943. 224 pp. Diagrams.

"Earlier edition, Macaulay, New York, 1931."

GUYOT, JULES. A Ritual for Married Lovers. Tr. by Gertrude M. Pinchot. Baltimore, Md.: Waverly, 1931. 130 pp.

"From the French 'Breviaire de l'Amour Expérimental,' 1859."

HALL, WINFIELD SCOTT. Love and Marriage. Philadelphia, Pa.: Winston, 1929. 367 pp.

HAMILTON, ELEANOR. Partners in Love: The Modern Bride Book of Sex and Marriage. Rev. ed. South Brunswick, N.J.: Barnes, 1968. 221 pp.

Earlier edition published by Ziff-Davis in 1961.

1971 edition by Bantam, New York.

HARLEY, RICHARD. Womanhood and Marriage: A Manual of Sexual Hygiene. London, Eng.: Bentley, 1928. 146 pp.

HARPER, ROBERT ALLAN, and W. R. STOKES. 45 Levels to Sexual Understanding and Enjoyment. Englewood Cliffs, N.J.: Prentice-Hall, 1971. 231 pp.

HART, A. J. The Sex Ritual. Detroit, Mich.: Physical Information Bureau, 1918. 199 pp.

HARVEY, WILL. How to Find and Fascinate a Mistress (and Survive in Spite of It All). San Francisco, Calif.: Montgomery Street Press, 1971. 163 pp.

HASTINGS, DONALD WILSON. A Doctor Speaks on Sexual Expression in Marriage. 2nd ed. Boston, Mass.: Little, Brown, 1971. 190 pp. Illus.

Earlier edition, 1966.

HAVEMANN, ERNEST. Men, Women and Marriage. Garden City, N.Y.: Doubleday, 1962. 227 pp.

HAVIL, ANTHONY. The Making of a Woman. London, Eng.: Wales, 1969. 160 pp.

HAVIL, ANTHONY. The Technique of Sex: Towards a Better Understanding of Sexual Relationship. New ed., completely rev., enl., and reset. London, Eng.: Wales, 1968. 159 pp. Illus.

Earlier edition, 1939.

HEGELER, INGE, and S. HEGELER. The XYZ of Love: Frank Answers to Every Important Question about Sex in Today's World. New York: Crown, 1970. 248 pp. Illus.

Translation of "Spørg Inge & Sten."

Also 1970 British edition.

HENDRY, JAMES PARKER. Secrets of Love and Marriage. Ed. by Edward Podolsky. New York: Herald, 1939. 151 pp. Illus.

HERBERT, FANNY SEGALLER. Sex Lore: A Primer on Courtship, Marriage, and Parenthood. London, Eng.: Black, 1918. 147 pp. Illus.

HIRSCH, EDWIN WALTER. Modern Sex Life. Completely rev. and rewritten. New York: New American Library, 1957. 160 pp.

First published in 1947 under the title "Sex Power in Marriage, with Case Histories."

HIRSCH, EDWIN WALTER. The Power to Love. Rev. ed. London, Eng.: New English Library, 1968. 380 pp.

"First published in 1948, by Citadel, New York."

HORNSTEIN, FRANZ XAVER VON, and A. FALLER, eds. Sex, Love and Marriage: A Handbook and Guide for Catholics. Tr. by A. V. O'Brien and W. J. O'Hara. New York: Herder and Herder, 1964. 387 pp. Illus.

Translation of "Gesundes Geschlechtsleben."

HOTEP, I. M. [pseud.]. Love and Happiness: Intimate Problems of the Modern Woman. New York: Knopf, 1938. 235 pp.

HOWARD, WILLIAM LEE. Facts for the Married. 2nd ed. London, Eng.: Rider, 1931.

Earlier edition, published in 1912, by Clode, New York.

HOWARTH, VYVYAN. Secret Techniques of Erotic Delight. New York: Stuart, 1966. 319 pp. Illus.

HUNTER, THOMAS ALEXANDER ALDRED, ed. Manual of Sex and Marriage. New York: Arc Books, 1966. 272 pp. Illus.

Earlier edition, 1964.

English edition under the title "Newnes Manual of Sex and Marriage."

HUNTER, THOMAS ALEXANDER ALDRED, ed. Newnes Manual of Sex and Marriage. London, Eng.: Newnes, 1964. 272 pp. Illus.

1966 edition by Arc Books, New York.

HUTTON, ISABEL GALLOWAY EMSLIE. The Sex Technique in Marriage. Selections from the original Intro. by Ira S. Wile. Rev. and enl. ed. New York: Emerson, 1961. 191 pp. Illus.

1929 English edition has the title "The Hygiene of Marriage."

JAFFÉ, GABRIEL VIVIAN. Design for Loving. London, Eng.: Mayflower, 1965. 189 pp.

JORGENS, ANDERS. Love Positions. London, Eng.: Canova, 1969. 187 pp. Illus.

JOY, JOHN A. New Concepts in Human Sexuality and Marriage for the College Student. Dubuque, Iowa: Kendall/Hunt, 1971. 64 pp.

JOYCE, MARY ROSERA, and R. E. JOYCE. New Dynamics in Sexual Love: A Revolutionary Approach to Marriage and Celibacy. Collegeville, Minn.: St. John's University Press, 1970. 182 pp.

KALYANAMALLA. Ananga-ranga: Or The Hindu Art of Love. Cosmopoli, for the Kama Shastra Society of London and Benares, and for private circulation only, 1885. 144 pp. Illus.

"Tr. from the Sanskrit, and annotated by F. F. Arbuthnot and Sir R. F. Burton."

Reprinted by Putnam, New York, in 1969

Several other versions published.

KARSH, EDWARD. The Membrum Virile. San Francisco, Calif.: Penury Publishing Co., 1969. 520 pp. Illus.

KAUFMAN, JOSEPH J., and G. BORGESON. Man and Sex: A Practical Manual of Sexual Knowledge. New York: Simon & Schuster, 1961. 254 pp. Illus.

KELLY, GEORGE LOMBARD. Sex Manual for Those Married or about to Be. Augusta, Ga.: Southern Medical Supply Co., 1961. 91 pp. Illus.

Several earlier editions.

KISCH, ENOCH HEINRICH. The Sexual Life of Woman in Its Physiological, Pathological and Hygienic Aspects. Only authorized tr. into English from the German by Eden Paul. New York: Rebman, 1910. 686 pp. Illus.

Translation of "Das Geschlechtsleben des Weibes in Physiologischer... Beziehung."

Also abbreviated and condensed version of above work in English, published in 1916.

KITCHING, EDWIN HOWARD. Sex Problems of the Returned Veteran. Fwd. by Ernest R. Groves. New York: Emerson, 1946. 124 pp.

English title, "Sex Problems of the Returning Soldier."

KLEMER, RICHARD HUDSON, ed. Counseling in Marital and Sexual Problems: A Physician's Handbook. Baltimore, Md.: Williams & Wilkins, 1965. 309 pp

KLEMER, RICHARD H., and M. G. KLEMER. Sexual Adjustment in Marriage. Public Affairs Pamphlet, No. 397. New York: Public Affairs Pamphlets, 1966. 28 pp. Illus.

KLING, SAMUEL G., and E. B. KLING, eds. Marriage Reader: A Guide to Sex Satisfaction and Happiness in Marriage, an Anthology. New York: Vanguard, 1947. 489 pp.

KOLLE, OSWALT. The Wonder of Love. Tr. from the German. London, Eng.: Sphere, 1970. 267 pp.

"Originally published in Zurich, Switzerland, by Ferenczy in 1967."

KORDEL, LELORD. Lady, Be Loved! Cleveland, Ohio: World, 1953. 209 pp.

KRICH, ARON M., ed. Men: The Variety and Meaning of Their Sexual Experiences. Intro. by Margaret Mead. New York: Dell, 1954. 319 pp.

KRICH, ARON M., ed. Women. Intro. by Margaret Mead. New York: Dell, 1953. 317 pp. Illus.

KUPFERBERG, TULI. 1001 Ways to Make Love. New York: Grove, 1969. 354 pp. Illus.

LAMARE, NOEL. Love and Fulfilment in Woman. Tr. by Adrienne and Ralph Case. New York: Macmillan, 1957. 179 pp.

Translation of "Connaissance Sensuelle de la Femme."

LAZARSFELD, SOFIE. Woman's Experience of the Male. Intro. by Norman Haire. Rev. ed. London, Eng.: Encyclopaedic Press, 1967. 446 pp.

Translation of "Wie Die Frau Den Mann Erlebt," published in Leipzig, Germany in 1931.

Reprinted by Wehman, Hackensack, N.J., circa 1969.

LEWIN, SAMUEL AARON, and J. GILMORE. Sex after Forty. New York: Medical Research Press, 1952. 200 pp. Illus.

LEWIN, SAMUEL AARON, and J. GILMORE. Sex without Fear. 2nd ed. rev. by Norman Applezweig. New York: Medical Research Press, 1956. 125 pp. Illus.

LEWIS, BARBARA. The Sexual Power of Marijuana. New York: Wyden, 1970. 177 pp.

LIBER, BENZION. Sex Life and Marriage (Essays on Sex Life — Married Life — Pregnancy and Childbirth). New York: Rational Living, 1933. 100 pp.

LIEDERMAN, EARLE E. The Hidden Truth about Sex. New York: Earle E. Liederman, 1926. 179 pp.

LIGNAC, De. A Physical View of Man and Woman in a State of Marriage. Tr. from French. London, Eng.: Vernor and Hood, 1798. 2 vols.

Translation of "De l'Homme et de la Femme," published in France, 1772.

LISWOOD, REBECCA. First Aid for the Happy Marriage. New York: Pocket Books, 1971. 247 pp.

Earlier edition, 1965, published by Trident, New York.

LISWOOD, REBECCA. A Marriage Doctor Speaks Her Mind about Sex. New York: Dutton, 1961. 192 pp. Illus.

LONG, HARLAND WILLIAM. Sane Sex Life and Sane Sex Living: Some Things That All Sane People Ought to Know about Sex Nature and Sex Functioning, Its Place in the Economy of Life, Its Proper Training and Righteous Exercise. Authorized ed. New York: Eugenics Publishing Co., 1922. 151 pp.

Reprinted by Wehman, Hackensack, N.J., circa 1969.

LOVELL, PHILIP M. Sex and You: A Care of the Body Book. Los Angeles, Calif.: Wolfer, 1940. 158 pp.

LYNN, ENVY F. The Drama of Sex: A Manual for Married Men Only. Omaha, Neb.: E. F. Lynn, 1961. 169 pp. Illus.

M. [pseud.]. The Sensuous Man: The First How-to-Book for the Man Who Wants to Be a Great Lover. New York: Stuart, 1971. 253 pp.

McCARTNEY, JAMES LINCOLN. The Drama of Sex. New York: Stratford, 1946. 147 pp. Illus.

MACAULAY, MARY HOPE. The Art of Marriage. Rev. ed. Sherborne, Eng.: Delisle, 1970. 135 pp.

Earlier edition, 1952.

MACAULAY, MARY HOPE. Marriage for the Married: A Sequel to the Art of Marriage. Sherborne, Eng.: Delisle, 1964. 216 pp.

McCARY, JAMES LESLIE. Human Sexuality: Physiological and Psychological Factors of Sexual Behavior. Princeton, N.J.: Van Nostrand, 1967. 374 pp. Illus.

McCORKLE, LOCKE. How to Make Love. New York: Grove, 1970. 147 pp.

1971 reprint has the subtitle "The Spiritual Nature of Love."

McCOWAN, DON CABOT. Love and Life: Sex Urge and Its Consequence. Chicago, Ill.: Covici, 1928. 205 pp.

MACFADDEN, BERNARR ADOLPHUS. Man's Sex Life. New York: Macfadden, 1942. 153 pp.

Reprint of 1935 edition.

MACFADDEN, BERNARR ADOLPHUS. Womanhood and Marriage: 53 Lessons in Sex Hygiene Exclusively for Women. New York: Physical Culture Publishing Co., 1918. 21 pt.

Another edition, 1923, published by Macfadden, New York.

MACFADDEN, BERNARR ADOLPHUS. Woman's Sex Life. New York: Macfadden, 1937. 152 pp.

Reprint of 1935 edition.

MALLESON, JOAN BILLSON. Any Wife, or Any Husband: Toward a Better Understanding of Sex in Marriage. New York: Random House, 1952. 237 pp.

Earlier edition published in 1950, by Heinemann, London, Eng.

MANDAL, SANT RAM. Sex and Love. Los Angeles, Calif.: Sant Ram Mandal, 1931. 92 pp. Illus.

MANNIN, ETHEL EDITH. Practitioners of Love: Some Aspects of the Human Phenomenon. New York: Horizon, 1970. 196 pp.

MANTEGAZZA, PAOLO. The Art of Taking a Wife. London, Eng.: Gay & Bird, 1894. 310 pp.

MANTEGAZZA, PAOLO. Husband. Tr. by G. C. Charton. London, Eng.: Gay & Bird, 1904. 322 pp.

MANTEGAZZA, PAOLO. Physiology of Love. Tr. from the Italian by Herbert Alexander. Ed. with Intro. by Victor Robinson. New York: Eugenics Publishing Co., 1936. 237 pp.

Translation of "Fisiologia Dell'Amore."

1917 translation has the title "The Book of Love."

This work, with "Hygiene of Love" and "The Sexual Relations of Mankind" comprises the "Love Trilogy" ("Trilogia Dell-Amore").

MANTEGAZZA, PAOLO. The Sexual Relations of Mankind. Tr. from the latest Italian ed., as approved by the author, by Samuel Putnam. Ed. with Intro., by Victor Robinson. New York: Eugenics Publishing Co., 1935. 335 pp.

"Translation of "Gli Amori Degli Uomini."

"This work, with the two already published, the 'Physiology of Love' ('Fisiologia Dell'Amore') and the 'Hygiene of Love' ('Igiene Dell'Amore'), completes the 'Love Trilogy' ('Trilogia Dell'Amore')." — Preface to the first edition.

Other editions published under the title "Anthropological Studies of Sexual Relations of Mankind."

Marriage, Courtship and Sex: by a Surgeon. London, Eng.: Allen & Unwin, 1964. 59 pp. Illus.

MATHERS, ANN C. The Astrology Love Book. New York: New American Library, 1969. 128 pp.

Maxims and Cautions for the Ladies: Being a Complete Oeconomy for the Female Sex. In Five Parts: I. On Courtship. II. Management of a Husband. III. Intrigues and Diversions. IV. On Separation or Divorce. V. On Widowhood and Second Marriages. By a Lady. London, Eng.: W. Owen, 1752. 103 pp.

MELENDY, MARY REIS. The Ideal Woman, for Maidens — Wives — Mothers: A Book Giving Full Information on All the Mysterious and Complex Matters Pertaining to Women. A Complete Medical Guide for Women. Chicago, Ill.(?) 1911. 488 pp.

Published in 1903 under the title "Perfect Womanhood."

MELENDY, MARY REIS, and M. H. FRANK. Modern Eugenics for Men and Women: A Complete Medical Guide to a Thorough Understanding of the Principles of Health and Sex Relations. New York: Preferred Publications, 1928. 542 pp. Illus.

MESSENGER, ERNEST CHARLES. Two in One Flesh. 2nd ed. Westminster, Md.: Newman, 1956. 3 vols. in 1.

"In three parts: An Introduction to Sex and Marriage. The Mystery of Sex and Marriage. The Practice of Sex and Marriage."

Earlier edition, 1949.

MILES, HERBERT JACKSON. Sexual Happiness in Marriage: A Christian Interpretation of Sexual Adjustment in Marriage. Grand Rapids, Mich.: Zondervan, 1967. 158 pp.

MOORE, DORIS LANGLEY-LEVY. The Technique of the Love Affair. Rev. and enl. with a new chapter for the use of men. London, Eng.: Rich & Cowan, 1936. 227 pp. Illus.

Earlier edition, 1928, reprinted by Knickerbocker, New York in 1946.

MOORE, MARCIA, and M. DOUGLAS. Diet, Sex, and Yoga. Rev. ed. York, Me.: Arcane, 1970. 281 pp. Illus.

Earlier edition, 1966.

MORAN, JIM. Why Men Shouldn't Marry. New York: Stuart, 1969. 96 pp.

MORLAN, GEORGE KOLMER. Guide for Young Lovers. South Brunswick, N.J.: Barnes, 1969. 148 pp.

MUKERJEE, RADHAKAMAL. The Horizon of Marriage. Bombay, India: Asia Publishing House, 1957. 375 pp.

About marriage in Asia.

MÜLLER-LYER, FRANZ CARL. Evolution of Modern Marriage: A Sociology of Sexual Relations. Tr. by Isabella C. Wiggleworth. New York: Knopf, 1930. 248 pp.

Translation of the German work "Phasen Der Liebe" published by Langen, Munich, Germany in 1913.

NAPHEYS, GEORGE HENRY. The Transmission of Life: Counsels on the Nature and Hygiene of the Masculine Function. Philadelphia, Pa.: McKay, 1898. 362 pp.

Previous edition, 1871.

NAYLOR, PHYLLIS REYNOLDS. How to Find Your Wonderful Someone: How to Keep Him/Her If You Do; How to Survive If You Don't. Philadelphia, Pa.: Fortress, 1972. 86 pp.

Also 1971 edition.

OAKLEY, ERIC GILBERT. Astrology and Sex: How the Stars Control Your Sex Life. London, Eng.: Walton, 1965. 323 pp. Illus.

OAKLEY, ERIC GILBERT. Sane and Sensual Sex. London, Eng.: Walton, 1963. 248 pp. Illus.

O'CONNER, L. R. The Photographic Manual of Sexual Intercourse. Intro. by Albert Ellis. New York: Pent-R Books, 1969. 256 pp. Illus.

OLIVEN, JOHN F. The Doctor Talks to Newlyweds. Philadelphia, Pa.: Lippincott, 1966. 32 pp. Illus.

A manual for doctors.

OLIVEN, JOHN F. Sexual Hygiene and Pathology. Philadelphia, Pa.: Lippincott, 1965. 621 pp.

Previous edition, 1955.

O'RELLY, EDWARD. Sexercises, Isometric and Isotonic. New York: Crown, 1967. 130 pp. Illus.

Also 1968 reprint.

PAGAN, SANCHA [pseud.]. One Woman vs. Kinsey. New York: Pageant, 1963. 121 pp.

The Picture Book of Sexual Love. New York: Cybertype, 1969. 320 pp. Illus.

PODOLSKY, EDWARD. The Modern Sex Manual. New York: Cadillac, 1942. 204 pp.

PODOLSKY, EDWARD. Sex Technique for Husband and Wife. New York: Cadillac, 1960. 158 pp. Illus.

Previous edition, 1949.

PODOLSKY, EDWARD. Sex Today in Wedded Life. Doctor's Confidential Advice, by Winfield Scott Pugh. New York: Simon, 1947. 239 pp. Illus.

Previous edition, 1942.

RAINER, JEROME, and J. RAINER. Sexual Adventure in Marriage. New York: Messner, 1965. 317 pp.

1966 edition published by Blond, London, England.

RAINER, JEROME, and J. RAINER. Sexual Pleasure in Marriage. Rev. ed. New York: Simon and Schuster, 1969. 187 pp.

1959 edition published by Messner, New York.

RAYNER, CLAIRE. People in Love: A Modern Guide to Sex in Marriage. London, Eng.: Hamlyn, 1968. 160 pp. Illus.

1969 edition published by Tri-Ocean in San Francisco, Calif.

REUBEN, DAVID R. Any Woman Can! Love and Sexual Fulfillment for the Single, Widowed, Divorced...and Married. New York: McKay, 1971. 364 pp.

REUBEN, DAVID R. Everything You Always Wanted to Know about Sex, but Were Afraid to Ask. New York: McKay, 1969. 342 pp.

Reprinted in 1971 by Bantam, New York.

ROBIE, WALTER FRANKLIN. The Art of Love. Rational Sex Series. North Hollywood, Calif.: Brandon, 1966. 386 pp.

1921 edition published in Boston by Badger.

ROBIE, WALTER FRANKLIN. Rational Sex Ethics: A Physiological and Psychological Study of the Sex Lives of Normal Men and Women, with Suggestions for a Rational Sex Hygiene. Boston, Mass.: Badger, 1916. 356 pp.

Several other versions published.

ROBIE, WALTER FRANKLIN. Sex and Life: What the Experienced Should Teach and What the Inexperienced Should Learn. Ithaca, N.Y.: Rational Life, 1924. 424 pp.

Also 1920 edition published by Badger in Boston.

ROBIE, WALTER FRANKLIN. Sex Histories. North Hollywood, Calif.: Brandon, 1966. 303 pp.

Previous edition 1921.

Also reprinted in 1970 under two different titles: "Joys of Sex" and "Pleasure of Love."

ROBINSON, CONSTANCE. Passion and Marriage. New York: Morehouse, 1965. 86 pp.

ROBINSON, WILLIAM JOSEPHUS. America's Sex and Marriage Problems: Based on Thirty Years Practice and Study. New York: Eugenics Publishing Co., 1928. 475 pp.

ROBINSON, WILLIAM JOSEPHUS. Woman: Her Sex and Love Life. New York: Eugenics Publishing Co., 1938. 344 pp.

"Including a 32-page Supplement of a Portfolio of Illustrations Containing a Picture-story of Woman's Sexual Life."

Also 1917 edition.

ROGET, MARIE, and H. ROGET. Swingers Guide for the Single Girl: Key to the New Morality. Los Angeles, Calif.: Holloway House, 1968. 224 pp.

ROTHENBERG, ROBERT E., ed. The Doctors' Premarital Medical Adviser. Written and prepared by Medbook Publications. New York: Grosset & Dunlap, 1969. 244 pp. Illus.

Reprinted in 1971.

ROUGE, JOHN. Love or Marriage? A Frank, Honest and Logical Review of Past, Present and Future Psychological and Physical Conditions Relating to an Ever Present and Particularly Fascinating Subject. New York: Peter Eckler, 1915. 128 pp.

ROUGEMONT, DENIS De. Love in the Western World. Tr. by M. Belgion. New York: Pantheon, 1956. 336 pp.

British edition has the title "Passion and Society."

Previously published in 1940.

Translation of "L'Amour et l'Occident."

ROWAN, ROBERT L. Horizontal Exercises. New York: Award Books, 1970. 173 pp.

"A doctor's long-tested program on how you can reach your sexual peak in your middle and later years."

RUBIN, ISADORE. Sexual Life after Sixty. New York: Basic, 1965. 274 pp.

RUBIN, ISADORE. Sexual Life in the Later Years. New York: Sex Information and Education Council of the U.S., 1970. 33 pp.

RUTGERS, JOHANNES. How to Attain and Practice the Ideal Sex Life: Ideal Sex and Love Relations for Every Married Man and Woman.... New York: Falstaff, 1937. 397 pp.

Translation by N. Haire of "Das Sexualleben in Seiner Biologischen Bedeutung."

SADLER, WILLIAM SAMUEL. Courtship and Love. New York: Macmillan, 1952. 209 pp. Illus.

SADLER, WILLIAM SAMUEL. Living a Sane Sex Life. New York: Perma Giants, 1950. 344 pp. Illus.

Also 1938 edition.

SADLER, WILLIAM SAMUEL, and L. K. SADLER. Sex Life, Before and After Marriage. Chicago, Ill.: American Publishers, 1938. 2 vols.

Vol. 1: Sexual Hygiene. Vol. 2: Marriage.

ST. JOHN, FREDERICK. Sex and Love As It Is Written, Illustrated with Emotional and Other Charts by Which the Sex and Love Natures of Men and Women May be Determined. Kansas City, Mo.: American Institute of Grapho Analysis, 1937. 150 pp. Diagrams.

SALTMAN, JULES, comp. Sex, Love, and Marriage: by David R. Mace, et al. New York: Grosset & Dunlap, 1968. 160 pp.

"Edited for the Public Affairs Committee."

SALTUS, EDGAR EVERTSON. Historia Amoris: A History of Love, Ancient and Modern. New York: AMS Press, 1970. 278 pp.

Reprint of the 1922 edition.

1906 edition published by Kennerley in New York.

SANGER, MARGARET. Happiness in Marriage. Elmsford, N.Y.: Maxwell Reprint, 1969. 231 pp.

1926 edition published by Brentano, New York.

SARGENT, WILLIAM EWART. Sex, Its Meaning and Purpose. The Teach Yourself Books. New York: Roy, 1956. 154 pp. Illus.

Also 1951 British edition.

SCHINDLER, GORDON WENCZEL [Porter Davis]. Handbook for Husbands and Wives: A Complete Guide for Sexual Adjustment in Marriage. El Segundo, Calif.: Banner, 1949. 127 pp.

Several reprints.

SCHOENFELD, EUGENE. Dear Doctor Hip Pocrates: Advice Your Family Doctor Never Gave You. New York: Grove, 1968. 112 pp.

Also 1970 edition.

SCHWAB, LAURENCE, and K. MARKHAM. Stop It! I Love It! Woodbridge, Conn.: Apollo, 1971. 215 pp.

SCHWARTZ, WILLIAM A. Sophisticated Sex Techniques in Marriage. New York: Lancer, 1967. 157 pp.

SCHWARTZ, WILLIAM ALEXANDER [L. T. Woodward]. You and Your Sex Life. Derby, Conn.: Monarch, 1963. 157 pp.

SCOTT, GEORGE RYLEY. New Art of Love: A Practical Guide for the Married and Those about to Marry. Library of Modern Sex Knowledge, No. 2. 3rd ed. London, Eng.: Torchstream, 1946. 96 pp.

SCOTT, GEORGE RYLEY. Sex in Married Life: A Practical Handbook for Men and Women. Complete rev. and enl. ed. London, Eng.: Luxor, 1965. 128 pp. Illus.

Also 1946 edition.

SCOTT, JAMES FOSTER. The Sexual Instinct: Its Use and Dangers as Affecting Heredity and Morals; Essentials to the Welfare of the Individual and the Future of the Race. 3rd ed. rev. and enl. Chicago, Ill.: Login Brothers, 1930. 473 pp.

Issued also under the title "Heredity and Morals...."

SEGAL, HAROLD S. Secret of Love and Happy Marriage. Boston, Mass.: Branden, 1969. 247 pp.

SEGALL, JAMES LEO. Sex Life in America: Its Problems and Their Solution. New York: Marks, 1934. 288 pp.

SHA, KOKKEN. A Happier Sex Life: Study in Modern Japanese Sexual Habits. Tr. by Robert Y. Tatsuoka and Sen Kozuka. Tokyo, Japan: Ikeda Shoten, 1964. 188 pp. Illus.

This famed Japanese picture book contains over 210 sexual positions illustrated by over 400 photographs.

Translation of "Seiseikatsu no Chie."

SIMONS, GEOFFREY LESLIE. Sex in the Modern World. London, Eng.: New English Library, 1970. 220 pp.

SMITH, JOHN ANTHONY JAMES. Sexual Fulfilment. London, Eng.: Marsland, 1970. 107 pp.

SMYTH, MARGARET. Sex in Marriage. Family Doctor Booklet. London, Eng.: British Medical Assn., 1966. 30 pp.

SPOTNITZ, HYMAN, and L. FREEMAN. The Wandering Husband: Love, Sex and the Married Man. Englewood Cliffs, N.J.: Prentice-Hall, 1964. 224 pp.

STEIN, JOSEPH. Maturity in Sex and Marriage. New York: Coward-McCann, 1963. 318 pp. Illus.

STEPHENSON, ELI FRANK. Love in the Future. Ed. by W. J. R. New York: Eugenics Publishing Co., 1929. 90 pp.

STERN, EDITH MENDEL. Men Are Clumsy Lovers. New York: Vanguard, 1934. 95 pp.

STOKES, WALTER RAYMOND. Married Love in Today's World. New York: Citadel, 1962. 157 pp.

STONE, CHESTER TILTON. Sexual Power. New York: Appleton-Century, 1937. 172 pp.

Half-title: Appleton Popular Health Series.

STONE, HANNAH MAYER. Drs. Hannah and Abraham Stone's A Marriage Manual: the Famous Guide to Sex and Marriage Recommended by Doctors and Educators. New ed., rev. by Gloria Stone Aitken and Aquiles J. Sobrero. New York: Simon and Schuster, 1968. 316 pp. Illus.

Earlier edition published in 1935, under the title "A Marriage Manual."

STOPES, MARIE CHARLOTTE CARMICHAEL. Enduring Passion: Further New Contributions to the Solution of Sex Difficulties, Being the Continuation of Married Love. Pref. by Morris L. Ernst. 4th ed. New York: Putnam, 1931. 181 pp.

STOPES, MARIE CHARLOTTE CARMICHAEL. Married Love: A New Contribution to the Solution of Sex Difficulties. New York: Putnam, 1939. 177 pp.

Also 1918 edition.

STREETER, HERBERT A. Help for Marital Hang-ups. Anderson, Ind.: Warner, 1970. 127 pp.

SWAROOP, R., ed. Increase Your Sexual Efficiency. Lucknow, India: Madhuri, 1960. 101 pp. Illus.

TALMEY, BERNARD SIMON. Love: A Treatise on the Science of Sex-attraction. 5th ed., newly rev. and enl. New York: Eugenics Publishing Co., 1933. 500 pp. Illus.

"For the physicians and students of medical jurisprudence."

Earlier edition, 1915.

TAMBA, YASUYORI. The Tao of Sex: An Annotated Translation of the Twenty-eighth Section of the Essence of Medical Prescriptions (Ishimpō), by Akira Ishihara and Howard S. Levy. Yokohama, Japan, 1968. 241 pp. Illus.

Reprint of original Chinese text (Ansei edition, 1948).

TEEHAN, MICHAEL FABIAN. Mirror of Life. Topeka, Kans.: Standard, 1925. 404 pp. Illus.

TENENBAUM, JOSEPH LEIB. Sex Happiness in Marriage: Up-to-date Answers to the Riddle of Sex. New York: Nelson-Hall, 1945. 362 pp.

First published under the title "The Riddle of Sex; the Medical and Social Aspects of Sex, Love and Marriage."

THORNTON, HENRY, and F. THORNTON. How to Achieve Sex Happiness in Marriage. New York: Vanguard, 1939. 155 pp.

1949 edition published by Citadel.

THORP, RODERICK, and R. BLAKE. Wives: An Investigation. New York: Evans, 1971. 356 pp.

TOFT, MOGENS. Sexual Techniques: An Illustrated Guide. London, Eng.: Souvenir, 1969. 143 pp. Illus.

Translation of "Tegninger af mie luf."

TRAINER, JOSEPH BYRON. Physiologic Foundations for Marriage Counseling. Saint Louis, Mo.: Mosby, 1965. 287 pp. Illus.

TREVOR, CHARLES T. Sex and the Athlete. 2nd ed. London, Eng.: Mitre, 1945. 40 pp. Illus.

TRIDON, ANDRE. Sex Happiness. New York: Rensselaer, 1938. 250 pp.

TRIMBOS, CORNELIS JOHANNES BAPTIST JOSEPH. Married or Single?
Healthy Attitudes towards Love and Sex. London, Eng.: Chapman, 1964.
224 pp. Illus.

Translation of "Gehuwd & ongehuwd."

TRIMMER, ERIC JAMES. Femina: What Every Woman Should Know about
Her Body. New York: Stein & Day, 1967. 191 pp.

"Deals with the female reproductive system, its functions and malfunc-
tions."

Also 1966 London edition.

TURNER, JOHN, VICAR OF GREENWICH. A Discourse on Fornication
Shewing the Greatness of That Sin: and Examining the Excuses Pleaded for
It, from the Examples of Antient Times; to Which Is Added an Appendix
Concerning Concubinage; As Also a Remark on Mr. Butler's Explication of
Hebrews xiii, 4, in His Late Book on That Subject. London, Eng.: Wyat,
1698. 62 pp.

TWEEDIE, DONALD F. Of Sex and Saints. Grand Rapids, Mich.: Baker,
1965. 73 pp. Illus.

TYRER, ALFRED H. Sex Satisfaction and Happy Marriage: A Practical Handbook of Sexual Information. Fwd. by R. L. Dickinson. 2nd rev. ed. New
York: Emerson, 1951. 160 pp.

UMAR IBN MUHAMMAD, AL-NAFZAWI. The Perfumed Garden of the
Shaykh Nefzawi. Tr. by R. F. Burton. New York: Gramercy, 1964. 271 pp.

The classic sixteenth-century Arabian treatise on physical love.

Several translations.

VALENSIN, GEORGES. The French Art of Sexual Love. Tr. from the French
by Lowell Bair. New York: Berkley, 1966. 221 pp.

VATSYAYANA, called MALLANAGA. The Kama Sutra: The Classic Hindu
Treatise on Love and Social Conduct. Tr. by R. F. Burton. Fwd. by
Santha Rama Rau. New York: Dutton, 1962. 252 pp.

Translation from Sanskrit text.

Several other versions.

VELDE, THEODOR HENDRIK Van De. Ideal Marriage: Its Physiology and
Technique. Tr. by Stella Browne. Rev. ed. New York: Random, 1968.

Earlier edition, 1929.

"The book is the first part of a trilogy."

"Deals with the physiology of conjugal life and sex technique."

VELDE, THEODOR HENDRIK Van De. Sex Efficiency through Exercises:
Special Physical Culture for Women, with 480 Cinematographic and 54
Full-page Illustrations. London, Eng.: Heinemann, 1933. 163 pp.

VELDE, THEODOR HENDRIK Van De. Sexual Tensions in Marriage;
Their Origin, Prevention and Treatment. Tr. by Hamilton Marr. New
York: Random, 1948. 330 pp.

"The second volume of ... (the author's) trilogy on married happiness."

"First published in English under the title 'Sex Hostility in Marriage.'"

VINCK, JOSE De. The Virtue of Sex. New York: Hawthorn, 1966. 255 pp.

VINCK, JOSE De, and J. T. CATOIR. The Challenge of Love: Practical Advice for Married Couples and Those Planning Marriage. New York: Hawthorn, 1969. 241 pp. Illus.

Volin, Michael, and N. PHELAN. Sex and Yoga. London, Eng.: Pelham, 1967. 175 pp. Illus.

Von URBAN, RUDOLF. Sex Perfection and Marital Happiness. New York: Dial, 1949. 263 pp.

WALKER, KENNETH MacFARLANE. Marriage, Sex, and Happiness: A Frank and Practical Guide to Harmony and Satisfaction in Conjugal Life. New York: Arco, 1965. 301 pp.

Reprint of 1963 edition, published by Odham, London, Eng.

WALLIS, JACK HAROLD. The Challenge of Middle Age. London, Eng.: Routledge, 1962. 147 pp.

WALTON, ALAN HULL. Stimulants for Love: A Quest for Virility. London, Eng.: Tandem, 1966. 255 pp.

Originally published in London in 1956 with the title "Love Recipes Old and New"; issued in 1958 in New York with the title "Aphrodisiacs: From Legend to Prescription." The present edition is an expansion and revision of the original.

WARREN, JOY. How to Be an Erotic Woman. New York: Award Books, 1971.

WARREN, ROGER. How to Be an Erotic Man. New York: Award Books, 1971. 152 pp.

WECK-ERLEN, L. Van Der. The Golden Book of Love: 600 Coital Positions for Human Sexual Proficiency. Intro. by Steve Hult. Portrayed by V. Incio. New York: Land's End Press, 1971. 1 vol. Unpaged. Illus.

Translation of "Das Goldene Buch der Liebe."

WEDECK, HARRY EZEKIEL. Love Potions through the Ages. London, Eng.: Vision, 1963. 336 pp. Illus.

WEINBERGER, SAMUEL S. Sex, Love and Marriage. New York: The Natural Health Assn., 1932. 124 pp.

WILLIAMS, LANE. Love Versus Marriage. Hollywood, Calif.: Academy, 1955. 144 pp.

WOLBARST, ABRAHAM LEO. Generations of Adam; Healthy Sex Life and How to Achieve It. New York: Stokes, 1930. 354 pp.

1934 edition published by Grosset under the title "Healthy Sex Life."

WOLF, HEINRICH FRANZ. Male Approach. Pref. by Alfred Adler. New York: Covici, Friede, 1929. 220 pp.

WORSLEY, ALLAN. Woman and Happy Marriage: A Psychological Study of the Feminine Mind in Relation to Marriage and the Problems of Everyday Life. Birmingham, Eng.: Cornish, 1949. 318 pp.

"Gives very practical and useful advice for men and women, on sexual relations and their psychological and temperamental aspects, before and during marriage."

WRAGE, KARL HORST. Man and Woman: The Basics of Sex and Marriage. Tr. by Stanley S. B. Gilder. Philadelphia, Pa.: Fortress, 1969. 259 pp. Illus.

Subtitle of London edition, 1969, is "The Basis of Their Relationship."

WRIGHT, HELENA. The Sex Factor in Marriage: A Book for Those Who Are or Are about to Be Married. 4th ed. London, Eng.: Williams & Norgate, 1946. 96 pp.

"Gives detailed information about the ways in which the physical intimacies of married life may be successfully managed."

1931 edition published by Vanguard, New York.

WRIGHT, HELENA. Sex Fulfilment in Married Women: A Sequel to "The Sex Factor in Marriage." London, Eng.: Williams & Norgate, 1947. 96 pp.

"Suitable for the reader who takes a specialized interest in the subject of sex. An attempt is made to discuss the relative functions of the clitoris and the vagina in the sexual act."

WYDEN, PETER, and B. WYDEN. Inside the Sex Clinic. New York: World, 1971. 244 pp.

Also published by New American Library, New York, in 1971.

WYLIE, BURDETT, ed. Sex and Marriage: A Guide to Marital Relations. Cleveland, Ohio: World, 1949. 348 pp. Illus.

"This book consists of extracts from the works of fifteen well-known sexologists, including Havelock Ellis, Wilhelm Stekel, Eustace Chesser, and Kenneth Walker, covering various phases of sex life. A comprehensive manual for men and women about to enter marriage."

12.
SEX REPRODUCTION

ARTIFICIAL INSEMINATION

Artificial Human Insemination. Report of a Conference held in London under the Auspices of the Public Morality Council. London, Eng.: Heinemann, 1947. 81 pp.

"A verbatim report of a number of speakers representing different professions and diverse points of view. The purpose of the Conference was not to reach conclusions, but to uncover the implications of the practice."

BEAL, OSCAR R. The Degeneration of Man. New York: Exposition, 1969. 126 pp.

CHURCH OF ENGLAND. ARCHBISHOP OF CANTERBURY'S COMMISSION ON ARTIFICIAL HUMAN INSEMINATION. Artificial Human Insemination, The Report. London, Eng.: S.P.C.K., 1948. 70 pp.

DAVIS, HENRY. Artificial Human Fecundation. New York: Sheed, 1951. 20 pp.

FINEGOLD, WILFRED J. Artificial Insemination. Fwd. by Alan F. Guttmacher. Springfield, Ill.: Thomas, 1964. 121 pp.

FRANCOEUR, ROBERT T. Utopian Motherhood: New Trends in Human Reproduction. Garden City, N.Y.: Doubleday, 1970. 278 pp.

GLOVER, WILLIAM KEVIN. Artificial Insemination among Human Beings: Medical, Legal and Moral Aspects. Catholic University of America. Studies in Sacred Theology, Series 2, No. 15. Washington, D.C.: Catholic University of America, 1948. 177 pp.

Thesis, Catholic University of America.

ROHLEDER, HERMANN. Test Tube Babies: A History of the Artificial Impregnation of Human Beings. New York: Panurge, 1934. 248 pp.

"Including a detailed account of its technique, together with personal experiences, clinical cases, a review of its literature, and the medical and legal aspects involved."

SCHELLEN, ANTONIUS MARTINUS CORNELIS MARIA. Artificial Insemination in the Human. New York: Elsevier, 1957. 420 pp. Illus.

"Translation by M. E. Hollander of 'De Artificiële Inseminatie bij de Mens.'"

SULLIVAN, JOSEPH T. Human Artificial Insemination According to Right Reason. Steubenville(?), Ohio: n.p., 1959. 117 pp.

Thesis, Pontificium Athenaeum Angelicum, Rome.

BIRTH CONTROL
AND CONTRACEPTION

ABHAYARATNE, O. E. R., and C. H. S. JAYEWARDENE. Family Planning in Ceylon. Colombo, Ceylon: Colombo Apothecaries, 1968. 188 pp.

AMERICAN ASSOCIATION OF PLANNED PARENTHOOD PHYSICIANS. Proceedings of the Annual Meeting. Cambridge, Mass.: Schenkman, 1964- Vol. 1- . Illus.

Each volume also has a distinctive title.

AMERICAN PUBLIC HEALTH ASSOCIATION. PROGRAM AREA COMMITTEE ON POPULATION AND PUBLIC HEALTH. Family Planning: A Guide for State and Local Agencies. New York: American Public Health Assn., 1968. 154 pp. Illus.

ASIA FAMILY PLANNING ASSOCIATION. Family Planning in Japan. Tokyo, Japan: Asia Family Planning Assn., 1961. 44 pp. Illus.

AUSTIN, COLIN RUSSELL, and J. S. PERRY, eds. A Symposium on Agents Affecting Fertility. Boston, Mass.: Little, 1965. 319 pp. Illus.

At the head of the title: Biological Council, Co-ordinating Committee for Symposium on Drug Action.

BANKS, JOSEPH AMBROSE. Prosperity and Parenthood: A Study of Family Planning among the Victorian Middle Classes. London, Eng.: Routledge, 1965. 240 pp.

BANKS, JOSEPH AMBROSE, and O. BANKS. Feminism and Family Planning in Victorian England. Studies in Sociology. New York: Schocken, 1964. 142 pp.

"List of relevant books and pamphlets on the woman question, published in Great Britain in the period 1792 to 1880."

BARRETT, MARY. Birth Regulation: The Non-Contraceptive Method of Family Planning. London, Eng.: Longmans, 1965. 53 pp. Illus.

BATES, MARSTON. The Prevalence of People. New York: Scribner, 1962. 283 pp

Previous edition published in 1955.

BEARD, ROLAND MAURICE CHARLES GEORGES. Contraception without the Pill: An Authoritative Guide to Non-Oral Contraceptive Techniques Written for Australian Conditions and Including a Chapter on the Sexual Difficulties Which Normal People May Encounter. Melbourne, Australia: Sun, 1970. 43 pp. Illus.

BEHRMAN, SAMUEL J., et al. Fertility and Family Planning: A World View. Ann Arbor, Mich.: University of Michigan Press, 1969. 503 pp.

"Papers from a conference held November 15-17, 1967, as part of the University of Michigan's sesquicentennial observance."

BENDER, STEPHEN J., and S. FELLERS. Contraception: By Choice or by Chance. Contemporary Topics in Health Science Series. Dubuque, Iowa: Brown, 1972. 60 pp. Illus.

Previously published in 1971.

BENJAMIN, ANNETTE FRANCIS. New Facts of Life for Women. Englewood Cliffs, N.J.: Prentice-Hall, 1969. 243 pp.

BERELSON, BERNARD. Family Planning Programs: An International Survey. New York: Basic, 1969. 310 pp.

"Originated as a series of talks in the Forum program of the Voice of America."

BERRILL, NORMAN JOHN. The Person in the Womb. New York: Dodd, 1968. 179 pp.

BEST, WINFIELD, and F. S. JAFFE, eds. Simple Methods of Contraception: An Assessment of Their Medical, Moral and Social Implications. New York: Planned Parenthood Federation of America, 1958. 63 pp. Illus.

Based on a symposium held in New York, October 15, 1957.

BLOOM, PHILIP M. Modern Contraception. London, Eng.: Delisle, 1968. 48 pp. Illus.

"A short but comprehensive survey explaining clearly, in every-day language, which contraceptives are to be recommended and why. Deals also with marriage preparation, breast feeding, and the 'change of life' in relation to contraception." Several editions published since 1949.

BOGUE, DONALD JOSEPH, et al. How to Improve Written Communication for Birth Control. Chicago, Ill.: Community and Family Study Center, University of Chicago Press, 1963. 90 pp.

BROMLEY, DOROTHY DUNBAR. Catholics and Birth Control: Contemporary Views on Doctrine. Fwd. by Richard Cardinal Cushing. New York: Devin, 1965. 207 pp.

BUMPASS, LARRY L., and C. F. WESTOFF. The Later Years of Childbearing. Princeton, N.J.: Princeton University Press, 1970. 168 pp.

CALDERONE, MARY STEICHEN. Sexual Health and Family Planning. New York: American Public Health Assn., 1968. 36 pp.

CALDERONE, MARY STEICHEN, ed. The Manual of Family Planning and Contraceptive Practice. Baltimore, Md.: Williams & Wilkins, 1970. 475 pp.

"A comprehensive reference text book for professionals in the family planning field. The second and greatly expanded edition contains several sections on the relationship of sexual attitudes and family planning behavior. First edition (with mostly different contributions) published in 1964 under the title 'Manual of Contraceptive Practice.'"

CALDWELL, JOHN CHARLES. Population Growth and Family Change in Africa: the New Urban Elite in Ghana. New York: Humanities, 1969. 222 pp.

Earlier edition published in London, England by Hurst, 1968.

CALLAHAN, DANIEL J. Ethics and Population Limitation. Occasional Papers of the Population Council. New York: Population Council, 1971. 45 pp.

CALLAHAN, SIDNEY CORNELIA. Christian Family Planning and Sex Education. Notre Dame, Ind.: Ave Maria, 1969. 72 pp. Illus.

CARR, JO, and I. SORLEY. Intentional Family. Nashville, Tenn.: Abingdon, 1971. 144 pp.

CARTWRIGHT, ANN. Parents and Family Planning Services. New York: Atherton, 1970. 293 pp. Illus.

CATHOLIC CHURCH. POPE PAULUS VI. On the Regulation of Birth. Humana Vitae Encyclical Letter, Pope Paul VI, July 25, 1968. Washington, D.C.: United States Catholic Conference, 1968. 21 pp.

Several other translations are in existence.

CHAKRABERTY, CHANDRA. Birth Control and Conception Techniques. Ed. by Saktipada Bhattacharjee. New York: Omin, 1952? 69 pp.

CHANDRASEKHAR, SRIPATI. India's Population: Facts, Problems, and Policy. Mystic, Conn.: Verry, 1967. 76 pp.

First published by Prakashan, Meerut, India, in 1967.

"Lecture delivered at the Centre for Population Studies, Harvard University, February, 1966."

CHANDRASEKHAR, SRIPATI. Population and Planned Parenthood in India. Fwd. by Jawaharlal Nehru. Intro. by Julian Huxley. 2nd rev. and enl. ed. New York: Macmillan, 1961. 137 pp.

CHASTEEN, EDGAR R. The Case for Compulsory Birth Control. Englewood Cliffs, N.J.: Prentice-Hall, 1971. 230 pp.

CHESSER, EUSTACE. A Practical Guide to Birth Control. Library of Modern Sex Knowledge, No. 11. London, Eng.: Torchstream Books, 1950. 127 pp.

First published 1947 under the title "Children by Choice"; reissued 1950. "Analyses the meaning of freedom in marriage—freedom from fears, selfishness, and emotional immaturity, but not from obligations. It should be read by all young people before entering into marriage as well as afterwards."

CHURCH OF ENGLAND. NATIONAL ASSEMBLY. BOARD FOR SOCIAL
RESPONSIBILITY. Sterilization: An Ethical Enquiry. London, Eng.: Church
Information Office, 1962. 46 pp.

CONSUMER REPORTS. The Consumers Union Report on Family Planning: A
Guide to Contraceptive Methods and Materials for Use in Child Spacing,
Techniques for Improving Fertility, and Recognized Adoption Procedures.
2nd ed. Mount Vernon, N.Y.: Consumer Reports, 1966. 191 pp. Illus.

First edition, 1962. "Prepared by the editors of Consumer Reports, Alan
F. Guttmacher, and others."

CONSUMERS' ASSOCIATION. Contraceptives: A "Which?" Supplement. 3rd
ed. London, Eng.: Consumers' Assn., 1970. 79 pp. Illus.

COOK, ROBERT CARTER. Human Fertility: The Modern Dilemma. Intro. by
Julian Huxley. Westport, Conn.: Greenwood, 1971. 380 pp. Illus.

"Chapters 2 and 3 were originally published in the Atlantic Monthly under
the title "Puerto Rico: An Explosion of People.'" Earlier edition published by Sloane, New York, 1951.

CURRAN, CHARLES E., ed. Contraception: Authority and Dissent. New
York: Herder, 1969. 237 pp. Illus.

Deals with the religious point of view on contraception.

DANDEKAR, KUMUDINI. Communication in Family Planning: Report on an
Experiment. Gokhale Institute of Politics and Economics, Poona, India.
Studies, No. 49. New York: Asia Publishing House, 1967. 109 pp.

DAVID, HENRY PHILIP. Family Planning and Abortion in the Socialist
Countries of Central and Eastern Europe: A Compendium of Observations
and Readings. New York: Population Council, 1970. 306 pp.

"Prepared by the International Research Institutes for Research, Washington, D.C."

DAVIS, HUGH J. Intrauterine Devices for Contraception: The IUD. Baltimore, Md.: Williams & Wilkins, 1971. 210 pp. Illus.

DAVIS, MORRIS EDWARD. Natural Child Spacing: The Body Temperature
Method of Child Planning. Fwd. by Morris Fishbein. Garden City, N.Y.:
Hanover, 1953. 67 pp. Diagrams.

DENNETT, MARY WARE. Birth Control Laws: Shall We Keep Them, Change
Them, or Abolish Them? New York: Da Capo, 1970. 309 pp. Illus.

Reprint of 1926 edition.

DERRICK, CHRISTOPHER. Honest Love and Human Life: Is the Pope Right
about Contraception? New York: Coward, 1969. 158 pp.

Also published by Hutchinson, London, England, 1969.

A discussion of "Humanae Vitae."

DICKINSON, ROBERT LATOU. Techniques of Conception Control: A Practical
Manual Issued by the Planned Parenthood Federation of America, Inc. 3rd
ed. Baltimore, Md.: Williams & Wilkins, 1950. 59 pp. Illus.

Earlier edition, 1941.

DICKINSON, ROBERT LATOU, and L. S. BRYANT. Control of Conception: An Illustrated Medical Manual. 2nd ed. Baltimore, Md.: Williams & Wilkins, 1938. 390 pp. Illus.

"Medical aspects of human fertility."

"A clinical manual, with numerous illustrations by the author. Describes anatomy, physiology, chemistry, technique of contraception, contraceptives and methods, sterilization, abortion, clinics."

DICKINSON, ROBERT LATOU, and C. J. GAMBLE. Human Sterilization: Techniques of Permanent Conception Control. Baltimore, Md.: n.p., 1950. 40 pp. Illus.

DICZFALUSY, EGON, and U. BORELL, eds. Control of Human Fertility. New York: Wiley, 1971. 354 pp. Illus.

"Proceedings of the 15th Nobel Symposium held May 27-29, 1970 at Södergan, Lidingö, Sweden."

DUFFY, BENEDICT J., and M. J. WALLACE. Biological and Medical Aspects of Contraception. Notre Dame, Ind.: University of Notre Dame, 1969. 133 pp. Illus.

"Presents current information for the general reader on the biology of reproduction and the medical aspects of fertility control."

FAGLEY, RICHARD MARTIN. Population Explosion and Christian Responsibility. New York: Oxford University Press, 1960. 260 pp.

FAMILY PLANNING ASSOCIATION OF GREAT BRITAIN. Family Planning in the Sixties: Report. London, Eng.: Family Planning Assn. of Great Britain, 1963. 1 vol.

FELDMAN, DAVID MICHAEL. Birth Control in Jewish Law: Marital Relations, Contraception, and Abortion as Set Forth in the Classic Texts of Jewish Law. New York: New York University Press, 1968. 322 pp.

"In this extensive and carefully documented study, the legal-moral teachings of Judaism through history are set forth on such themes as sexual responsibility of the husband and wife, sexual pleasure as an independent aspect of marital relationships, contraception, abortion, and masturbation."

FIELDING, MICHAEL [pseud.]. Parenthood: Design or Accident? A Manual of Birth Control. New (7th) ed. rev. under the auspices of the Family Planning Association, by Eleanor Mears. London, Eng.: Williams & Norgate, 1958. 95 pp. Illus.

Earlier edition, 1934.

FINCH, BERNARD EPHRAIM, and H. GREEN. Contraception Through the Ages. Springfield, Ill.: Thomas, 1964. 174 pp.

'Traces the practice of contraception from the time of the Pharaohs until the present. First published in London, England, 1963, by Owen."

FRANK, RICHARD, and C. TIETZE. Successful Family Planning Made Easy and Inexpensive: A Birth Control and Marriage Manual, with Special Sections on the Rhythm Method and How to Improve the Sexual Side of Your Marriage. Chicago, Ill.: Community and Family Study Center, University of Chicago, 1963. 56 pp. Illus.

"Prepared under the medical supervision of the authors."

FRIENDS, SOCIETY OF. AMERICAN FRIENDS SERVICE COMMITTEE. Who Shall Live: Man's Control over Birth and Death: A Report. New York: Hill, 1970. 144 pp. Illus.

FRYER, PETER. The Birth Controllers. New York: Stein and Day, 1966. 384 pp. Illus.

"A history of the chief pioneers of birth control from antiquity to contemporary days."

GANDHI, MOHANDAS KARAMCHAND. Through Self-Control. Ed. by Anand T. Hingorani. Bombay, India: Bharatiya Vidya Bhavan, 1964. 108 pp.

Several other versions and translations of the author's works on birth control are in existence.

GEORG, IWAN EUGEN. Truth About Rhythm. New York: Kenedy, 1962. 212 pp. Illus.

"Translation of 'Die Frau und Die Ehe,' 1957. First published under the title 'Eheleben und Kindersegen.' "

GILLETTE, PAUL J. The Vasectomy Information Manual. Fwd. by Jim Bouton. New York: Outerbridge & Lazard, 1972. 235 pp. Illus.

"Prepared with the cooperation of the Association for Voluntary Sterilization. First published under the title 'Vasectomy: The Male Sterilization Operation.' "

GREENBLATT, ROBERT BENJAMIN, ed. Progress in Conception Control: The Sequential Regimen. Philadelphia, Pa.: Lippincott, 1966. 88 pp.

"Report of a scientific discussion held in Chicago at the time of the Fourteenth Annual Meeting of the American College of Obstetricians and Gynecologists, May 1966."

GUTTMACHER, ALAN FRANK, et al. Birth Control and Love: The Complete Guide to Contraception and Fertility. 2nd rev. ed. New York: Macmillan, 1969. 337 pp.

"A wholly revised and expanded edition of 'The Complete Book of Birth Control,' written by officials of Planned Parenthood-World Population in 1961 and published also in 1964 under the title 'Planning Your Family.' "

HALLER, JÜRGEN. Hormonal Contraception. Tr. from the 2nd German ed. by Herbert Gottfried. Los Altos, Calif.: Geron-X, 1969. 288 pp. Illus.

"Translation of 'Ovulationshemmung durch Hormone.' "

HARDIN, GARRETT JAMES. Birth Control. Biological Sciences Curriculum Study Book. Science and Society Series. New York: Pegasus, 1970. 142 pp. Illus.

HARDIN, GARRETT JAMES, ed. Population, Evolution, and Birth Control: A Collage of Controversial Ideas. 2nd ed. San Francisco, Calif.: Freeman, 1969. 386 pp.

Earlier edition, 1964.

HARDIN, GARRETT JAMES. Science and Controversy: Population, A Case Study. San Francisco, Calif.: Freeman, 1969. 30 pp.

"Intended to accompany the author's 'Population, Evolution, and Birth Control.'"

HAVIL, ANTHONY. Birth Control and You: A Full Medical Description for Every Man and Woman. London, Eng.: Wales, 1951. 100 pp. Illus.

HAWTHORN, GEOFFREY. The Sociology of Fertility. Themes and Issues in Modern Sociology. London, Eng.: Collier-Macmillan, 1970. 161 pp.

Deals with human fertility and family planning.

HENSHAW, PAUL STEWART. Adaptive Human Fertility. New York: McGraw, 1955. 322 pp. Illus.

"Dr. Henshaw has provided a summary of the case for wide dissemination of birth control knowledge, by giving a review of the biology of reproduction and of the nature of population growth, and a survey on fertility management."

HIMES, NORMAN EDWIN. Medical History of Contraception. New York: Schocken, 1970. 521 pp. Illus.

"Medical foreword by Robert L. Dickinson. Preface by Alan F. Guttmacher. A thorough study of the history of the control of conception from antiquity to the present day, and dealing with all countries of the world. Fully documented and scientific in treatment." Reprint of 1936 edition, published by Williams & Wilkins, Baltimore, Maryland.

HIMES, NORMAN EDWIN, and A. STONE. Planned Parenthood: A Practical Guide to Birth Control Methods. Rev. and expanded by J. J. Rovinsky. New York: Collier, 1965. 316 pp. Illus.

"A manual of contraceptive practice, clear and comprehensive with a pleasant philosophical turn, well illustrated. Includes a short history of contraception, and a consideration of related matters, such as abortion." First published in 1938 under the title 'Practical Birth-Control Methods,' with a foreword by Havelock Ellis and introduction by Robert L. Dickinson.

HONDA, TATSUO, ed. Fourth Public Opinion Survey on Birth Control in Japan. Institute of Population Problems, Tokyo. Population Problems Series, No. 15. Tokyo, Japan: Mainichi Newspapers, 1958. 59 pp. Tables.

HORNIBROOK, ETTIE A. ROUT. Practical Birth Control: A Revised Version of "Safe Marriage." London, Eng.: Heinemann, 1940. 82 pp.

"This little book gives practical information about the use of contraceptives. The method recommended is fully described, and other methods in use are mentioned. Some interesting remarks are added on the ethics of sexual practices, and a useful list of birth-control clinics is given."

HOYT, ROBERT G., ed. The Birth Control Debate. Kansas City, Mo.: National Catholic Reporter, 1970. 224 pp.

Reprint of 1968 edition. "Consists chiefly of material first published in the 'National Catholic Reporter.'"

HUGHES, J. E. Eugenic Sterilization in the United States: A Comparative Summary of Statutes and Review of Court Decisions. Supplement No. 162, Public Health Report. Washington, D.C.: Dept. of Health, Education, and Welfare, 1940. 45 pp.

INTERNATIONAL PLANNED PARENTHOOD FEDERATION. Directory of Selected Training Facilities in Family Planning and Allied Subjects. 2nd ed. London, Eng.: International Planned Parenthood Federation, 1968. 178 pp.

INTERNATIONAL PLANNED PARENTHOOD FEDERATION. Family Planning in Five Continents. London, Eng.: International Planned Parenthood Federation, 1970. 40 pp.

INTERNATIONAL PLANNED PARENTHOOD FEDERATION. World List of Family Planning Agencies. London, Eng.: International Planned Parenthood Federation, 1970. 12 pp.

JOHNSON, STANLEY. Life without Birth: A Journey through the Third World in Search of the Population Explosion. London, Eng.: Heinemann, 1970. 364 pp. Illus.

JOYCE, MARY ROSERA. The Meaning of Contraception. Staten Island, N.Y.: Alba, 1970. 148 pp.

The subject is discussed from a Catholic point of view.

KANABAY, DONALD, and H. KANABAY. Sex, Fertility, and the Catholic. Staten Island, N.Y.: Alba, 1965. 144 pp. Illus.

KENDALL, KATHERINE A., ed. Population Dynamics and Family Planning: A New Responsibility for Social Work Education. New York: Council on Social Work Education, 1971. 159 pp.

"Proceedings of the International Conference on Social Work Education, Population, and Family Planning. Sponsored by the Council on Social Work Education in cooperation with the East-West Center."

KENNEDY, DAVID M. Birth Control in America: The Career of Margaret Sanger. Yale Publications in American Studies, 18. New Haven, Conn.: Yale University Press, 1970. 320 pp. Portraits.

KIPPLEY, JOHN F. Covenant, Christ and Contraception. Staten Island, N.Y.: Alba, 1970. 160 pp.

KNAUS, HERMANN. Human Procreation and Its Natural Regulation. New York: Obolensky, 1965. 86 pp. Illus.

"Translation of 'Die Fruchtbaren und Unfruchtbaren Tage Der Frau und Deren Sichere Berechnung.'" Earlier English translation under the title "The Fertile and Infertile Days of Women and Their Definite Calculation."

KRISHNA MURTHY, K. G. Research in Family Planning in India. Delhi, India: Sterling, 1968. 108 pp.

"This book has been brought out in collaboration with the Social Research Division of the Central Family Planning Institute, New Delhi."

LADER, LAWRENCE. Breeding Ourselves to Death. Fwd. by Paul R. Ehrlich. New York: Ballantine, 1971. 115 pp. Illus.

LADER, LAWRENCE, ed. Foolproof Birth Control: Male and Female Sterilization. Boston, Mass.: Beacon, 1972. 286 pp. Illus.

LAUMAS, K. R. Review of Research Work in India on Intra-Uterine Contraceptive Devices. New Delhi, India: Indian Council of Medical Research, 1969. 227 pp. Illus.

"Proceedings of a seminar held jointly under the auspices of Indian Council of Medical Research and Central Family Planning Institute, September 11-13, 1968."

LEDNICER, DANIEL, ed. Contraception: The Chemical Control of Fertility. New York: Dekker, 1969. 269 pp. Illus.

Deals with oral contraceptives.

LINDNER, HANS R. Hormones, Fertility and Birth Control. Science Research for the Progress of Man. New York: American Committee for the Weizmann Institute of Science, 1970. 16 pp. Portraits.

"An interview with Dr. Hans R. Lindner, Head, Department of Biodynamics, The Weizmann Institute of Science."

LORAINE, JOHN ALEXANDER. Sex and the Population Crisis: An Endocrinologist's View of the Twentieth Century. St. Louis, Mo.: Mosby, 1970. 200 pp. Illus.

British edition published by Heinemann, London, 1970.

MARSHALL, JOHN. The Infertile Period: Principles and Practice. Rev. ed. Baltimore, Md.: Helicon, 1969. 123 pp. Illus.

Earlier edition, 1963, and new edition, 1967, published by Darton, London, England.

MARSHALL, JOHN. Planning for a Family: An Atlas of Temperature Charts. London, Eng.: Faber, 1965. 159 pp. Illus.

MEDAWAR, JEAN, and D. PYKE, eds. Family Planning. Baltimore, Md.: Penguin, 1971. 256 pp. Illus.

MILBANK MEMORIAL FUND. Approaches to Problems of High Fertility in Agrarian Societies. Proceedings of the Annual Conference, 1951. New York: Milbank Memorial Fund, 1952. 171 pp.

"Papers presented at the 1951 annual conference of the Milbank Memorial Fund."

MILBANK MEMORIAL FUND. Current Research in Human Fertility. Proceedings of the Annual Conference, 1954, Pt. 2. New York: Milbank Memorial Fund, 1955. 162 pp.

"Papers presented at the 1954 annual conference of the Milbank Memorial Fund."

MINTZ, MORTON. The Pill: An Alarming Report. Boston, Mass.: Beacon, 1970. 140 pp.

"This discussion of oral contraceptives brings together antipill testimony and offers an indictment of the drug industry, the regulatory agencies, and the medics."

MURPHY, JOHN PATRICK, and J. D. LAUX. The Rhythm Way to Family Happiness: A Lifetime Reference for the Use of the Rhythm Method. New and rev. 3rd ed. New York: Hawthorn, 1969.

"First edition by Rhythm Indicator, Inc., Elmira, New York, published in 1950 under the title 'The Rhythm Way for Birth Control.' A practical manual for application of the medical findings of Dr. K. Ogino and Dr. H. Knaus."

NEUBARDT, SELIG B. Contraception. New York: Simon and Schuster, 1968. 157 pp.

"Clearly and accurately presents the techniques of contraception, not as a mechanical way of avoiding undesired pregnancy, but as an integral part of the sexual life of the couple." Original title: "A Concept of Contraception."

NOONAN, JOHN T. Contraception. Cambridge, Mass.: Harvard University Press, 1966. 561 pp.

"Traces the evolution of Roman Catholic thought and teachings on birth control and discusses attitudes the Roman Church has historically held towards various methods of contraception."

NORTMAN, DOROTHY. Population and Family Planning Programs: A Factbook. New York: Population Council, 1969. 48 pp.

At the head of the title: Reports on Population/Family Planning.

O'BRIEN, JOHN ANTHONY. Family Planning in an Exploding Population. New York: Hawthorn, 1968. 222 pp.

PARKER, VALERIA HOPKINS. The Illustrated Birth Control Manual. New York: Cadillac, 1957. 392 pp. Illus.

PECK, ELLEN. The Baby Trap. New York: Geis Associates, 1971. 245 pp.

PEEL, JOHN, and M. POTTS. Textbook of Contraceptive Practice. London, Eng.: Cambridge University Press, 1969. 297 pp. Illus.

"Written by a sociologist and a medical expert, this is an accurate and authoritative textbook for the medical student and practicing physician."

PINCUS, GREGORY, ed. The Control of Fertility. New York: Academic Press, 1965. 360 pp. Illus.

PLACE, FRANCIS. Illustrations and Proofs of the Principle of Population. New York: Houghton, 1930. 354 pp.

"Being the first work on population in the English language recommending birth control . . . demonstrating Francis Place as the founder of the modern birth control movement." Edition of 1822 published in London, England, by Longman.

POHLMAN, EDWARD. How to Kill Population. Philadelphia, Pa.: Westminster, 1971. 169 pp.

POHLMAN, EDWARD. The Psychology of Birth Planning. Cambridge, Mass.: Schenkman, 1969. 496 pp. Illus.

POLGAR, STEVEN, ed. Culture and Population: A Collection of Current Studies. Carolina Population Center Monograph 9. Chapel Hill, N.C.: Carolina Population Center, 1971. 196 pp.

POLLOCK, MARY, ed. Family Planning: A Handbook for the Doctor. Baltimore, Md.: Williams & Wilkins, 1966. 190 pp. Illus.

1963 edition published by New English Library, London, England.

Progress and Problems of Fertility Control Around the World: Two or Three Children — That's Enough. Demography, Vol. 5, No. 2. Washington, D.C.: Population Assn. of America, 1968. 539 pp. Illus.

PYLE, LEO, ed. The Pill and Birth Regulation: The Catholic Debate, Including Statements, Articles, and Letters from the Pope, Bishops, Priests, and Married and Unmarried Laity. Baltimore, Md.: Helicon, 1964. 225 pp.

QUINN, FRANCIS X., ed. Population Ethics. Washington, D.C.: Corpus, 1968. 144 pp.

RAINWATER, LEE. And the Poor Get Children: Sex, Contraception, and Family Planning in the Working Class. Social Research Studies in Contemporary Life, No. 1. Chicago, Ill.: Quadrangle Books, 1967. 202 pp

"A report of the findings of a family planning study of a very small group of lower socio-economic white and black couples. The verbatim recording of portions of the interviews give insight into the attitudes of one segment of the population." Reprint of 1960 edition.

REID, SUE TITUS, comp. Population Crisis: An Interdisciplinary Perspective. Glenview, Ill.: Scott, 1972. 220 pp.

ROBINSON, JAMES FREDERICK. Family Planning. 2nd ed. Edinburgh, Scotland: Livingstone, 1967. 72 pp.

ROBINSON, WILLIAM JOSEPHUS. Fewer and Better Babies: Birth Control, or, The Limitation of Offspring by Prevenception. New York: Eugenics Publishing Co., 1936. 257 pp.

Several editions are in existence. 1915 edition published by The Critic and Guide Co. in New York.

ROSSMAN, ISADORE. Sex, Fertility, and Birth Control. New York: Stravon, 1967. 224 pp. Illus.

RYAN, JOHN. Family Limitation: Modern Medical Observations on the Use of the "Safe Period." New York: Sheed and Ward, 1960. 68 pp.

Other editions previously published.

SABONIS-CHAFEE, B. Birth Control: Moral Error or Moral Necessity. New York: Vantage, 1968. 75 pp.

ST. JOHN-STEVAS, NORMAN. The Agonising Choice: Birth Control, Religion, and the Law. Bloomington, Ind.: Indiana University Press, 1971. 340 pp.

SALTMAN, JULES. The Pill: Its Effects, Its Dangers, Its Future. New York: Grosset, 1970. 124 pp.

SANGER, MARGARET. Appeals from American Mothers. New York: Womans Publishing Co., 1921. 16 pp.

"Letters to Margaret Sanger."

SANGER, MARGARET. Family Limitation. Rev. 6th ed. New York(?) 1917.
16 pp. Illus.

SANGER, MARGARET. Margaret Sanger: An Autobiography. New York:
Norton, 1938. 504 pp.

SANGER, MARGARET. Motherhood in Bondage. Elmsford, N.Y.: Maxwell
Reprint, 1970. 446 pp.

Selections from letters sent to Margaret Sanger by mothers in the United
States and Canada. Reprint of 1928 edition.

SANGER, MARGARET. My Fight for Birth Control. New York: Farrar, 1931.
360 pp.

SANGER, MARGARET. Pivot of Civilization. New York: Brentano's, 1922.
284 pp.

SANGER, MARGARET. Woman and the New Race. Pref. by Havelock Ellis.
New York: Brentano's, 1923. 234 pp.

SANGER, MARGARET, and HANNAH M. STONE. The Practice of Contraception: An International Symposium and Survey. Baltimore, Md.: Williams
& Wilkins, 1931. 316 pp.

"A report of a discussion by many experts, of the technical problems of
contraception, at an International Birth Control Conference at Zurich in
1931."

SCOTT, GEORGE RYLEY. Birth Control: A Practical Guide for Working
Women. London, Eng.: Laurie, 1936. 60 pp. Illus.

SCOTT, GEORGE RYLEY. Facts and Fallacies of Practical Birth Control,
Including an Examination of the "Natural Method" of Contraception, of the
Gräfenberg Ring, and Sterilization. London, Eng.: Laurie, 1935. 156 pp.
Illus.

SCOTT, GEORGE RYLEY. Male Methods of Birth Control, Their Technique
and Reliability: A Practical Handbook for Men. London, Eng.: Laurie, 1937.
96 pp. Illus.

SCOTT, GEORGE RYLEY. Modern Birth Control Methods. 2nd ed. completely
rev. London, Eng.: Torchstream, 1947. 156 pp. Illus.

"Gives clear directions for the successful application of all known methods
of birth control, with an appendix on the facilitation of conception for those
who desire children."

SEAMAN, BARBARA. The Doctors' Case Against the Pill. New York: Wyden,
1969. 279 pp.

SHANNON, WILLIAM HENRY. The Lively Debate: Response to Humanae
Vitae. New York: Sheed and Ward, 1970. 216 pp.

SPITZER, WALTER O., and C. L. SAYLOR, eds. Birth Control and the
Christian. Wheaton, Ill.: Tyndale, 1969. 590 pp.

"Conference jointly sponsored by the Christian Medical Society and
Christianity Today in Portsmouth, New Hampshire, 1968."

STALLWORTHY, JOHN, et al. Problems of Fertility in General Practice. 2nd ed. London, Eng.: Cassell, 1953. 259 pp. Illus.

STOPES, MARIE CHARLOTTE CARMICHAEL. Birth Control and Libel: The Trial of Marie Stopes. Ed. by Muriel Box. South Brunswick, N.J.: Barnes, 1968. 392 pp.

First published in 1967 under the title "The Trial of Marie Stopes."

STOPES, MARIE CHARLOTTE CARMICHAEL. Birth Control Today: A Practical Handbook for Those Who Want to Be Their Own Masters in This Vital Matter. 12th ed., rev. and brought up to date. London, Eng.: Hogarth, 1957. 177 pp. Illus.

1939 edition published by Heinemann, London, England.

STOPES, MARIE CHARLOTTE CARMICHAEL. Contraception (Birth Control), Its Theory, History, and Practice: A Manual for the Medical and Legal Professions. 7th ed. rev. New York: Putnam, 1949. 491 pp.

"The pioneer work on the subject, revised and brought up to date, giving much useful information, including descriptions of contraceptives in use, a summary of the history of family limitation and contraception from the earliest days to the present time, and a chapter on birth-control clinics."

Several editions are in existence since 1923.

STOPES, MARIE CHARLOTTE CARMICHAEL. Preliminary Notes on Various Technical Aspects of the Control of Conception, Based on the Analysed Data from Ten Thousand Cases Attending the Pioneer Mother's Clinic, London. London, Eng.: Mother's Clinic for Constructive Birth Control, 1930. 44 pp.

STOPES, MARIE CHARLOTTE CARMICHAEL. Wise Parenthood: The Treatise on Birth Control for Married People, a Practical Sequel to "Married Love." 20th ed., rev. London, Eng.: Putnam, 1936. 95 pp.

SUBBIAH, B. V. The Tragedy of a Papal Decree (in a Crowded World). New York: Vantage, 1971. 144 pp.

SWAROOP, R. Birth Control for the Layman. Lucknow, India: Madhuri, 1955. 128 pp. Illus.

TAYLOR, ROSALIE. Inside Information on Sex and Birth Control. London, Eng.: Dickens, 1969. 126 pp. Illus.

THOMAS, JOHN L. Marriage and Rhythm. Westminster, Md.: Newman, 1957. 180 pp.

THOMSON, CLAIRE. A Christian Approach to Family Planning. Madras, India: Christian Literature Society, 1963. 42 pp. Illus.

"Published for the Christian Medical Association of India."

TUNNADINE, L. P. D. Contraception and Sexual Life: A Therapeutic Approach. Mind and Medicine Monographs, 19. Philadelphia, Pa.: Lippincott, 1970. 80 pp.

TYLER, EDWARD T., ed. Birth Control: A Continuing Controversy. Springfield, Ill.: Thomas, 1967. 182 pp. Illus.

"Proceedings of a symposium sponsored by the Postgraduate Medical Extension Division of U. C. L. A., January 29-30, 1966."

UNITED STATES CONGRESS. SENATE. COMMITTEE ON GOVERNMENT OPERATIONS. Establish a Commission on Population Growth and the American Future. Washington, D.C.: U. S. Govt. Printing Office, 1969. 244 pp. Illus.

"Hearing...Ninety-first Congress, first session on S. 2701, a bill to establish a Commission on Population Growth and the American Future, September 15, 1969."

VAUGHAN, PAUL. The Pill on Trial. New York: Coward-McCann, 1970. 244 pp.

WEINBERG, ROY DAVID. Laws Governing Family Planning. New York: Oceana, 1968. 118 pp.

WELTON, THURSTON SCOTT. Rhythm Birth Control: The Modern Method of Birth Control. Rev. and enl. ed. New York: Grosset, 1960. 170 pp. Illus.

Previously published under the title "The Modern Method of Birth Control."

WESTOFF, CHARLES F., et al. Family Growth in Metropolitan America. Princeton, N.J.: Princeton University Press, 1961. 433 pp. Tables.

"A study and analysis of the results of a sample survey conducted in 1957 by National Analysts, Inc., Philadelphia, Pennsylvania."

WESTOFF, LESLIE ALDRIDGE, and C. F. WESTOFF. From Now to Zero: Fertility, Contraception, and Abortion in America. Boston, Mass.: Little, Brown, 1971. 358 pp.

WHELPTON, PASCAL KIDDER, et al. Fertility and Family Planning in the United States. Princeton, N.J.: Princeton University Press, 1966. 443 pp.

"Based on an interview survey conducted in 1960 under the direction of the Survey Research Center, University of Michigan and The Scripps Foundation, Miami University. Makes projections of births and population to 1985."

WILLIAMS, GLANVILLE LLEWELYN. The Sanctity of Life and the Criminal Law. New York: Knopf, 1957. 350 pp.

"A British jurist examines society's attitudes toward the control of conception, sterilization, artificial insemination, abortion, suicide, and euthanasia."

WOLFERS, D., ed. Post-Partum Intra-Uterine Contraception in Singapore. New York: Excerpta Medica, 1970. 193 pp. Illus.

WOOD, CLIVE. Birth Control Now and Tomorrow. London, Eng.: Davies, 1969. 210 pp. Illus.

WOOD, HORATIO CURTIS. Sex without Babies. Philadelphia, Pa.: Whitmore, 1967. 229 pp.

"A review of voluntary sterilization as a method of birth control by an official of the Association for Voluntary Sterilization."

WRAGE, KARL HORST. Children: Choice or Chance. Philadelphia, Pa.: Fortress, 1969. 119 pp.

WRIGHT, HELENA. Birth Control: Advice on Family Spacing and Healthy Sex Life. 5th ed. London, Eng.: Cassell, 1958. 76 pp.

A simple guide to birth control by an eminent worker in the field. Discusses moral and practical issues, and explains clearly the use of accepted methods.

WRIGHT, HELENA. Contraceptive Technique: A Handbook for Medical Practitioners and Senior Students. With the assistance of H. Beric Wright. 3rd ed. London, Eng.: Churchill, 1968. 96 pp. Illus.

CAUSE AND DETERMINATION OF SEX

ABBOUD, MICHAEL BEN. Love, Life, and Truth. Boston, Mass.: Christopher, 1951. 60 pp.

ABBOUD, MICHAEL BEN. The Secret of Sexes, Revealed and Controlled: From the Bible. Hazleton, Pa.: n.p., 1947. 58 pp.

ACENA, J. F. Determination of Sex by Foetal Heart Rate. Newark, N.J.: Marquette, 1931. 35 pp.

BACCI, GUIDO. Sex Determination. New York: Pergamon, 1965. 306 pp. Illus.

BENEDICT, ARTHUR LINCOLN. Choose the Sex of your Children: Or, Factors Determining Sex. New York: Ross, 1950. 281 pp. Illus.

CREW, FRANCIS ALBERT ELEY. Sex-Determination. 4th ed. rev. New York: Dover, 1965. 188 pp.

Earlier edition, 1933.

DAVEY, D. MURRAY. Son or Daughter? Sex Determination in Theory and Practice. London, Eng.: Wales, 1942? 104 pp.

DAWSON, ERNEST RUMLEY. The Causation of Sex in Man: A New Theory of Sex Based on Clinical Materials. 3rd ed. London, Eng.: Lewis, 1921. 226 pp. Illus.

"Together with chapters on forecasting or predicting the sex of the unborn child and on the determination or production of either sex at will." Also 1909 edition.

DONCASTER, LEONARD. The Determination of Sex. New York: Putnam, 1914. 172 pp. Diagrams.

Also published by Cambridge University Press, Cambridge, England, 1914.

JACKSON, ROY CLAY. The Cause and Control of Sex in Human Offspring. Tacoma, Wash.: Roy C. Jackson, 1926. 205 pp. Illus.

LANE, CORNELIUS W. A Treatise on the Influence of Mind over Matter in Solving the Great Problem of How to Previously Determine the Sex. Chicago, Ill.: n.p., 1899. 290 pp.

LUPATKIN, MORDE. The Diagnosis of Chromosomal Sex Using the Oral Mucosal Smear as the Simplest Method. Zurich, Switzerland, n.p.: 1957. 22 pp. Illus.

Inaugural dissertation, Zurich.

MOORE, CARL RICHARD. Embryonic Sex Hormones and Sexual Differentiation. American Lecture Series, No. 8. American Lectures in Endocrinology. Springfield, Ill.: Thomas, 1947. 81 pp. Illus.

ØKLAND, FRIDTHJOF. Is It a Boy? Sex-Determination According to Superstition and to Science. London, Eng.: Allen, 1932. 92 pp. Illus.

RICHARD, S. Y. The Science of the Sexes, or How Parents May Control the Sex of their Offspring, and Stock-Raisers Control the Sex of Stock. 5th ed. Cincinnati, Ohio; Spinning, 1879. 315 pp.

RORVIK, DAVID M. Your Baby's Sex: Now You Can Choose. New York: Dodd, 1970. 126 pp. Illus.

Also published by Bantam, New York, in 1971.

SANDELL, DAVID HUGH. Boy or Girl? How Parents Can Decide the Sex of Their Child. New York: n.p., 1939. 112 pp. Illus.

1939 edition published by Cassell, London, England.

Von BOROSINI, AUGUST J. Choosing the Sex of your Child: A Guide to Sex Predetermination. New York: Exposition Press, 1953. 78 pp. Illus.

Translated from the German.

REPRODUCTION

ASPLUND, JAN, and S. GENELL, eds. Proceedings of Symposium on the Uterine Cervix as a Fertility Factor, Held on January 25, 1958, in Malmo, Sweden. Acta obstetricia et gynecologica Scandinavica, Vol. 38. Supplement 1. Lund, Sweden: n.p. 130 pp. Illus.

Articles in English and German.

AUERBACH, ALINE SOPHIE BUCHMAN, and H. S. ARNSTEIN. Pregnancy and You. New York: Child Study Assn., 1962. 31 pp.

BENEDEK, THERESE FRIEDMAN. Psychosexual Functions in Women. Chicago Institute for Psychoanalysis. Studies in Psychosomatic Medicine. New York: Ronald, 1952. 435 pp. Illus.

Chapters 1-11, by T. Benedek and B. B. Rubenstein, published in 1942 under the title ''The Sexual Cycle in Women.''

BENEDEK, THERESE FRIEDMAN, and B. B. RUBENSTEIN. The Sexual Cycle in Women: The Relation between Ovarian Function and Psychodynamic Processes. Washington, D.C.: Committee on Problems of Neurotic Behavior, Division of Anthropology and Psychology, National Research Council, 1942. 307 pp.

"Monograph based on a study of 152 cycles of fifteen women of childbearing age, carried out as a research project of the Institute for Psychoanalysis, Chicago."

BERGMAN, PER. Sexual Cycle, Time of Ovulation, and Time of Optimal Fertility in Women: Studies on Basal Body Temperature, Endometrium, and Cervical Mucus. Acta obstetricia et gynecologica Scandinavica, Vol. 29, Supplement 4. Lund, Sweden: n.p. 139 pp. Illus.

BONDI, HERMANN, et al., eds. How Life Is Created. London, Eng.: Marshall Cavendish, 1969. 64 pp. Illus.

BURNS, JOHN. The Anatomy of the Gravid Uterus, with Practical References Relative to Pregnancy and Labour. Glasgow, Scotland: Mundell, 1799. 248 pp.

Published also by Cushing and Appleton, Salem, and Joshua Cushing, Boston, 1808.

CARR, DONALD EATON. The Sexes. Garden City, N.Y.: Doubleday, 1970. 252 pp.

"Examines human sexuality from the viewpoint of biological history, in order to pose solutions to the possibility of a disastrous population explosion."

CLYMER, REUBEN SWINBURNE. How to Create the Perfect Baby, by Means of the Art or Science Generally Known as Stirpiculture, or Prenatal Culture and Influence in the Development of a More Perfect Race. Quakertown, Pa.: Philosophical Publishing Co., 1950. 144 pp.

CORNER, GEORGE WASHINGTON. Hormones in Human Reproduction. New York: Atheneum, 1963. 281 pp. Illus.

First published in 1943 and revised in 1947 by Princeton University, Princeton, New Jersey. "Represents, with considerable additions, the substance of the Vanuxem Lectures, given at Princeton University in 1942."

DANIELS, GUY. The Beauty of Birth, by Colette Portal. Adapted from the French by Guy Daniels. New York: Knopf, 1971. 26 pp. Illus.

"Brief text and color illustrations follow the process of human reproduction from the production of ovum and sperm to the birth of the baby."

DAVIS, MAXINE. Facts about the Menopause. New York: McGraw-Hill, 1951. 172 pp.

DEMAREST, ROBERT J., and J. J. SCIARRA. Conception, Birth and Contraception—A Visual Presentation. Intro. by Mary S. Calderone. New York: McGraw-Hill, 1969. 129 pp. Illus.

"This atlas presents the basic facts about human reproduction, beautifully illustrated with sixty-one full color plates."

DIAMOND, MILTON, ed. Perspectives in Reproduction and Sexual Behavior. Bloomington, Ind.: Indiana University Press, 1968. 532 pp. Illus.

Symposium held in collaboration with the 1966 San Francisco meeting of the American Association of Anatomists.

DICK-READ, GRANTLY. Dick-Read's Childbirth without Fear: The Principles and Practice of Natural Childbirth. 5th ed., ed. by Linton Snaith and Alan Coxon. London, Eng.: Heinemann, 1968. 241 pp. Illus.

First edition published in 1942 under the title "Revelation of Childbirth." Explains that childbirth is a natural function, and that pain in civilized labor is due to emotional causes which can be avoided in cases of normal and uncomplicated labor. The mother should experience the intense joy of motherhood if birth takes place under natural conditions.

DICK-READ, GRANTLY. Introduction to Motherhood. London, Eng.: Heinemann, 1960. 88 pp.

"Simply written instructions for a woman who is going to have a baby. Explains method by which natural childbirth may be attained."

DREYFUS, ALFRED. Information, Please! For Women Only. Incorporating the Dunhill Chart. New York: Vantage, 1961. 556 pp. Illus.

EL-FATTAH, ALI ABD. Sterility and Fertility and Sexual Disorders in Male. Post-graduate Lecture Series. Cairo, Egypt: n.p. 98 leaves.

ENGLE, EARL THERON, ed. Menstruation and Its Disorders. Springfield, Ill.: Thomas, 1950. 338 pp. Illus.

"Proceedings of a conference held under the auspices of the National Committee on Maternal Health."

ENGLE, EARL THERON, ed. Studies on Testis and Ovary, Eggs and Sperm. Springfield, Ill.: Thomas, 1952. 237 pp. Illus.

"Proceedings of a conference for studies on human reproduction, held in New York in 1950 and sponsored by the Committee on Human Reproduction, National Research Council."

FARRIS, EDMOND JOHN. Human Ovulation and Fertility. Philadelphia, Pa.: Lippincott, 1956. 159 pp. Illus.

FLANAGAN, GERALDINE LUX. The First Nine Months of Life. New York: Simon and Schuster, 1962. 95 pp. Illus.

"A description of what happens to the human organism during the nine months between fertilization and birth. Photographs illustrate the changing form of the unborn child as it develops."

FORD, CLELLAN S. A Comparative Study of Human Reproduction. Yale University Publications in Anthropology, No. 32. New Haven, Conn.: Human Relations Area Files Press, 1964. 111 pp.

"Reprinted from 1945 edition."

FORD, CLELLAN S. Field Guide to the Study of Human Reproduction. Behavior Science Field Guides, Vol. 2. New Haven, Conn.: Human Relations Area Files Press, 1964. 60 leaves.

GALLIEN, LOUIS. Sexual Reproduction. Tr. by Paul Capon. New York: Walker, 1963. 146 pp. Illus.

Translation of "La Sexualité," published by Presses Universitaires de France in Paris.

GRABILL, WILSON H., et al. The Fertility of American Women. Census Monograph Series. New York: Wiley, 1958. 448 pp. Illus.

"Research for this monograph was done for the Social Science Research Council in cooperation with the United States Department of Commerce, Bureau of the Census."

GRAY, MADELINE. The Changing Years: The Menopause without Fear. New rev. ed. Garden City, N.Y.: Doubleday, 1967. 279 pp.

Earlier edition, with different subtitle, published in 1951.

1970 reprint by New American Library, New York.

GREENBLATT, ROBERT BENJAMIN, ed. Ovulation: Stimulation, Suppression, and Detection. Philadelphia, Pa.: Lippincott, 1966. 341 pp. Illus.

"A compilation of modern theories of the mechanics and physiology of ovulation by more than thirty authorities, who treat every important aspect of the subject in depth."

HAMILTON, WILLIAM JAMES, and H. W. MOSSMAN. Human Embryology: Prenatal Development of Form and Function. 2nd ed. Cambridge, Eng.: Heffer, 1952. 432 pp. Illus.

HARRISON, RICHARD JOHN. The Child Unborn. London, Eng.: Routledge, 1951. 226 pp. Illus.

HARRISON, RICHARD JOHN. Reproduction and Man. New York: Norton, 1971. 134 pp. Illus.

British edition, 1967 published by Oliver, London, England.

HARTMAN, CARL G. Science and the Safe Period: A Compendium of Human Reproduction. Baltimore, Md.: Williams & Wilkins, 1966. 294 pp. Illus.

HIPPOCRATES. On Intercourse and Pregnancy: An English Translation of "On Semen and On the Development of the Child," by Tage U. H. Ellinger. Intro. by Alan F. Guttmacher. New York: Schuman, 1952. 128 pp.

Translations of "De Genitura" and "De Natura Pueri."

JEFFRIES, LILIAS BLACKETT. The Change of Life and Its Problems. London, Eng.: Gollancz, 1952. 125 pp.

KISER, CLYDE VERNON, et al. Trends and Variations in Fertility in the United States. Vital and Health Statistics Monographs. Cambridge, Mass.: Harvard University Press, 1968. 338 pp. Illus. Map.

KLEIN, ROBERT A., and B. J. SCHUMAN. How to Have a Baby: Techniques for Fertile Marriage. New York: Hermitage House, 1951. 224 pp. Illus.

KUIPERS, KATHARINA DOROTHEA [Katharina Dalton]. The Menstrual Cycle. New York: Pantheon, 1969. 149 pp. Illus.

British edition published by Penguin, Harmondsworth, England, in 1969.

LAMAZE, FERNAND. Painless Childbirth, Psychoprophylactic Method. Chicago, Ill.: Regnery, 1970. 192 pp. Illus.

Translation of "Qu'est-ce que L'Accouchement sans Douleur?" Published in Paris, France, in 1956.

Deals with the method of natural childbirth.

LAMBERT, BENGT. The Frequency of Mumps and of Mumps Orchitis: And The Consequences for Sexuality and Fertility. Uppsala, Sweden: Almqvist, 1951. 166 pp. Illus.

Akademisk avhandling — Uppsala. Also published as "Acta genetica et statistica medica," Vol. 2, Supplement 1, 1951.

LEBKICHER, ROBERT E. An Advanced Concept and Timing of the Human Reproductive Cycle. Philadelphia, Pa.: n.p., 1958. 74 pp. Illus.

LEHRMAN, ROBERT L. The Reproduction of Life. New York: Basic Books, 1964. 246 pp. Illus.

LEVINE, LENA, and B. DOHERTY. The Menopause. New York: Random, 1952. 198 pp.

LIMNER, ROMAN RECHNITZ. Sex and the Unborn Child: Damage to the Fetus Resulting from Sexual Intercourse during Pregnancy. Fwds. by Alan F. Guttmacher and Theodor Reik. New York: Julian, 1969. 229 pp.

LINCOLN, MIRIAM. You'll Live through It: Facts about the Menopause. New and enl. ed. New York: Harper, 1961. 221 pp. Illus.

Earlier edition, 1950. British edition has the title "Woman: Her Change of Life."

LLOYD, CHARLES W., ed. Human Reproduction and Sexual Behavior. Philadelphia, Pa.: Lea and Febiger, 1964. 564 pp. Illus.

"A comprehensive handbook by various contributors, addressed primarily to physicians."

LORAINE, JOHN A., and E. T. BELL. Fertility and Contraception in the Human Female. Baltimore, Md.: Williams & Wilkins, 1968. 392 pp. Illus. Tables.

British edition published by Livingstone, London, England, 1968.

MACY CONFERENCE ON TEACHING THE BIOLOGICAL AND MEDICAL ASPECTS OF REPRODUCTION TO MEDICAL STUDENTS. Teaching the Biological and Medical Aspects of Reproduction to Medical Students: Report. New York: Hoeber, 1966. 151 pp.

"Sponsored by the Josiah Macy, Jr. Foundation and held in Princeton, New Jersey in 1965."

MALLESON, JOAN BILLSON [Medica]. Change of Life: Facts and Fallacies of Middle Age. London, Eng.: Delisle, 1949. 76 pp.

"This book, written for the lay reader by a distinguished medical consultant explains how assistance can be given to a woman who finds herself in difficulty at the change of life. This is a matter of vital importance, not only to women, but also to their husbands and families."

MARSHALL, FRANCIS HUGH ADAM. Physiology of Reproduction. Ed. by A. S. Parkes. 3rd ed. London, Eng.: Longmans, 1960-1962. 2 vols. in 3.

Reprint of 1952 edition. Earlier edition, 1910.

MILLEN, JAMES W. Nutritional Basis of Reproduction. American Lecture Series, Publication No. 485. A monograph in American Lectures in Living Chemistry. Springfield, Ill.: Thomas, 1962.

MILNER, ESTHER, ed. The Impact of Fertility Limitation on Women's Life — Career and Personality. New York Academy of Sciences, Annals. Vol. 175, Art. 3. New York: New York Academy of Sciences, 1970. Pp. 783-1065.

"Papers presented at a workshop held by the Academy on February 19-21, 1970."

MONTAGU, ASHLEY. Life Before Birth. Fwd. by Alan F. Guttmacher. New York: New American Library, 1964. 244 pp.

"A progress report on our growing understanding of the ways in which a child can be influenced before birth. It reveals that during the nine-month gestation period a human being is more susceptible to his environment than he will ever be again in his life."

NAG, MONI. Factors Affecting Human Fertility in Nonindustrial Societies: A Cross-Cultural Study. Yale University Dept. of Anthropology. Publication in Anthropology, No. 66. New Haven, Conn.: Human Relations Area File Press, 1968. 227 pp.

Reprint of 1962 edition.

PARKES, ALAN STERLING. Sex, Science and Society: Addresses, Lectures and Articles, annotated by the author and illus. by A. G. Wurmser. Newcastle-upon-Tyne, Eng.: Oriel, 1966. 324 pp. Illus.

PHILLIPP, ELLIOT ELIAS. Having Your Baby. London, Eng.: Educational Productions, 1970. 48 pp. Illus.

PILKINGTON, ROGER. Males and Females. London, Eng.: Delisle, 1948. 92 pp.

"A fascinating book, enlivened by touches of humour, written primarily for the adolescent or young adult, but will be read with interest by older people. Explains very lucidly human reproduction in terms of heredity."

REID, DUNCAN E., et al. Principles and Management of Human Reproduction. Philadelphia, Pa.: Saunders, 1972. 915 pp. Illus.

RHODES, PHILIP. Reproductive Physiology for Medical Students. London, Eng.: Churchill, 1969. 308 pp. Illus.

RHODES, PHILIP. Woman: A Biological Study of the Female Role in the Twentieth Century Society. London, Eng.: Corgi, 1969. 192 pp. Illus.

ROBINSON, JAMES FREDERICK. Having a Baby. 3rd ed. Edinburgh, Scotland: Livingstone, 1965. 116 pp. Illus.

Previous edition, 1954.

ROBSON, JOHN MICHAEL. Recent Advances in Sex and Reproductive Physiology. London, Eng.: Churchill, 1949. 348 pp.

"A treatise for the specialist, dealing essentially with the sexual and reproductive phenomena in the female in relation to the activity of the sex hormones, and the mode of action of the hormones in relation to the physiological processes."

Also published in 1934 by Churchill, England, and in 1940 by Blakiston in Philadelphia.

ROESSLIN, EUCHARIUS. The Byrth of Mankynde, Otherwyse Named the Womans Booke. Set forth in English from the Latin of E. Roesslin by T. Raynalde . . . and by him . . . augmented, etc. London, Eng.: n.p., 1626.

Issued originally in German, Strassburg, 1513 under the title "Der Swangern Frauwen und Behamen Rosegarten." Several translations and versions are in existence.

ROSEN, JAMES ALAN. Fertility in Men and Women; The How and Why of Having Children. New York: Coward, 1952. 177 pp. Illus.

RUBIN, HERMAN HAROLD. Glands, Sex, and Personality. New York: Funk, 1952. 205 pp. Illus.

RUGH, ROBERTS, and L. B. SHETTLES. From Conception to Birth: The Drama of Life's Beginnings. New York: Harper, 1971. 262 pp.

RYDER, NORMAN B., and C. F. WESTOFF. Reproduction in the United States, 1965. Princeton, N.J.: Princeton University Press, 1971. 419 pp.

SHARMAN, ALBERT. The Middle Years: The Change of Life. Edinburgh, Scotland: Livingstone, 1962. 80 pp.

SIEGLER, SAMUEL LEWIS. Fertility in Women: Causes, Diagnosis and Treatment of Impaired Fertility. Fwd. by Robert Latou Dickinson. Philadephia, Pa.: Lippincott, 1944. 450 pp.

SMYTH, MARGARET. Woman: The Middle Years. Family Doctor Book. London, Eng.: British Medical Assn., 1970. 30 pp.

SOLOMONS, MICHAEL. Life Cycle: Facts for Adults. Dublin, Ireland: Figgis, 1963. 120 pp.

SPENGLER, JOSEPH JOHN. France Faces Depopulation. Westport, Conn.: Greenwood, 1968. 313 pp.

Also published in 1938.

SWYER, GERALD ISAAC MACDONALD. Reproduction and Sex. Survey of Human Biology, Vol. 2. London, Eng.: Routledge, 1954. 280 pp. Illus.

SYMPOSIUM ON SEX AND REPRODUCTION, MINAKAMI, 1966. Sex and Reproduction. Gunma Symposia on Endocrinology, Vol. 4. Maebashi, Japan: Institute of Endocrinology, 1967. 235 pp. Illus.

UNITED NATIONS. DEPARTMENT OF ECONOMIC AND SOCIAL AFFAIRS. Human Fertility and National Development: A Challenge to Science and Technology. New York: United Nations, 1971. 140 pp. Illus.

United Nations Document.

VELARDO, JOSEPH THOMAS, ed. The Endocrinology of Reproduction. New York: Oxford University Press, 1958. 340 pp. Illus.

VELARDO, JOSEPH THOMAS, ed. Essentials of Human Reproduction: Clinical Aspects, Normal and Abnormal. New York: Oxford University Press, 1958. 270 pp. Illus.

VELLAY, PIERRE. Sex Development and Maternity: Childbirth without Pain by the Psycho-Prophylactic Method. London, Eng.: Hutchinson, 1968. 186 pp. Illus.

Translation of "Développement Sexuel et Maternité." American edition has the title "Childbirth with Confidence."

WIJSENBEEK, I. A., ed. Abstracts of Main Lectures, of Major Papers and of Free Communications of the World Congress on Fertility and Sterility held in Amsterdam, 1959. New York: Excerpta Medica Foundation, 1959. 77 pp.

"Sponsored by the International Fertility Association."

WILLIAMS, PETER LLEWELLYN, et al. Basic Human Embryology. Philadelphia, Pa.: Lippincott, 1966. 136 pp. Illus.

"Designed to supplement the medical student's knowledge of the field."

WOOD, CLIVE. Sex and Fertility. London, Eng.: Thames, 1969. 216 pp. Illus.

13.
SEXUAL ETHICS

ACLAND, RICHARD, et al. Sexual Morality: Three Views. Ed., with Intro., by R. Sadler. London, Eng.: Arlington, 1965. 82 pp.

Contents: Chastity or What? by R. Acland; The New Morality: a Christian Comment, by G. B. Bentley; Sexual Morality, by C. L. Gough.

ADAM, AUGUST. The Primacy of Love. Tr. from the German by E. C. Noonan. Westminster, Md.: Newman, 1958. 217 pp.

Deals with Christian sexual ethics.

ADAMS, CHARLES FRANCIS. Some Phases of Sexual Morality and Church Discipline in Colonial New England. Cambridge, Mass.: Wilson, 1891. 43 pp.

"Reprinted from the Proceedings of the Massachusetts Historical Society, June, 1891."

ANCHELL, MELVIN. Sex and Sanity. New York: Macmillan, 1971. 310 pp. Illus.

ARMITAGE, ROBERT B. Never Told Stories: How Girls Are Deceived. Chicago, Ill.: Advanced Thought, 1918. 239 pp.

ARMSTRONG, RINALDO WILLIAM. Sex, Temperance and Right Thinking. Ottawa, Canada: Graphic Publishers, 1931. 170 pp.

ARUNACHALAM, PONNAMBALAM. Light from the East: Being Letters on Gñanam, the Divine Knowledge. Ed. by Edward Carpenter. London, Eng.: Allen & Unwin, 1927. 156 pp.

ATKINSON, RONALD F. Sexual Morality. New York: Harcourt, 1966. 191 pp.

1965 edition published by Hutchinson, London, England.

BANOWSKY, WILLIAM SLATER. It's a Playboy World. Old Tappan, N.J.: Revell, 1969. 126 pp.

BASSETT, MARION PRESTON. A New Sex Ethics and Marriage Structure, Discussed by Adam and Eve. New York: Philosophical Library, 1961. 332 pp.

BAX, CLIFFORD. That Immortal Sea. London, Eng.: Dickson, 1933. 248 pp.

"A meditation upon the future of religion and of sexual morality."

BERGE, ANDRÉ, et al. Body and Spirit: Essays in Sexuality. Tr. by Donald Attwater. New York: Longmans, 1940. 200 pp.

Translations of essays selected from "Problèmes de la Sexualité." "First published in 1939." Contents: Preface, by Jacques de Lacretelle; Sex and the Child, by André Berge; The Relation of Sexuality and the Person, by Xavier de Lignac; Sex and Personality According to Freud, by Théo Chentrier; Biology and Sexual Morality, by Abbé Manchanin; Sexual Hygiene or Sexual Purity? by Father Benoît Lavand; Marriage and Society, by P. H. Simon; The Senses and the Spirit, by Gustave Thibon; Woman's Metaphysical Mission, by Peter Wust; The Verdict of Animality, by Daniel Rops.

BERTOCCI, PETER ANTHONY. The Human Venture in Sex, Love, and Marriage. New York: Association Press, 1963. 143 pp.

First published in 1949. "The author is concerned rather with the qualitative values of sex and love, than the biological aspect as in Kinsey."

BERTOCCI, PETER ANTHONY. Sex, Love, and the Person. New York: Sheed and Ward, 1967. 173 pp.

"The author answers questions concerning sex, locating them less in ethics than in the insights of the personality sciences. He contends that . . . expressions of sexual involvement should be related to marriage."

BLACKWELL, ELIZABETH. The Human Element in Sex: Being a Medical Inquiry into the Relation of Sexual Physiology to Christian Morality. New ed. London, Eng.: Churchill, 1894. 76 pp.

Several other editions are in existence.

BOYD, N. E. To the Studious and Thoughtful, about Our Sexual Nature. 3rd ed. Pamphlets on Medicine, Vol. 7, No. 6. Washington, D.C.: Darby, 1887. 19 pp.

"Published by the Washington Society for Moral Education."

BRASEFIELD, NELL R. Commandment Seven. Boston, Mass.: Christopher, 1931. 81 pp.

BRILL, EARL H. Sex Is Dead, and Other Postmortems. New York: Seabury, 1967. 127 pp.

"The author discerns a swing back from an overemphasis on sex on the campus and in modern literature and drama."

BRITISH COUNCIL OF CHURCHES. Sex and Morality. New York: Fortress, 1966. 77 pp.

Also published in London by S.C.M. Press. "Discusses the Christian attitude toward premarital abstinence, examining various positions within the churches and pointing to the great need for dialogue and further study." "Report of a working party appointed by the Council in 1964."

BROWN, S. SPENCER N. Understanding Love and Sex. Waco, Texas: Texian, 1967. 198 pp.

BROWN, WILLIAM HERBERT. The Sex Life of Boys and Young Men. Cincinnati, Ohio: Standard Pub. Co., 1917. 146 pp.

BUREAU, PAUL. Towards Moral Bankruptcy. London, Eng.: Constable, 1925. 546 pp.

"Authorized translation from the original French 'L'Indiscipline Des Moeurs.'" Deals with French moral conditions.

CALVERTON, VICTOR FRANCIS. The Bankruptcy of Marriage. New York: Macaulay, 1928. 341 pp.

"Stresses the impermanence of sex attitudes."

CARPENTER, EDWARD. Homogenic Love, and Its Place in a Free Society. Manchester, Eng.: Labour Press, 1894. 51 pp.

CARPENTER, EDWARD. Love's Coming-of-Age: A Series of Papers on the Relations of the Sexes. Enl. ed. London, Eng.: Allen & Unwin, 1948. 221 pp.

First published in 1896 in England.

CARPENTER, EDWARD. Sex-Love and Its Place in a Free Society. Manchester, Eng.: Labour Press, 1894. 25 pp.

CHANCE, JANET. The Cost of English Morals. London, Eng.: Williams & Norgate, 1932. 127 pp.

"Aims to analyse the conventional code of English morals in its effect on sexual life; to show that it causes much suffering, and to ask whether it is worth the price that is paid."

CHESSER, EUSTACE. Is Chastity Outmoded? London, Eng.: Heinemann, 1960. 122 pp.

"A consideration of the arguments for and against premarital intercourse."

COMFORT, ALEXANDER. Barbarism and Sexual Freedom: Lectures on the Sociology of Sex from the Standpoint of Anarchism. London, Eng.: Freedom Press, 1948. 68 pp.

"A dissertation on the limitations of sexual freedom under the present social conditions which are described by the author as industrial barbarism. He rejects the conception of power in society as antisocial and biologically unsound, condemns coercive marriage as it exists in modern societies, and considers what pattern of sexual conduct would be appropriate to the free and anarchical society in which he believes."

CONFERENCE ON CHRISTIAN POLITICS, ECONOMICS AND CITIZENSHIP. The Relation of the Sexes. C.O.P.E.C. Commission Reports, Vol. 4. New York: Longmans, 1924. 219 pp.

"Report presented in Birmingham, Eng., April 5-12, 1924."

CORBIN, CAROLINE FAIRFIELD. A Woman's Philosophy of Love. Boston, Mass.: Lee and Shepard, 1893. 302 pp.

COWAN, JOHN. The Science of a New Life. New York: Source Book Press, 1970. 405 pp. Illus.

Reprint of 1874 edition, published by Cowan, New York.

CRAIG, ALEC. Sex and Revolution. London, Eng.: Allen & Unwin, 1934. 144 pp.

"Discusses the conflict between orthodox sexual morality and modernist sexual ethics, and urges that political revolution should be accompanied by sexual revolution."

CROLY, DAVID GOODMAN. The Truth about Love: A Proposed Sexual Morality Based upon the Doctrine of Evolution and Recent Discoveries in Medical Science. New York: Wesley, 1872. 259 pp.

First edition has a different subtitle, "A Book For Adults."

DARST, DAVID, and J. FORGUE. Sexuality on the Island Earth. New York: Paulist Press, 1970. 64 pp.

Contents: Sexuality on the Island Earth, by D. Darst and J. Forgue; All Relative Things Are Not Equally Relative, by J. M. Gustafson; We Are Born in Ambiguity and We Never Totally Escape It, by G. Baum; Meanings Given from Within, by S. Callahan; When Love Becomes the Problem, by R. May.

DAVIS, ANDREW JACKSON. The Genesis and Ethics of Conjugal Love. New York: Davis, 1874. 142 pp.

DEDEK, JOHN F. Contemporary Sexual Morality. New York: Sheed and Ward, 1971. 170 pp.

DEWAR, LINDSAY. Marriage without Morals: A Reply to Mr. Bertrand Russell. London, Eng.: Society for Promoting Christian Knowledge, 1931. 48 pp.

DOLAN, ALBERT HAROLD. A Modern Messenger of Purity. Chicago, Ill.: Carmelite Press, 1932. 188 pp.

"Sermons concerning the sixth commandment, delivered at the Eastern shrine of the Little Flower."

DOROTHY, CHARLES V. God Speaks Out on the New Morality. Pasadena, Calif.: Ambassador College, 1964. 324 pp. Illus.

"By a collaboration of faculty members of Ambassador College, Graduate School of Theology."

DRAKEFORD, JOHN W. The Great Sex Swindle. Nashville, Tenn.: Broadman, 1966. 128 pp.

"Discusses the trend away from the conventional concepts of morality, and the reasons for the new 'permissive' attitudes."

DUMAS, ALEXANDRE, THE YOUNGER. Man-Woman: Or, The Temple, the Hearth, the Street. Tr. and ed. by George Vandenhoff. With a Memoir of the Author. Philadelphia, Pa.: n.p., 1873. 113 pp.

Translation of L'Homme-Femme," published in 1872.

DUMAS, FRANCINE. Man and Woman: Similarity and Difference. Tr. from the French by Margaret House. Geneva, Switzerland: World Council of Churches, 1966. 88 pp.

Translation of "Homme et Femme, Similitude et Alterité."

DUVALL, SYLVANUS MILNE. Men, Women, and Morals. New York: Association Press, 1952. 336 pp.

ELLER, VERNARD. The Sex Manual for Puritans. Fwd. by Richard Armour. Nashville, Tenn.: Abingdon, 1971. 78 pp. Illus.

ELLIS, ALBERT. The Case for Sexual Liberty. Tucson, Ariz.: Seymour, 1965. 1 vol.

"Convincingly argues in favor of the replacement of enforced monogamy by a much freer code of premarital and marital relationships."

FISCHER, JACQUES. Love and Morality: An Attempt at a Physiological Interpretation of Human Thought. Tr. from the French by C. A. Phillips. New York: Knopf, 1927. 291 pp.

Translation of "L'Amour et La Morale," published by Payot, Paris, 1925.

FRASER, IAN M. Sex as Gift. Philadelphia, Pa.: Fortress, 1967. 80 pp.

British edition, published by Student Christian Movement Press, London, has the subtitle "A Personal Account of Work Undertaken for the Committee of Scottish Churches' House."

GALLICHAN, WALTER MATTHEW. The Great Unmarried. New York: Stokes, 1916. 224 pp.

"The author considers the causes of celibacy in many men and women and suggests some positive remedies."

GANDHI, MOHANDAS KARAMCHAND. Self-Restraint versus Self-Indulgence. Ahmedabad, India: Navajivan, 1958. 208 pp.

Earlier edition, 1928.

GOOD, FREDERICK L., and O. F. KELLY. Marriage, Morals and Medical Ethics. New York: Kenedy, 1951. 202 pp.

GRIFFITH, EDWARD FYFE. Morals in the Melting Pot. London, Eng.: Methuen, 1948. 295 pp.

"Entirely rewritten and brought up to date." First edition published in 1938 by Gollancz, London.

GRIFFITH, EDWARD FYFE. Sex and Citizenship. London, Eng.: Methuen, 1948. 240 pp.

"The theme of this book is the relationship between religion and sex, the social and ethical aspects of sex, and the significance of personal behaviour in the problems of social morality facing us today." Earlier edition published by Gollancz, London, in 1941.

GRUMMAN, DONALD L., et al. Sexuality: A Search for Perspective; Based on a Colloquy held at Michigan State University. New York: Van Nostrand Reinhold, 1971. 356 pp.

Colloquy held during the winter quarter of 1969.

GUYON, RENÉ. The Ethics of Sexual Acts. New York: Knopf, 1948. 383 pp.

Translation of "La Légimité Des Actes Sexuels" which constitutes Vol. 1 of the author's "Studies in Sexual Ethics." First published in 1929 and translated into English by J. C. and Ingeborg Flugel in 1933. British edition has the title "Sex Life and Sex Ethics."

GUYON, RENÉ. Sexual Freedom. Tr. from the French by Eden and Cedar Paul, with Intro. by Norman Haire. New York: Knopf, 1950. 344 pp.

Translation of "La Liberté Sexuelle" which constitutes Vol. 2 of the author's "Studies in Sexual Ethics." First published in 1933 and translated into English in 1939.

GUYON, RENÉ. Studies in Sexual Ethics. New York: Knopf, 1948-1950. 2 vols.

French title: "Études D'Éthique Sexuelle," 6 vols, 1929-1938. Contents: Vol. 1. The Ethics of Sexual Acts. Vol. 2. Sexual Freedom. "Translation of the first two volumes of a monumental work, planned to cover the whole field of sex ethics in ten volumes. After six volumes had been published in France the war stopped further progress, and it has not yet been possible to publish the remainder. Only the first two volumes have so far been translated into English. The author's argument is founded on the hypothesis that the sexual urge is a natural instinct entirely distinct from the reproductive function; that all sexual acts, including even those generally regarded as abnormal, are natural expressions of that instinct and are legitimate provided they cause no injury to anyone; and that sex behaviour should be removed from the sphere of morals and of law."

HAMLET, JOSEPH. Sex Dominates Life. Sydney, Australia: Currawong, 1944. 136 pp.

HEFNER, HUGH MARSTON. The Playboy Philosophy. Chicago, Ill.: HMH, 1963-1965. 194 pp.

"Reprinted installments from 'Playboy' magazine, December 1962-February 1965, of the columns in which Mr. Hefner spells out his philosophy about sex."

HERBERT, SOLOMON. Fundamentals in Sexual Ethics: An Inquiry into Modern Tendencies. London, Eng.: Black, 1920. 350 pp.

HILTNER, SEWARD. Sex and the Christian Life. New York: Association Press, 1957. 128 pp.

A discussion by a leading Protestant theologian and pastoral counselor, in which he draws from his earlier work, "Sex Ethics and the Kinsey Reports," published by Association Press, New York, 1953.

HODANN, MAX. History of Modern Morals. Tr. by Stella Browne. London, Eng.: Heinemann, 1937. 354 pp.

"A history of the development of the new science of sexology. The fight for Darwinism; against venereal disease; for birth control; for legalized abortion; for sex education; against the traditional taboos of patriarchal society."

HUTCHINSON, EVALINE DEMEZY SHIPLEY. Creative Sex. London, Eng.: Allen & Unwin, 1936. 122 pp.

"A revaluation of sex, based on the ethics of religion, discarding outworn conventions and dogmas, free from any conception of sin, accepting the teaching of modern science and philosophy."

INGRAM, KENNETH. Sex Morality Tomorrow. London, Eng.: Allen & Unwin, 1940. 176 pp.

"Describes the changes in the code of pre-war sex morality, analyses the imperfections of this code, and proposes constructive principles for a 'new morality.' Written from a progressive Christian standpoint." American edition published by Norton, New York, 1940.

JEFFS, C. Sex and Salvation: The World's Master Pet Sin—God Defeated. London, Eng.: Page & Thomas, 1950? 180 pp.

KARDINER, ABRAM. Sex and Morality. Indianapolis, Ind.: Bobbs-Merrill, 1954. 266 pp.

"A psychoanalyst examines the sexual practices of modern American men and women and the changes in marital and sex relations which he believes have resulted from a widespread relaxation of sexual morality in our culture." British edition published by Routledge, London, 1955.

KENNEDY, EUGENE C. The New Sexuality: Myths, Fables, and Hang-ups. Garden City, N.Y.: Doubleday, 1972. 212 pp.

KIMMEL, VIOLA MIZELL. The Double Standard of Conduct for Men and Women Today: Its Origin and Results. New York: n.p., 1916. 57 pp.

KIRCHWEY, FREDA, ed. Our Changing Morality: A Symposium. New York: Boni, 1924. 249 pp.

Partial Contents: Styles in Ethics, by B. Russell; Changes in Sex Relations, by Elsie C. Parsons; Toward Monogamy, by Charlotte P. Gilman; Dominant Sexes, by M. Vaerting; Can Men and Women be Friends? by F. Dell; Communist Puritans, by L. Fischer; Women and the New Morality, by Beatrice M. Hinkle.

KNAPP, JESSIE THOMAS. Taking "Forth the Precious from the Vile"—Jer. XV, 19, Including They Shall Know Themselves into One. Rev. and enl. Menasha, Wis.: Bantam, 1920. 220 pp.

"A study in higher mental hygiene, correlating biology, science, philosophy and religion."

KÖHN-BEHRENS, CHARLOTTE. Eros at Bay: The Illusion of Modern Love. Tr. from the German by D. and E. L. Rewald. London, Eng.: Putnam, 1962. 216 pp.

Translation of "Der Bedrohte Eros: Eine Kritik der Modernen Liebe," published by Biederstein, Munich, Germany, 1960.

LANDAU, ROM. Sex, Life and Faith: A Modern Philosophy of Sex. London, Eng.: Faber, 1946. 319 pp.

LANGDON-DAVIES, JOHN. Sex, Sin and Sanctity. London, Eng.: Gollancz, 1954. 358 pp.

LEWIS, D. Chastity: Or, Our Secret Sins. New York: n.p., 1890. 320 pp.

Listen, Son: A Father's Talks on the Facts of Life and Catholic Ideals of Social Conduct. Chicago, Ill.: Franciscan Herald, 1957. 72 pp.

LOWRY, OSCAR. A Virtuous Woman: Sex Life in Relation to the Christian Life. Grand Rapids, Mich.: Zondervan, 1938. 160 pp.

LOWRY, OSCAR. The Way of a Man with a Maid: Sexology for Men and Boys. Grand Rapids, Mich.: Zondervan, 1940. 160 pp.

"A companion volume to the author's 'A Virtuous Woman.' "

LUDER, WILLIAM FAY. A New Approach to Sex. Boston, Mass.: Farnsworth, 1966. 103 pp.

LYS, CLAUDIA De. To Be or Not to Be a Virgin. New York: Speller, 1960. 224 pp.

McDERMOTT, JOHN FRANCIS, ed. The Sex Problem in Modern Society: An Anthology. New York: Modern Library, 1931. 404 pp.

McGLOIN, JOSEPH T. Yearn a Little! Or, Why did God Come up with Two Sexes? Milwaukee, Wis.: Bruce, 1961. 134 pp. Illus.

Book 2 of the author's "Love—and Live."

MacKENZIE, IAIN FRASER. Social Health and Morals: An Analysis and A Plan. London, Eng.: Gollancz, 1947. 173 pp.

"Considers that, whereas our moral code used to be clear and well-defined, since the 1914-18 War our sexual morality has become chaotic. It is recognized that sexual abstinence of the unmarried is difficult and is injurious physically and psychically, but the only remedy suggested is early marriage, subsidized by the State."

MacKINNON, DONALD MacKENZIE, et al. God, Sex and War. Philadelphia, Pa.: Westminster, 1965? 127 pp.

Partial Contents: Ethical Problems of Sex, by H. Root; Personal Relations before Marriage, by H. Montefiore. Lectures delivered at Cambridge University, Cambridge, England, Easter term, 1962 and published by Collins, London, 1963.

McPARTLAND, JOHN. Sex in our Changing World. New York: Rinehart, 1947. 280 pp.

MACE, DAVID ROBERT. Does Sex Morality Matter? London, Eng: Rich and Cowan, 1943. 160 pp.

"A reasoned defence of the Christian standards of chastity and fidelity, a book for confused people, and others. Deals with such questions as free love, trial marriage, venereal disease, birth control, and divorce."

MANN, CHARLES HOLBROOK. Spiritual Sex Life: A Study in Swedenborg. Elkhart, Ind.: Bell, 1914. 63 pp.

MARGOLD, CHARLES WILLIAM. Sex Freedom and Social Control. Chicago, Ill.: University of Chicago Press, 1926. 143 pp.

Doctoral thesis, University of Michigan, 1925.

MEISEL-HESS, GRETE. The Sexual Crisis: A Critique of Our Sex Life. Authorized tr. by E. and C. Paul. New York: Critic and Guide Co., 1917. 345 pp.

Translation of "Die Sexuelle Krise," 1909.

MONEY-KYRLE, ROGER ERNLE. Aspasia, the Future of Amorality. London, Eng.: Paul, 1932. 141 pp.

NEWSOM, GEORGE ERNEST. The New Morality. London, Eng.: Nicholson, 1932. 319 pp.

1933 edition published in New York by Scribner.

OLFORD, STEPHEN F., and F. A. LAWES. The Sanctity of Sex. Westwood, N.J.: Revell, 1963. 128 pp.

O'NEIL, ROBERT P., and M. A. DONOVAN. Sexuality and Moral Responsibility. Washington, D.C.: Corpus, 1968. 154 pp.

ORAISON, MARC. The Human Mystery of Sexuality. New York: Sheed and Ward, 1967. 180 pp.

"A French priest-psychiatrist analyzes the influence of sex in personality development from the embryo to old age." Translation of original "Le Mystère Humain de la Sexualité," Paris, Seuil, 1966.

PEDERSEN, VICTOR COX. The Man a Woman Marries: Problems in Consideration. New York: Minton, 1929. 266 pp.

"This volume . . . is the companion or counterpart of my first book: 'The Woman a Man Marries.'"—Preface.

PEDERSEN, VICTOR COX. The Woman a Man Marries: An Analysis of Her Double Standard. New York: Doran, 1927. 276 pp.

POMERAI, RALPH De. Aphrodite: Or, The Future of Sex Relationships. London, Eng.: Paul, 1931. 96 pp.

POMERAI, RALPH De. The Future of Sex Relationships. London, Eng.: Paul, 1936. 132 pp.

"This volume, originally intended to be no more than an enlargement of my 'Aphrodite,' has turned out a completely new book."—Preface.

POMEROY, HIRAM STERLING. The Ethics of Marriage. New York: Funk & Wagnalls, 1888. 197 pp.

POST, LOUIS FREELAND. Ethical Principles of Marriage and Divorce. Chicago, Ill.: Public Publishing Co., 1906. 138 pp.

PUGH, WINFIELD SCOTT. The Doctor Discusses Morals. New York: William-Frederick, 1946. 75 pp.

RANKIN, WILLIAM HENRY. A Bachelor Defends American Women. New York: Thunder Enterprises, 1966. 252 pp.

1967 edition published by Pyramid in New York has the title "A Sexual Defense of American Women."

REE-BARTLETT, LUCY. Sex and Sanctity. London, Eng.: Longmans, 1912. 104 pp.

REICH, WILHELM. The Invasion of Compulsory Sex-Morality. New York: Farrar, 1971. 215 pp.

Translation of "Der Einbruch der Sexualmoral."

REICH, WILHELM. The Sexual Revolution: Towards a Self-governing Character Structure. New York: Orgone Press, 1945. 273 pp.

"Translated from the German in 1935; argues that repressions (in a general sense) bind energies which might otherwise be available for useful activity. The failure of the Russian sex reform movement is also discussed."

Original title "Die Sexualität im Kulturkampf." Several editions are in existence, latest 1971, Octagon, New York.

REICHE, REIMUT. Sexuality and Class Struggle. Tr. from the German by S. Bennett. New York: Praeger, 1971. 175 pp.

Translation of "Sexualität und Klassenkampf," Frankfurt, 1968. "The author argues that today's sexual revolution is actually establishment-serving."

RICHARDSON, NORMAN EGBERT. Sex Culture Talks to Young Men. New York: Eaton & Mains, 1912. 93 pp.

ROAN, CARL MARTIN. Home, Church, and Sex. New York: Washburn, 1930. 325 pp.

ROBINSON, WILLIAM JOSEPHUS. Sexual Truths versus Sexual Lies, Misconceptions, and Exaggerations. 2nd ed. Hoboken, N.J.: American Biological Society, 1932. 400 pp.

Also edition of 1919.

ROBINSON, WILLIAM JOSEPHUS, et al. Sex Morality: Past, Present, and Future. New York: Critic Guide Co., 1912. 192 pp.

1928 edition, Eugenics Publishing Co., New York.

ROSSITER, FREDERICK MAGEE. The Torch of Life: A Key to Sex Harmony. New York: Eugenics Publishing Co., 1932. 214 pp.

Several other editions are in existence.

ROVER, CONSTANCE. Love, Morals and the Feminists. London, Eng.: Routledge, 1970. 183 pp. Illus.

ROY, RUSTUM, and D. ROY. Honest Sex. New York: New American Library, 1968. 209 pp. Illus.

"Develops a religious ethic which is based on respect and love for each human individual rather than on dogmatic rules."

Reprinted in 1969.

ROYDEN, MAUDE. Sex and Commonsense. New York: Putnam, 1922. 211 pp.

Other editions are in existence.

RUSSELL, BERTRAND. Marriage and Morals. New York: Liveright, 1970. 316 pp.

"A survey of the changes in marital morality resulting from changes in social conditions from the dawn of history to the present day." Reprint of 1929 edition.

RUSSELL, GEORGE LAWRENCE. Sex Problems in War-Time. London, Eng.: Published for the Church of England by The Student Christian Movement, 1940. 63 pp.

RUSSELL, LAO. Love: A Scientific and Living Philosophy of Love and Sex. Swannanoa, Va.: University of Science and Philosophy, 1966. 207 pp. Illus.

SCANZONI, LETHA. Sex and the Single Eye. Grand Rapids, Mich.: Zondervan, 1968. 142 pp.

"In our sex-saturated society, young people are faced with conflicting codes and attitudes—and they are looking for a truly Christian philosophy or orientation toward sex."

SHERMAN, HAROLD MORROW. Your Key to Romance: A Frank Approach to Love for the Young Woman of Today. Hollywood, Calif.: House-Warven, 1951. 144 pp.

SMITH, ERNEST PARKINSON, and A. GRAHAM IKIN. Morality, Old and New. Derby, Eng.: Smith, 1964. 155 pp.

Original edition under the title "Sex Problems and Personal Relationships," published by Heinemann, London, 1956.

STOCKHAM, ALICE BUNKER. Karezza: Ethics of Marriage. New and rev. ed. Chicago, Ill.: Stockham, 1903. 141 pp.

Previous edition published in 1896.

SWEDENBORG, EMANUEL. The Delights of Wisdom Concerning Conjugial Love: After Which Follow the Pleasures of Insanity Concerning Scortatory Love. Philadelphia, Pa.: Bailey, 1796. 521 pp.

Translation of "Delitiae sapientiae de amore conjugali," Amsterdam, Netherlands, 1768. Several other editions and versions are in existence. 1938 edition published by the Swedenborg Publishing Association in New York has the title "Marital Love, Its Wise Delights."

TAYLOR, MICHAEL J., comp. Sex: Thoughts for Contemporary Christians. Garden City, N.Y.: Doubleday, 1972. 262 pp.

THIELICKE, HELMUT. The Ethics of Sex. New York: Harper, 1964. 338 pp.

"A Protestant view of human sexuality which combines theological and scientific thinking."

TOLSTOI, LEO NIKOLAEVICH. The Relations of the Sexes. New and enl. ed. London, Eng.: Free Age Press, 1908? 88 pp.

Translation from private letters, diaries, and unpublished manuscripts.

TOON, MARK. The Philosophy of Sex According to St. Thomas Aquinas. Catholic University of America. Philosophical Studies, No. 156. Washington, D.C.: Catholic University of America, 1954. 33 pp.

Abstract of thesis—Catholic University of America.

TROBISCH, WALTER, et al. Essays on Love: Or, "His" Reader on Love and the Christian View of Marriage. Chicago, Ill.: Inter-Varsity, 1968. 120 pp. Illus.

A collection of articles that had originally appeared in "His" magazine.

WALKER, BROOKS R. The New Immorality. Garden City, N.Y.: Doubleday, 1968. 228 pp.

"This work provides the kind of insights desperately needed by anyone trying to understand what has happened to the old morality."

WALKER, KENNETH MacFARLANE. Sex: And a Changing Civilization. London, Eng.: Lane, 1935. 135 pp.

"A psychological study of sex, and the effect of social changes on sexual ethics."

WALKER, MARY EDWARDS. Unmasked, Or The Science of Immorality. Philadelphia, Pa.: Boyd, 1878. 146 pp.

"To Gentlemen. By a Woman Physician and Surgeon."

1888 edition published by Walker, Jersey City, N.J.

WALSH, MOLLY. Sex and the People We Are: A Woman's Angle. New York: Paulist, 1967. 123 pp.

British edition, Darton, London, 1967.

WAYNE, T. G. [pseud.]. Morals and Marriage: The Catholic Background to Sex. New York: Longmans, 1936. 81 pp.

WELTMER, SIDNEY ABRAM. Regeneration: A Discussion of the Sex Question from a New and Scientific Standpoint. Nevada, Mo.: Weltmer Institute of Suggestive Therapeutics, 1908. 156 pp.

Previous editions published in 1889 and 1900.

WHITE, DOUGLAS. Modern Light on Sex and Marriage. London, Eng.: Skeffington, 1932. 127 pp.

WHITELEY, CHARLES HENRY, and W. M. WHITELEY. Sex and Morals. New York: Basic Books, 1967. 135 pp.

British edition published by Batsford, London.

WILLARD, ELIZABETH OSGWOOD GOODRICH. Sexology as the Philosophy of Life, Implying Social Organization and Government. Chicago, Ill.: Walsh, 1867. 483 pp.

WOOD, FREDERIC C. Sex and the New Morality. New York: Association Press, 1968. 157 pp.

"A former college chaplain discusses situation ethics as it applies to sexual morality with the ideal of love as the basis of morality and exploitation as the essence of immorality." "A book for young adults and those who counsel them."

WOODLING, MARVIN E. Who Are We?: Or Moral Degeneracy and Its Attendant Evils. New York: Abbey, 1902. 157 pp.

WRIGHT, HELENA. Sex and Society. Seattle, Wash.: University of Washington, 1969. 140 pp.

1968 edition published by Allen & Unwin, London, England.

WYNN, JOHN CHARLES, ed. Sexual Ethics and Christian Responsibility: Some Divergent Views. New York: Association Press, 1970. 224 pp.

14.
SOCIAL-SEXUAL PROBLEMS

ABORTION

The Abortion Act 1967. London, Eng.: Pitman Medical, 1969. 115 pp.

"Proceedings of a symposium held by the Medical Protection Society, in collaboration with the Royal College of General Practitioners, at the Royal College of Obstetricians and Gynaecologists, London, 7 February 1969. Includes the text of the act."

Abortion: Murder or Mercy? As Told to Margaret Witte Moore. Greenwich, Conn.: Fawcett, 1962. 128 pp.

ABORTION LAW REFORM ASSOCIATION. A Guide to the Abortion Act, 1967. London, Eng.: Abortion Law Reform Association, 1968. 25 pp.

An Alra publication. Includes the text of the Act.

APTEKAR, HERBERT. Anjea: Infanticide, Abortion and Contraception in Savage Society. New York: Godwin, 1931. 192 pp.

ARÉN, PER. On Legal Abortion in Sweden: Tentative Evaluation of Justification of Frequency during Last Decade. Acta obstetricia et gynecologica Scandinavica, Vol. 37, Supplement 1. Lund, Sweden: n.p., 1958. 75 pp. Illus.

"Based on three articles by Arén and others which were issued in 'Svensk läkartidningen,' 1957-58."

BATES, JEROME E., and E. S. ZAWADZKI. Criminal Abortion: A Study in Medical Sociology. Peoria, Ill.: Thomas, 1964. 250 pp.

BENNETT, JOHN TUSON. Abortion Law Reform? South Yarra, Victoria, Australia: John T. Bennett, 1968. 28 pp.

BROWNE, FRANCES WORSLEY STELLA, et al. Abortion. London, Eng.: Allen & Unwin, 1935. 143 pp.

Contents: The British Law as to Abortion; The Right to Abortion, by F. W. S. Browne; The Case Against Legalized Artificial Abortion, by A. M. Ludovici; The Problem of Deliberate Abortion, by Dr. Harry Roberts.

BURNS, JOHN. Observations on Abortion, Containing an Account of the Manner in Which It Takes Place, the Causes Which Produce It, and the Method of Preventing or Treating It. 2nd American ed. Springfield, Ill.: Thomas, 1809. 138 pp.

CALDERONE, MARY STEICHEN. Abortion in the United States. New York: Hoeber, 1958. 224 pp. Illus.

"A conference sponsored by the Planned Parenthood Federation of America, Inc., at Arden House and the New York Academy of Medicine. This report contains papers from authorities in the field concerning illegal and therapeutic abortion as a social as well as a legal problem. It includes a section on abortion statistics in the United States."

CALIFORNIA. POPULATION STUDY COMMISSION. Report to the Governor. Berkeley, Calif.: Dept. of Public Health, 1967. 108 pp. Illus.

CALLAHAN, DANIEL. Abortion: Law, Choice and Morality. New York: Macmillan, 1970. 524 pp.

CHURCH OF ENGLAND. NATIONAL ASSEMBLY. BOARD FOR SOCIAL RESPONSIBILITY. Abortion: An Ethical Discussion. London, Eng.: Church Information Office, 1965. 70 pp.

CLÉMENT, GUSTAVE. Thou Shalt Not Kill: A Doctor's Brief for the Unborn Child. Authorized tr. from the fourth French ed. Philadelphia, Pa.: Reilly, 1930. 152 pp.

Translation of "Le Droit de L'Enfant à Naître."

COOKE, NICHOLAS FRANCIS. Licensed Foeticide. Detroit, Mich.: American Observer Office, 1878. 15 pp.

COOKE, ROBERT E., et al. The Terrible Choice: The Abortion Dilemma. Fwd. by Pearl S. Buck. New York: Bantam, 1968. 110 pp. Illus.

"This book discusses the many issues involved in abortion without coming to any conclusions. Based on the proceedings of an International Conference on Abortion held in 1967 in Washington, D. C. Written under the auspices of the Joseph P. Kennedy, Jr. Foundation."

DAVID, HENRY PHILIP. Family Planning and Abortion in the Socialist Countries of Central and Eastern Europe: A Compendium of Observations and Readings. New York: Population Council, 1970. 306 pp.

"Prepared by the International Research Institutes for Research, Washington, D. C."

DEVEREUX, GEORGE. A Study of Abortion in Primitive Societies: A Typological, Distributional, and Dynamic Analysis of the Prevention of Birth in 400 Preindustrial Societies. New York: Julian, 1955. 394 pp.

DICKENS, BERNARD MORRIS. Abortion and the Law. London, Eng.: Mac-
Gibbon, 1966. 219 pp. Tables.

DONNER, JAMES [pseud.]. Women in Trouble: The Truth about Abortion in
America. Derby, Conn.: Monarch, 1959. 256 pp.

DUFFY, EDWARD A. The Effect of Changes in the State Abortion Laws.
Public Health Service Publication No. 2165. Rockville, Md.: U. S. Maternal
and Child Health Service, 1971. 28 pp. Illus.

EBON, MARTIN. Every-Woman's Guide to Abortion. New York: Universe
Books, 1971. 256 pp.

Also published in 1971 by Pocket Books, New York.

EKBLAD, MARTIN. Induced Abortion on Psychiatric Grounds: A Follow-Up
Study of 479 Women. Tr. from the Swedish. Acta psychiatrica et neuro-
logica Scandinavica. Supplement 99. Stockholm, Sweden: n.p., 1955. 237 pp.

FERRIS, PAUL. The Nameless: Abortion in Britain Today. London, Eng.:
Hutchinson, 1966. 173 pp.

Forum on Abortion, Brisbane, 1969. Kingston, Australia: Australian Frontier,
1969. 27 pp.

GALBALLY, R. T. J., et al. The Right to Be Born. A.C.T.S. Publications,
No. 1568. Melbourne, Australia: Australian Catholic Truth Society, 1970.
31 pp.

GEBHARD, PAUL H., et al. Pregnancy, Birth, and Abortion. New York:
Harper, 1958. 282 pp. Diagrams.

"The authors are all staff members of the Institute for Sex Research under
whose auspices the research was done. Utilizes data from the same sample
of 8,000 women which was used in the Kinsey report on the human female."

GLASS, ROBERT H., and N. G. KASE. Woman's Choice: A Guide to Contraception, Fertility, Abortion, and Menopause. New York: Basic Books, 1970.
144 pp. Illus.

GRANFIELD, DAVID. The Abortion Decision. Garden City, N.Y.: Doubleday,
1969. 240 pp.

Reissued in 1972.

GRISEZ, GERMAIN GABRIEL. Abortion: The Myths, the Realities and the
Arguments. New York: Corpus, 1970. 559 pp.

GROUP FOR THE ADVANCEMENT OF PSYCHIATRY. COMMITTEE ON PSY-
CHIATRY AND LAW. The Right to Abortion: A Psychiatric View. New
York: Scribner, 1970. 75 pp.

GUTTMACHER, ALAN FRANK, ed. The Case for Legalized Abortion Now.
Berkeley, Calif.: Diablo, 1967. 154 pp.

HALE, EDWIN MOSES. A Systematic Treatise on Abortion. Chicago, Ill.:
Halsey, 1866. 347 pp. Illus.

HALL, ROBERT ELLIOTT, ed. Abortion in a Changing World. New York: Columbia University Press, 1970. 2 vols. Illus.

"The proceedings of an international conference convened in Hot Springs, Virginia, November 17-20, 1968, by the Association for the Study of Abortion."

HALL, ROBERT ELLIOTT. A Doctor's Guide to Having an Abortion. New York: New American Library, 1971. 68 pp. Illus.

HART, THOMAS M., ed. Proceedings of the First American Symposium on Office Abortion Procedures. San Francisco, Calif.: Society for Humane Abortion, 1970. 49 pp.

"Sponsored by the Society for Humane Abortion, the symposium was held on May 16, 1970."

HENDIN, DAVID. Everything You Need to Know About Abortion. New York: Pinnacle, 1971. 192 pp.

HINDELL, KEITH, and M. SIMMS. Abortion Law Reformed. London, Eng.: Owen, 1971. 269 pp. Illus.

"Appendix 2 (pages 249-253) includes the Abortion act 1967."

United States publisher is Humanities, New York.

HORDERN, ANTHONY. Legal Abortion: The English Experience. New York: Pergamon, 1971. 322 pp.

JAVERT, CARL THEODORE. Spontaneous and Habitual Abortion. New York: Blakiston, 1957. 450 pp. Illus.

JENKINS, ALICE. Law for the Rich. Rev. ed. London, Eng.: Skilton, 1964. 96 pp.

Earlier edition, 1960, published by Gollancz, London, England.

"A plea for the reform of the abortion law."

JOYCE, ROBERT E., and M. R. JOYCE. Let Us Be Born: The Inhumanity of Abortion. Chicago, Ill.: Franciscan Herald, 1970. 98 pp.

KINDREGAN, CHARLES P. Abortion, the Law, and Defective Children: A Legal-Medical Study. Washington, D.C.: Corpus, 1969. 57 pp.

KINDREGAN, CHARLES P. The Quality of Life: Reflections on the Moral Values of American Law. Milwaukee, Wis.: Bruce, 1969. 120 pp.

KOLSTAD, PER. Therapeutic Abortion: A Clinical Study Based upon 968 Cases from a Norwegian Hospital, 1940-53. Oslo, Norway: n.p., 1957. 72 pp.

"The Norwegian Research Council for Science and the Humanities. Section: Medicine. E408-1. T."

KUMMER, JEROME M., ed. Abortion: Legal and Illegal, a Dialogue between Attorneys and Psychiatrists. 2nd ed. Santa Monica, Calif.: Kummer, 1969. 63 pp.

"Discussion taken from a panel conference and workshop sponsored by the Southern California Society of Psychiatry and the law in Los Angeles on November 23, 1963."

LADER, LAWRENCE. Abortion. Indianapolis, Ind.: Bobbs-Merrill, 1966. 212 pp.

"An authoritative and documented report on the laws and practices governing abortion in the United States and around the world. The author discusses religious positions on abortion and recommends reforms in our abortion laws." Reprinted by Beacon, Boston, in 1967.

LEE, NANCY HOWELL. The Search for an Abortionist. Chicago, Ill.: University of Chicago Press, 1969. 207 pp.

"Based on the author's thesis, Harvard University, 1968, entitled 'Acquaintance Networks in the Social Structure of Abortion.'"

LINDAHL, JAN. Somatic Complications Following Legal Abortion. Tr. from the Swedish. Stockholm, Sweden: n.p., 1958. 180 pp.

"Akademisk avhandling - Karolinska Institutet, Stockholm."

LIOTTA, MATTHEW A. The Unborn Child. New York: Little and Ives, 1931. 44 pp.

LOWE, DAVID. Abortion and the Law. Completed by Harriet Van Horne Lowe. New York: Pocket Books, 1966. 116 pp.

MACE, DAVID ROBERT. Abortion: The Agonizing Decision. Nashville, Tenn.: Abingdon, 1972. 144 pp.

MEDICAL DEFENCE UNION. Memoranda on the Abortion Act 1967, and the Abortion Regulations, 1968. London, Eng.: The Union, 1968. 29 pp.

MIETUS, NORBERT J. The Therapeutic Abortion Act: A Statement in Opposition. Sacramento, Calif.(?): n.p., 1967. 104 pp.

MONDRONE, DOMENICO. Mamma, Why Did You Kill Me? Tr. from the Italian original's 3rd ed. by Dino Soria. Baltimore, Md.(?): n.p., 1970. 47 pp.

Deals with the religious aspects of abortion.

NEW JERSEY. COMMISSION TO STUDY THE NEW JERSEY STATUTES RELATING TO ABORTION. Final Report to the Legislature. Trenton, N.J.: n.p., 1969. 135 pp.

NEWMAN, SIDNEY H., et al. Abortion Obtained and Denied: Research Approaches. New York: Population Council, 1971. 203 pp.

Workshop held at Bethesda, Maryland, 1969.

NOONAN, JOHN T., et al. The Morality of Abortion: Legal and Historical Perspectives. Cambridge, Mass.: Harvard University Press, 1970. 276 pp.

OVERSTREET, EDMUND W., ed. Therapeutic Abortion and Sterilization. Fluid, Electrolyte, and Acid-Base Problems, ed. by Roy W. Bonsnes. Clinical Obstetrics and Gynecology, Vol. 7, No. 1. New York: Hoeber, 1964. 255 pp. Illus.

PILPEL, HARRIET F., and K. P. NORWICK. When Should Abortion Be Legal? Public Affairs Pamphlet, No. 429. New York: Public Affairs Committee, 1969. 24 pp. Illus.

REITERMAN, CARL, ed. Abortion and the Unwanted Child. By the California Committee on Therapeutic Abortion. New York: Springer, 1971. 181 pp.

Conference held in San Francisco, California, in 1969.

ROBINS, SHARON, and B. GRANGER. Having a Wonderful Abortion. New York: Exposition Press, 1971. 152 pp.

A personal narrative.

ROBINSON, JOHN ARTHUR THOMAS, Bp. Abortion: Beyond Law Reform. London, Eng.: Abortion Law Reform Association, 1966. 10 pp.

Lecture delivered by the Bishop of Woolwich on October 22, 1966 to a meeting of the Abortion Law Reform Association.

RONGY, ABRAHAM JACOB. Abortion: Legal or Illegal? New York: Vanguard, 1933. 212 pp.

"Describes the position regarding induced abortion in the U. S. A., where the practice of abortions by qualified doctors is becoming extensive, apparently without interference from the governing bodies in the medical profession. The author expresses the opinion that inducement of abortion should be legally permissible on a number of grounds."

ROSEN, HAROLD. Abortion in America: Medical, Psychiatric, Legal, Anthropological, and Religious Considerations. Boston, Mass.: Beacon, 1967. 368 pp.

1954 edition published under the title "Therapeutic Abortion."

SCHAEFER, GEORGE, ed. Legal Abortions in New York State: Practical Aspects for the Physician. Modern Treatment, Vol. 8, No. 1. New York: Medical Dept., Harper, 1971. 221 pp. Illus.

Includes papers from the Symposium on Legal Abortion held October 28-November 1, 1970, at the annual meeting, District II of the American College of Obstetricians and Gynecologists in Nassau, Bahamas.

SCHULDER, DIANE, and F. KENNEDY. Abortion Rap. New York: McGraw-Hill, 1971. 238 pp.

SHAW, RUSSELL B. Abortion on Trial. London, Eng.: Hale, 1969. 176 pp.

Also published by Pflaum, Dayton, Ohio, in 1968.

SLOANE, BRUCE, ed. Abortion: Changing Views and Practice. New York: Grune and Stratton, 1971. 182 pp. Illus.

At the head of the title: "Seminars in Psychiatry. Reprinted in large part from the August 1970 issue (Vol. 2, No. 3) of Seminars in Psychiatry."

SMITH, DAVID T., comp. Abortion and the Law. Cleveland, Ohio: Press of Western Reserve, 1967. 237 pp.

"All essays except the Commentary were originally published in Vol. 17 of the 'Western Reserve Law Review' under the auspices of the Western Reserve University School of Law."

STREETER, JOHN SOPER. Practical Observations on Abortion. London, Eng.: Sherwood, 1840. 70 pp.

TARNESBY, HERMAN PETER. Abortion Explained: A Sunday Times Guide to Abortion within the Law. London, Eng.: Sphere, 1969. 110 pp. Illus.

TAYLOR, HOWARD C. The Abortion Problem. Baltimore, Md.: Williams & Wilkins, 1944. 182 pp.

"Proceedings of the Conference on Abortion Problems held under the auspices of the National Committee on Maternal Health, Inc. at New York Academy of Medicine, June 19th and 20th, 1942."

Van De WARKER, ELY. The Detection of Criminal Abortion and a Study of Foeticidal Drugs. Boston, Mass.: Campbell, 1872. 88 pp.

WEDGE, FLORENCE. Shall Baby Be Born or Aborted? Pulaski, Wis.: Franciscan, 1971. 84 pp.

WHITEHEAD, JAMES. On the Causes and Treatment of Abortion and Sterility. 2nd ed. Philadelphia, Pa.: Lea, 1854. 320 pp.

WILSON, PAUL R. The Sexual Dilemma: Abortion, Homosexuality, Prostitution, and the Criminal Threshold. St. Lucia, Australia: University of Queensland, 1971. 172 pp.

"A frank and systematic discussion of abortion, homosexuality and prostitution — categories of behavior which, in most of their manifestations are still illegal in many countries. The author attempts to solve the dilemma of having to decide whether these activities should remain illegal or whether public policy should be changed so that they no longer fall within the scope of criminal law."

WORLD HEALTH ORGANIZATION. Abortion Laws: A Survey of Current World Legislation, Geneva, Switzerland: World Health Organization, 1971. 78 pp.

"This survey was originally published in the International Digest of Health Legislation, 1970, Vol. 21, pages 437-512."

WRIGHT, HENRY CLARKE. The Unwelcome Child: Or The Crime of an Undesigned and Undesired Maternity. Boston, Mass.: Marsh, 1858. 120 pp.

X, DR. The Abortionist, by Dr. X as Told to Lucy Freeman. Garden City, N.Y.: Doubleday, 1962. 216 pp.

ILLEGITIMACY

BARRETT, ROBERT. Care of the Unmarried Mother. Alexandria, Va.: Robert Barrett, 1929. 224 pp.

"List of philanthropic maternity homes for unmarried mothers in the United States, pages 201-213."

BERNSTEIN, ROSE. Helping Unmarried Mothers. New York: Association Press, 1971. 187 pp.

BRUCE, ANN. Why Should I Be Dismayed? London, Eng.: Faber, 1958. 190 pp.

CHESSER, EUSTACE. Unwanted Child. London, Eng.: Rich and Cowan, 1947. 172 pp.

"Intended for all those concerned with the interest of the community and the future generations. The psychological and other causes of the problem of the unwanted child are analyzed, with many case-histories."

De FORD, MIRIAM ALLEN. Love-Children: A Book of Illustrious Illegitimates. New York: Dial, 1931. 302 pp.

Contents: Love-Children; The Bastard as King: William the Conqueror; The Bastard as Statesman: Alexander Hamilton; The Bastard as Scholar: Erasmus; The Bastard as Painter: Leonardo da Vinci; The Bastard as Scientist: D'Alembert; The Bastard as Composer: Borodin; The Bastard as Littérateur: Strindberg and Dumas, Fils; Finale.

DEWAR, DIANA. Orphans of the Living: A Study of Bastardy. London, Eng.: Hutchinson, 1968. 208 pp.

The Human Rights of Those Born out of Wedlock: A Consideration of Needs and How They Might be Met. London, Eng.: National Council for the Unmarried Mother and Her Child, 1969. 86 pp.

Proceedings of the Golden Jubilee Conference of National Council for the Unmarried Mother and Her Child, in honour of United Nations Human Rights Year, Thursday 21st November-Friday 22nd November 1968.

KRAUSE, HARRY D. Illegitimacy: Law and Social Policy. Indianapolis, Ind.: Bobbs, 1971. 379 pp.

LEAGUE OF NATIONS. CHILD WELFARE COMMITTEE. Study of the Position of the Illegitimate Child Based on the Information Communicated by Governments. Boston, Mass.: World Peace Foundation, 1929. 107 pp.

LUSHINGTON, GUY. Lushington's Law of Affiliation and Bastardy, with States, Notes, Forms, etc. 6th ed., by Albert Lieck. London, Eng.: Butterworth, 1936. 252 pp.

NATIONAL CONFERENCE ON SOCIAL WELFARE. Illegitimacy: Today's Realities. New York: National Council on Illegitimacy, 1971. 77 pp.

"Papers presented at the 1970 National Conference on Social Welfare."

OSOFSKY, HOWARD. The Pregnant Teen-Ager: A Medical, Educational, and Social Analysis. Springfield, Ill.: Thomas, 1968. 124 pp.

"A discussion of the medical, social and educational problems of the pregnant teenager."

RAINS, PRUDENCE MORS. Becoming an Unwed Mother: A Sociological Account. Chicago, Ill.: Aldine-Atherton, 1971. 207 pp.

ROBERTS, ROBERT W., ed. The Unwed Mother. New York: Harper, 1966. 270 pp.

"A collection of articles on unwed mothers and the social problem of illegitimacy which have appeared in various books and scholarly journals."

SCHATKIN, SIDNEY B. Disputed Paternity Proceedings. 2nd ed. Albany, N.Y.: Banks and Co., 1947. 614 pp.

Previous edition published in 1942.

VINCENT, CLARK EDWARD. Unmarried Mothers. New York: Free Press, 1969. 308 pp.

PROSTITUTION

ACTON, WILLIAM. Prostitution. Ed., with Intro. and notes, by Peter Fryer. New York: Praeger, 1969. 251 pp.

"Abridged from the second, expanded edition of 1870."

ACUNA, CHILE MAPOCHA. Women for Sale. New York: Godwin, 1931. 201 pp.

Deals with prostitution in New York City.

ADDAMS, JANE. A New Conscience and an Ancient Evil. New York: Macmillan, 1913. 219 pp.

Much of the material has been published in "McClure's" magazine.

Cf. Preface.

ADDITON, HENRIETTA SILVIS. City Planning for Girls: A Study of the Social Machinery for Case Work with Girls in Philadelphia. Social Service Monographs, No. 5. Chicago, Ill.: University of Chicago Press, 1928. 150 pp.

"With comments on present methods, brief histories of past experiments, and recommended plans for the future. Survey made by the Big Sister Association of Philadelphia with the co-operation of the leading agencies interested in work with girls. Cf. pages 2-3."

AGNIHOTRI, VIDYADHAR. Fallen Women: A Study with Special Reference to Kanpur. Kanpur, India: Maharaja Printers, 1954(?) 99 pp. Illus.

AMERICAN SOCIAL HYGIENE ASSOCIATION. The Case against the Red Light District. U. S. Public Health Service. V. D. No. 54. Issued by the Treasury Dept., U. S. Public Health Service, Washington, D. C. Washington, D.C.: Government Printing Office, 1920. 7 pp.

"Prepared for the United States Public Health Service and the various state boards of health by the American Social Hygiene Association, New York City."

ANDREWS, EDMUND. Prostitution and Its Sanitary Management. St. Louis, Mo.: n.p., 1871. 31 pp.

ARCHDALE, RICHARD LATHAM. Prostitution and Persecution. London, Eng.: Pall Mall Press, 1960. 30 pp.

"Some comments on the Street Offences Act."

BARLAY, STEPHEN. Bondage: The Slave Traffic in Women Today. New York: Funk & Wagnalls, 1968. 263 pp.

British edition has the title "Sex Slavery: A Documentary Report on the International Scene Today."

BARNES, CLAUDE TEANCUM. White Slave Act: History and Analysis of Its Words, Other Immoral Purpose. Salt Lake City, Utah: Claude T. Barnes, 1946. 49 pp.

BENJAMIN, HARRY, and R. E. L. MASTERS. Prostitution and Morality: A Definitive Report on the Prostitute in Contemporary Society and an Analysis of the Causes and Effects of the Suppression of Prostitution. Intro. by Walter C. Alvarez. New York: Julian, 1964. 495 pp.

British edition, Souvenir, London, England, 1965.

BEOTRA, B. R. The Suppression of Immoral Traffic in Women and Girls Act, 1956, with States Rules. 2nd ed. Allahabad, India: Law Book Co., 1970. 390 pp.

Deals with prostitution in India.

BÉRAUD, F. F. A. The Public Women of Paris: Being an Account of the Causes of Their Depravation, Their Several Classes, Their Means and Ways of Living, Their Arts, Habits, and Practices. New York: Dewitt and Davenport, 1849. 293 pp.

BULLOUGH, VERN L. The History of Prostitution. New Hyde Park, N.Y.: University Books, 1964. 304 pp.

"An historical survey of prostitution from primitive and ancient times to the present."

BURGESS, WILLIAM. The World's Social Evil: A Historical Review and Study of the Problems Relating to the Subject. Chicago, Ill.: Saul, 1914. 413 pp.

CARLEBACH, JULIUS. Juvenile Prostitutes in Nairobi. East African Studies, No. 16. Kampala, Uganda: Applied Research Unit, East African Institute of Social Research, 1962. 50 pp.

CHICAGO. VICE COMMISSION. The Social Evil in Chicago. New York: Arno, 1970. 399 pp. Illus.

"A study of existing conditions, with recommendations by the Vice Commission of Chicago, a municipal body appointed by the mayor and City council of the city of Chicago. Originally published in 1911 for distribution by the American Vigilance Association."

CLOUZET, MARYSE CHOISY. Psychoanalysis of the Prostitute. New York: Philosophical Library, 1961. 138 pp. Illus.

Also published by Pyramid, New York, in 1962.

COCKS, ORRIN GIDDINGS. The Social Evil and Methods of Treatment. Sex Education Series, Study No. 5. New York: Association Press, 1912. 68 pp.

"Designed for use as a basis and outline for discussion in groups of lay-men, such as men's clubs in churches."

CROSS, HAROLD H. U. The Lust Market. New York: Citadel, 1956. 256 pp.

De BECKER, JOSEPH ERNEST. The Sexual Life of Japan: Being an Exhaustive Study of the Nightless City or the "History of the Yoshiwara Yukwaku." New York: American Anthropological Society, 1934. 386 pp. Illus.

First edition published in 1899 by Maruya, Yokohama, Japan, under the title "The Nightless City."

De LEEUW, HENDRIK. Cities of Sin. New York: Wiley, 1947. 297 pp.

Appendix (pages 243-297) contains citations from the official records of the League of Nations. "Sketches in broad outlines the systems of white slavery and prostitution that exist in the most important Oriental cities." First published in 1933.

De LEEUW, HENDRIK. Sinful Cities of the Western World. New York: Citadel, 1949. 285 pp.

First published in 1934.

De MENTE, BOYE. The Pleasure Girls and Fleshpots of Japan. London, Eng.: Ortolan, 1966. 159 pp. Illus.

De MENTE, BOYE. Some Prefer Geisha: The Lively Art of Mistress-Keeping in Japan. Rutland, Vt.: Tuttle, 1966. 167 pp. Illus.

ELLIOTT, ALBERT WELLS. The Cause of the Social Evil. 3rd ed. Macon, Ga.: Elliott, 1919. 122 pp.

First and second editions are under the title "The Cause of the Social Evil and the Remedy."

FREED, LOUIS FRANKLIN. The Problem of European Prostitution in Johannesburg: A Sociological Survey. Cape Town, South Africa: Juta, 1949. 430 pp.

Thesis, University of Pretoria.

FRICHET, HENRY. Fleshpots of Antiquity: The Lives and Loves of Ancient Courtesans. Tr. from the French with Fwd., Intro., Essays, and Notes by A. F. Niemoeller. New York: Panurge, 1934. 249 pp.

Translation of "Courtisanes dans L'Antiquité."

GLOVER, EDWARD. The Psychopathology of Prostitution. 2nd ed. London, Eng.: Institute for the Study and Treatment of Delinquency, 1957. 20 pp.

GOLDMAN, EMMA, and A. SHULMAN. The Traffic in Women and Other Essays on Feminism. New York: Times Change Press, 1971. 63 pp. Illus.

Contents: Alix Shulman: The Most Dangerous Woman in the World. Emma Goldman: The Traffic in Women; Marriage and Love; Woman Suffrage.

The essays by Emma Goldman were first published in 1910 in a collection entitled "Anarchism and Other Essays."

GOSLING, JOHN, and D. WARNER. The Shame of a City: An Inquiry into the Vice of London. London, Eng.: W. H. Allen, 1960. 208 pp.

GOULD, GEORGE, and R. E. DICKERSON, comps. Digest of State and Federal Laws Dealing with Prostitution and Other Sex Offenses, with Notes on the Control of the Sale of Alcoholic Beverages as It Relates to Prostitution Activities. American Social Hygiene Assn., Publication No. A-422. New York: American Social Hygiene Assn., 1942. 453 pp.

"Published with the cooperation of the United States Public Health Service."

GREENWALD, HAROLD. The Elegant Prostitute: A Social and Psychoanalytic Study. New York: Walker, 1970. 305 pp.

"A revised edition, with new material, of 'The Call Girl,' published in 1958 by Ballantine, New York. This study shows us that the 'Elegant Prostitute,' when really confronted with herself is not so elegant but emerges as a human being with feelings."

HALL, GLADYS MARY. Prostitution in the Modern World: A Survey and a Challenge. New York: Emerson, 1936. 200 pp.

"Substance of book written as a thesis for the University of Liverpool. London edition, Williams and Norgate, 1933, has the title 'Prostitution: A Survey and a Challenge.'"

HANWAY, JONAS. Letters Written Occasionally on the Customs of Foreign Nations in Regard to Harlots, the Lawless Commerce of the Sexes, the Repentance of Prostitutes, the Great Humanity and Beneficial Effects of the Magdalene Charity in London, and the Absurd Notions of the Methodists. London, Eng.: Rivington, 1761. 597 pp.

HENRIQUES, FERNANDO. Prostitution and Society: A Survey. Chapter head designs by Rosamund Seymour. London, Eng.: MacGibbon, 1962-68. 3 vols. Illus.

Contents: Vol. 1. Prostitution and Society. Vol. 2. Prostitution and the New World. Vol. 3. Modern Sexuality.

"A sociological survey of prostitution from classical times to the present. 1961 edition published under the title 'Stews and Strumpets.'"

HUND, JOHN. The Physician and the Social Evil: A Study of the Development of the Medical Science under Religious Influence with Special Reference to the Social Evil. Milwaukee, Wis.: Enterprise, 1911. 44 pp.

INTERNATIONAL REVIEW OF CRIMINAL POLICY. Prostitution. International Review of Criminal Policy, No. 13. Paris, France: United Nations, 1958. 184 pp. Illus.

United Nations, Document ST.SOA/Ser. M/13. Text in English, French, or Spanish.

JAMES, DONALD H. Sex and Business. New York: Macfadden, 1971. 192 pp.

KEMP, TAGE. Prostitution: An Investigation of Its Causes, Especially with Regard to Hereditary Factors. Copenhagen, Denmark: Levin and Munksgaard, 1936. 253 pp. Diagrams.

"Translated from the Danish."

KHALAF, SAMIR. Prostitution in a Changing Society: A Sociological Survey of Legal Prostitution in Beirut. Beirut, Lebanon: Khayats, 1965. 163 pp.

KIMBALL, NELL. Nell Kimball: Her life as an American Madam, by Herself. Ed. with Intro. by Stephen Longstreet. New York: Macmillan, 1970. 286 pp.

LACROIX, PAUL [Pierre Dufour]. History of Prostitution among All the Peoples of the World, from the Most Remote Antiquity to the Present Day. Tr. from the French by Samuel Putnam. New ed. New York; Covici, 1931. 2 vols.

Earlier edition, 1926. Translation of "Histoire De La Prostitution Chez Toux Les Peuples Du Monde," published in Paris, France, 1851-1853.

LEAGUE OF NATIONS. ADVISORY COMMITTEE ON SOCIAL QUESTIONS. Enquiry Into Measures of Rehabilitation of Prostitutes. New York: Columbia University Press, 1938. 4 pts. in 3 vols.

Pt. 1. Prostitutes: Their Early Lives. Pt. 2. Social Services and Venereal Disease. Pt. 3. Methods of Rehabilitation of Adult Prostitutes. Pt. 4. Conclusions and Recommendations.

LONGSTREET, STEPHEN, and E. LONGSTREET. Yoshiwara: City of the Senses. New York: McKay, 1970. 225 pp. Illus.

Deals with prostitution in Tokyo.

McCABE, JOSEPH. The Story of the World's Oldest Profession: Prostitution in the Ancient, Medieval and Modern Worlds. Girard, Kans.: Haldeman-Julius, 1932. 123 pp.

MARSH, MARGUERITE. Prostitutes in New York City: Their Apprehension, Trial, and Treatment, July 1939-June 1940. New York: Welfare Council, 1941. 178 pp.

"Mimeographed."

MINER, MAUDE EMMA. Slavery of Prostitution: A Plea for Emancipation. New York: Macmillan, 1916. 308 pp.

First published as a doctoral thesis at Columbia University, New York, in 1916.

O'CALLAGHAN, SEAN. Damaged Baggage: The White Slave Trade and Narcotics Trafficking in the Americas. New York: Roy, 1970. 191 pp.

O'CALLAGHAN, SEAN. The Slave Trade Today. New York: Crown 1962. 191 pp.

"Reports on slave traffic which the author maintains is prevalent in many African and Middle East areas."

O'CALLAGHAN, SEAN. The White Slave Trade. London, Eng.: New English Library, 1967. 159 pp.

1965 edition published by Hale in London.

O'CALLAGHAN, SEAN. The Yellow Slave Trade: A Survey of the Traffic in Women and Children in the East. London, Eng.: Blond, 1968. 140 pp.

POWELL, AARON MACY, ed. The National Purity Congress, Its Papers, Addresses, Portraits: An Illustrated Record of the Papers and Addresses of the First National Purity Congress, Held under the Auspices of the American Purity Alliance in Baltimore, October 14, 15 and 16, 1895. New York: American Purity Alliance, 1896. 453 pp.

RANGA, RAO M., and J. V. R. RAO. The Prostitutes of Hyderabad: A Study of the Socio-Cultural Conditions of the Prostitutes of Hyderabad. Hyderabad, India: Assn. for Moral and Social Hygiene in India, Andhra Pradesh Branch, 1970? 79 pp.

REITMAN, BEN LEWIS. Second Oldest Profession: A Study of the Prostitute's Business Manager. New York: Vanguard, 1931. 266 pp.

ROSS, ALLEN V. Vice in Bombay. London, Eng.: Tallis, 1969. 192 pp. Plates.

American edition has the title "Bombay after Dark."

RUBIN, THEODORE ISAAC. In the Life. New York: Macmillan, 1961. 166 pp.

A prostitute's story of her life as told to the author who was Chief Psychiatrist at the Women's House of Detention, New York.

RYAN, MICHAEL. Prostitution in London, with a Comparative View of That of Paris and New York. London, Eng.: Baillière, 1839. 447 pp.

SANGER, WILLIAM W. History of Prostitution: Its Extent, Causes, and Effects throughout the World. New York: Harper, 1858. 685 pp.

"Being an official report to the Board of Alms-House Governors of the city of New York." Several editions are in existence.

SCHREIBER, HERMANN [Lujo Bassermann]. The Oldest Profession. New York: Stein and Day, 1968. 300 pp.

1967 edition published in London by Barker. Translation of "Das Älteste Gewerbe, Eine Kulturgeschichte."

SCOTT, BENJAMIN. A State Iniquity: Its Rise, Extension, and Overthrow. New York: Kelley, 1968. 401 pp.

Deals with prostitution in Great Britain. Reprint of the 1890 edition.

SCOTT, GEORGE RYLEY. A History of Prostitution from Antiquity to the Present Day. Rev. and enl. London, Eng.: Torchstream, 1952. 320 pp.

"Deals objectively with the causes of prostitution from ancient times, the practice of prostitution today in various countries, regulated versus uncontrolled prostitution, and the future of prostitution." 1936 edition published by Greenberg, New York.

SPINGARN, ARTHUR BARNETT. Laws Relating to Sex Morality in New York City. Publications of the Bureau of Social Hygiene. New York: Century, 1926. 171 pp.

First published 1917.

STERN, MICHAEL. The White Ticket: Commercialized Vice in the Machine Age, from the Official Records at the New York District Attorney's Office. New York: National Library Press, 1936. 255 pp.

TABOR, PAULINE. Pauline's. Louisville, Ky.: Touchstone, 1971. 295 pp. Illus.

This is the autobiography of the owner/operator of a house of prostitution.

TAIT, WILLIAM. Magdalenism: An Inquiry into the Extent, Causes, and Consequences of Prostitution in Edinburgh. 2nd ed. Edinburgh, Scotland: Rickard, 1842. 360 pp.

Earlier edition, 1840.

TALBOT, JAMES BEARD. The Miseries of Prostitution. 3rd ed. London, Eng.: Madden, 1844. 80 pp.

UNITED NATIONS. SECRETARIAT. Study on Traffic in Persons and Prostitution: Suppression of the Traffic in Persons and of the Exploitation of the Prostitution of Others. New York: Dept. of Economic and Social Affairs, 1959. 57 pp.

United Nations. Document.

VINTRAS, ACHILLE. On the Repressive Measures Adopted in Paris Compared with the Uncontrolled Prostitution of London and New York. London, Eng.: Hardwicke, 1867. 86 pp.

WAKE, CHARLES STANILAND. Sacred Prostitution and Marriage by Capture. n.p., 1929. 114 pp.

Originally included in the author's "Serpent-Worship, and Other Essays," published in London, England, by Redway, 1888. This work also contains a chapter on totemism.

WARDLAW, RALPH. Lectures on Magdalenism: Its Nature, Extent, Effects, Guilt, Causes, and Remedy. New York: Redfield, 1843. 172 pp.

First published in Glasgow, Scotland, by Maclehose in 1842 under the title "Lectures on Female Prostitution." "The lectures were delivered and published by special request of forty ministers of the gospel, and eleven hundred fellow-Christians."

WARREN, JOHN H. Thirty Years' Battle with Crime. New York: Arno, 1970. 400 pp. Illus.

1874 edition has the subtitle "Or the Crying Shame of New York; as Seen under the Broad Glare of an Old Detective's Lantern."

WATERMAN, WILLOUGHBY CYRUS. Prostitution and Its Repression in New York City, 1900-1931. Columbia University. Columbia Studies in the Social Sciences, No. 352. New York: AMS Press, 1968. 164 pp.

Reprint of 1932 edition, published by Columbia University Press, New York.

WINICK, CHARLES, and P. M. KINSIE. The Lively Commerce: Prostitution in the United States. Chicago, Ill.: Quadrangle, 1971. 320 pp.

SEX OFFENSES AND OFFENDERS

AHMAD, EJAZ. Law Relating to Sexual Offenses. Lucknow, India: Law Book Mart, 1963. 372 pp.

Deals with sex crimes in India and Great Britain.

ALABAMA. GOVERNOR'S COMMISSION TO STUDY SEX OFFENSES. Interim Report. Birmingham, Ala.: 1967. 27 leaves.

Deals with sex crimes in Alabama.

AMIR, MENACHEM. Patterns in Forcible Rape. Chicago, Ill.: University of Chicago Press, 1971. 394 pp.

BAILEY, DERRICK SHERWIN. Sexual Offenders and Social Punishment. Westminster, Eng.: Church Information Board, 1956. 120 pp.

"Being the evidence submitted on behalf of the Church of England Moral Welfare Council to the Departmental Committee on Homosexual Offences and Prostitution, with other material relating thereto. Statutes relating to homosexual offences and prostitution, pages 112-120."

Bibliographical footnotes.

BECKER, HAROLD K., et al. New Dimensions in Criminal Justice. Metuchen, N.J., Scarecrow, 1968. 279 pp.

Deals with the sexual sterilization of criminals.

BIGGS, EARL R. How to Protect Your Child from the Sex Criminal: Rules and Suggestions for the Protection of Children from Sexual Molestation, Assault and Murder. Portland, Oreg.: New Science Book Co., 1950. 63 pp.

BLACKER, CHARLES PATON. Voluntary Sterilization. New York: Oxford University Press, 1934. 145 pp.

"Advocates the legalization of voluntary sterilization as recommended by the Eugenics Society and the Brock Report. Of interest to doctors and laymen, written mainly for the latter."

BREMER, JOHAN. Asexualization: A Follow-Up Study of 244 Cases. New York: Macmillan, 1959. 366 pp.

Deals with the castration of criminals and defectives in Norway.

BURTON, LINDY. Vulnerable Children: Three Studies of Children in Conflict, Accident Involved Children, Sexually Assaulted Children, and Children with Asthma. London, Eng.: Routledge, 1968. 277 pp.

CALIFORNIA. LANGLEY PORTER NEUROPSYCHIATRIC INSTITUTE, SAN FRANCISCO. Final Report on California Sexual Deviation Research. California. Legislature. Assembly. Assembly Interim Committee Reports, 1953-1955. Vol. 20, No. 1. Sacramento, Calif.: Printed by the Assembly of the State of California, 1954. 160 pp.

CALIFORNIA. LEGISLATURE. ASSEMBLY. INTERIM COMMITTEE ON JUDICIAL PROCESS. Preliminary Report of the Subcommittee on Sex Crimes. Sacramento, Calif.: Assembly of the State of California, 1950. 269 pp.

CALIFORNIA. LEGISLATURE. ASSEMBLY. INTERIM COMMITTEE ON JUDICIAL SYSTEMS AND JUDICIAL PROCESSES. Report of the Subcommittee on Sex Crimes. Sacramento, Calif.: Assembly of the State of California, 1952. 64 pp.

CAMBRIDGE. UNIVERSITY. DEPARTMENT OF CRIMINAL SCIENCE. Sexual Offences: A Report. English Studies in Criminal Science, Vol. 9. New York: St. Martin's, 1957. 553 pp.

CANADA. ROYAL COMMISSION ON THE CRIMINAL LAW RELATING TO CRIMINAL SEXUAL PSYCHOPATHS. Report. Ottawa, Canada: Royal Commission on the Criminal Law..., 1958. 200 pp. Tables.

CHURCH OF ENGLAND MORAL WELFARE COUNCIL. The Law on Sexual Offences: A Practical Handbook for the Clergy and Social Workers. Westminster, Eng.: Church Information Board, 1956. 22 pp.

CLAYTON, GEORGE. Sex and Crime. New York: Macfadden, 1971. 192 pp.

DALY, CAHAL B. Morals, Law, and Life. Chicago, Ill.: Scepter, 1966. 228 pp.

English edition published by Burns, London, in 1962 has the subtitle: "An Examination of the Book — 'The Sanctity of Life and the Criminal Law' " (written by G. L. Williams).

De FRANCIS, VINCENT. Protecting the Child Victim of Sex Crimes Committed by Adults: Final Report. Denver, Colo.: American Humane Assn., Children's Division, 1969. 230 pp.

De RIVER, JOSEPH PAUL. The Sexual Criminal: A Psychoanalytical Study. 2nd ed. Springfield, Ill.: Thomas, 1956. 375 pp. Illus.

Earlier edition, 1949.

De RIVER, JOSEPH PAUL. Crime and the Sexual Psychopath. Springfield, Ill.: Thomas, 1958. 346 pp. Illus.

DOSHAY, LEWIS JACOB. The Boy Sex Offender and His Later Career. Fwd. by George W. Henry. Montclair, N.J.: Patterson Smith, 1969. 206 pp. Illus.

Reprint of 1943 edition published by Grune, New York.

DRUMMOND, ISABEL. The Sex Paradox. New York: Putnam, 1953. 369 pp.

Deals with the laws on sex in the United States.

DRZAZGA, JOHN. Sex Crimes. Springfield, Ill.: Thomas, 1960. 242 pp.

DUFFY, CLINTON T. Sex and Crime. Garden City, N.Y.: Doubleday, 1965. 203 pp.

"The author, ex-warden of San Quentin Prison, believes that sex is the cause of nearly all deviant behavior."

EAST, SIR WILLIAM NORWOOD. Sexual Offenders. London, Eng.: Delisle, 1955. 101 pp.

With extracts from the "Psychological Treatment of Crime," by East and Hubert; a postscript on sexual perversions, by Desmond Curran; and an epilogue, by Clifford Allen.

ELLIS, ALBERT, and R. BRANCALE. The Psychology of Sex Offenders. American Lecture Series, Publication No. 297. The Bannerstone Division of American Lectures in Public Protection. Springfield, Ill.: Thomas, 1956. 132 pp.

FISHMAN, JOSEPH FULLER. Sex in Prison: Revealing Sex Conditions in American Prisons. New York: Padell, 1951. 256 pp.

1934 edition published by National Library Press in New York.

Also published by Lane, London, England.

FOXE, ARTHUR NORMAN. Crime and Sexual Development: Movement and Fixation of the Libido in Criminotic Individuals. New York: Monograph, 1936. 91 pp.

FRANKEL, EMIL. Psychiatric Characteristics of Sex Offenders. Trenton, N.J.: Dept. of Institutions and Agencies, 1950. 28 leaves.

A statistical analysis of 250 sex offenders examined at the New Jersey State Diagnostic Center at Menlo Park made in collaboration with the Center's director, Ralph Brancale and members of the staff.

FRISBIE, LOUISE V. Another Look at Sex Offenders in California. California Mental Health Research Monograph, No. 12. Sacramento, Calif.: Dept. of Mental Hygiene, Bureau of Research and Statistics, 1969. 272 pp. Illus.

FRISBIE, LOUISE V., and E. H. DONDIS. Recidivism among Treated Sex Offenders. California Mental Health Research Monograph, No. 5. Sacramento, Calif.: Dept. of Mental Hygiene, Bureau of Research and Statistics, 1965. 159 pp. Illus.

"A study of 1921 male dischargees from a California State Hospital."

GEBHARD, PAUL H., et al. Sex Offenders: An Analysis of Types. New York: Harper, 1965. 923 pp. Illus.

"A study by the Institute for Sex Research which contrasts the case histories of men in prison for sex offenses and a control group of males never convicted."

GIBBENS, TREVOR CHARLES NOEL, and J. PRINCE. Child Victims of Sex Offences. London, Eng.: Institute for Study & Treatment of Delinquency, 1963. 23 pp.

GIGEROFF, ALEX K. Sexual Deviations in the Criminal Law: Homosexual, Exhibitionistic, and Pedophilic Offences in Canada. Clarke Institute of Psychiatry. Monograph Series, 2. Toronto, Canada: University of Toronto, 1968. 218 pp.

"Published for the Clarke Institute of Psychiatry."

GREAT BRITAIN. HOME DEPARTMENT. Report of the Departmental Committee on Sexual Offences against Young Persons. Parliament. Papers by Command. Cmd. 2561. London, Eng.: H.M. Stationery Office, 1925. 103 pp.

GUPTA, RAM LAL. The Medico-Legal Aspects of Sexual Offences. Lucknow, India: Eastern Book Co., 1964. 344 pp. Illus.

Deals with sex offenses in India.

GUTTMACHER, MANFRED SCHANFARBER. Sex Offenses: The Problem, Causes, and Prevention. New York: Norton, 1951. 159 pp.

HARDIE, GARTH M., and G. F. HARTFORD. Commentary on the Immorality Act (Act No. 23 of 1957). Cape Town, South Africa: Juta, 1960. 113 pp.

Deals with sex crimes laws in South Africa.

HART, HERBERT LIONEL ADOLPHUS. Law, Liberty and Morality. New York: Oxford University Press, 1968. 88 pp.

Reprint of 1963 edition published by Stanford University Press, Stanford, California. Originally given as part of Harry Camp Lectures at Stanford University in 1962.

HOPPER, COLUMBUS B. Sex in Prison: The Mississippi Experiment with Conjugal Visits. Baton Rouge, La.: Louisiana State University Press, 1969. 160 pp. Illus.

"A professor of sociology, Dr. Hopper evaluates the program of conjugal visits at the Mississippi State Penitentiary at Parchman and their effects on prison and family life, suggesting that such a program warrants serious consideration for possible application to other penal institutions."

HUMAN BETTERMENT FOUNDATION, CALIFORNIA. Collected Papers on Eugenics Sterilization in California: A Critical Study of Results in 6,000 Cases. Intro. by E. S. Gosney. Pasadena, Calif.: Human Betterment Foundation, 1930. 26 vols. in 1. Illus.

"The first work of assembling and analyzing the case histories of California institutions was turned over to Paul Popenoe ... and most of the papers collected in this volume bear his name." — Introduction.

ILLINOIS. COMMISSION ON SEX OFFENDERS. A Report to the 74th General Assembly and the Governor, the Honorable Otto Kerner. Evanston, Ill.: n.p., 1965. 54 leaves.

KARPMAN, BENJAMIN. The Sexual Offender and His Offenses: Etiology, Pathology, Psychodynamics, and Treatment. New York: Julian, 1954. 744 pp. Diagrams.

KLING, SAMUEL G. Sexual Behavior and the Law. New York: Pocket Books, 1969. 294 pp.

First published in 1965 by Geis, New York. "Deals with the laws on sex in popular question and answer form."

KRAFFT-EBING, RICHARD. The Sexual Offender. Selected with Intro. by Robert H. V. Ollendorff. London, Eng.: Ortolan, 1967. 159 pp.

Selected translations from "Psychopathia Sexualis," written by Krafft-Ebing in the nineteenth century.

LINDNER, HAROLD. An Analysis of the Psychological Characteristics of a Selected Group of Imprisoned Sexual Offenders. College Park, Md.: n.p., 1951. 216 leaves. Illus.

Thesis, University of Maryland. Typescript.

LINDSEY, BENJAMIN BARR, and W. EVANS. The Revolt of Modern Youth. New York: Boni, 1925. 364 pp.

"Observations by Judge Lindsey, made in the Juvenile Court of Denver, Colorado, of unconventional developments in social and especially in sexual behavior among American adolescent youths and girls."

MacDONALD, JOHN MARSHALL. Rape Offenders and Their Victims. With a chapter by Hunter S. Thompson. Springfield, Ill.: Thomas, 1971. 342 pp.

MASTERS, ROBERT E. L., and E. LEA. Sex Crimes in History: Evolving Concepts of Sadism, Lust-Murder, and Necrophilia, from Ancient to Modern Times. Including: A Historical Survey of Sex Savages and Sexual Savagery in the East by Allen Edwardes. New York: Matrix House, 1966. 323 pp.

1963 edition published by Julian Press, New York.

MAY, GEOFFREY. Social Control of Sex Expression. New York: Morrow, 1931. 307 pp.

"A study of the efforts of the State to control the sexual life of the individual. Traces the development of the doctrine of sex repression among primitive peoples and by the Christian Church, and its enforcement in England and America."

MELLER, NORMAN. Sexual Psychopaths. Hawaii. University, Honolulu. Legislative Reference Bureau, Report, 1949, No. 2. Honolulu, Hawaii: Legislative Reference Bureau, University of Hawaii, 1949. 35 leaves.

MICHIGAN. GOVERNOR'S STUDY COMMISSION ON THE DEVIATED CRIMINAL SEX OFFENDER. Report. Lansing, Mich.: n.p., 1951. 245 pp. Illus.

MINNESOTA. DEPARTMENT OF CORRECTIONS. SECTION ON RESEARCH AND STATISTICS. The Sex Offender in Minnesota. St. Paul, Minn.: n.p., 1964. 43 leaves.

"A descriptive study of 149 felons sentenced to the State Prison or the State Reformatory for Men for sex and associated offenses from July 1, 1960 through June 30, 1962. Director of Research: Nathan G. Mandel."

MINNESOTA. LEGISLATURE. INTERIM COMMISSION ON PUBLIC WELFARE LAWS. Sex Psychopath Laws: Report. St. Paul, Minn.: n.p., 1959. 41 pp.

MOHR, JOHANN W. A Documentary Follow-Up of Sexual Offenders Referred to the Forensic Out-Patient Clinic. Seminar No. 34. Toronto, Canada: Toronto Psychiatric Hospital, 1960. 35 pp.

Mimeographed.

MORLAND, NIGEL. An Outline of Sexual Criminology. New York: Hart, 1967. 160 pp.

First published by Tallis, Oxford, England, in 1966.

MUELLER, GERHARD O. W. Legal Regulation of Sexual Conduct. New York: Oceana, 1961. 159 pp.

NEVADA. LEGISLATIVE COUNSEL BUREAU. Rehabilitation of Sex Offenders in Nevada: An Evaluation. Carson City, Nev.: n.p., 1962. 81 pp. Illus.

NEVADA. LEGISLATIVE COUNSEL BUREAU. Nevada Sexual Deviation Research. Bulletin No. 24. Carson City, Nev.: n.p., 1955. 24 pp.

NEW YORK STATE. DEPARTMENT OF MENTAL HYGIENE. Final Report: Research Project for the Study and Treatment of Persons Convicted of Crimes Involving Sexual Aberrations, June 1952 to June 1955. New York: n.p., 1956. 401 pp. Illus.

Initial report, issued by the Commissioners of Mental Hygiene and Correction, has the title "Report on Study of 102 Sex Offenders at Sing Sing Prison."

OREGON, LEGISLATIVE ASSEMBLY. INTERIM COMMITTEE ON SOCIAL PROBLEMS. Report on the Care, Treatment and Rehabilitation of Sex Offenders to the Fifty-Second Legislative Assembly, State of Oregon. Salem, Oregon: n.p., 1962. 63 pp.

OREGON. LEGISLATIVE ASSEMBLY. INTERIM COMMITTEE ON SOCIAL PROBLEMS. Selected Background Materials on the Problem of Sex Offenders. Salem, Oregon: n.p., 1962. 1 vol.

PARKER, TONY. The Hidden World of Sex Offenders. Indianapolis, Ind.: Bobbs-Merrill, 1969. 242 pp.

British edition by Hutchinson in London has the title "The Twisting Lane: Some Sex Offenders."

PENNSYLVANIA. DEPARTMENT OF JUSTICE. BUREAU OF CORRECTION. Characteristics of "Barr-Walker" Cases in the Bureau of Correction. Harrisburg, Pa.: n.p., 1957. 27 pp. Tables.

Deals with the laws on sex in the state of Pennsylvania.

PENNSYLVANIA. GENERAL ASSEMBLY. JOINT STATE GOVERNMENT COMMISSION. PANEL OF MEDICAL ADVISORS ON HEALTH AND WELFARE. The Dangerous Sex Offender: A Report to the Joint State Government Commission, General Assembly of the Commonwealth of Pennsylvania. Harrisburg, Pa.: n.p., 1963. 40 pp. Tables.

PLOSCOWE, MORRIS. Sex and the Law. Rev. ed. New York: Ace, 1962. 288 pp.

1951 edition published by Prentice-Hall, New York. "A judge shows the confusion and differences that exist in our current sex laws in each state. He makes a case for the need for drastic change in our laws governing marriage, divorce, and many other aspects of sexual behavior."

POLLAK, OTTO, and A. S. FRIEDMAN, eds. Family Dynamics and Female Sexual Delinquency. Palo Alto, Calif.: Science and Behavior Books, 1969. 210 pp.

"This is a series of scholarly papers on the family factors in sexual delinquency as well as socio-economic, cultural, and psychodynamic factors and their application for family therapy. The book grew out of a seminar and a special training and demonstration project of the Philadelphia Psychiatric Center and the United States Department of Health, Education, and Welfare."

POLLENS, BERTRAM. The Sex Criminal. New York: Macaulay, 1938. 211 pp. Illus.

POPENOE, PAUL BOWMAN, and E. S. GOSNEY. Twenty-Eight Years of Sterilization in California. 3rd ed. Princeton, N.J.: Birthright, Inc., 1946. 44 pp.

1939 edition published by Human Betterment Foundation, Pasadena, California.

RADIN, EDWARD D. Crimes of Passions. New York: Putnam, 1953. 247 pp.

RADIN, EDWARD D. Web of Passion: A Dramatic Collection of True Crime Cases. New York: Popular Library, 1955. 126 pp.

REINHARDT, JAMES MELVIN. Sex Perversions and Sex Crimes. Springfield, Ill.: Thomas, 1957. 340 pp.

RODGERS, RAYMOND SPENCER. Sex and Law in Canada: Text, Cases and Comment. Ottawa, Canada: Policy Press, 1962. 80 pp.

ROEBURT, JOHN. Sex-Life and the Criminal Law: A New Book. New York: Belmont, 1963. 157 pp.

Sex Offenses. Law and Contemporary Problems, Vol. 25, No. 2. Durham, N.C.: School of Law, Duke University, 1960. Pp. 216-375.

Sexual Crime Today: Papers read by Max Grunhut, Rudolf Sieverts and Jacob M. van Bemmelen at a Symposium Organized by the Institute of Criminal Law and Criminology of the University of Leiden. Strafrechtelijke en criminologische onderzoekingen. Nieuwe reeks, 4, deel. The Hague, The Netherlands: Nijhoff, 1960. 86 pp. Diagrams.

SHERWIN, ROBERT VEIT. Sex and the Statutory Law in All 48 States: A Comparative Study and Survey of the Legal and Legislative Treatment of Sex Problems. New York: n.p., 1949. 2 pts. in 1 vol.

SHULTZ, GLADYS DENNY. How Many More Victims? Society and the Sex Criminal. Philadelphia, Pa.: Lippincott, 1965. 363 pp.

SLATER, MANNING R. [pseud.]. Sex Offenders in Group Therapy: The Personal Experiences of a Clinical Psychologist in Criminal Group Therapy by Manning R. Slater as told to George Bishop. Los Angeles, Calif.: Sherbourne, 1964. 159 pp.

SLOVENKO, RALPH, ed. Sexual Behavior and the Law. Springfield, Ill.: Thomas, 1965. 886 pp.

"A comprehensive collection of original articles by forty-seven authorities on various aspects of sexual behavior and on legislation dealing with sex. Includes bibliographies."

STÜRUP, GEORG KRISTOFFER. Treatment of Sexual Offenders in Herstedvester, Denmark: The Rapists: The Third Isaac Ray Lecture. Acta Psychiatric Supplement 204. Copenhagen, Denmark: Munksgaard, 1968. 63 pp.

TAPPAN, PAUL W. The Habitual Sex Offenders: Report and Recommendations of the Commission on the Habitual Sex Offender. Trenton, N.J.: State of New Jersey, 1950. 68 pp.

TRAINI, ROBERT. Murder for Sex, and Cases of Manslaughter under the New Act. London, Eng.: W. Kimber, 1960. 267 pp. Illus.

TRIVEDI, HARI DAR DUTTA. Law Relating to Sexual Offences. Allahabad, India: Central Law Agency, 1963. 132 pp.

WARD, DAVID A., and G. G. KASSEBAUM. Women's Prison: Sex and Social Structure. Chicago, Ill.: Aldine, 1967. 269 pp.

"A study by two sociologists of the dynamics of prison behavior. Questioning of inmates and staff indicated that the predominant female response to the pains of imprisonment was homosexual behavior."

WILLIAMS, BERNARD [William Bernard]. Jailbait: The Story of Juvenile Delinquency. Garden City, N.Y.: Garden City Books, 1951. 216 pp.

WILLIAMS, GLANVILLE LLEWELYN. The Sanctity of Life and the Criminal Law. New York: Knopf, 1957. 350 pp.

"A British jurist examines society's attitudes toward the control of conception, sterilization, artificial insemination, abortion, suicide, and euthanasia."

WOODSIDE, MOYA. Sterilization in North Carolina: A Sociological and Psychological Study. Chapel Hill, N.C.: University of North Carolina, 1950. 219 pp.

Deals with the sterilization of criminals in North Carolina.

WORTHINGTON, GEORGE E., and R. TOPPING. Specialized Courts Dealing with Sex Delinquency: A Study of the Procedure in Chicago, Boston, Philadelphia and New York. New York: Hitchcock, 1925. 460 pp.

Publication of the Bureau of Social Hygiene.

WULFFEN, ERICH. Woman as a Sexual Criminal. North Hollywood, Calif.: Brandon House, 1967. 363 pp.

Translated from the third revised German edition of "Das Weib als Sexualverbrecherin." 1934 edition published by the American Ethnological Press in New York.

AUTHOR INDEX

TITLE INDEX

Manual of Exotica Sexualia, 77
Manual of Family Planning and Con-
traceptive Practice, 211
Manual of Sex and Marriage, 194
Manual of Sex Education for Parents,
Teachers and Students, 141
Manual of Sex Magick, 189
Manual on Sex Education, 147
Many Faces of Love, 35
Many Faces of Sex, 53
Marquesan Sexual Behavior, 83
Marquis and the Chevalier, 38
Marquis de Sade, the Man and His
Age, 106
Marquis de Sade's 120 Days of
Sodom, 106
Margaret Sanger; An Autobiography,
220
Margaret Sanger: Pioneer of Birth
Control, 153
Margaret Sanger: Woman Rebel, 170
Marital Breakdown, 22
Marital Counseling, 31
Marital Infidelity, 68
Marital Love, Its Wise Delights, 242
Marriage (Blood), 19
Marriage (Blum), 20
Marriage (Groves), 25
Marriage (Harper), 25
Marriage (Lipke), 27, 156
Marriage (Mair), 28
Marriage: A Medical and Sacra-
mental Study, 26, 63
Marriage, A Topical Outline, 5
Marriage and Family among
Negroes, 19
Marriage and Family Counseling;
Perspective and Prospect, 29
Marriage and Family Interaction, 18
Marriage and Family Life, 25
Marriage and Family Relationships,
24
Marriage and Fertility of Women
Suffering from Schizophrenia or
Affective Disorders, 120
Marriage and Freedom, 188
Marriage and Legitimate Birth Con-
trol, 192
Marriage and Morals, 30, 241
Marriage and Personal Develop-
ment, 19
Marriage and Rhythm, 221
Marriage and the Bible, 33, 67
Marriage and the Christian Tradi-
tion, 21
Marriage and the Family (Baber), 18
Marriage and the Family (Christen-
sen and Johnson), 21

Marriage and the Family (Zimmer-
man), 33
Marriage and the Sex Problem, 144
Marriage and the Unconscious, 24
Marriage Art, 190
Marriage as a Trade, 25
Marriage Bed, 41
Marriage, Before and After, 29
Marriage Counseling and Concilia-
tion, 4
Marriage Counseling in Medical
Practice, 29
Marriage Counselling in the Com-
munity, 25
Marriage, Courtship and Sex,
198
Marriage Doctor Speaks Her Mind
about Sex, 196
Marriage Education and Counselling,
21
Marriage, Family and Society: A
Reader, 30
Marriage for Moderns, 20
Marriage for the Married, 197
Marriage Guidance, 32
Marriage Happiness or Unhappi-
ness, 15, 19
Marriage Has Many Faces, 23
Marriage Is What You Make It, 29
Marriage Is a Bad Habit, 17
Marriage Is for Adults Only, 24
Marriage Is for Grownups, 19
Marriage Is for Two, 31
Marriage Is the First Step toward
Divorce, 28
Marriage Laws in the Bible and the
Talmud, 23
Marriage Manual. See Drs. Hannah
and Abraham Stone's A Marriage
Manual, 203
Marriage, Morals and Medical
Ethics, 236
Marriage, Morals, and Sex in Amer-
ica, 22, 87
Marriage: Past and Present, 21
Marriage, Past, Present and Future,
29
Marriage Reader, 195
Marriage Relationship, 30
Marriage, Sex, and Happiness, 206
Marriage, the Family, and Society,
32
Marriage under Stress, 30
Marriage Without Morals, 22, 235
Marriages Are Not Made in
Heaven, 29
Married Life, 30
Married Love, 204

ANALYTICAL SUBJECT INDEX